THE BIBLE IN MODERN SCHOLARSHIP

THE BIBLE IN MODERN SCHOLARSHIP

PAPERS READ AT THE 100TH MEETING OF THE SOCIETY OF BIBLICAL LITERATURE • DECEMBER 28-30, 1964

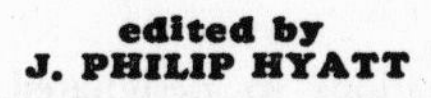
edited by
J. PHILIP HYATT

ABINGDON PRESS
nashville
new york

THE BIBLE IN MODERN SCHOLARSHIP

Library of Congress Catalog Card Number: 66-11059

SET UP, PRINTED, AND BOUND BY THE PARTHENON PRESS, AT NASHVILLE, TENNESSEE, UNITED STATES OF AMERICA

CONTRIBUTORS

Kurt Aland, Professor of Theology, University of Münster/Westfalen, Germany.

Martin A. Cohen, Associate Professor of Jewish History, Hebrew Union College-Jewish Institute of Religion, New York, New York.

Ernest Cadman Colwell, President, School of Theology at Claremont, Claremont, California.

Hans G. Conzelmann, Professor of New Testament, University of Göttingen, Germany.

W. D. Davies, Edward Robinson Professor of Biblical Theology, Union Theological Seminary; Adjunct Professor of Religion, Columbia University, New York, New York.

Roland de Vaux, O.P., Director, École Biblique et Archéologique Française, Jerusalem.

Avery Dulles, S.J., Professor of Fundamental Theology, Woodstock College, Woodstock, Maryland.

Floyd V. Filson, Dean and Professor of New Testament Literature and History, McCormick Theological Seminary, Chicago, Illinois.

David Noel Freedman, Professor of Hebrew and Old Testament Literature, San Francisco Theological Seminary and the Graduate Theological Union, San Anselmo, California.

Stanley Brice Frost, Professor of Old Testament Language and Literature and Dean of Graduate Studies and Research, McGill University, Montreal, Canada.

Moshe Greenberg, Professor of Biblical Studies, University of Pennsylvania, Philadelphia, Pennsylvania.

Hans Jonas, Professor of Philosophy, Graduate Faculty, New School for Social Research, New York, New York.

Arvid S. Kapelrud, Professor of Old Testament, University of Oslo, Norway.

Helmut H. Koester, John H. Morrison Professor of New Testament Studies, The Harvard Divinity School, Cambridge, Massachusetts.

Herbert G. May, Finney Professor of Old Testament Language and Literature, Graduate School of Theology, Oberlin College, Oberlin, Ohio.

George E. Mendenhall, Professor, Department of Near Eastern Languages and Literatures, University of Michigan, Ann Arbor, Michigan.

Bruce M. Metzger, George L. Collord Professor of New Testament Language and Literature, Princeton Theological Seminary, Princeton, New Jersey.

James Muilenburg, Gray and Seminary Professor of Old Testament, San Francisco Theological Seminary, San Anselmo, California.

†Johannes Munck, Professor of New Testament Exegesis, University of Aarhus, Denmark.

James Bennett Pritchard, Curator, Biblical Archaeology, The University Museum, and Professor of Religious Thought, University of Pennsylvania, Philadelphia, Pennsylvania.

G. Quispel, Professor of Early Church History, University of Utrecht, Holland.

James M. Robinson, Professor of Religion, Claremont Graduate School, Claremont, California.

David M. Stanley, S.J., Dean of Theological Faculty, Regis College, Willowdale, Ontario, Canada.

Krister Stendahl, Frothingham Professor of Biblical Studies, The Harvard Divinity School, Harvard University, Cambridge, Massachusetts.

Bruce Vawter, C.M., Professor of Sacred Scripture, Kenrick Seminary, St. Louis, Missouri.

Robert McLachlan Wilson, Senior Lecturer, St. Mary's College, University of St. Andrews, Scotland.

James Philip Hyatt, *Editor,* Professor of Old Testament, Vanderbilt University, Nashville, Tennessee.

† Deceased.

ABBREVIATIONS

BA	*Biblical Archaeologist*
BASOR	*Bulletin of the American Schools of Oriental Research*
BJRL	*Bulletin of the John Rylands Library*
BZAW	*Beiheft zur Zeitschrift für die alttestamentliche Wissenschaft*
CBQ	*Catholic Biblical Quarterly*
EvTh	*Evangelische Theologie*
FRLANT	*Forschungen zur Religion und Literatur des Alten und Neuen Testaments*
HNT	*Handbuch zum Neuen Testament*
HTR	*Harvard Theological Review*
HUCA	*Hebrew Union College Annual*
IB	*Interpreter's Bible*
IDB	*Interpreter's Dictionary of the Bible*
IEJ	*Israel Exploration Journal*
JBL	*Journal of Biblical Literature*
JBR	*Journal of Bible and Religion*
JNES	*Journal of Near Eastern Studies*
JSS	*Journal of Semitic Studies*
JTS	*Journal of Theological Studies*
NT	New Testament
NTS	*New Testament Studies*
OrChr	*Oriens Christianus*
OT	Old Testament

RB	*Revue Biblique*
RGG	*Die Religion in Geschichte und Gegenwart*
SBT	*Studies in Biblical Theology*
ThR	*Theologische Rundschau*
TLZ	*Theologische Literaturzeitung*
VigChr	*Vigiliae Christianae*
VT	*Vetus Testamentum*
ZAW	*Zeitschrift für die alttestamentliche Wissenschaft*
ZNW	*Zeitschrift für die neutestamentliche Wissenschaft und die Kunde der älteren Kirche*
ZTK	*Zeitschrift für Theologie und Kirche*

FOREWORD

The Society of Biblical Literature and Exegesis was born in 1880. On January 2nd of that year eight scholars gathered in the study of Professor Philip Schaff at 42 Bible House, New York, New York, and resolved to take steps to form the Society "for the purpose of promoting a thorough study of the Scriptures by the reading and discussion of original papers." The first meeting of the Society was held on June 4th and 5th in the study of the Reverend E. A. Washburn at 103 East Twenty-first Street, New York, with eighteen members present. Thirty-three persons had accepted invitations to membership. In the course of three sessions the constitution and bylaws were adopted, officers were elected, and six papers were read and discussed, seven being held over for presentation at later meetings. The first paper was read by Philip Schaff under the title, "The Pentecostal and the Corinthian Glossalalia."

The 100th meeting of the organization—known officially as The Society of Biblical Literature since 1962—was held in New York, December 28-30, 1964. Union Theological Seminary served as host, and most of the sessions were held in the spacious assembly halls of The Riverside Church. Nearly a thousand persons were in attendance, and the Society now had a total of 2,185 members. This was the 100th *meeting,* but not the 100th *year* of the Society. From the first year through 1896 it held semiannual meetings, and since that time has met only once every year.

The present volume contains all the papers read at the 100th meeting and at the meeting of the American Textual Criticism Seminar, a daughter organization, which was held immediately following the close of the Society's meeting. The only paper not published here is the presidential address, delivered by Frederick V. Winnett of Toronto University on "Re-Examining the Foundations." His address was published in the March, 1965 issue of the *Journal of Biblical Literature,* pages 1-19. The chapters of the present volume, indicated by roman numerals, correspond to the sessions of the meeting. The order of the chapters does not, however, follow the order of the successive sessions, but has been arranged to follow a roughly chronological order of the biblical topics.

At the banquet of the Society on the evening of December 29th, Douglas M. Knight, President of Duke University, delivered an address on "Literature, Faith and the Bible." Henry J. Cadbury, a member since 1911 and Secretary for many years, spoke on the history of the Society, giving many delightful personal reminiscences.

Those who read papers on the program of the 100th meeting were invited by the program committee to write on specified topics, but were given much freedom in their writing. The topics were chosen with a view to covering the principal problems and concerns of current biblical scholarship, with a backward look to the past two or three generations of scholarship and a forward look to the immediate future. Some participants chose to survey research of the past with a statement of the problems as they now appear to stand; others preferred to treat one or two detailed subjects in depth; some attempted to anticipate the course of study in the biblical field in the years lying ahead. Readers will see that the papers do not conform to fixed patterns laid down in advance, and they will find varying points of view expressed with vigor.

In discussing their topics the authors often deal with the problem of method in biblical study. Various problems associated with history, its meaning and its importance, come again and again into the discussions. While the committee sought to cover the most important problems of current scholarship, some of the prominent concerns of the present are not specifically treated in separate papers—for example, the Qumran materials and form criticism. Yet these receive treatment or reference in several papers. Taken as a whole the papers should give the reader a representative cross section of biblical scholarship of the present and the recent past. It is not a parochial scholarship. The papers herein were written by scholars from many parts of the world, and from Protestant,

Roman Catholic, and Jewish circles. Thus the scholarship of these pages is both interfaith and international—ecumenical in the broadest sense. Perhaps the most amazing conclusion to which some readers will come is that the agreements among the writers outnumber their disagreements.

The committee which planned the program over the course of two years consisted of the following: Samuel Sandmel, provost of Hebrew Union College-Jewish Institute of Religion, chairman; John L. McKenzie, S.J., of Loyola University, Chicago; and the undersigned. The late Kendrick Grobel of Vanderbilt University, Executive Secretary of the Society of Biblical Literature, served on the committee throughout 1964. He contributed to the planning of the program, invited the individual participants, and gave close attention to all of the details of the program.

It is a pleasure to acknowledge the assistance of many persons in the preparation of this volume. The twenty-six authors, who were participants in the programs that have been described, have given splendid cooperation in submitting their papers and granting permission for their publication. Members of the planning committee, named above, have given counsel at several points. Pierce Ellis, a member of the editorial staff of the Abingdon Press, has taken an unusual personal interest in this volume since the time his press first considered publishing it, and has worked closely with me at all stages. Roy Wells, a graduate fellow at Vanderbilt in 1964-65 and now a faculty member at Austin College, gave valuable assistance in preparing several papers for publication. We have attempted to publish the papers virtually as they were delivered in New York, but this was more strictly possible for some than others. Some authors revised their papers slightly in view of the New York discussions. In general, however, the authors have not sought to bring their papers up to date beyond the time they were read.

This volume is dedicated to the memory of Kendrick Grobel, a devoted member of the Society of Biblical Literature and my longtime friend and colleague. He became a member of the Society in 1934. After that he read papers at meetings, contributed articles and book reviews to the *Journal,* and served in several official positions: New Testament book review editor (1948) and assistant editor (1949) of the *Journal,* president of the Southern Section (1956), and Secretary of the Society (1962-64). He became the first Executive Secretary when the new position was created in December, 1963, and he died in office on February 2, 1965. He was to have been co-editor of this volume, and he contributed more to the success of the 100th meeting than any other single individual. This volume of papers and the 100th meeting at which they were presented are enduring monuments to his efficient service to the Society and his intense devotion to the cause of biblical scholarship.

J. PHILIP HYATT
Vanderbilt University
July 8, 1965

CONTENTS

1

ROLAND
de VAUX, O.P.

Method in the Study of Early Hebrew History

The title proposed for this paper limits it to the most ancient periods of Hebrew history: the patriarchs, the sojourn in Egypt, the exodus, and the conquest; and it asks us to consider only problems of method. It is not a question of saying what we can know of these periods, but to decide how we can seek to know something.

All History (with a capital) is a construction and an interpretation. The event which appears once, in space and time, the naked fact, unique, isolated, has in itself no sense for the historian. It is a stone of the building which he is to build, but he will not know whether this stone is a foundation, a support, or the keystone until he has assembled many of these stones, of these facts, and has compared them and arranged them according to a certain order. The event does not become a part of History until it is interpreted.

The historical interpretation of the OT can be done in different ways. These ways have different points of view, use different methods, and reach different results.

1. There is the point of view of just the historian. Israel is one of the peoples of the ancient Near East whose place and role he puts in general history. He reconstructs its political and economic history, studies its social, political, and religious institutions and its culture, as he does or would do for any other people. The Bible is for him a document of history which he criticizes, and controls, and supplements by the information which he can obtain outside of the Bible. The result is a history of Israel.

2. There is the point of view of the historian of religions. The Bible is for him a document of religious history. The OT is the collection of the sacred books of Israel. They are the expression of the faith of Israel. This faith is historical; it is founded on the conviction that God has directed all the history of the people whom he has chosen, Israel. The historian of religions is not particularly interested in knowing in what measure this interpretation of facts corresponds to authentic history. He is writing a history of the religion of Israel, and he does it with as much sympathy, but also with as much objectivity, as he would study any other religion of antiquity, and he can bring his work to a proper conclusion without sharing the faith of Israel.

3. The point of view of the theologian differs from the historian of religions in that he accepts the OT as containing the revelation of *his* God, revealed first to Israel in history but destined also to *himself* who is the spiritual heir of Israel. He accepts, as coming from God, the interpretation which the Bible gives of the events of history, and this biblical history is, for him, the history of God revealing himself to men.

In other words, the historian seeks to find how the history of Israel is explained and inserted in the history of the world; the historian of religions seeks how Israel itself has interpreted its history; the theologian seeks what God wanted to explain to Israel and to himself by this history. The three methods of research are different and reach different results. There is nevertheless an internal relationship between these three ways of looking at the history of Israel. The theologian takes for his starting point the conclusions of the historian of religions, and he judges of their validity, not only according to the criteria of rational science, but according to their conformity to the established truths of his faith. He then goes beyond these conclusions by integrating them into the whole of the revelation. The connection between religious history and objective history, between the history believed by Israel and the true history of Israel, is apparently more difficult to establish; however, it must be established in the eyes of the believer, for if the historical faith of Israel is not in a certain way founded in *history,* this faith is erroneous and cannot command my assent.[1]

[1] This especially against G. von Rad, who wrote a *Theologie des Alten Testaments* which, in my opinion, is only a "history of Israel's religion." He stresses the opposition between the "believed" and the "true history; he judges that the historian cannot

These three ways of looking at the history of Israel are all legitimate, provided that each one keeps to the methods which are peculiar to it and does not go beyond its limits. We are concerned here only with the first, the objective history, and with the most ancient part of this history, the origins of Israel.

A prejudicial question arises. The history of Israel begins only when this group has acquired its unity and its stability by settling in Canaan, and by the establishment of the League of the Twelve Tribes, when Israel became a "nation." Has the historian the right or the means to go back farther, to seek where this people came from, from what human group it was detached, how it was formed?

Yes, the historian has the right to do so; it is even his duty. For he must pass judgment on the memories which Israel itself had kept of its origins. In the Bible, which is the document the historian uses, these traditions are found in the Pentateuch and the book of Joshua, and they fill more pages than the whole history of Israel, from the League of the Tribes to the ruin of Jerusalem, from the book of Judges to the end of Chronicles. The problem is not only urgent for the historian. It matters also very much for the historian of religions and for the theologian, for the faith of Israel is founded on acts of God: the call of Abraham and the promises made to the patriarchs, the deliverance from Egypt, the revelation of Sinai, the choice of the people, and the gift of the Promised Land are together parts of the creed and events of the history, and these acts all fall in the period of the origins.

But what value can history recognize in these traditions? Certain recent authors have given a negative or restricted answer to this question.

For G. E. Mendenhall [2] the idea of Israel as "people" is posterior to the constitution of the League of the Tribes. Israel began as a specifically religious community, a group of captive slaves escaped from Egypt, united only by their worship of a common deity. This group polarized

---

reach the facts on which Israel's confession of faith is founded and that, besides, it does not matter for the believer. One must consider also his more recent, and more balanced paper, "Offene Fragen im Umkreis einer Theologie des Alten Testaments," in *TLZ*, Vol. XXCVIII (1963), cols. 401-19.

[2] G. E. Mendenhall, "The Hebrew Conquest of Palestine," *BA*, XXV (1962), 66-87. He had expressed more "classical" views in "Biblical History in Transition," in *The Bible and the Ancient Near East. Essays in Honor of W. F. Albright*, ed. by G. Ernest Wright (1961), pp. 32-53 (his contribution is dated 1957).

the resistance of the peasants of Canaan against the system of the city-states. There was no invasion, peaceful or warlike; there was no conquest. In this perspective, no more can there be a "patriarchal" history, since "Israel" has no ancestors different from the Canaanites from whom it separated by a socio-political process.

Martin Noth [3] begins his *History of Israel* with the constitution of the League of the Tribes. These tribes had specific traditions about their ancestors and the events prior to their settling in Canaan, which have been combined in the composition of the Pentateuch. He recognizes that these traditions have an historical basis but he considers that the historian cannot reach the facts upon which these traditions rest; we can say nothing about the time and the place, the antecedents and the circumstances of the life of the patriarchs; we cannot ascertain the events which have been associated with the exit from Egypt; etiological accounts have transformed into a warlike conquest what had been a peaceful infiltration into Canaan.

Opposed to these negative judgments there are very positive affirmations. The same year that Martin Noth was publishing his *History of Israel,* W. F. Albright wrote: "As a whole the picture in Genesis is historical, and there is no reason to doubt the general accuracy of the biographical details and the sketches of personality which bring the Patriarchs to life with a vividness unknown to a single extrabiblical character in the whole vast literature of the ancient Near East." [4] He judged in the same way the value of the accounts of the exodus and the conquest. A few years later John Bright criticized sharply the "nihilism" of Noth;[5] then he gave, in his *History of Israel,* his own conclusions: on the patriarchs "enough can be said to justify the assertion that its account is rooted in historical events"; on the events of the desert, "we may be sure that the tradition accurately reflects historical occurrences"; on the conquest, "there is no reason to doubt that this conquest was, as the book of Joshua depicts it, a bloody and brutal business." [6] G. E. Wright defended, against Noth, the synthesis

[3] Martin Noth, *Geschichte Israels,* 1950, rev. English tr., 1960, pp. 123, 115, 82.

[4] W. F. Albright, *The Biblical Period From Abraham to Ezra. An Historical Survey,* 1950. Without change in the 1963 ed., p. 5.

[5] John Bright, *Early Israel in Recent History Writing,* 1956. The word reappears as a refrain, pp. 52, 54, 64, 67, 72, 82, 83, 87.

[6] John Bright, *A History of Israel,* 1959, pp. 69, 110, 117, 127.

of Bright [7] and presented in his *Biblical Archaeology* the same positive conclusions on the history of the origins of Israel.[8]

Such oppositions between authors who have an equal concern for objective truth evidently brings into question the methods which they use. It is true that all agree in saying that the same rules must be applied to the biblical narratives as to any document of history, literary criticism analyzing written sources, form criticism examining the formation of traditions and their *Sitz im Leben,* historical criticism appreciating the value of traditions according to their likelihood inside the Bible and their agreement with the evidence outside the Bible. But they all do not apply these different criticisms in the same way and do not give to each one the same importance.

Some start from an analysis of the biblical narratives, study their literary form, and go back to the traditions which they used; considering the long time during which these oral or written traditions have been handed down with eliminations, additions, combinations, they judge that the value of these traditions is not verifiable historically and that all the "external evidence" which we have and that we will ever have is of little help.

Others are struck by the close parallels which accumulate between the documents outside the Bible and the narratives of the Bible. They recognize a general connection between the historical milieu from which these documents come and that which the Bible supposes, and therefore they are led to appreciate more favorably the historical value of these accounts. It is significant that on the one hand Martin Noth, before publishing his history, should have written two big books of literary criticism and history of traditions and a commentary on the book of Joshua, and that he was working at the same time on a commentary on the book of Exodus. It is significant, on the other hand, that W. F. Albright has written a considerable number of studies on linguistics, archaeology, and the texts of the ancient Near East, but that his work contains few specific studies on the exegesis and literary criticism of the Bible. At the risk of deforming by simplifying too much, one could say that the historical value of the traditions is approached from the inside by the one and from the outside

[7] G. E. Wright, "Modern Issues in Biblical Studies: History of the Patriarchs," in *The Expository Times,* LXXI (1959-1960), 292-96.

[8] G. E. Wright, *Biblical Archaeology,* 1957. Rev. ed., 1962.

by the other. The ideal method would be to associate the two points of view according to an exact balance. Is this possible?

Since the biblical narratives are documents of history which we possess and which must be explained, it is from them that we must start, and literary criticism is foremost and indispensable. The enormous work accomplished in this domain for a century cannot be neglected. Many points remain debatable, but the principal lines of the distinction of the sources and their relative age must be accepted. Because Y. Kaufmann refuses certain established conclusions of literary criticism, the picture which he presents of the conquest of Canaan cannot satisfy an historian.[9] For a long time the mistake has been to consider that the documents detected by literary criticism supplied valid evidence only for the history of the period where they had been put down in writing. The classical expression of this judgment has been given by J. Wellhausen: from the accounts of Genesis, he says, "One cannot gather any historical knowledge about the Patriarchs, but only about the time when the narratives which concern them took shape in the people of Israel." [10] Since then literary criticism has evolved. It is no longer exclusively concerned with the great "documents" in their final writing (whose dates moreover have been put back), but it considers also the preliterary state of these documents and the oral "traditions" from which they have come.

It is admitted that late as these written documents are, they can preserve—and they do in fact preserve—memories which are authentic. As G. E. Mendenhall has observed, in antiquity "writing is used to preserve, not, as in the modern scholarly world, to create." [11] E. A. Speiser has analagous expressions: "His task [the narrator's] was to retell, not to originate." [12] I accept these statements, but with this reservation, that the writing is the last link of a living tradition and that it adds to this tradition its personal mark by the choice, the combination, the presentation, and the appreciation of the traditional material which it uses.

Literary criticism by itself does not bring a sufficient answer

[9] Y. Kaufmann, *The Biblical Account of the Conquest of Palestine,* 1953; *The Religion of Israel* (tr. by Greenberg), 1962.

[10] J. Wellhausen, *Prolegomena zur Geschichte Israels,*[3] 1886, p. 331.

[11] G. E. Mendenhall, "Biblical History in Transition," *loc. cit.,* p. 34.

[12] E. A. Speiser, "The Biblical Idea of History in its Common Near Eastern Setting," *IEJ,* VII (1957), 201-16; the quotation is p. 214. See also G. E. Wright, *JBL,* LXXVII (1958), 45-46.

to the questions of the historian, and he, beyond the texts, must go back to the study of the traditions. Recently the accuracy of the oral tradition has been greatly insisted upon, especially in the Near East and especially among the people who did not use writing, or used it very little.[13] This affirmation needs serious restrictions.[14] The oral transmission of an account achieves a certain fixity only when this account has received a poetic or rhythmic form, and this fixity is helped if there is a parallel written tradition which controls and sustains it. Neither in the Near East nor elsewhere are historic memories transmitted for long without being deformed if there is only an oral transmission. On the other hand, certain characteristics attached to names, places, sanctuaries, or rites are preserved with astonishing persistence.

These reservations made, the form and the content of the ancient biblical traditions permit one to think that they have preserved accurate memories of the origins of Israel. They contain indeed certain of those elements which oral tradition preserves best, they retain ancient poetic compositions, and they refer to two (or one?) collections of poems or epic tales, the "Book of the Wars of Yahweh" (Num. 21:14) and the "Book of the Braves" (Josh. 10:13).[15]

But the tradition does not only preserve, it constructs also. For the book of Joshua, it is "all Israel" which, together, conquers the Promised Land. In Exodus and Numbers it is "all Israel" which comes out of Egypt, receives the revelation of Sinai, accomplishes the marches in the desert. This "all Israel" is the offspring of the twelve sons of Jacob, who have come to Egypt and who are themselves the descendants of Abraham. The global presentation is certainly artificial; the origins of Israel are infinitely more complex, and this tradition which has become common to Israel is the result of the combination of particular traditions.

Nevertheless, this unification itself must retain the attention of the historian; it expresses the conviction Israel had of a certain common

[13] Cf. the works of H. S. Nyberg, H. Birkeland and, generally, E. Nielsen, *Oral Tradition*, 1954.

[14] Cf. among others J. van der Ploeg, "Le rôle de la tradition orale dans la transmission du texte de l'Ancien Testament," *RB*, LII (1947), 5-41; W. F. Albright, *From the Stone Age to Christianity*,[2] 1957, pp. 64-76.

[15] S. Mowinckel, "Hat es ein israelitisches Nationalepos gegeben?" *ZAW*, LIII (1935), 130-52. But cf. N. H. Tur-Sinai, "Was there an Ancient 'Book of the Wars of the Lord'?" *Bulletin of Israel Exploration Society*, XXIV (1959-1960), 146-48.

origin founded on blood ties, and this conviction cannot be deprived of all historical justification. The principal reproach that one can make to the recent theory of G. E. Mendenhall on the "conquest" is that it rejects this fundamental exigency of the tradition of Israel.[16]

The reason or the excuse for these divergent opinions is that the Hebrew *'am* is insufficiently translated by "people," or rather, that Israel's idea of people is different from ours.[17] It denotes essentially ties of consanguinity. Of the dead it is said that they are reunited with their *'am* (Gen. 25:17, etc.). A priest must not make himself impure by contact with a corpse of anyone of his *'am,* except his nearest relatives (Lev. 21:1-2). There is no reason to distinguish between two different words, as most of the dictionaries do: *'am* indicates first a close consanguine, the word used collectively means kin, and the "people" is an extension of the family. The marriages between the clan of Jacob and the inhabitants of Shechem would have made a single *'am* out of the two groups (Gen. 34:1-6). The "people of Israel" are the *bene Israel,* the descendants of the sons of Jacob. Abraham leaving Harran with his wife, his nephew Lot, and all of his house is already the kernel of an *'am* and for the Israelites the history of their "people" began with that of their ancestor Abraham.

This does not exclude—and the example which I gave of the Shechemites supposes it—that the growth of this "people" could be made by the integration of groups of foreign blood either by intermarriage or by all sorts of agreements. The Bible presents examples of it, such as the Calebites incorporated in the tribe of Judah, or the treaty with the Gibeonites. The history of the Arab tribes, ancient or modern, furnishes many parallels. These groups bring their own traditions which become part of the common patrimony. But even as these groups are inserted in an existing line, so their particular traditions are combined and harmonized with a central tradition which unifies them. For Israel, this tradition is a religious one, that of Yahwism. Now Yahwism contains three indivisibles: *one God,* Yahweh, who has chosen *one people,* Israel, the people of Yahweh, and has given to this people *one land,* Canaan, the land of Yahweh. This is the interpretation which Israel has given of

[16] See n. 2.

[17] Cf. L. Rost, "Die Bezeichnungen für Land und Volk im Alten Testament," in *Festschrift Otto Procksch,* 1934, pp. 125-48; E. A. Speiser, "'People' and 'Nation' of Israel," *JBL,* LXXIX (1960), 157-63.

its history, it is the expression of a faith, but it is so basic that the historian must take it into account if he wishes to understand this history.

It is legitimate and necessary that the historian should seek how these traditions, special or common, have been formed and from whence they come. But he must avoid a mistake in method. Literary criticism has often been paralyzed by a too minute distinction of sources which pulverizes the texts and makes them unintelligible. The analysis of the common tradition of Israel in a great number of special, and at first independent, traditions makes incomprehensible the formation of the final tradition and even the development of history. An example of this excess is the thesis of E. Nielsen on the traditions of Shechem.[18] Another example, more serious in its consequences, is the distinction made by Noth in the Pentateuch of five principal themes and several secondary themes, which would have been first so many independent traditions, and then artificially combined between them. The unity of the Israelite tradition having been thus destroyed, the very existence of Israel and its faith becomes impossible to explain.[19]

We have said that tradition preserves and also constructs. Besides this does tradition invent? If tradition creates it ceases to be a witness of history. This creative power has been attributed to two elements in the formation of tradition: etiology and worship.

Often in the Pentateuch and in the book of Joshua the name of a person or the name of a place, a custom, a monument or ruin, or even a natural formation is explained by the account of an action, a situation, or an event. The account often ends by recalling the custom or the monument "which stands to this day," and which is proposed as the evidence and proof of the truth of this history. According to certain authors, and especially to Martin Noth on the accounts of the conquest,[20] these explanations are invented; they are etiological accounts. One must point out, however, that a name, a custom, a monument always has its explanation.[21] It happens that this explanation may be unknown or forgotten, and then the human need to understand impels tradition to in-

[18] E. Nielsen, *Shechem. A Traditio-Historical Investigation,* 1955.

[19] Cf. J. Bright, *Early Israel,* p. 84.

[20] M. Noth, *Das Buch Josua,* 1938, 2nd ed., 1953.

[21] Cf. especially W. F. Albright, *BASOR,* LXXIV (1939), 12-17, and my review of M. Noth in *RB,* XLVII (1938), pp. 462-64.

vent an explanation. These false etymologies and false interpretations belong to all time and all places. It is possible, it is likely, and in certain cases it is sure that such and such an explanation of the Bible is etiological, but it is not possible that all explanations are, and that a whole tradition should be founded only on etiology. If there had never been a conquest of Canaanite cities one would never have dreamed of explaining such and such a ruin by an account of conquest. One must decide in each case whether the account is historical or whether it is invented, whether the explanation is authentic or etiological. Etiology has certainly not had a primary role in the formation of tradition.

Worship is also presented as a creative factor of tradition. In every sanctuary a *hieros logos* was recited, a foundation legend which attributed the origin of worship to the action of an ancestor in response to a divine manifestation.[22] The liturgy of the festivals in Egypt and Mesopotamia was the representation and the reenactment of mythical events. The religion of Israel was founded on the belief in the interventions of Yahweh in history in favor of his people; the liturgy commemorated and reenacted this history of salvation which was then told by epic accounts.[23]

It is correct that certain elements of the narratives can be explained in this fashion: for example, in the story of the founding of the sanctuary of Bethel, Jacob promises to pay the tithe (Gen. 28:20-22); later Jacob and his family go on a pilgrimage to Bethel (Gen. 35:1-7). It is probably the reflection of later customs: the tithe is attested by Amos 4:4, the pilgrimage by I Sam. 10:3. Likewise one finds in the narrative of the first Passover in the book of Exodus the reflection of later liturgical practices. It is inevitable that worship should have colored the narratives, but it did not create them. Precisely because the religion of Israel is historical, worship expresses the religious interpretation which Israel has given to the events of its past: Passover and Unleavened Bread are a "memorial" to the deliverance from Egypt. In reverse, the two other great festivals of Israel, the Tents and the Weeks, which are of Canaanite origin, have not given birth to any tradition; on the contrary they were later tied to the events

[22] See, for example, C. A. Keller, "Über einige alttestamentliche Heiligtümerlegenden," *ZAW*, LXVII (1955), 141-68; LXVIII (1956), 85-97.

[23] See mostly J. Pedersen, "Passahfest und Passahlegende," *ZAW*, LII (1934), 161-75; G. von Rad, *Das formgeschichtliche Problem des Hexateuch*, 1938 (*Gesammelte Studien*, 1958, pp. 9-86).

of the history of salvation, the sojourn in the desert and the Sinai covenant. Tradition is prior to the worship; it is only remodeled afterwards to be adapted to the liturgy; worship is not the creator of the tradition.[24]

The thorough faithfulness of the traditions thus deserve to be considered with favorable presumption by the historian. On the other hand, the enlargements which they have received, the etiological elements which they have been able to welcome, the modifications which worship has imprinted upon them—all this requires that before being used in the construction of history they should be controlled by external evidence. But from where can this evidence come and what can it bring?

Ethnography has been called upon, and the study of human groups which can presently be observed which in the same areas or in similar conditions lead the same kind of life and are of the same social status as the ancestors of the Israelites. Actually, it means the study of the nomadic Arab tribes of the Near East. Recently G. E. Mendenhall has vigorously opposed this use of "Bedouinism" to explain the origins of Israel.[25] This reaction is justified but it goes too far. The comparisons which can be made in this domain are limited. The ancestors of the Israelites were never true nomads, camel breeders. The accounts of the patriarchs represent them as sheep grazers. (To answer, incidentally, to a recent opinion, I cannot find in the texts that instead of shepherds they were caravan merchants.) These shepherds live on the border of cultivated lands and begin to settle. We can notice in modern times the same pastoral life and the same evolution among seminomadic tribes in Syria and Transjordania. We can study among them and find in the Arab texts a social structure founded on the family, the organization of the tribe, its growth by the integration of individuals or foreign groups, the union between tribes, later expressed by supposed geneological ties. The legitimacy of these comparisons with the Bible is confirmed in a curious way: the life and journeys of the sheep-raiser are ordered by climatic and geographical conditions; it is to be noted that all the stops of the patriarchs are situated in the climatic zone which best suits this pastoral life. However, another observation limits the breadth of the comparisons: the modern tribes in the process of settling, glory in—with more or less reason—an heroic past

[24] Cf. G. E. Wright, "Cult and History. A Study of a Current Problem in Old Testament Interpretation," *Interpretation,* XVI (1962), 3-20.

[25] G. E. Mendenhall, *BA,* XXV (1962), 66-87.

of pure nomadism; the epic of the patriarchs has not kept such memories because the great nomadism did not yet exist; there was not as there was later a "desert civilization."

But it is above all from archaeology that an external confirmation is demanded of the value of traditions, and it is on its use that the challengers of the opposed tendencies, which we have pointed out, dispute. It is unjust to reproach Martin Noth for a "complete refusal to make use of archaeological data."[26] Only, Martin Noth sees the limits of the evidence which archaeology can bring, and he protests against a sometimes abusive use of archaeology.[27] This reaction is exaggerated but it is salutary.

For the epic of the patriarchs, the most recent researches seek the confirmation of the biblical traditions in the following facts: (1) N. Glueck and S. Rothenberg have discovered numerous sites of the Intermediary Period between the Early and the Middle Bronze Ages in the Negev and the Sinai where the patriarchs sojourned or crossed. (2) There are names and places in the narratives of Genesis which are found again in the extrabiblical texts of the second millennium B.C. (3) The texts of Mari, which contain some of these names, inform us on the history and the ethnic and social situation of Upper Mesopotamia and furnish an adequate setting for these patriarchal narratives. (4) The texts of Nuzi contain parallels to patriarchal customs. But these documents concern different periods: the sites of the Negev and of the Sinai were abandoned in the course of the nineteenth century; the texts of Mari are of the eighteenth century; the texts of Nuzi of the fifteenth century; the names parallel to those of the Bible are found in texts which cover the whole of the second millennium B.C. On the other hand, the narratives concerning the life of the patriarchs in the Negev (to say nothing of Sinai) do not require, perhaps they even exclude, an occupation of the kind which is attested by archaeology. As for the customs of Nuzi, if they are limited to this region and to this period they cannot be used to enlighten the history of the patriarchs who were never east of the Tigris; if they are

[26] G. E. Wright, *JBL,* LXXVII 1958), 48.

[27] M. Noth, "Der Beitrag der Archäologie zur Geschichte Israels," in *Congress Volume. Oxford, 1959* (Suppl. to *VT,* VII, 1960), 262-82, and *Die Ursprünge des alten Israel im Lichte neuer Quellen,* 1961.

not limited to this region and this period they cannot be used to date the patriarchs.

Let us now take the history of the conquest. The only two detailed narratives which the Bible gives are those of the conquest of Jericho and the conquest of Ai. At first sight the results of the excavations at Jericho and at Ai do not confirm the biblical narratives; rather, they contradict them. Conversely, the excavations have established a destruction of Tell ed-Duweir = Lachish and of Tell Beit Mirsim = Debir towards the end of the thirteenth century B.C. The Bible mentions these two cities only in recapitulations of cities taken by Joshua; the redactional character of these lists is shown by literary criticism. The Bible says elsewhere that Debir was conquered not by the Israelites but by the Calebites. According to the latest excavations, Ashdod also was destroyed at the end of the thirteenth century. The book of Joshua says nothing of a conquest of this region and it seems to me very doubtful that this destruction should be attributed to the Israelites. It must rather be put in connection with the invasion of the Peoples of the Sea, or with the counterattack of Merneptah. But then would the explanation of other destructions of Palestinian cities not also be found in these troubles of the thirteenth century?

A positive evidence is at last brought by the excavations of Hazor. The city was severely destroyed at the end of the thirteenth century and it was not rebuilt till much later. This corresponds with the story of the capture and destruction of Hazor in Josh. 11:12-14 and to the mention of Jabin, king of Hazor in Josh. 11:1. Besides, the excavations confirm the prior importance of the city and the position of Hazor as "capital of all the Canaanite kingdoms" of the region (Josh. 11:10). This also helps the literary and historical criticism of Judg. 4 and shows that the name of Jabin, king of Hazor was introduced from Josh. 11 into this account of the battle of Kishon, launched against Sisera in the time of the judges. This last point brings out an important rule of method: the historian must perpetually confront the criticism of the traditions with the external evidence which he gathers. In the same way the negative results of archaeology at Jericho and at Ai demand a reappreciation of the first chapters of Joshua.

The study of the origins of Israel requires a coordinated application of all these methods. There remains to ask oneself what is the extent and value of the conclusions that can be thus obtained. The nature of the biblical traditions and the way by which they have been transmitted to us forbid hoping that they might be controlled in many of their details by extrabiblical documents. The nature of the events which they report and the character of the men they show in action do not permit the hope of ever finding in extrabiblical sources mention of these events or of these men. But this extrabiblical evidence and all the contacts it supplies permit one to establish the general probability of the traditions, and to fix the general historical setting which suits the events which they report. The historian can thus accept these traditions, insofar as he is satisfied by their intrinsic likelihood and as long as they are not contradicted by external evidence. But the content of these traditions, even thus reevaluated, is insufficient for him to write properly a history of the origins of Israel.

Indeed, these conclusions which I propose seem to be agreed to by the best representatives of the two tendencies which I have opposed at the beginning of this paper. In the last work in which he treated the problem of the patriarchs, Martin Noth brings in the texts of Mari and he concludes: "Thus the tradition of the Old Testament which seeks the starting point of the Patriarchs precisely in this region of Upper Mesopotamia appears at least as not only historically possible in itself but as likely." However, he adds: "About the details of the beginning of Israel it is only the tradition peculiar to Israel which up till now can give information and one can hardly expect that it will ever be otherwise. On the other hand it goes without saying that this tradition must be perpetually considered in relation to what is known to us of the oriental milieu of Israel." [28] On the other side John Bright writes: "It is, let it be admitted, impossible in the proper sense to write a *history* of Israel's origins, and that because of limitations in the evidence both from archaeology and from the Bible itself. . . . We know nothing of the lives of Abraham, Isaac, and Jacob save what the Bible tells us, the details of which lie beyond the control of archaeological data." And he adds: "The tradition that Israel's ancestors had come from Mesopotamia cannot, in the light of the evidence, be gainsaid. We may assume that among these migrating clansmen, though no contemporary text observed them, there moved an

[28] M. Noth, *Die Ursprünge* . . . pp. 32-33.

Abraham, an Isaac and a Jacob, chieftains of sizable clans who remembered their origins in the 'plain of Aram.' "[29] Both agree then about the method and hold about the same conclusions.

The biblical scholars will always, according to their temperament, emphasize either more the extent of the knowledge acquired or more the limits of our possible knowledge, but they must accept the same principles of method: the rigorous use of the internal criticism of the biblical traditions combined with the criticism of the external evidence to the Bible.[30]

[29] J. Bright, *A History of Israel,* pp. 67, 86.

[30] This conflict between archaeologists and literary critics on the historical value of tradition is not restricted to our field of biblical studies. I cannot resist quoting from a discussion on *The Trojan War* by M. I. Finley, J. L. Caskey, G. S. Kirk, D. L. Page, published in *The Journal of Hellenic Studies,* LXXXIV (1964), 1-20, which reached me after this paper had been written. M. I. Finley: "The *Iliad* and *Odyssey* . . . tell us much about the society in the centuries after the fall of Troy and scattered bits about the society earlier (and also later, in the time of the monumental composers), but nothing of any value about the war itself in the narrative sense, its causes, conduct, or even the peoples who took part in it," p. 9. J. L. Caskey: "Material evidence from the site of Troy has indeed not proven that the place was captured by Mycenaean Greeks. *Proofs,* of the kind Mr. Finley demands and that we all should like to have, rarely come to light in any archaeological excavation," p. 9. G. S. Kirk: "I am quite prepared to agree with Finley that the total picture of life given in the *Iliad* and *Odyssey* owes almost as much to the circumstances of the early Iron Age as to those of the real Achaean world of the later Bronze Age. . . . But can we believe that the interruption of the tradition, whether poetical or non-poetical, caused by the upheavals at the end of the Bronze Age can have been so severe as to destroy not merely the details but the very outlines of the whole substance of events belonging to the last heroic period of the Achaean civilization?", pp. 15 and 16. D. L. Page: "The evidence of Homer, that Greeks from the mainland sacked Troy . . . cannot be proven to the exclusion of other possibilities. That is frankly admitted," but "the Homeric account has been confirmed since 1870 to an extent unimaginable before that time. It is very likely the true account; at least it is the only one which claims the support of various and abundant evidence in both literary and archaeological records," pp. 17 and 19. The parallel is striking with our own problems, and the same different answers are given.

GEORGE E. MENDENHALL

RESPONSE TO ROLAND de VAUX'S "Method in the Study of Early Hebrew History"

Professor de Vaux has described in very lucid fashion both the present methods in biblical history, and the conclusions reached which stand in paradox with one another. It seems probable that no competent scholar would disagree with his insistence that biblical and extrabiblical evidence must now be combined in any serious historical method. Historical conclusions ought to be based on, or at least be compatible with, all relevant evidence. It is true, however, that scholars in any field of academic inquiry will trust methods and draw conclusions from evidence which they themselves can control. This may well be one reason for the great difference in emphasis, to which Professor de Vaux referred; but is this the only reason for the wide disparity in opinions now held? What happens when rigorous biblical criticism reaches conclusions which are in opposition to conclusions drawn from extrabiblical sources? Above all, what is the process by which a scholar concludes that extrabiblical documents are actually relevant to the biblical history? There is now hardly a culture of the ancient Near East which has not contributed some evidence that has been used for interpretation of the Bible. A comparative method has developed without a very careful examination of the presuppositions involved, and with very little attention to its further implications.

Anthropologists generally accuse historians of working with a maximum of unexamined presuppositions, and this charge is one which biblical historians must face seriously. Professor de Vaux has pointed out the interrelationships between the three academic traditions in biblical interpretation, namely, the historical, history of religion, and theological (in reverse order of their chronological development). It is now necessary to ask, however, whether or not this traditional division of academic labor has resulted in very great inadequacies in the methods of each. The scholar in modern academic life has, of course, a vested interest in the continuity of his own particular academic tradition and method; yet there can be little doubt that the traditional academic compartmentalizations which the modern university has inherited do not correspond to any objective reality, and are in fact becoming increasingly a part of the problem of knowing, not part of the answer.

Surely the historian cannot ignore the history of religion, particularly in biblical history, except under an untenable assumption that there is no relationship between event and ideology, or even between ideology and the recording of history in the Bible itself. Surely the historian who wishes to deal with the Bible cannot proceed upon an assumption that he has no theological presuppositions, even if they are more akin to the religious nationalism of Assyria than to the Bible. On the other hand, the relationship between event and ideology, so characteristic of the Bible, is something which must involve the theologian in history itself; but this is a difficult problem for the historian dealing with non-theological fields as well. As Crane Brinton put it in his work *The Anatomy of Revolution*,[1] "No ideas, no revolution. This does not mean that ideas *cause* revolutions, or that the best way to prevent revolutions is to censor ideas. It merely means that ideas form part of the mutually dependent variables we are studying." When we deal with much more accessible discontinuities in human history, the problem is evidently now insoluble. Yet there can be little doubt that it is precisely this insoluble problem which the biblical traditions pose for us in an inescapable manner. That which secular historians call ideology consists in biblical history at least of very deeply held religious convictions of human beings, which are bound up with historical events in the closest possible way, for they are determinants of human behavior.

If the separation of history from the history of religion results in a method which does not fit the materials we have, a second inadequacy is very closely related, which similarly has to do with underlying presuppositions. When direct evidence is lacking or very difficult to evaluate historically, as in the case of early Hebrew history, it is inevitable that basic assumptions concerning the historical process will be very largely responsible for dictating conclusions. It is in this fact that the wide disparity of scholarly views most probably have their explanation. On the

[1] (New York: Vantage Books 1957), p. 52.

one hand, scholarly work *can* doubtless proceed upon the assumption that we have no usable historical sources. This is merely to give up the historical task as hopeless, and to reduce the scholarly problem simply to a description of the process by which the Bible was written. On the other hand, biblical history today is in a predicament analogous to that of nuclear physics; our fundamental historical particles of data derived very largely from archaeological excavations are far too numerous to fit into the received picture of early Hebrew history, either of religious or academic tradition. The nineteenth-century ideas about the evolution of culture are still deeply engrained into the "collective unconscious" of biblical scholars, as are also concepts of cultural change which constitute a very serious handicap to further progress. The sedentarization of nomads, for example, is an historical process appealed to for explanation by both biblical scholars, and ancient orientalists; it illustrates the pitfalls involved in the correlation of biblical with extrabiblical evidence, for if scholars in both fields are working with the same erroneous assumption, there will arise a confidence in results which it may take a century to rectify. The principles which apply to biblical history apply also to the extra-biblical evidence, and method consists first of all in the careful examination of the specific data. Historical generalizations must be derived from the concrete evidence, not imposed upon it. In a forthcoming essay, S. Talmon argues very persuasively from the biblical evidence itself, that the Bible really contains little indication that the Israelite tribes were ever true nomads; and careful examination of the Mari archives yields abundant evidence that the contrast between shepherds and villagers was, in most cases, of very little significance, socially or religiously.

It is no longer possible to treat early Israel as a primitive, unsophisticated group of cultureless barbarians who gradually became civilized. The historical context of Israel's emergence was not that of outside barbarians inundating the civilized land of Canaan—the very historicity of the patriarchal traditions is the best proof of this. The context is that which is true also of the entire eastern Mediterranean region, a mystery which has been very little examined. The context is that of the breakdown of a system of civilizations, the breaking in of a Dark Age which spread eventually over Egypt, Greece, Anatolia, Syria, and Mesopotamia for a couple of centuries. During this Dark Age, foundations were being laid in several areas for new cultural syntheses and political systems. It is of course difficult to trace the relationship between Solomon's empire and the cultural traditions of the Bronze Age; but this is just as difficult a problem in the case of the Phoenicians and Arameans, to say nothing of the Greeks who suffered from a very severe case of arrested development until the sixth century.

It is already abundantly evident from the important contributions of de Vaux and others, that the biblical history must be studied within the context of ancient Near Eastern history, in order to avoid the usual process of imposing modern concepts, thought patterns, and concerns upon the materials received. Probably most historians now have a deep distrust of *a priori* concepts of historical development; but since working hypotheses are inevitable, it is necessary that every aspect of the hypothesis be checked to determine that it is actually a cultural feature of the ancient peoples and their ways of thought and behavior, not ours. Furthermore, biblical scholars ought at least be aware of trends in other fields; the increasing rejection of the idea that any important cultural change implies an ethnic change must at least induce us to reexamine the evidence, including the biblical tradition. The overwhelming evidence of language alone makes it impossible to conclude that the linguistic differences between the early Hebrews and Canaanites were any greater than the differences within either group. A great ethnic contrast between the two groups becomes therefore inconceivable.

The breakdown of civilizations and empires at the end of the Late Bronze Age included, in fact was, a very rapid social and cultural change. But the old theory of invading barbarian hordes engaging in the wholesale slaughter of populations in the name of Yahweh is simply impossible. Ironically enough, the only detailed narratives concerning the *ḥerem* during the period of the conquest have to do with Jericho and Ai, both of which seem to have lacked any significant population at that time according to presently available archaeological evidence. (It is very tempting to conclude that the best candidates for the *ḥerem* were those which were already in ruins.) To be sure, such periods of political chaos do encourage migrations, but *from* areas of population density and social catastrophe *to* the fringe areas, except for bands well organized and well armed for military operations, such as the Philistines—and one must add now, the band of soldiers who crossed the Jordan with Joshua. The Bible knows of no migration into Palestine during the period of conquest, except that from Egypt—and of those only two persons reached Palestine proper. What the Bible does tell of is the crossing of the Jordan by the military band derived from a population base in Transjordan to assist in the overthrow of *kings,* who were in age-old fashion hastily mobilizing their combined forces for a concerted resistance against a movement, not a migration. Where the ark was, from the point of view of the biblical historiographers, there was all Israel, but the sacred history forgot that most of the year those who were Israel spent the time in their villages tending fields and flocks; and movements of the ark are not identical with mass migrations of all those who had become by covenant the *'am* which God had created (not Abraham), and which was not reckoned among the *goyim* until David or Solomon.

If guiding hypotheses are derived from processes we know to be at work during the period involved, both in and beyond the biblical tradition, the conclusions are not always compatible with the biblical histories —but this is a constant, true of every theory now held. Early Israel was a specifically religious movement which grew by the adherence of already existing tribes as tribes; in the process, it created a great contrast between Israelite and Canaanite upon a radically new foundation, where contrasts had been previously of a different order. It created a discontinuity; even though innumerable individual features of daily life and thought remained the same, others were radically reinterpreted, such as the old agricultural festivals which have always been a problem. Their historicizing, like that of the Roman Saturnalia in a later historic epoch, was inevitable.

The major function of a leading hypothesis is to suggest new contexts and relationships between those incidental details of evidence available, so that we may proceed to a reconstruction of history in a way that will account for as much of our evidence as is possible. Such a leading hypothesis ought also to account for the discrepancies between the reconstruction and the content of biblical traditions. Under the present hypothesis, the patriarchal narratives seem to be a problem, as de Vaux has pointed out. Why should so very much space have been devoted to the pre-Israelite traditions? Again, the first procedure is to examine those narratives within the context of the historical periods from which they derive as we now have them. It is generally conceded that the earliest sources come from the time of Solomon, a time when a very thorough modernization and reformation of Israelite religion was taking place. It is a characteristic of every religious reformation to appeal to a more remote past against the recent past. Following the conquest of the old Canaanite cities by King David, the reign of Solomon seems to have resulted in a virtually total integration of the old Canaanite population and the old Israelite; many of the Israelite tribes are heard of no more, and it is very difficult to see any evidence of an ethnic contrast later, particularly in the South. As Speiser has recently argued, there is little reason to doubt that the Abraham traditions, like those of Daniel, Noah, and Job, were shared by the entire population of Palestine during the Late Bronze Age. The existence of two forms of Abraham's name demonstrates further that the traditions were current in two contrasting linguistic groups in the Bronze Age, since neither form could have been later invented. In addition, the very fact that Abraham is regarded as kin or ancestor of the Transjordanian populations as well as early Arab tribes, indicates some connection with those groups. It is no accident that Abraham furnishes a good example to all his numerous progeny and kinfolk, by bringing the tithe to the king of Salem. The land promised to Abraham in Genesis corresponds similarly to the extent of the Empire of David. The patriarchal traditions of Abraham and Isaac (Jacob is a radically different problem) are not demonstrably referred to in premonarchical sources, but as a tradition common to both Israel and Canaan they became very useful during the United Monarchy, and entered permanently into the mainstream of biblical history and had constantly to be reinterpreted, particularly after the destruction of the Monarchy.

Method cannot be discussed satisfactorily in isolation from specific problems. The citation of specific problems in this paper is intended to illustrate the necessity of dealing simultaneously with biblical and extra-biblical evidence, and also the more difficult problem of attempting to understand the driving convictions which led ancient scribes to utilize and reinterpret old traditions to make them valuable and relevant to their own time. Ps. 78 assures us that the historical traditions constitute a *mashal;* they are even *ḥidot*. Biblical history constantly illustrates the "uses of the past" for instructing and guiding the present; it is a manner of thought unfashionable in academic circles at present, yet as scholars we are not called upon to judge, but to understand. Such uses of historical tradition later developed into the wildness of allegorical interpretation, a form of prolonged metaphor in which typically a series of actions are symbolic of other actions. Ultimately perhaps, the essential distinction between wild allegory and responsible historical interpretation of the Bible lies in understanding the mind of its Ultimate Author, but for this there is no academic method. As scholars we must understand the minds of its authors by seeing how they used their word-labels, not ours, and seeing life as they saw it—and they were not Christians; nor were they rabbinic Jews.

MOSHE GREENBERG

RESPONSE TO ROLAND de VAUX'S "Method in the Study of Early Hebrew History"

One is filled with admiration at the balance Père de Vaux has struck between claiming too much and too little, between pessimism and optimism. Such circumspection and scope are the fruits of lifelong study, research, and discovery, a constant striving to understand particulars in themselves as well as their place in the larger framework. Our discipline is fortunate to have such masters in its vanguard, and we may congratulate ourselves for having evoked this lucid statement from Père de Vaux on a most vexed theme.

The layman—such do I count myself in this area—must regard with wonder and envy the assurance shown by most of the scholarly jousters in this field. After years of training the philologist reaches a point where he relies on his sense of the context to help him decide the meaning of an obscure word, phrase, or passage. Yet in spite of all our advances no insider need be told how far we are from understanding many of the most familiar passages of Hebrew narrative, not to speak of prophecy and poetry. When we seek the context of early Israel's history we find that not only is the tradition spotty and sporadic, but the external environing context is uncommonly defective. The contemporary Near East was undergoing upheavals in which old civilizations were dissolving, or had retired into their shells, while new peoples were just beginning to erupt upon the scene. Records are meager even for the established civilizations; of the impression Israel made on its neighbors during the centuries between the patriarchs and the founding of the monarchy we have virtually no external trace. It is no wonder that opinion on the incorporation of the patriarchal stories into general history is sharply divided. Once the traditions are required to validate themselves by external tests, the slightness of the evidence upon which such validation can rest proves to be equalled only by the flimsiness of the arguments that call it into question.

Père de Vaux has done well to remark the often extreme indirectness of philological and archaeological "attestations" of preconquest traditions. Mesopotamian law of largely prepatriarchal times, Nuzi customs geographically remote (though Harran was in the Mittannian state), Mari names—these and the like do indeed establish the verisimilitude of biblical traditions, their agreement with ancient Near Eastern practice at large. Insofar as certain practices, such as adoption, fail to appear in later times, the authenticity of the tradition in these respects is supported. But the skeptic is right in insisting that such evidence does nothing to authenticate a single one of the patriarchs, or enable us to locate them in a particular external framework. For answering the questions, who were the patriarchs? how did they live? what relations had they with their neighbors? we are never likely to have any resort other than biblical traditions. Recent remodelings of the patriarchal image along the lines of international merchants or caravaneers seem perverse, just because an externally verifiable picture of patriarchal life is gained by sacrificing the sole witness to the phenomenon: if the tradition is wrong about their way of life (and it is quite unequivocal about their shepherd-nomad status), why put any trust in it at all?

One of the potent solvents of confidence in the historicity of Israel's early traditions is the etiological approach to them. It cannot be denied that etiology is a prime motive of the tradition; the popular historiography of every people is etiological through and through; it seeks to preserve those memories of the past that make the present meaningful. To conclude from this that popular historiography is a collection of *ad hoc* invented etiologies of contemporary institutions and values is both a non-sequitur and a tax on credulity. The traditions of a migrant nation with a strongly developed historical sense will of course attach to places, persons, and tribes, since events necessarily occur to persons and tribes at given places. But to suppose that places—sanctuaries, stoneheaps, ruins, towns, for example—can generate peculiar, non-patterned stories such as are found in the conquest traditions is another tax on credulity.

Those events that survive the etiological interpretation are often regarded as having had but local significance at first. The issue here is the antiquity of the union of clans called Israel, the bearer of the traditions. Here I find myself differing with our learned master. Had there not been, however constituted, an entity called Israel prior to the occupation of Canaan, that planned and executed, however imperfectly, an invasion and settlement of both sides of the Jordan, I fail to see how subsequently the tribal confederacy of Israel in Canaan could have arisen. That confederacy, for the first time in history, united populations on both sides of the Jordan, along the whole length of the inland, and even jumped over the Canaanite valley of Jezreel to embrace the Galilean tribes. Such an unprecedented unity in an area that by nature encourages ethnic and political fragmentation is intelligible to me only on the assumption of a prior union of its elements. Again, when the entire tradition speaks of general hostility between the Israelites and the natives—the exception of Shechem being accounted for in the tradition itself (the Dinah episode, Jacob's blessing to Joseph)—I cannot comprehend why a peaceful, gradual interpenetration of populations (as the Israelite occupation is sometimes alleged to have been) should have been so contrarily represented.

All the foregoing is by way of a preliminary to the assertion that the loosely connected tales of the conquest tradition no more require the assumption of an originally disconnected batch of local etiological tales than do the similar varied traditions of the seventh-century Moslem conquest of Palestine-Syria. Who imagines that the loosely juxtaposed, and inconsistently ordered accounts of the battles of Ajnadain, Fihl, Damascus, Yarmuk, and Caesarea were originally *ortsgebundenen* etiologies? The traditions of the Moslem invasion were *volksgebundenen;* they were preserved in the memories of men caught up in a powerful religio-national movement. There is no better parallel to the general character of the Israelite invasion as described in the book of Joshua and Judg. 1. But, you say, the contradictions! Who, after all, conquered Hebron? Was Joshua the leader all along? of the whole union? Was the conquest accomplished at one blow, or in stages? A cursory reading of the confused records of the Arab conquest will provide parallels galore to such difficulties and contradictions. The order of the battles and the time elapsed differ in Medinan and Iraqi traditions. The time and extent of activity of the heroic figure of the conquest, Khâlid ibn al Walîd, "The Sword of Allah," who deposed him, when and why—are shrouded in confusion. Yet the general outline is clear: a prior assignment of territory to be conquered among three or four camps; a few crucial campaigns under a unified command ranging from south to north and in Transjordan; then mopping-up operations in various sectors under the local generals.[1] The parallel in gross to the tradition of Israel's conquest is remarkable. Of course there is disharmony among the biblical data; of course there are signs of editions; of course criticism is indispensable to make one's way through the divergences. But to reject the main lines of the tradition in favor of a concocted picture of a peaceful infiltration seems to be hazardous in the extreme.

Anyone acquainted at first hand with the material, biblical and extra-biblical, knows how tenuous are the constructions we make to bridge the gaps between our deplorably fragmentary data. We string cobwebs of theory over the chasms, cobwebs that may be shredded by tomorrow's deliberation or later reconsideration. Our mainstay, logical inference, fails to take into account the irrationality of real events, or the exent of our ignorance. A beautiful illustration of the trap into which inferences are apt to lead the historian comes from last week's newspaper. "Mr. Trevor-Roper, professor of history at Oxford wrote in *The Sunday Times* of London this week that the commission investigating President Kennedy's assassination had left important matters unresolved. First, he said, [Oswald] was questioned for 12 hours after his arrest by the FBI and the police. Oswald was warned that any statement [he made] could be used against him. Yet, supposedly, no notes or tape recordings were kept. That could not be true, the professor said. 'How could any statement made by Oswald be used against him if his statements were unrecorded?' " The inference is compelling: written records must have been made; something is being kept from the public. I continue from the news item: "According to Warren Commission staff members and persons familiar with the police methods, this question . . . is simply based on unfamiliarity with the situation. The fact is that few police forces tape or transcribe interviews with suspects. Characteristically, the suspect is questioned at some length. If he makes incriminating admissions, a stenographer will be called in and a confession dictated and signed." [2]

[1] Classic critical treatments of the Arab accounts of the conquest of Syria are J. Wellhausen, *Skizzen und Vorarbeiten,* VI (1899), 1-7, 51-68; M. J. de Goeje, *Mémoire sur la conquête de la Syrie* (1900). A specimen of Arab historiography on this period is available in English in P. Hitti, *The Origins of the Islamic State* (1916), a translation of part of Baladhuri's account of the Moslem wars. A modern soldier's appraisal of these battles is J. B. Glubb, *The Great Arab Conquests* (1963).

[2] *New York Times,* Dec. 17, 1964.

We cannot, of course, abandon inference. But we can strive to maintain a becoming humility and open-mindedness, keeping in view our appalling handicaps. The many tacit assumptions, mostly unexamined, which we habitually make ought to be kept at the forefront of our consciousness:

The canon of literary criticism that an interruption of chronological order or a mixture of styles indicates composition—resting on the assumption that original creations in biblical times were chronologically ordered and stylistically homogeneous.

The correlate of the above, that composition implies lateness—resting on the peculiar notion that compilers could not have been contemporaries of the several authors whose work they compiled.

The assumption that fantasy or legend implies a real distance from the event at the bottom of the legend—in the face of abundant evidence that legends can accompany heroes during their lifetime, not to speak of the years immediately after their death.

Form criticism too, as suggestive as it has been, is grossly abused when it is made to serve chronology. The pure or original forms abstracted by the form critic are no more than mental constructs, useful for the esthetic and literary criticism of a piece. Rarely, however, does a passage in our texts actually display this ideal form; usually we meet with mixtures. Now the assumption that mixed or skewed forms signify editorial or transmissional tampering is a gratuitous denial of a poet's right or even inclination to create from the first a novel form for his creation. There is impressive evidence that in the course of time forms deteriorated; but that at any moment in the history of biblical literature only pure forms were in use is the merest assumption. Hence the notion that by stripping a piece of its form-corrupters one can get back to its original kernel is unproved. Above all, conjectures on the absolute dating based on form criteria seem to be better repressed at this stage of our knowledge.

We are hardly in a position to speak even of "probability" in most of these matters. Our "probability" is more often than not an impression gotten from one or two stray instances. The only honest way to write or talk on these matters is with liberal doses of "ifs," "perhapses," and "maybes" that will leave no doubt to our readers and students what the true state of our knowledge is.

It seems to me that the materials of ancient near Eastern literature have not yet been tapped adequately by tradition and form criticism. These materials have enabled scholars to recreate the civilizations that were the milieu of biblical Israel; they offer cultural and religious analogues and contrasts to Israelite creativity. But a study of their literary styles and habits, especially with an eye to the differences between our expectations and their performance, would put solid ground under the feet of the man who would speak confidently about what may and may not be expected in a piece of ancient near Eastern literature. In his comparative study of Egyptian literature, T. Eric Peet displayed irritation at the awkwardness of Egyptian narrations. "This incident," he writes of a passage in the Tale of the Shipwrecked Sailor, "is an excrescence. It has no relation to the rest of the story and it holds up the action. It is probably an allusion to some myth . . . and the mythologist has here got the better of the story-teller, to the disadvantage of the story." Or again of the style of Sinuhe: "At one point the whole action is held up while he delivers a metrical panegyric on the present king of Egypt. . . . When the moment of [his] recall comes, a long, bombastic and extravagant court document is blatantly inserted, and no attempt is made to weave it into the texture of the narrative. It is even brutally labelled *Copy of the decree which was brought to the humble servant concerning his return to Egypt,* and we are not even spared a copy of Sinuhe's acknowledgement of this decree, couched in terms only less stilted. After these interludes, which, be it noted, are of considerable length Sinuhe returns to his narrative, which flows smoothly and uninterruptedly to its finish." [3] Note well: though annoyed by such roughness, Peet does not believe Sinuhe therefore to be an editorial patchwork.

Of this sort of evidence concerning the native modes of ancient writing we cannot have enough. Yet hardly a beginning has been made. But until we have solid studies of the styles of ancient near Eastern writing, how can we speak with confidence about what is in and out of order, an editorial excrescence or an original "awkwardness"—from our viewpoint —in biblical writing? Not, mind you, that one has any right automatically to equate biblical style with extrabiblical. But if the evidence goes the way I suspect it will, the same sort of verisimilitude that Mari, Nuzi, and Hammurabi have given the customs of patriarchal times is likely to

[3] T. E. Peet, *A Comparative Study of the Literatures of Egypt, Palestine, and Mesopotamia* (1931), pp. 31 f., 37 f.

be lent to the present styles of biblical writing, changing our conception of the editor's hand in creating them.

To conclude: after allowances have been made for and against the historicity of biblical tradition, and counting in all the near Eastern materials relevant and presently available, a history of Israel's beginnings satisfying the standards of a modern historian still cannot be written. One can rehearse the traditional accounts, assessing fully and candidly grounds of doubt and indications of verisimilitude where they exist, showing forth the inner coherence and freedom from pattern of the tradition, insofar as they exist. If there is one dictate commanded by our present condition it is this: that we speak in the language of humility and contingency. Père de Vaux's masterly survey is a model of obedience to this dictate.

2

ARVID S.
KAPELRUD

The Role of the Cult in Old Israel

The fourth chapter of Genesis tells about the offerings of Cain and Abel. As the books of the OT are arranged, that is the first time the note of the cult is sounded, and it grows to a melody which is heard through the whole work, mostly harmoniously, but some times also in a cacophony of disharmony.

Nevertheless, the cult is only one, if complicated, feature of the OT, and since the middle of last century other features have been brought to the fore by an army of scholars. That was done to such a degree by the Wellhausen school and its recent followers that when the tides turned, the new stress on the cult and its importance in Israel caused some irritation, opposition, and even accusations of high church theology, revolving around cult and ritual, institutions and offices.[1] A protest against a point of view which underlines the importance of the cult in Israel too much is found in Martin Noth's *History of Israel,* a book which is much used by students not only in Germany, but also in other countries. Noth admits that the central feature in the amphictyony was the common cult at the central holy place in front of Yahweh, i.e. the ark (Judg. 20:26 f.). Details about this cult are, however, unknown.[2] In this connection Noth draws some far-reaching conclusions. According to him cultic acts were apparently not regarded as of prime importance in Israel, and it is not accidental that compared with religious documents from neighboring countries, e.g. Ugarit, the OT shows surprisingly little interest in purely

[1] G. Fohrer, *JBL,* LXXX (1961), 318.
[2] Noth, *Geschichte Israels,* 3. Aufl., Göttingen, 1956, p. 94. English tr., p. 97.

cultic events and problems.[3] It is tempting to reply with his own words here: "No wonder, because it is not usual to tell much about regularly working and therefore not very remarkable institutions." [4] It is also necessary to draw attention to the following statement from the same context: "Just because the constitution of the amphictyonic confederation of the twelve tribes remained a permanent and therefore self-evident institution, so little is told about it in the OT." [5] Noth has not applied this interesting principle to the cult in the OT, but other scholars have.

Even without use of this principle it is necessary to contend that life in old Israel was permeated by cultic thinking, cultic acts, and cultic expressions. Religious life in Israel expressed itself in cult and had to be expressed in that way. If we cut out the cult, we cut out the covenant, and in cutting out the covenant we also take the ground away under Israelite morality.

But before we go into details it is necessary to discuss briefly what cult really is. Different opinions on controversial matters in the field of the cult do not seldom depend on the fact that scholars have different definitions of cult. Cult is much more than sacrifices and offerings. According to Paul Tillich, "all religious acting is cultic acting," and offerings are thus "the central, cultic symbol." [6] This definition seems very wide, but a wide definition is preferable if our picture of religion in old Israel shall be a right one. Mowinckel defines cult in the following way: "Cult or worship may generally be defined as the socially established and regulated holy acts and words, through which the encounter and communion of God with the congregation is established." [7] Cult is, according to him, "the visible and auditive expression of the relation between God and the congregation." [8] Personally I should prefer a definition which is a trifle wider: cult is religious life in certain regulated forms, expressing the relationship between God and man and intended for use in a society.

Historically seen, the cult was present at the earliest stages of the history of Israel; in any case the old traditionists were of this opinion. The historical narratives do not say very much about *how* cult was performed,

[3] *Ibid.*, p. 96. English tr., p. 99.
[4] *Ibid.*, p. 94. English tr., p. 97.
[5] *Ibid.*
[6] *Religionsphilosophie,* Stuttgart, 1962, pp. 105, 109.
[7] *Offersang og Sangoffer,* Oslo, 1951, p. 15. English tr., p. 15.
[8] *Ibid.*, p. 16. English tr., p. 16.

they just tell that cult took place. The narratives of the cultic acts and words of the patriarchs are not told in order to convey an historical fact to posterity alone. There may be reason to leave out the question of historicity here, on which de Vaux has recently uttered a well-balanced judgment.[9] The decisive point in the Yahwistic tradition is to give a picture of the patriarchs as cult founders and as persons who took no definite step in their lives without cultic acts.[10] Sanctuaries were erected principally in places where God had shown himself in a theophany, all along the route the patriarchs traveled.[11] There is scarcely any important center of patriarchal habitation that was not marked by an altar.[12]

This is a dominating point of view not only in the Yahwistic tradition, but also in the group of traditions which are called Elohistic. In Gen. 12:6 ff. it is told that Abraham first stopped at Shechem when he came to Canaan, at the *māqôm* where the Oak of Moreh stood, probably an old oracle place and a Canaanite sanctuary. But what Abraham met there was no Canaanite god, it was Yahweh, who promised him the country which he had entered. Abraham then built an altar for Yahweh. As pointed out by de Vaux, we have here a typical story about the foundation of a sanctuary: theophany, divine message, and beginning of the cult.[13]

But it is more than that. The role played by Yahweh is worth observing. The traditionist does not hide the fact which could not be hidden: that the cult place was an old Canaanite one. He tries, however, to show that Yahweh was the God who was actually present at this place, and that the Canaanite cult had to be replaced by an Israelite. That means that ancient Canaanite cult was a factor that could not be neglected. It was a power which could be defeated only by a new strong power: an Israelite cult, instituted by the patriarchs.

This is plainly said in the Elohistic traditions, which tell that Jacob bought a piece of land outside Shechem and set up an altar there. He called it "El, God of Israel" (Gen. 33:18-20). The name of this altar is a program, indicating that El was not only the god who was worshiped at Shechem by the Canaanites, but also the God of Israel. That is an in-

[9] *Ancient Israel,* New York, 1962, p. 289.
[10] E.g. Gen. 12:7, 8; 13:4, 18; 15:7 ff.; 26:25.
[11] De Vaux, *op. cit.,* p. 289.
[12] R. J. Thompson, *Penitence and Sacrifice in Early Israel Outside the Levitical Law,* Leiden, 1963, p. 53.
[13] *Op. cit.,* p. 289.

dication of the same process of identification which went on until the time of David when it reached its final stage. This process reveals something about the importance of the cult at this time: it was a power which the Israelites had to master if they would survive and not be submerged in the Canaanite religion. The main question was not whether it was El who was worshiped or Yahweh. As the Yahwistic tradition underlines, the decisive fact was that cult had to be performed because it was necessary for a continued life in the new country, the promised land of Canaan.

It is possible to apply the same point of view to what happened at other cult places: Bethel, Hebron (or Mamre), Beersheba, Mizpah, Shiloh, Gilgal, Gibeon, Ophrah, and Dan, but that would only accumulate evidence and not bring us further. It would, however, give us a lively picture of Hebrew groups, trying to establish themselves in a new country and trying hard to find balance of life through a cult which meant more to them at this stage than did the fact who the god was whom they worshiped.

Just as intense in their cult, but with another mighty revelation of God's direct acts in history, were the groups coming into Canaan from the south. Most probably they brought with them two important cult objects which were to play a central role: the tent of meeting and the ark of Yahweh.[14] According to the old traditions (J and E layers), the tent of meeting was a place where Israelites who wanted an oracle could get it (Exod. 33:7). This indicates that it was a movable sanctuary, which the tribes brought with them, simply because they could not do without a cult place and oracle place like this one. The picture which the Priestly tradition gives of the tent (Exod. 36 and 40) is a late idealization which has led many scholars to see the tent as mere fiction, which it surely was not, as ancient and modern Bedouin usage indicates.[15]

An even more central role was played by the ark of Yahweh. As it is described in the Priestly tradition in Exod. 25:10-22 and 37:1-9 the ark was a chest made of acacia wood, with a plate of gold, the *kappōreth,* and two cherubim who covered it with their wings. It was most probably an ark of this form which was kept at Shiloh (I Sam. 3:3) and carried into the battle at Aphek (I Sam. 4:3 f.), later kept at Kiriath-jearim (I

[14] *Ibid.,* pp. 294-302.
[15] So also *ibid.,* p. 296.

Sam. 5:7—7:1) and then brought up to Jerusalem in a procession by David (II Sam. 6). This procession was regularly repeated, as Pss. 132 and 25 seem to indicate. The ark was a cultic symbol, constantly signalizing the presence of Yahweh among his people, in war and peace, and especially at the great festivals. The tent of meeting and the ark of Yahweh linked the Israelite everyday cultically with Yahweh and the holy sphere.

From the south came also the *pesaḥ*-festival, a cultic event which more and more became the dominating event in the spring. The origin of this feast cannot be discussed on this occasion, but to sketch the importance of it, a few words have to be said. The Passover was first a rite practiced by shepherds, nomads or seminomads. It was a springtime sacrifice of a lamb, in order to secure fecundity for the flock.[16] After the invasion of the Israelites into Canaan the feast of Unleavened Bread, *maṣṣôth,* was combined with the Passover. This feast was a great event, starting with the reaping of the first sheaf at the barley harvest, and lasting a whole week (Exod. 12:16, 23:15, 34:18, Lev. 23:6-8, Deut. 16:8). It was kept in the month of Abib, the month when the Passover also took place.

These feasts were common in ordering unleavened bread used,[17] but they were even more combined through an ideological complex, which must surely have had some base in the ancient form and ideology of the feasts. The overwhelming experience which the tribes made who were able to march unhurt out of Egypt, colored and destined the Yahweh religion for all future. It also colored the Israelite cult and gave it an historical impress which is original and not found among the neighboring peoples.

There is no reason to doubt that there was an important historical event which impressed the Israelite tribes who fled from Egypt. The story about this event was told and retold hundreds of times, and the result of this can be seen in Exod. 1—15. Those chapters are neither a pure historical narrative nor a mere "cultic expression of a myth about Yahweh's struggle with his enemies," [18] but rather a combination of both

[16] *Ibid.,* p. 489.
[17] *Ibid.,* p. 491, and *Les sacrifices de l'Ancien Testament,* Paris, 1964, pp. 24 f.
[18] De Vaux, *Ancient Israel,* p. 492. De Vaux here probably alludes to Johannes Pedersen's point of view in his *Israel,* III-IV, London and Copenhagen, 1940, pp. 384-415, 728-37.

phenomena. The solemn introduction in Exod. 1, leading over to the legend about the birth of Moses, the many wonderful events, demonstrating the power and the glory of Yahweh, and in the end the hymn in Exod. 15, glorifying Yahweh as a man of war, as a victorious king, who would reign for ever and ever, this is all so cultically colored that the fact cannot be denied. On the other hand the whole attitude of the Israelite tribes would be completely incomprehensible, if there were not historical facts behind.

This encounter between cult and history is not accidental in old Israel. We meet it again and again, and it takes us to a first conclusion: Yahweh's acting in history, his choice of his people and the patriarchs, his leading the tribes safely out of Egypt, were memorialized and made living to the people, continuously through the cult. The role of the cult was no matter of secondary importance: it transformed history into experience. The narrator in Exod. 12:26 f. has himself indicated this clearly.

But no cult can live from history alone, even when it is transformed. Cult requires an encounter; its main interest lies in what happens here and now and what is going to happen in the next future. Yahweh revealed himself as victorious king (Exod. 15:7), who would make the earth swallow his enemies, as he had made horse and chariot disappear in the sea under the exodus from Egypt (Exod. 15:1-12).

Yahweh's mighty deeds were renewed and actualized in the Passover. That was the overtone in the old spring feast in the month of Abib. But there were strong undertones also, springing directly from the need and anxiety of man. Both God's answer and man's desire were concentrated in the cult, so long as it was a living cult and no mere mechanical repetition of ancient rites.

The old festival components of the spring feast, the shepherds' simple Passover and the *maṣṣôth* feast, were answers to man's need. They promised fecundity and prosperity for the flock, and the blood smeared upon the tent-poles or the door-stiles drove away evil powers (Exod. 12:23). The *maṣṣôth* were made at the beginning of the barley harvest, from the new grain, without old leaven (Exod. 13:5-8, 23:15, 34:18). The unleavened bread announced and started something new and was most probably part of an ancient fertility rite.[19] This character of something

[19] De Vaux, *Ancient Israel,* pp. 490 f. Kraus, *Gottesdienst in Israel,* 2. Aufl., Munich, 1962, pp. 65 ff.

new is still present in the narrative in Josh. 5:10-12, where Passover and the feast of Unleavened Bread are kept apart.

Both the original Passover and the *maṣṣôth* feast were kept to secure fertility in the next coming future, the Passover for the herds and the *maṣṣôth* for the fields and the crops. In this respect they were part of a New Year ideology, into which the narrative of the breaking up from Egypt and starting a new life for the tribes could very well go.[20] As Yahweh had revealed his power and glory in his struggle with the Egyptians and let his chosen servant Moses lead the people through the dangers of the sea and the desert, so he would be ready to save his people again and take it to a better future.

What role this combined spring-time feast played in Israel in the time of the kings, is not known. When King Josiah in 622 B.C. swept away the foreign cult in Jerusalem and Judah, the Passover was given a prominent place, in its full, combined form (II Kings 23:9, 21-23). Directions for a full-form Passover are found in Deut. 16:1-8, and here it is expressly ordered that the people should go up to Jerusalem to have their Passover at the holy abode, Deut. 16:2, 5 f. This was surely in line with the interests of the Deuteronomists, to have all cult centralized at one place, in Jerusalem, where it could be kept under complete control.

There are, however, probably also other intentions behind this move. In the story of Josiah's reform it is told that the Passover had not been kept according to the book of the covenant since the days of the judges (II Kings 23:21 f.). That may mean that the feast was now held in its full form, at the holy place. But what is more important is the fact that Josiah (and the Deuteronomists and the Priestly author) obviously make the Passover the central and dominating feast in the Yahweh cult. That was the end of a long line, started already with the Yahwistic traditions within Exod. 1—15.

The questions may then arise: why was the importance of this feast underlined so strongly at this time? why was it placed in the foreground so demonstratively?

The Deuteronomist point of view is already mentioned, but that was probably not the original answer to the question. The first answer is found in the reform of King Josiah. The king turned out of the temple

[20] J. B. Segal, *The Hebrew Passover from the Earliest Times to A.D. 70,* London, 1963, p. 117.

several priests of foreign gods, pictures of these gods, and their altars, and he put an end to their cult (II Kings 23). The foreign cult had reached immense dimensions and must have left a most perceptible vacuum. This vacuum had to be filled at once, so that any falling back into the foreign practice could be avoided. Genuine Israelite feasts had to come instead of a cult that was colored by foreign influence. The Mesopotamian annual festival, the *akîtu,* which was celebrated as a New Year's feast in the spring,[21] probably also played a role in Jerusalem, in a temple cult where features from Canaanite, Phoenician, and Assyro-Babylonian cult were constantly filtering in in the century before Josiah. The Assyrian influence was strong already at the time of Ahaz, and the press did not decrease until the time of Josiah (cf. II Kings 16).

Seen against this background we can better understand the sudden interest which Josiah and his high priest Hilkiah took in renewing the Passover and making it the central feast. They needed a feast of a genuine Israelite character, and preferably a feast that was celebrated in the spring, so that it could keep the *akîtu* out. That gave them no choice: it had to be the Passover, with all the elements which could be gathered into it, i.e. the fully combined Passover.

In this operation the Deuteronomists and later the Priestly author followed up, thus finishing a development which had started earlier in the standing struggle in the time of the kings between ancient Yahwistic features in Israel's religion and a strong foreign religious influence, now Canaanite, now Phoenician, now Assyro-Babylonian. The religion of Israel was no constant, fixed entity; it was a religion finding its content and form in a never-ceasing struggle—speaking theologically, in a history of revelation.

The history of the cult in old Israel is a real mirror of this struggle, as is already indicated. It reflects the changing tendencies and indicates what is going on.

The Josian and Deuteronomist revolution, which it, for lack of a better name, may be called, caused many changes and revaluations. When the Passover was placed definitely in the foreground, other cultic events declined into the background. The old rivalry between the spring-time feast and the autumn feast ended here, and as the situation was, it ended with

[21] Sv. Aage Pallis, *The Babylonian Akitu Festival,* Copenhagen, 1926, p. 301.

the victory of the Passover, which could, however, never substitute for the old New Year and autumn festival.

The Josian and Deuteronomist revolution made the ancient New Year and autumn feast fall to pieces, and that was done deliberately. The ancient feast was seen by the circle behind the revolution as too much colored with Assyro-Babylonian features. That is a conclusion which must announce itself to the mind when we consider the whole tendency of Josiah's reform and the Deuteronomistic history writing.

The old feast crumbled to pieces. What remained was, according to Deut. 16, the feast of Tents (*sukkôth*), at ingathering time, to be celebrated for seven days with joy at the place which Yahweh would choose. This feast would then ensure the blessing of Yahweh (vss. 13-15). According to Deut. 31 the Law was read publicly to all Israel at the feast of Tents, every seventh year (vss. 9-13).

The features mentioned by the Deuteronomists surely give some important aspects of an ancient autumn festival that could not easily be put away. It was a feast at ingathering time, a feast of joy, with the rich blessing of Yahweh, to whom gifts were brought (Deut. 16:16 f.) and homage paid, as to a king, a feast where the Psalms paying homage to Yahweh as king (Pss. 47, 93, 95, 96, 97, 98, 99) could well be used.[22] In addition comes the indication in Deut. 31 that the Law should be read every seventh year at the feast of Tents, which has made scholars think of a renewal of the covenant at this feast, mentioned, e.g. by Mowinckel, already in 1927.[23] Von Rad combined Deut. 31 with Josh. 24, and his conclusion is: "The feast of tents was in old time just the feast to which the congregation made a pilgrimage. So there is no other conceivable solution than that the feast of covenant renewal between Yahweh and the people was identical with this feast." [24]

Artur Weiser goes farther in his commentary to the Psalms. To him the covenant festival was the great central feast, which cannot be reconstructed in all its details, but whose basic elements and essential character can be apprehended. The feast was in essence a cultic drama in the course of which the fundamental events in the history of man's salvation

[22] S. Mowinckel, *The Psalms in Israel's Worship,* Vol. I, New York and Oxford, 1962, pp. 106 ff.

[23] *Le décalogue,* Paris, 1927, pp. 119 f.

[24] *Das formgeschichtliche Problem des Hexateuch,* p. 31 (=*Gesammelte Studien,* Munich, 1958, p. 42).

were reenacted, through recitation of the cult narrative with more or less dramatic emphasis. The congregation attending the feast experienced this as something which happened in its presence (Josh. 24), and thereby participated in the assurance and realization of salvation which was the real purpose of the festival.[25] Weiser is also of the opinion that the basic form of the narrative passages of the Pentateuch had its foundation in the cultic tradition of the sacral confederacy of the twelve tribes.[26]

Mowinckel took his point of departure from the Psalms praising Yahweh as king (mentioned above), which he combined with the Elohistic and Yahwistic notices in Exod. 23:16 and 34:22 about the feast of Ingathering at the end of the year. This feast was the ancient New Year festival when the foundations of the new year were laid, through a cultic drama where Yahweh was praised by his people and enthroned anew. He took his seat as a king, after having defeated his enemies, who were often seen as chaos monsters (Ps. 74:12 ff., Ps. 104), and judged them. Creation and victory over the Egyptians in the exodus were seen as two of his greatest deeds.

As Ringgren has recently pointed out,[27] we have here two different interpretations of a series of partly identical features: Mowinckel has stressed the connection with the Babylonian New Year festival which had impressed the whole Middle Eastern area, while von Rad and Weiser have tried to underline the Israelite features connected with the covenant of Yahweh. One interpretation does not quite exclude the other, and it seems likely that together they indicate the roots of the Israelite New Year festival, as it can be reconstructed from the Psalms, as an aspect of the feast of Tents.[28]

Now it is possible to answer some questions about the New Year festival. First: it is mentioned in the Yahwistic and Elohistic traditions as the feast of Ingathering at the end of the year (Exod. 34:22 and 23:16). Nothing more is said about this feast than about other feasts. To use Martin Noth's words: "Just because [it] . . . remained a permanent and therefore self-evident institution, so little is told about it in the OT." [29]

[25] Weiser, *The Psalms,* London and Philadelphia, 1962, p. 28.
[26] *Ibid.,* p. 26.
[27] Ringgren, *Israelitische Religion,* Stuttgart, 1963, p. 178.
[28] So also Ringgren, *op. cit.,* p. 178.
[29] See above, n. 5.

To the second question: why did it disappear in Israel? the answer was given above. And disappear it did, there is no doubt about that. Because of its character, which must have been more in line with the description of Mowinckel than with that of von Rad and Weiser, it gathered, rather easily, Canaanite and Babylonian features which gave it a foreign color. Probably the feast was originally Canaanite, with El as the main figure, and directly taken over by David in his policy of reconciling Israelites and Canaanites. That does not mean, however, that the Israelites took over a complete cultic pattern. Several features, which cannot be discussed here, were taken over, but a standing, complete pattern never existed.

For the third: how do we know that it did disappear? That can easily be seen from Neh. 8, where it is told how Ezra restarted the feast of Tents, and the people kept it seven days and had a solemn assembly on the eighth, according to Lev. 23. All the people built tents or huts from branches and bushes and took part in the feast (Neh. 8:14). And it is not hard to see what is new in this action.[30] It is the whole celebration of the feast in the ancient manner, as is said directly in the text, with some overstatement: "for from the days of Jeshua the son of Nun to that day the people of Israel had not done so" (Neh. 8:17). When we substitute Josiah for Jeshua the statement is probably historically correct.

At the time of Ezra and Nehemiah neither Canaanite nor Babylonian religion could seriously influence the feast of Tents; the situation was changed and the old feast could reappear. And in one of the latest chapters of the OT, from late, post-exilic time,[31] Zech. 14, we read a triumphant song, that can only reflect a feast with a character as indicated by Mowinckel: "Then everyone that survives of all the nations that have come against Jerusalem shall go up, year after year, to worship the King, Yahweh Sebaoth, and to keep the feast of Tents. And if any of the families of the earth do not go up to Jerusalem to worship the King, Yahweh Sebaoth, there will be no rain upon them. And if the family of Egypt do not go up and present themselves, then upon them shall come the plague with which Yahweh afflicts the nations that do not go up to keep the feast of Tents" (Zech. 14:16-18).

What, then, does this discussion of the great spring-time and autumn

[30] Against de Vaux, *Ancient Israel,* p. 497.
[31] Benedikt Otzen, *Studien über Deuterosacharja,* Copenhagen, 1964, p. 212.

festivals in old Israel show? It shows that the whole religious life of Israel is reflected in the cult. Only the prophets have not been discussed so far, but a few words will be said about them. The great religious reforms as well as the great collections of traditions, those of the Deuteronomists, the Priestly author, and the Chronicler, all expressed themselves through the cult. The cult was the fertile soil in which ideas were born—and lived. There the ancient traditions were given their form and handed down to posterity; there the psalms were composed and used. In it the hope, the joy, the fear, the anxiety, and the desperation of the people were expressed; in it Yahweh's answers came to them. The cult was nothing accidental; it was a living core in the relation between Yahweh and his people.

That this core needed to be under a strict and constant control the prophets have shown. They criticized many sides of the cult, as, for example, did Amos (5:21-27), and especially they attacked the sacrifices (Isa. 1:11-17, 7:21 ff., Hos. 6:6, Mic. 6:6-8). There can be no doubt that those of the prophets who took this position were of the opinion that the cult, first and foremost the sacrifices, had gained an importance which tended to cover and move into the background features in Israel's religion which were more central.

There is, however, a common agreement among most scholars of today that the prophets did not want to abolish the cult, which actually was an inconceivable idea to them. What they wanted to underline were important features within the covenant: a firm belief in God and a life in accordance with his will and with ancient customs and statutes, as they were laid down, orally or written, in the covenant. The prophets did not need to mention the covenant so much, as they lived completely within it, in their points of view, in their preaching.

The observation that the prophets used the language and literary forms of the cult[32] has recently made scholars form a theory that the preaching of the prophets was a regular part of the cult. The cultic occasion for Amos, for example, according to this point of view should have been the covenant festival.[33] Even the prophet who is considered to be most

[32] Underlined, e.g. by myself in *Joel Studies,* Uppsala and Leipzig, 1948, and *Central Ideas in Amos,* Oslo, 1956, new ed., 1961.

[33] Henning Graf Reventlow, *Das Amt des Propheten bei Amos* (*FRLANT,* Heft 80), Göttingen, 1962.

personal in his preaching, Jeremiah, is characterized as "lacking just the individual features which distinguish the individual in modern meaning." [34] His "I" is only part of his "we" as representative and embodiment of the congregation. (There is naturally a difference between this "I" of the prophet and the "I" of Yahweh in Yahweh's oracles.)

This is neither the place nor the time to discuss these theories. They may go too far, but they have to be taken seriously. The prophets did not come in straight from the desert or from some village to speak to their people in a language and a literary form which was often complicated, and which could only be learnt during a long stay at the temple, or some other central place which could supply a teacher. The prophets learned from the cult, they took part in it, more or less, and it is impossible to form a picture of an Israelite prophet without a solid cultic background.

Then, to end where we started: in his dream at the cult place of Bethel Jacob dreamed that there was a ladder set up on the earth, and the top of it reached to heaven, and the angels of God were ascending and descending on it (Gen. 28:12). That ladder symbolizes the role of the cult in old Israel.

[34] Reventlow, *Liturgie und prophetisches Ich bei Jeremia*, Gütersloh, 1963, p. 239.

BRUCE VAWTER, C.M.

RESPONSE TO ARVID S. KAPELRUD'S "The Role of the Cult in Old Israel"

It is, perhaps, always somewhat premature to speak of consensuses in a science as vigorous and as questing as that of biblical interpretation. We know too well how many of the assured positions of the past century have been subjected to a complete reexamination in our own. However, we also know how much that is lasting and unassailable has been bequeathed us by the literary and historical criticism of the nineteenth century. Particular conclusions have altered, only to reveal their underlying principles as more firmly established. In much the same way, we can perceive an emerging consensus in the form critical studies of the twentieth century. In respect to the role of the cult in Israel's formation, as Professor Kapelrud has described it in his paper, it is hardly conceivable that anyone here would be seriously disposed to question the fact that that role was an extensive one. The principle is sound, and none have done more to demonstrate its soundness than the distinguished succession of Scandinavian scholars to which Professor Kapelrud belongs. What remains to be determined is just how extensive the role of the cult has been and what specific role it has played at various times.

As far as extent is concerned, I would only note as my impression that less than adequate justice has been accorded this factor in some of the recent attempts to synthesize the history of Israel and its religion. The Psalms, it is true, have been conceded, or very nearly conceded, to the cult. But even today the relation of the prophets to the cult is too likely to be confined to a rehash of the pros and cons and the nuances of the prophetic denunciations of ritual and sacrifice. Of cultic influence on the prophets little if anything is said. And far too little is said about the role of the cult in the formation and preservation of Israel's historical traditions.[1]

It is on this last point that I should like to dwell in this brief response

[1] Cf. G. E. Wright, "Cult and History," *Interpretation*, XVI (1962), 3-20.

to Professor Kapelrud's paper. I shall confine myself to the matter with which he began, the patriarchal legends of the book of Genesis.

That cultic concerns more ancient than the sources of Genesis, more ancient even than the sources of these sources, lie at the background of the patriarchal stories, has long been recognized. The precise nature of these concerns has been variously assessed, but the term "cult saga" has occurred with persistent regularity. Hermann Gunkel perceived in the association of Abraham with Beersheba and Hebron (Mamre), of Jacob with Bethel, Shechem, and Penuel, in the frequent evocation of sacred wells, trees, and other sites, the clew to the cult interests that had once been formative in the composition of these popular sagas. These interests, however, Gunkel concluded, appear only vestigially in most of the stories, which owe their finished form to the art of non-cultic story tellers.[2] In Gen. 22:1-14, for example, the cult saga of Jeruel lies at the background of the patriarchal story, but the foreground has been preempted for other, quite diverse, preoccupations of the biblical authors.[3] As they stand in the Bible, the patriarchal legends have been woven from the threads of many etiologies, etymological, geographic, and ethnic as well as the cultic, so that it is difficult if not impossible to disentangle them satisfactorily.[4]

Later authors have taken up where Gunkel left off, attempting to unravel the threads and to seek in the disparate cultic elements of these stories the key to their prehistory. For Martin Noth, as is well known, the *Ortsgebundenheit* of the cult sagas implicit in the patriarchal legends is the index to their separate origins in the local cult centers of Canaan, where they once served thematic purposes quite independent of their later inclusion in the Israelite national epic of the Pentateuch/Hexateuch.[5] The legends were historicized into the Pentateuch first through the figure of Jacob (cf. Deut. 26:5), which led to the assimilation of the Joseph story; both of these cycles originated in central Palestine. The

[2] Hermann Gunkel, *Genesis* (Göttingen: Vandenhoeck & Ruprecht,[5] 1922), pp. lxix ff. *Idem, The Legends of Genesis* (tr. W. H. Carruth: Chicago: Open Court, 1901), pp. 106 f. (reprinted as a paperback by Schocken, 1964). See also Wright, *op. cit.*, p. 14, and John Skinner, *Genesis* (New York: Scribners, 1917), pp. xxviii-xxxii, on the nature of the traditions and their transmission.

[3] Gunkel, *Genesis*, pp. 240 ff.

[4] *Ibid.*, pp. xxx ff., 159 ff.; *Legends*, pp. 18-36.

[5] Martin Noth, *Überlieferungsgeschichte des Pentateuch* (Stuttgart: Kohlhammer, 1948), pp. 58-62.

final stage was to preface to these the southern traditions about Abraham and Isaac. The disparate origins of these legends are signalled by the disparate cult interests that underlie them, and to these the patriarchal history as such can often be a secondary appendage. Behind Jacob's association with Shechem, for example, lies an ancient cult pilgrimage from Shechem to Bethel,[6] and an Israelite enclave in Shechem (cf. Gen. 33:19), where a covenant ritual took place at the sanctuary of El Berith.[7] Isaac, who, together with Ishmael was associated with Gerar/Beer-lahai-roi through the cult of El Roi (Gen. 16:13), was only later connected with Abraham, a figure preserved in the cult history of Hebron/Mamre.[8]

That the geographical details of the stories mainly owe their existence to local cult interests, has become the common assumption of many subsequent writers, who have sought only to fill in supplementary details. Recently, for example, F. F. Hvidberg has found in the "oak of weeping" at Bethel (Gen. 35:8) the historicization of a site originally connected with the cult of the mother goddess Astarte (Gen. 35:14 shows the connection of this site with the cult).[9] The same association, he believes, may be discerned in the location of Rachel's tomb at Ramah (cf. Gen. 35:19, I Sam. 10:2, Jer. 31:15-17).

It must be admitted that Noth's reconstruction of the patriarchal history makes sense. That is to say, it offers an hypothesis that reasonably accounts for the phenomena. Things very well could have happened this way. However, form critical hypotheses must be tested by some standard other than their intrinsic reasonableness if they are to avoid the easy pitfall of circular arguments. It would not be altogether unreasonable to assume that the entire Hexateuchal story of Moses and Joshua (that is to say, Ἰησοῦς) is an etiological invention to explain John 1:17 and the rest of the Moses-Jesus typology of the NT, did we not know better. John Bright has offered an illuminating series of instances in American history where etiologies could be just as reasonably assumed, and just as incorrectly.[10] This sort of thing does not, of course, prove that Noth and Alt

[6] Cf. Albrecht Alt. "Die Wallfahrt von Sichem nach Bethel," *Von Bulmerincq Memorial* (Riga: Ernst Plates, 1938), pp. 218-30 (=*Kleine Schriften zur Geschichte des Volkes Israel* [Munich: Beck, 1953] I, 79-88).

[7] Noth, *op. cit.*, pp. 86-95.

[8] *Ibid.*, pp. 112-27.

[9] *Weeping and Laughter in the Old Testament* (Leiden: Brill, 1962), pp. 106 f.

[10] *Early Israel in Recent History Writing* (Naperville, Illinois: Allenson, 1956), pp. 94-110.

were wrong, but it does put us on our guard against too easily acceding to an hypothesis merely because it is plausible.

In respect to the patriarchal legends we obviously have nothing quite as satisfactory as American history to control our hypotheses. We do, however, have a centrally important historical fact, so basic and so much taken for granted that it can become lost from sight in the complexity of its details. That fact is Israel itself. Bright is of the opinion that the hypothesis of Alt and Noth as applied to the patriarchal history leaves Israel to this extent without an adequate explanation, and I am inclined to agree. The historical fact of Israel seems to require rather more that is historical about the patriarchal stories than Alt and Noth were prepared to allow. For prehistorical though they may have been, the patriarchs were part and parcel of Israel's history. They were such for the Yahwist, and they were such for the "cultic credos" that preceded him (cf. Deut. 26:5 ff., Josh. 24:2 ff., I Sam. 12:8), the antiquity of which has been ably argued by von Rad.[11]

The late T. W. Manson, opposing an exaggerated form criticism that could see only the creative influence of the Christian community as the explanation of the Gospel materials, once reminded his readers that it was conceivable that Jesus was no less interesting, for his own sake, to people of the first century than to historians of the twentieth.[12] *Positis ponendis,* something of the same thing may be said of the patriarchs. The fact that their role in the biblical narrative is primary and not incidental to a series of cult legends, could suggest that this was their role primordially in the traditions that were later incorporated into the national epic of Israel. Alt, it seems to me, actually recognized something of this kind in the patriarchal figures, when in his fundamental work on the subject he acknowledged them as first and foremost recipients of revelation and authors of cult, who were only secondarily associated with the sanctuaries of Canaan after the Israelite *Landaufnahme*.[13]

It has been claimed that the Hexateuchal stories have made a conscious

[11] *Das formgeschichtliche Problem des Hexateuch* (Stuttgart: Kohlhammer, 1938), pp. 50-57 (=*Gesammelte Studien zum Alten Testament* [Munich: Kaiser Verlag, 1958], pp. 62-70).

[12] "Present-day Research in the Life of Jesus," *Dodd Festschrift* (Cambridge University Press, 1955), pp. 213 f.

[13] *Der Gott der Väter* (Stuttgart: Kohlhammer, 1929), pp. 49-73 [*Kleine Schriften* 1, pp. 45-67].

effort to preserve the cult legends of precisely those shrines which were of the most interest to early Israel, places like Shiloh, Shechem, Mizpah, Ramah, Gibeon, Gilgal, Bethel, Dan, Ophrah, and Beersheba. That there is something to this, no one would care to deny. Nevertheless, the role played by the sanctuaries in these stories is not at all simple, but highly complex and even ambiguous. De Vaux, for example, has pointed out that the sanctuaries associated with the patriarchs were not the most popular ones in the period of the judges and from the time of the monarchy could have become suspect to orthodox Yahwists (cf. Amos 4:4, 5:5, Hos. 5, etc.) ; in this fact he sees a factor to be weighed in considering the historical likelihood of the patriarchal stories.[14]

As defined by Mowinckel, the cult legend of which we have been speaking is a narrative derived from the cultic myth of a sanctuary, the enacted mystery recast as a message.[15] He conceives of the transformation of this myth into epic through the art of professional or semiprofessional saga-tellers created by the demands of pilgrims on the occasions of the great festivals, either attached to the sanctuary in question or as wandering "men of God," Levites, seers, *nᵉḇî'îm,* saints, miracle-workers. Versions would rise and be combined, and larger complexes of traditions would be formed, poetic in style and structure, in which the connection with the cult and cult places would always remain more or less recognizable. Because the Pentateuchal stories are not like this, he insists that in Israel the historical tradition existed from the beginning as a preoccupation independent of the cultic; there has been an influence on the former from the latter, but it has been secondary. Though the historical tradition was likewise experienced in the cult as a real history of salvation, as *mythos,* still it does not appear that any of the traditions as they have been handed down to us in the Pentateuch could ever have been used as "festival legend" in his defined sense of the word. They are, rather, historical saga.[16]

It is very difficult, as a matter of fact, to imagine a cult legend, even a vestigial cult legend, that would be content with identifying a sacred

[14] *Ancient Israel, Its Life and Institutions* (tr. John McHugh; New York: McGraw-Hill, 1962) , p. 289.

[15] Sigmund Mowinckel, *Religion und Kultus* (Göttingen: Vandenhoeck & Ruprecht, 1953) , pp. 108-15.

[16] *Idem, The Psalms in Israel's Worship* (tr. D. R. Ap-Thomas; Oxford: Blackwell, 1962) , I, 166-69.

well as "between Kadesh and Bered" (Gen. 16:14) or an ancient altar as merely "having Bethel on the west and Ai on the east" (Gen. 12:8). It is hard to credit an enduring cultic interest in locations like the land of Moriah (Gen. 22:2) or the valley of Shaveh (Gen. 14:17), the identity of which was evidently no longer known to those who so carefully preserved these details of the patriarchal stories.

But if we can conceive of an early cult interest that transcended the local and that was itself historical, we can perhaps also conceive of a cultic *Sitz im Leben* for the Pentateuchal stories that is not as distinct from the historical as Mowinckel would make it. Is the prose story of Deborah in Judg. 4 more or less "historical" than the Song of Deborah in Judg. 5, which is doubtless an extract from the cultic "Book of the Wars of Yahweh" (Num. 21:14)? The continuing interest of the biblical authors in the patriarchal stories lay not so much in the locales which were their setting as in the theophanies that had taken place there. The theophanies were in themselves the important thing, not the theophanies as sanctifying a particular place of cult. Despite the importance of Shechem to amphictyonic Israel, of Bethel to the Israel of the monarchy, and of Beersheba as a place of pilgrimage for both Israel and Judah in the time of the Yahwist, nothing is really brought out either in praise or blame of these sites: they are important only as places where God had appeared to the patriarchs. Similarly, Gilgal is the site of a theophany in the continuing Hexateuchal narratives (Josh. 5:13-15), as is Ophrah (Judg. 6:11-15), and so on.

It may also be noted that some of these names at least were remembered not only as of sites associated with theophanies but also as of divine titles which had been identified with Yahweh. Roi is consciously recalled as such a title in connection with Beer-lahai-roi (Gen. 16:13 f.). Bethel, too, which can now be identified certainly as such a title, appears to have been so remembered in Gen. 31:13, 35:7.[17] Other instances are not equally clear. Sheba, for example, appears as a divine title only elsewhere

[17] The very least that can be said of MT in these passages is that it is equiprobable with the alternatives that have been proposed. Cf. Otto Eissfeldt, "Der Gott Bethel," *Archiv für Religionswissenchaft,* XXVIII (1930), 1-30 (=*Kleine Schriften* [Tübingen: Mohr, 1962], I, 206-33). RSV "the God of Bethel" for *hāʾēl bêt-ʾēl* of Gen. 31:13 is, of course, impossible. The Confraternity and Anchor Bible (Speiser) translations have supplied a phrase from LXX and the Targum which, however, is uncertain and, in any case, a *lectio facilior.*

in the OT, represented in such names as Bath-sheba, Elisheba, Jehosheba, and so forth.[18] On the other hand, that names like Elyon or Shaddai have lost whatever specific geographic associations they once possessed shows how secondary the interest in places could be.

May we not ask whether this state of affairs does not fairly reflect a cultic situation in its own right underlying the patriarchal legends, a cultic situation that remains living in these stories and has not been artificially produced through the reworking of sanctuary cult legends? As Eissfeldt has insisted more than once, too much stress has been laid on what is local in these stories and not enough on what is their consistent emphasis: to identify Yahweh with a single God, the El of patriarchal times.[19] As the stories appear in Genesis, there is nothing polemical about them; Yahweh is identified with, not substituted for El.[20] But if this was their emphasis for Yahwistic authors, could it not have been the original emphasis of the stories as they grew out of the lives of some of Israel's ancestors?

Our present knowledge of ancient Near Eastern history, its peoples and religions, has taught us to treat the patriarchal stories with respect as regards their historical memory for cultural and social detail. May we not properly presume an equally tenacious memory for religious and cultic detail? In this connection several thoughts occur to me. One is the recent suggestion of E. A. Speiser that in the Abraham story, reset in its historical context as we know it, we may find an authentic record of the beginning of the monotheistic biblical process.[21] It is no peremptory argument against such an hypothesis that there is no parallel to an El cult of this kind otherwise known to us from Canaan. The rather pathetic El of the Ugaritic texts, a god of empty titles tolerated as a kind of senile elder statesman, obviously is no model for the El of the Penta-

[18] Cf. Herbert Haag, "Erwägungen über Beer-Sheba," *Sacra Pagina: Miscellanea Biblica Congressus Internationalis Catholici de re Biblica* (Paris: Gabalda, 1959), I, 335-45. Francesco Vattioni, "Deus pestis Era," *Verbum Domini,* XXXVI (1958), 38-42, has suggested an affinity between the *ilSibi* of cuneiform texts and the god of pestilence Erra or Irra.

[19] Cf. "El and Yahweh," *JSS,* I (1956), 25-37; "Non dimittam te, nisi benedixeris mihi," *Mélanges Robert* (Paris: Bloud & Gay, 1957), pp. 77-81. See also de Vaux, *op. cit.,* p. 294.

[20] Cf. G. W. Ahlström, *Aspects of Syncretism in Israelite Religion* (Lund: Gleerup, 1963), pp. 12-14.

[21] *Genesis* (*Anchor Bible;* Garden City: Doubleday, 1964), pp. xlvi-lii.

teuch, and efforts to connect them must be in vain.[22] However, we are not concerned with the El of Ugarit but with the El of Israel's ancestors. And I submit that if Israel itself is unique in human history, we have some reason to suppose that its antecedents could be equally unique.

Certainly the Pentateuch has simplified some vast complexities, and this is especially true of the patriarchal history. Probably the most obvious simplification was the joining of the Joseph story, of Egyptian origin, with the remainder of these legends redolent of the soil and cult of Canaan. The Yahwistic coloration of the stories—not merely that of the Yahwist—is admittedly anachronistic. But the chronicle of a preamphictyonic cult of a single El who could be identified with Yahweh need be no anachronism at all.

I would only add that if we do, indeed, owe the preservation of these stories to their cultic associations, we may have an additional insight into the way in which they have retained accuracy of detail through many centuries. If the patriarchs were remembered primarily as founders of tribal religion, and not merely as connected with given shrines, their interest for the tradition would have been roughly what it was for Israel's earliest historians. It could have extended to such non-sanctuary concerns as the purchase of an ancestral tomb from a man named Ephron, and to intra- and extratribal relationships. Anyone who has had any dealings with a religion in which cult and its institutions are taken very seriously knows how conservative it can be in its tradition and how impatient it can be of change, even in the area of the peripheral. It was to such a tradition that the Yahwist fell heir at the emergence of Israel the nation.

[22] For Otto Eissfeldt's reading of text 53 (Gordon's 107), see his *El im ugaritischen Pantheon* (Berlin: Akademie-Verlag, 1951), pp. 60-70. Cf. the remarks of Marvin H. Pope, *El in the Ugaritic Texts* (Leiden: Brill, 1955), pp. 82-104.

HERBERT G. MAY

RESPONSE TO ARVID S. KAPELRUD'S "The Role of the Cult in Old Israel"

Professor Kapelrud's paper is a significant treatment of a topic which is at the heart of much contemporary OT research. Among other things, his subject involves a reconstruction of the probable cultic practices and associated beliefs of the patriarchs, the question of the existence and possible role of the amphictyonic organization of early Israel, the nature and origins of numerous cultic objects and institutions (such as sacrifices, priesthood, ark, tent of meeting and/or tabernacle, and the bull-throne of Yahweh), Canaanite and Mesopotamian influences on the Israelite cult, the role of the king in the cult, and the attitude of the prophets toward the cult and their participation in it. The subject also involves the festivals in ancient Israel, including such issues as the annual covenant renewal festival and its role in formulating and preserving the traditions and legal codes of Israel, the nature of the autumn festival and the relation of a New Year enthronement of Yahweh rite to it, and the origins and development of the combined festival of Passover and of Unleavened Bread as a springtime festival. Professor Kapelrud has made reference to most of these in his excellent paper.

Time limitation has prevented him from dealing directly with the historicity of the biblical presentation of the cultic acts and associated ideology of the patriarchs, or with the presupposition that the patriarchs were founders of separate cults in which deities were given names compounded with the personal names of the founders.[1] The patriarchs may well have had some historical association with the Canaanite sanctuaries,[2] and as Kapelrud says, the tradition cannot and does not hide the fact that the place was an old Canaanite one. These were the sanctuary sites which later Hebrews took over on entering Canaan. That at these Canaan-

[1] Albrecht Alt, "Der Gott der Väter," *Kleine Schriften zur Geschichte des Volkes Israel,* I, 1-78; cf. H. G. May, "The God of My Father," *JBR,* IX (1941), 155 ff.
[2] R. de Vaux, *Ancient Israel,* pp. 289-94.

ite shrines there was any continuous practice of a cult established by the patriarchs extending down to the time of the conquest of Canaan is most dubious.[3] Abram built an altar at Shechem and journeyed on. The J tradition would seem to presume that an Israelite cult was thus instituted, that Yahweh was worshiped there, and ignores completely the problem of a totally Canaanite milieu. The important Canaanite temple complex there was revealed by the excavations. The religion of the Hebrew tribes at Shechem before the conquest must remain conjectural; neither Yahweh nor Elohim is mentioned in Gen. 34.[4] Does the picture of Jacob setting up an altar near Shechem and calling it "El, the God of Israel" (Gen. 33:18-20) indicate that either the patriarchs themselves or the later Hebrews believed that El, the god worshiped at Shechem by the Canaanites, was also Yahweh, the God of Israel? Or is there here no conscious identification of the Canaanite deity with the Israelite deity, El, the God of Israel, being considered by the traditionalist as an ancient title of Yahweh, not as a Canaanite deity?[5] Either the actual identification of the Canaanite El with Yahweh or the association of the name and certain of the attributes of El of Shechem with Yahweh can be explained by Cross's very probable thesis that the pre-Mosaic backgrounds of Yahwism are to be interpreted in terms of Yahweh as originally a cultic name of El, eventually splitting off from El in the radical differentiation of his cultus,

[3] This would be particularly true if Abraham is to be placed in the 19th-20th century B.C. (N. Glueck, *Rivers in the Desert,* pp. 60-110; W. F. Albright, "Abraham the Hebrew: A New Archaeological Interpretation," *BASOR,* CLXIII (1961), 36-53); it is difficult to imagine Abraham as the founder of a cult with distinct ideology which continued differentiated from normative Canaanite religion down through the many centuries until the Hebrews occupied the Shechem area. Contrast C. H. Gordon, who places the patriarchs in the Amarna period ("The Patriarchal Narratives," *JNES,* XIII [1954], 56-59). See H. Cazelles, art. "Patriarchs," *Supplément au dictionnaire de la Bible,* VIIb Fasc. 36, 1961, cols. 81-153, and extensive bibliography of patriarchal period studies noted there.

[4] Walter Harrelson (*Interpreting the Old Testament,* p. 79) advances the hypothesis that Simeon and Levi may have worshiped Yahweh in pre-Mosaic days at Shechem, and through them Yahwism may have been mediated to Judah. But perhaps Gen. 49:5-7, representing a pre-Mosaic condition of these tribes (see G. von Rad, *Genesis,* pp. 418-19) indicates that Israel's God ("I" in vs. 7) would have nothing to do with them (H. H. Rowley, *From Joseph to Joshua,* pp. 5-6). Jacob and his sons are associated with Shechem, although intermittently (Gen. 33:18-20; 35:2-4; ch. 34). See E. F. Campbell, Jr. and J. F. Ross, "The Excavation of Shechem and the Biblical Tradition," *BA,* XXVI (1963), 2-26.

[5] Compare the obviously post-patriarchal mythopoeic association of Jacob and Israel in Gen. 32:28.

and ultimately ousting El from his place in the divine council.[6] Such a radical differentiation of Yahweh's cultus probably did not come before the time of Moses.

The question of a pre-Mosaic Yahwistic cult remains as difficult as ever. E. A. Speiser in his excellent new commentary on Genesis argues confidently not only for a patriarchal Yahwism, but for an Abrahamic monotheistic Yahwism.[7] The absence of biblical pre-Mosaic names with Yahweh compounds cannot be ignored, and the E and P reminiscences of Moses as the originator of the Hebrew Yahwistic cult must be explained. The earliest most certain extrabiblical appearance of Yahweh as a nominal form occurs among Asiatic place-names on an Amenhotep III (1413-1377) temple of Amon at Soleb in Nubia, where it (*Yhw3*) is associated with the semi-nomadic Shasu of the Seir-Edom region or south Palestine. It appears also on another later list of Ramses II.[8] The earlier Amorite onomastic data from Mari are variously interpreted. The first element in such names as *Yawi-Ilâ, Yawi-Addu, Yahwi-Il,* etc., has been most plausibly interpreted as verbal,[9] but André Finet interprets it as nominal, the name *Yawi-Ilâ* meaning "El (that is) Yawi," i.e., El in a syncretistic cult identified with a newcomer, Yawi.[10]

It may well be that the patriarchal narratives reflect how the patriarchs and Hebrew groups in Canaan in pre-Joshua days adjusted themselves through trying to find a balance through a cult which meant more to them at this stage than did the identity of the god (or gods?) they worshiped. Whatever the "theology" of Abraham, he seems to have had no difficulty in participating in a cultic meal with Melchizedek, accepting a blessing in the name of the Canaanite god (Gen. 14:18, 19), making a covenant with the Canaanite Abimelech probably at the Beer-sheba sanc-

[6] F. M. Cross, Jr., "Yahweh and the God of the Patriarchs," *HTR,* LV (1962), 225-59. Cf. J. Philip Hyatt, "The Origin of Mosaic Yahwism," in E. J. Vardaman and J. L. Garrett, eds., *The Teacher's Yoke: Studies in Memory of Henry Trantham* (1964), pp. 85-93.

[7] E. A. Speiser, *Genesis* (*The Anchor Bible*), pp. xliii-lii.

[8] Raphael Giveon, "Toponymes ouest-asiatiques à Soleb," *VT,* XIV (1964), 244, 255. Cf. W. F. Albright in *JBL,* LXVII (1947), 380. *Yw* at Ugarit can hardly be associated with Yahweh (see J. Gray, "The God *Yw* in the Religion of Canaan," *JNES,* XII [1953], 278-83).

[9] F. M. Cross, Jr., *op. cit.,* pp. 252-53. So also Th. Bauer, J. Gray, etc. H. B. Huffmon (*Amorite Personal Names in the Mari Texts,* 1965, pp. 70-73) also places these names in the verbal-sentence category.

[10] André Finet, "Iawi-ilâ, roi de Talhayum," *Syria,* XLI (1964), 117-42.

tuary (Gen. 21:27-33; cf. 26:23-33), and worshiping at Canaanite sanctuary sites with no sense of ideological conflict. All this was, however, before there was the stronger sense of separatism and distinctiveness which came with Mosaic Yahwism. Even afterwards the cultic syncretism should not be minimized, illustrated in the details of the sanctuary of Micah in Judg. 17 or in David's adoption of a Canaanite threshing floor sanctuary and its Canaanite priest Zadok.[11]

The cultic syncretism and at the same time the radical ideological differentiation in the period from Joshua on can be understood particularly if we accept Mendenhall's interpretation of the conquest of Canaan and his plausible thesis that a tribe might not be formed by kinship descended from a common ancestor, but might be a socio-political group formed in Canaan, a group withdrawn from the local community and accepting allegiance to a deity, Yahweh, who had been brought out of Egypt by a small group.[12] While such a tribe had its roots in the local scene, its view of deity was radically differentiated from that of Canaanite "paganism," even though Yahweh might originally have been a cultic name of El.[13]

Kapelrud suggests that the ark and tent of meeting in origin are probably to be associated with groups entering Canaan from the south, and that although P may present a late idealization of the tent, the tent was no mere fiction. The studies of Morgenstern, who would like very much to be at this centennial celebration,[14] Cross's discussion of the tabernacle from an archaeological and historical approach,[15] the more recent investigation of the sacred tent by Haran,[16] and von Rad's study of the tent

[11] H. H. Rowley, "Melchizedek and Zadok," in *Festschrift A. Bertholet*, pp. 461-72; W. Harrelson, *op. cit.*, pp. 177-78.

[12] G. E. Mendenhall, "The Hebrew Conquest of Canaan," *BA*, XXV (1962), 66-86. If what really happened was "a peasant's revolt against the network of interlocking Canaanite city states," not a nomadic invasion, then the influence of and continuation of Canaanite cultic practices in Israel, despite the religious and socio-political differentiation, is easily comprehended.

[13] Yahweh was differentiated from El as Israel's covenant God in a monolatrous system which introduced sharp distinctions and conflicts. Syncretism, but with ideological differentiation, appears in Jeroboam's Bethel and Dan cults, where, as Cross believes (*op. cit.*, pp. 257-58), Jeroboam did not invent a new cultus, but reintroduced an El cultus, with its bull symbolism; this Elijah, Elisha, and Amos did not criticize, despite their protagonism of Yahweh.

[14] J. Morgenstern, *The Ark, Ephod, and Tent of Meeting*.

[15] F. M. Cross, Jr., "The Tabernacle," *BA*, X (1947), 45-68.

[16] M. Haran, "The Nature of the *'Ohel Mo'edh* in Pentateuchal Sources," *JSS*, V (1960), 50-66; "*'Oṭfe, Maḥmal,* and *Ḳubbe,*" in *D. Neiger Memorial Volume*, pp. 215-

and ark,[17] and others indicate the complexity of the problems involved. The writer would naturally like to recall his theory that the ark had the form of a miniature temple and the possible implications of this for its origins.[18] The ark was early associated with the throne of Yahweh,[19] and was at home in the throne-room of the temple [20] and was related to the theophanic presence, the Glory of Yahweh.[21] It played a role in the festival of the enthronement of Yahweh in the temple,[22] regarded in part as a repetition of the procession in II Sam. 6.[23] Along with these early cultic institutions one might add the bull image throne of Yahweh. It has been suggested that this was one of the cult objects brought from the desert, in course of time to be repudiated and then reintroduced by Jeroboam I.[24] Alternatively, if Yahweh was originally an El figure, the bull image throne of Yahweh could also have been a natural development in Canaan. It does seem inconsonant with the imageless deity of Mosaic Yahwism in the desert.

The highlight of Kapelrud's paper comes in his analysis of the festivals of Israel, particularly the Passover and Unleavened Bread spring festival and its import in Josiah's reform.[25] Parenthetically, without denying the role of the cult in transforming the history of the exodus into experience, I would agree with de Vaux that there are other elements in Exod. 1—15 than ritual ones;[26] the cultic coloring of all of Exod. 1—15 as a cultic unit is not evident, nor is it apparent that the chapters took their present form

21; "The Tabernacle in the Priestly Source; Its Technical and Material Gradations," in *N. H. Tur-Sinai Jubilee Volume* (Hebrew), pp. 27-42.

[17] G. von Rad, "Zelt und Lade," *Gesammelte Studien zum Alten Testament* (1958), pp. 100-29.

[18] H. G. May, "The Ark—A Miniature Temple," *American Journal of Semitic Languages,* LII (1936), 215 ff. See R. Hartmann, "Zelt und Lade," *ZAW,* XXXVII (1917-18), 209-44, who holds the ark belonged to settled agricultural communities.

[19] II Sam. 6:2.

[20] Cf. the bull image throne of Yahweh at Dan and Bethel.

[21] I Sam. 4:21; cf. Isa. 6:1-3; Ezek. 43:1-5.

[22] See G. Henton Davies, art. "Ark of the Covenant" in *IDB*.

[23] See Ps. 132:8-10.

[24] See R. de Vaux, *op. cit.,* p. 334; W. Harrelson, *op. cit.,* pp. 96-97; H. J. Kraus, *Gottesdienst in Israel* (1962), pp. 149 ff.

[25] We may fittingly recall at this centennial celebration President Morgenstern's great contributions in this area, particularly in the numerous articles in *HUCA,* from its first volume in 1921 to the current issue in 1964.

[26] *Op. cit.,* p. 492.

as a result of being told and retold in the cult.[27] When the festival of the Passover and the festival of Unleavened Bread, the pastoral and agricultural spring festivals, were combined is uncertain.[28] Kapelrud rightly notes that the role of the combined Passover-Unleavened Bread festival in the period of the monarchy is unknown. The autumn festival seems to have played the primary role.[29] By contrast, the Deuteronomic legislation [30] stresses strongly the Passover, making it a rite for the central sanctuary alone, the Israelites then returning to their communities for the festival of Unleavened Bread. The emphasis is not coincidental, and accords with Josiah's great Passover celebration,[31] the first such Passover since the days of the judges. Before Josiah's time, as de Vaux suggests,[32] the Passover may have been a family festival.

Kapelrud's explanation is very convincing, namely that at this time the Passover filled the vacuum caused by the abolition of the pagan priests, gods, and altars from the Judean cult and cessation of what had become the great autumnal New Year festival with its features which the reformers would have regarded as pagan. Associated with its rites were doubtless the horses dedicated to the sun by generations of preceding kings and the chariots of the sun, removed in Josiah's reform.[33] Compare the chariot of Bel Marduk which was employed to convey the statue of the god from its home in Esagila to the *akîtu*-house during the New Year festival, mentioned in a newly published Babylonian chronicle as brought back from Assur to Babylon.[34] We may presume that in the

[27] Apart from this question, it is at least clear that a later ritual composition might be inserted into the historical narrative, or that the narrative might be composed to explain or serve as precedent for a later cultic practice. The former is illustrated in Exod. 15:1-18, composed to be sung in the Jerusalem temple (see vs. 17 and contrast F. M. Cross, Jr. and D. N. Freedman, "The Song of Miriam," *JNES,* XIV [1955], 237-50). The latter is obvious in Exod. 12:1-27, and most probable in Exod. 24:3-8, which cannot be read without the impression that the writer is putting into a historical setting the rites of the renewal of the covenant; see W. Beyerlin, *Herkunft und Geschichte der ältesten Sinaitraditionen,* pp. 44-57.

[28] See H. G. May, "The Relation of the Passover to the Festival of Unleavened Bread," *JBL,* LV (1936), 65 ff. See Exod. 23:15; 34:18 (34:25*b* is secondary, for Exod. 23:18 has the more original form of the regulation).

[29] I Kings 8:1 ff.; a comparison of texts suggests the ark procession in II Sam. 6:12 ff. may have been at this time of the year; cf. also I Kings 12:32; Judg. 21:19-21.

[30] Deut. 16:1-8.

[31] II Kings 23:21 ff.

[32] R. de Vaux, *op. cit.,* p. 488; W. Harrelson, *op. cit.,* pp. 83, 425.

[33] II Kings 23:11.

[34] A. R. Millard, "Another Babylonian Chronicles Text," *Iraq,* XXVI (1964), 14 ff., and see literature cited.

reaction after the death of Josiah, abundantly evidenced in Jeremiah, the pagan aspects of the solar cult and perhaps even the old New Year enthronement festival were reintroduced. Ezekiel alludes to the worship of the sun and other pagan aspects of the cultic practices in the temple courts as he knew them in the post–Josianic period,[35] and makes use of the New Year festival symbolism of the enthronement of Yahweh.[36]

By the time of Josiah's reform the corruptions in the cult, including those associated with the New Year festival, had become intolerable. They resulted in part from innovations introduced by Manasseh, who had been "brainwashed" during his exile in Assyria.[37] Zephaniah describes some of the corruptions in the cult in Josiah's days before the reform, and perhaps significantly uses the Day of Yahweh symbolism to announce the coming judgment.[38] That Josiah's Deuteronomic reform would have made the autumnal festival "fall to pieces" is not at all improbable, it now taking the form legislated for it in the regulations for the festival of Booths in Deut. 16:13-15. We may presume that it was thus celebrated during the rest of the days of Josiah, as is suggested by Kapelrud. It was apparently, however, soon after discontinued, to be reinstituted at the time of Ezra, when it was thought that its celebration had lapsed since the time of Joshua.[39]

Kapelrud rightly agrees with Ringgren and others that the interpretation of the fall festival by von Rad and Weiser as a covenant renewal festival and the interpretation of it by Mowinckel and others in terms of the New Year enthronement of Yahweh festival are two different interpretations of a series of partly identical features.[40] If this is so, and if the autumnal festival disintegrated from its usual form as a result of the Josianic-Deuteronomic reform, then any annual covenant renewal rites

[35] Ezek. 8:1-18.

[36] H. G. May, *Ezekiel, IB,* VI, pp. 69-70, 300-301; "The Departure of the Glory of Yahweh," *JBL,* LVI (1937), 309 ff.

[37] II Chr. 33:10-11; but after rather than before Manasseh's reform.

[38] Zeph. 1.

[39] Neh. 8. This would have been in 445, the twentieth year of Artaxerxes I.

[40] Weiser himself would agree: see A. Weiser, *The Old Testament: Its Formation and Development,* p. 34. The association of the covenant renewal rites and the enthronement of Yahweh New Year ideology is hinted in Exod. 24:3 ff.; the consummation of the blood rites and the reading of the book of the covenant in vss. 3-8 (=E, see Beyerlin, *loc. cit.,* pp. 19-23) is associated by E in vs. 10 with the theophany of the enthroned deity (cf. Ezek. 1:26-28), and P in vss. 15-18 also presents a picture of the Glory of Yahweh theophany (cf. Exod. 40:1, 17, 34-35, in a spring New Year setting).

associated with the autumnal festival [41] may have gone with it. The legislation in Deut. 31:10, 11 posits not an annual covenant renewal service, but rather specifies that the law shall be read at the sabbatical year celebration of the festival of Booths.[42] And it is not the Sinai-Horeb covenant which is thus to be confirmed by reading, but rather the testimonies, statutes, and ordinances which Moses spoke to Israel in Transjordan;[43] this is the law which Moses wrote and gave to the sons of Levi to be read every seven years.[44] Very probable is Eissfeldt's view that Deuteronomy was regarded as a literary substitute for the book of the covenant,[45] and Weiser's theory that it was intended to replace the book of the covenant also from the cultic standpoint.[46] With Josiah's reform the cultic covenant renewal ceremony may have become a sabbatical year occasion.

Time forbids discussion of the theories of the formulation and transmission of sacred history at the cultic festival.[47] One might compare and

[41] See Hans-Joachim Kraus, *Gottesdienst in Israel: Studien zur Geschichte des Laubhüttenfestes* (1954).

[42] The writer accords generally with the opinion that we must not relegate the production of the book of Deuteronomy *in its present form* too far away from the reform itself, that Deuteronomy and its reform owes its origin and effectiveness to the sacral traditions of the union of the twelve tribes with the historical conjunction of the circumstances of Josiah's policy, and that in Deuteronomy older heterogeneous materials are combined with novel tendencies and perspectives (A. Weiser, *op. cit.*, pp. 132-33; the book of Deuteronomy is composed of various strata of tradition: see J. Muilenburg, "The Form and Structure of the Covenantal Formulations," *VT*, IX (1959), 346-65). In any case, Deut. 31 does not belong to the earliest Deuteronomic strata. The sabbatical year covenant renewal may have had some specific relevance to Josiah's reform; contrast Alt's view of the antiquity of the sabbatical year sacral reading of the law (*Die Ursprünge des israelitischen Rechts*, pp. 63 ff.; 324 ff.); so also Kraus, Noth. Some suggest the annual renewal ceremony ceased with the monarchy. The antiquity of the sabbatical year reading hardly finds support in the seven-year period in Ugaritic myth (Kraus, *ibid.*, pp. 54-56, 129-32). By contrast, de Vaux doubts that in OT times the feast of Booths as such commemorated the covenant (*op. cit.*, p. 502).

The increased emphasis on the Passover in the Josianic-Deuteronomic reform is consonant with the relation of that reform to the national, political situation, which included, as Weiser says, an attempt on the part of Josiah to free himself of the declining world empire and to win over the north by a Davidic renaissance policy. The passover is associated with Yahweh's smiting of Israel's foe; the triumph of Yahweh over the Egyptians would have fallen in with the mood of Josiah's times.

[43] It has been suggested that this was also the original locale of the Covenant Code tradition.

[44] Deut. 31:9-11; cf. 4:44-46; 5:1.

[45] O. Eissfeldt, *Einleitung in das Alte Testament* (3rd ed.), pp. 292-97.

[46] A. Weiser, *op. cit.*, p. 131.

[47] A. Weiser, *op. cit.*, pp. 88-91; cf. G. von Rad, *Das Formgeschichtliche Problem des Hexateuch, Gesammelte Studien* (1958); H. G. Reventlow, *Das Heiligkeitgesetz.*

contrast the view that the JEPD sources are stages and types in the shaping of the tradition of sacral history which maintained itself by its sacral recitation at the feast of the covenant from the political division of the tribes to the reading of the Torah in the synagogues with the viewpoint of Speiser that P is the work of a school with unbroken history from earliest times, a standing scholastic committee, as it were, in regular session since the inchoate beginnings of ethnic consciousness in Israel, its final product being the Pentateuch.[48] Also deserving of special attention is the ceremony of the renewal of the covenant, which Harrelson has described as one of the most fruitful and solid discoveries of contemporary OT study, although one must confess that the evidence for it is as indirect as that for the enthronement of Yahweh New Year ceremony. Likewise deserving further discussion under the topic assigned for this session is the amphictyonic organization of early Israel, almost axiomatic in contemporary biblical scholarship even though variously interpreted,[49] and concerning which Orlinsky has raised serious questions.[50] But the time limit assigned to this paper has already expired, and much relevant material has been assigned to footnotes.

[48] E. A. Speiser, *op. cit.*, pp. xxiv-xxvi, xxxvi.

[49] See, for instance, Murray Newman, *The People of the Covenant,* who presumes a pre-Mosaic six-tribe amphictyony at Shechem, a twelve-tribe amphictyony organized by Joshua at Shechem, and a six-tribe pre-monarchial amphictyony at Hebron. Compare Noth's view of a twelve-tribe amphictyony constituted on the model of the six-tribe society.

[50] H. M. Orlinsky, "The Tribal System of Israel and Related Groups in the Period of the Judges," *Oriens Antiquus,* I (1962), 11 ff.

3
Prophecy And Apocalyptic

JAMES MUILENBURG

The "Office" of the Prophet in Ancient Israel

When one ventures to survey the course of scholarly inquiry into the OT records throughout the course of the period beginning with the organization of our Society in 1881 and to assess the present situation in OT studies in relation to that period, it soon becomes apparent that the most profound changes have taken place in two major areas. The first of these is clearly the book which bears the altogether infelicitous and certainly mistaken title of Deuteronomy, a work which has long been recognized as occupying a peculiarly strategic position not only in the history of Israel's literary compositions, but also in the history of her faith.[1] The second area where the transformation is most clear covers the extensive range of Israelite prophecy and of our understanding of the prophets.[2] The rigid separation between the law and the prophets, so characteristic of the time of Julius Wellhausen and his successors, is today universally regarded as mistaken, for we now see, as never before, how deeply prophecy has penetrated the so-called legal formulations, above all the sacral tra-

[1] Gerhard von Rad, *Deuteronomiumstudien, FRLANT*. N. F. XL (1947), Zweite Ausgabe. English tr., *Studies in Deuteronomy* in *SBT*, IX (1953), 37: "Deuteronomy is the beginning of a completely new epoch in Israel. In every respect, therefore, Deuteronomy is to be designated as the middle point of the Old Testament. The question of its derivation is possibly the most difficult in the history of the Old Testament traditions." See Muilenburg, "The Form and Structure of the Covenant Formulations," *VT* IX (1959), 347 f.

[2] Georg Fohrer, "Neuere Literatur zur alttestamentlichen Prophetie," *Theol. Rundschau* N.F., XIX (1951), 277-345; XX (1952), 193-271. See also his critical evaluation of recent trends in "Remarks on Modern Interpretation of the Prophets," *JBL*, LXXX (1961), 309-19.

ditions embodied in the book of Deuteronomy, and how much the prophets were indebted to Israel's legal traditions both for the form and for the substance of their proclamations.[3] We have gone a long way from the time of Bernhard Duhm[4] and Carl Cornill[5] and Gustav Hölscher,[6] or indeed from the days of John Skinner[7] and George Adam Smith[8]—to mention but a few of those who have contributed to our understanding of the prophets of Israel. One has only to compare the commentaries in the *Biblischer Kommentar* or the *Kommentar zum Alten Testament* or the *Handbuch zum Alten Testament* series with those of the *Handkommentar zum Alten Testament,* edited by W. Nowack (1892 ff.) or the *Kurzer Handcommentar,* edited by Karl Marti (1897 ff.) or the *International Critical Commentary,* edited by C. A. Briggs, S. R. Driver, and Alfred Plummer (1895 ff.) to appreciate something of the revolutionary change that has taken place.

The reasons for this striking change in our understanding of both Deuteronomy and the prophets are not far to seek. For one thing, we have come to see that the methodology of historical criticism, taken by itself, was unable to offer satisfactory answers to many of our most insistent

[3] Otto Procksch, *Theologie des alten Testaments,* pp. 561-63; Ernst Sellin, *Mose und seine Bedeutung für die israelitisch-jüdische Religionsgeschichte* (1922), pp. 6 f.: "Die weitere Untersuchung hat mir dann ergeben, dass gerade diese Mosetradition der rote Faden ist der durch die nachmosaischen Jahrhunderte bei den meisten Propheten sich findet und sie miteinander verbindet . . . dass für den göttlichen Willen, wie ihn nach jener Tradition Mose formuliert hat." Paul Volz, *Mose und seine Werk,* 1932, pp. 229 ff.; *idem, Prophetengestalten des alten Testaments,* 1938, pp. 74, 123 f. G. von Rad, *Old Testament Theology,* I (1962), 99: ". . . what stands unmistakably in the forefront of Deuteronomy is an interest in prophecy and the problems which it set." Compare, however, von Rad's observations in *Studies in Deuteronomy,* p. 69. For the prophetic employment of the legal traditions, cf. von Rad, *Theologie des alten Testaments,* II, 416: "Schärfer und bedrohlicher als durch die Propheten ist in Israel nicht mehr 'gesetz gepredigt' worden . . . Beim Deuteronomium und Deuteronomisten liegt unter allen Umständen eine Beeinflussung vor." See also Walther Eichrodt, *Theology of the Old Testament,* I, 293 f.; Yehezkel Kaufmann, *The Religion of Israel* (tr. and abridg. from Hebrew), 1960, pp. 224-29, esp. p. 228. Abraham J. Heschel, *The Prophets,* p. 472.

[4] *Das Buch Jesaia* (1892, 4th ed., 1923); *Das Buch Jeremia. Kurzer Handcommentar zum alten Testament* (1901); *Israels Propheten* (1916).

[5] *Das Buch Jeremia* (1905); *Das Buch des Propheten Ezechiel* (1886).

[6] *Die Propheten* (1914).

[7] *The Book of Ezekiel* in the Expositor's Bible (1895); *The Book of the Prophet Isaiah* in The Cambridge Bible for Schools and Colleges (1905); *Prophecy and Religion* (1922).

[8] *The Book of the Twelve Prophets,* 2 vols., in the Expositor's Bible (1896-98 and subsequent eds.); *The Book of Isaiah* in the Expositor's Bible (1889-90 and later eds.).

questions concerning the composition, function, and exegesis of the biblical texts. It was this impasse that gave rise to *Gattungsforschung,* associated above all with the name of Hermann Gunkel and his students.[9] Gunkel undertook to identify and describe the types and forms represented in our biblical material, to call our attention to the oral provenance of many of the traditions, to delineate, at least to a degree, something of the structure and rhetoric of a particular *Gattung,* and to point, so far as it is possible, to the concrete social or cultural milieu in which the *Gattung* was spoken, i.e. its *Sitz im Leben,* whether in the court of law or on the various occasions of celebration and festival. More recently we have advanced our form-critical investigations into an examination of the history of the traditions, and it is precisely in the manifold traditions preserved in the book of Deuteronomy and the prophetic literature where we have made our most notable and, as I believe, our most salutary advance. Intimately related to the foregoing ways of working with the biblical texts has been a stress upon the place of the cult in ancient Israel, best illustrated by the many contributions of Sigmund Mowinckel,[10] but also by perhaps the majority of OT scholars today. Scores of passages both in the historical and prophetic books, as well as in the book of Psalms, have been assigned to cultic forms and celebrations. *Pari passu* with the application of these newer methodologies to the biblical texts has been the recovery of the records from the peoples of the ancient Near East, records of many different forms and styles, which have cast a welcome light upon Israel's literary compositions as well as upon the motifs and modes of thought that they embody. To be sure,

[9] *Genesis übersetzt und erklärt* (1901); the introduction to Hans Schmidt's *Die grossen Propheten übersetzt und erklärt* in Die Schriften des alten Testaments, pp. ix-lxx (1905); "Die israelitische Literatur" in *Kultur Der Gegenwart,* ed. Paul Hinneberg I, 7, *"Die orientalischen Literaturen"* (1906), pp. 53-112; *Reden und Aufsätze* (1913), esp. "Die Grundprobleme der israelitischen Literaturgeschichte," pp. 29-38; *Einleitung in die Psalmen; Die Gattungen der religiösen Lyrik Israels,* zu Ende geführt von Joachim Begrich. See also Gunkel's various contributions to the first edition of *RGG,* esp. "Propheten seit Amos," IV, 1875 ff.

[10] Psalmenstudien II. *Das Thronbesteigungsfest Jahwäs und der Ursprung der Eschatologie* (1922); III. *Kultusprophetie und prophetische Psalmen* (1923); *Le Décalogue* (1927); *Religion og Kultus* (1950). German tr., *Religion und Kultus* (1953). Aubrey R. Johnson, *The Cultic Prophet in Ancient Israel,* 2nd ed., 1962. For a thorough and detailed treatment of the cult in the book of Deuteronomy, see Walter Brueggemann, *A Form-Critical Study of the Cultic Material in Deuteronomy: an Analysis of the Nature of Cultic Encounter in the Mosaic Tradition,* Dissertation, Union Theological Seminary (1961).

Gunkel availed himself of the extrabiblical texts and made exemplary use of them in his study of the forms and types of Israel's speech,[11] but many of the most important collections were discovered or translated after he had done his major work. It is noteworthy that these more recent materials have served to illuminate in a special way the traditions preserved in Deuteronomy and the prophets. One thinks of the compilations of laws, the international and other suzerainty treaties, the Mari letters, and other inscriptional materials.

Unhappily, there has been a proclivity to press our inquiries too far in all the areas to which I have referred. We are all aware, for example, of the excesses of source analysis in the early decades of our Society's existence, or of the reduction of literary compositions to mere snippets, or of the common confusion of strophes with independent poems, or of the dissection of traditio-historical criticism to such a degree that the original work all but vanishes or disintegrates beneath the deftness of our analytical skill. Or we have witnessed the invocation of the cult in every possible situation, with the upshot that psychological and historical understanding is somewhat cavalierly dismissed by the pejorative words liberalism and historicism. Yet these excesses by no means invalidate the methods themselves. Finally, let it be said that the results we achieve in our study will in large part be conditioned by the techniques we employ. The exclusive use of historical criticism will often yield one set of results; form criticism and traditio-historical criticism without reference to historical and literary criticism will often yield quite another.

We have proceeded in our investigations, then, from the identification of the *Gattung* and the comparison of various specimens of a particular *Gattung* to the determination of the *Sitz im Leben,* and today we are engaged in still another inquiry, one that was inevitable so long as we subjected a pericope to patient and careful scrutiny. I refer to the speakers who address us in the literary forms or to the "office" which they may represent or to the role they assume. A substantial literature has gathered about this legitimate concern.[12] Here I wish to emphasize what

[11] Above all, of course, Hugo Gressmann's *Altorientalische Texte und Bilder zum Alten Testament,* 2 vols. (1909, 2nd expanded ed., 1926-27), but also many other inscriptional materials (see, e.g., his *Reden und Aufsätze* and his commentaries on Genesis and the Psalms).

[12] Albrecht Alt, *Die Ursprünge des israelitischen Rechts* in *Kleine Schriften zur Geschichte des Volkes Israel,* I (1959), 278-332, esp. pp. 300-302; Martin Noth, "Das

has now become fairly common knowledge among us, that many of the materials, i.e. many of the forms which we seek to understand, have an oral provenance, and this holds particularly for the sacral traditions of the book of Deuteronomy and the prophetic traditions. As Klostermann saw long ago [13] and as G. von Rad has stressed recently,[14] the diverse materials assembled in Deuteronomy were originally designed for public proclamation. They were meant to be spoken to the gathered community of Israel. Now nowhere in the whole range of Scripture is the speaking style more in evidence than here. This is illustrated by the stirring and eloquent rhetoric of the book, by the character of its different literary genres, such as the sermon or the lawsuit or the treaty (or covenant), by the repeated summons to hearing and the numerous vocatives, by the ever-recurring appeals to contemporaneity and to Israel's own historic past, and by the passionate mood of the speakers. But if this is true, and I do not see how it can well be gainsaid, then we are confronted in an acute way with the problem of the speaker, i.e. the one who is

---

Amt des 'Richters Israels,'" *Bertholet Festschrift* (1950) pp. 404-17; *idem, Amt und Berufung im Alten Testament,* Bonner Akademische Reden 19 (1958); Ernst Würtwein, "Der Ursprung der prophetischen Gerichtrede," *ZAW,* XLIX (1952), 1-15; W. Zimmerli, "Ich bin Jahwe," in *Geschichte und das Altes Testament, Beiträge zur historischen Theologie, Alt Festschrift* (1953), pp. 179-210, esp. pp. 186-92; Hans-Joachim Kraus, *Gottesdienst in Israel,* 2nd enlarged ed.; *idem, Die prophetische Verkündigung des Rechts in Israel.* Theol. Studien 51 (1957); J. J. Stamm, *Der Dekalog im Lichte der neueren Forschung* (1958); Henning Graf Reventlow, "Das Amt des Mazkir," *Theol. Zeitschrift XV* (1959), 161-75; *idem,* "Prophetenamt und Mittleramt," *ZTK* LVIII (1961), 269-84; *Das Amt des Propheten bei Amos, FRLANT* LXXX (1962); *idem, Wächter über Israel* (1962) (Das prophetische Amt Ezechiels); *idem, Liturgie und prophetisches Ich bei Jeremia* (1963); Eberhard von Waldow, *Der traditionsgeschichtliche Hintergrund der prophetischen Reden, BZAW,* LXXXV (1963); Hans Wildberger, *Jahwes Eigentumsvolk,* Abhandlungen zur Theologie des Alten und Neuen Testaments 37 (1960); H. J. Boecker, "Erwägungen zum Amt des Mazkir," *Theol. Zeitschrift,* XVII (1961), 212-16.

[13] *Der Pentateuch, Beiträge zu seinem Verständnis und seiner Entstehungsgeschichte,* Zweite Auflage (1907), pp. 344 f.; "Aus dieser Untersuchung des Abschnittes Dt. 12-28 ergibt sich Erstens: dass auch er seiner literarischen Art nach kein für sich bestehendes und für sich zu verstehendes Gesetzbuch ist, sondern vielmehr eine Sammlung von Materielien für den öffentlichen Gesetzvortrag. Zweitens: der öffentliche Gesetzvortrag geschah bei den solennen Zusammenkünften am Heiligtum, wohin man ging 'um die Furcht Jahwes zu lernen' . . . Viertens: von anderen und älteren Gesetzsammlungen, welche die Form der Gottesrede hatten, unterschied diese Gesetzschrift charakterisch dadurch, dass sie ihren Inhalt als Rede eines autoritativen menschlichen Ichs, als Weisung eines anerkannten Dolmetschers des göttlichen Willens gab." See further, pp. 345-47.

[14] *Studies in Deuteronomy,* p. 15; *Das formgeschichtliche Problem des Hexateuchs,* =*Gesammelte Studien zum Alten Testament* (1958), pp. 37-41.

playing the role or taking the place of Moses. Who, then, is Moses or *mutatis mutandis* who is the Mosaic figure who addresses us in the sacral traditions of Deuteronomy, or, if we may anticipate ourselves, how are we to understand the figure of the prophet like Moses (Deut. 18:15 ff.)?[15] What is the relation of the prophetic speech of Deuteronomy to the speech of the prophets,[16] or what is the relation of the laws of Deuteronomy, notably the apodictic laws, and other legal formulations of the OT in their various forms and guises to the legal formulations of the prophets?[17]

Before we are able to render a decision on these matters, it is essential that we scrutinize the sacral traditions preserved in Deuteronomy in order to determine their character and to see what light they may shed upon the Mosaic figure and the various traditions associated with him. First a word about the provenance of the book. It is now generally recognized that the work as we have it before us represents a long period of development and growth. We clearly have to do with strata of tradition, the earliest of which were doubtless oral, but these are supplemented by accretions from later periods. Literary forms and types are transformed and expanded, often parenetically; at times they are reordered and refashioned in such a way as to revise or alter the original traditions.[18] The homiletical interests of the traditionists have left their stamp upon a large part of the book; both the historical narratives and the legal formulations come to us in the guise of preaching.

The affinities of the Deuteronomic traditions with those of the Elohist

[15] Ernst Sellin, *Mose und seine Bedeutung für die israelitisch-jüdische Religionsgeschichte,* p. 1: "Die letzte und wichtigste Frage aller israelitisch-jüdischen Religionsforschung wird immer die bleiben: Wer war Mose?"; Ludwig Köhler, *Der hebräische Mensch* (1953), p. 164; English tr., *Hebrew Man,* p. 144.

[16] Karl Budde, "Das Deuteronomium und die Reform König Josias," *ZAW,* XLIV (1926), 177-224. Cf. p. 220: "Somit nimmt das Prophetentum hier offen und unbestritten die Verfasserschaft des Deuteronomium für sich in Anspruch, und wir brauchen niemand weiter danach zu fragen. Eine schöne Bestätigung für diese abschliessende Stelle des Prophetentums in der Reihe der theokratischen Autoritäten erwächst uns in der Geschichte des Deuteronomium, oder besser der Vorlage der josianischen Reform, noch aus der Tatsache, dass das letzte Wort dabei dem Prophetentum zufällt." See also n. 3.

[17] See *infra,* pp. 83-84.

[18] Otto Eissfeldt, *Einleitung in das Alte Testament,* 3., neubearbeitete Auflage (1964), pp. 292-97; Artur Weiser, *The Old Testament: its Formation and Development* (tr. from the 4th German ed., 1957) (1961), pp. 131-32.

have long been observed.[19] Now in order to evaluate the relation of the two bodies of tradition it is essential to reconsider the date of the Eliohist.[20] The arguments supporting an eighth-century date are increasingly difficult to uphold, and it seems probable that we should assign it to a much earlier period. The writer has long maintained that the Yahwist depends upon the oral traditions of the northern Elohist, above all in the sections in Exodus which recount the conclusion of the covenant and the giving of the Torah. This, as we shall see, brings the origins of the sacral traditions of Deuteronomy and those of the Elohist into close temporal connection. In the opening sermons it is clear that Deuteronomy leans heavily upon the Elohist narrative traditions of the Tetrateuch.[21] The Elohist decalogue of Exod. 20:1-17 is repeated, albeit with characteristic alterations and additions. The Covenant Code of Exod. 20:23—23:33 is elaborated and reinterpreted within the contexts of later times and situations.[22] Indeed, von Rad has shown that the structure of Deuteronomy conforms completely with that of the Sinai pericope of Exod. 19—24, by far the greater part of which belongs to the Elohist.[23] The city of Shechem occupies a strategic place in the Deuteronomic sacral traditions, as is suggested by the not infrequent references to Gerizim

[19] See the introductions to the OT of C. Steuernagel, S. R. Driver, O. Eissfeldt, R. H. Pfeiffer, A. Weiser, W. O. E. Oesterley, and T. H. Robinson, the commentaries of Alfred Bertholet, Steuernagel, and S. R. Driver, and Johannes Hempel, *Die althebräische Literatur und ihr hellenistisch-jüdisches Nachleben* (1934), p. 139; Karl Budde, *op. cit.*, pp. 177-224; Adam C. Welch, *Deuteronomy: the Framework to the Code* (1932), *passim;* R. Brinker, *The Influence of Sanctuaries in Early Israel* (1945), pp. 196 f., p. 211: "*Deuteronomy* is almost entirely based on a document which is generally called E." Perhaps the most eloquent witness to the close affinities of the Elohist and Deuteronomic writers is the way in which the same passages have been assigned by some scholars to the Elohist, by others to the Deuteronomists. Many of the passages which were heretofore ascribed to the Elohist are now assigned to the Deuteronomist by Martin Noth and others.

[20] Note especially the work of Otto Procksch, *Das nordhebräische Sagenbuch: Die Elohimquelle,* pp. 307 f.; Martin Noth, *Überlieferungsgeschichte des Pentateuch,* pp. 248-49; Ephraim Speiser, *Genesis* (Anchor Bible, 1964), p. XXX, n. 5.

[21] This is recognized by the majority of scholars; for succinct statements, see especially A. C. Welch, *op. cit.,* p. 7; Brinker, *op. cit.,* pp. 197 f.

[22] S. R. Driver, *An Introduction to the Old Testament,* 9th ed. (1913), pp. 73-76. Note, however, the contention of Eissfeldt and Weiser that the intent of the Deuteronomist is to replace the Covenant Code. Be that as it may, the basis of Deuteronomic laws is the Covenant Code. The work of the Deuteronomic traditionists represents an illuminating illustration of Israelite hermeneutics.

[23] *Das formgeschichtliche Problem des Hexateuchs,* pp. 33-35; *Studies in Deuteronomy,* pp. 14 f.

and Ebal, and this obviously connects with the crucial report of Josh. 24, another prevailingly Elohist deposit, where the twelve tribes of Israel enter together into the covenant federation.[24]

The connection of the traditions associated with the Shechemite amphictyony with those in Deuteronomy is supported by many scholars, and it is agreed by most of these that they were originally employed in the celebrations of a festival of covenant renewal (Deut. 11:26-32; 27:1-26; Josh. 8:30-36).[25] A number of attempts have been made to articulate the structure of the covenant liturgies, and it is noteworthy that the Elohist and the *Urdeuteronomium* stand in the closest possible relation with one another here.[26] Since Shechem occupies so central a place in both traditions, it is not improbable that we should look to it for the *mise en scène* of both; i.e. we may assume that the various traditions in their

[24] A. Alt, *Die Ursprünge des israelitischen Rechts,* pp. 324 ff.; M. Noth, *Das System der zwölf Stämme Israels* (1930), pp. 140-51; *Die Gesetze im Pentateuch* (1940), pp. 29-33, =Gesammelte Aufsätze (1957), pp. 53-58; G. von Rad, *Das formgeschichtliche Problem des Hexateuchs,* pp. 41-48; *Studies in Deuteronomy,* p. 40; G. Ernest Wright, *IB,* II (1953), 326; *Shechem: the Biography of a Biblical City* (1964), pp. 20 f.; H. J. Kraus, *Die prophetische Verkündigung des Rechts in Israel,* p. 5; Murray Lee Newman, *The People of the Covenant,* pp. 108 ff. and *passim;* Eduard Nielsen, *Shechem* (1955), ch. IX; Bernhard Anderson, *Biblical Archaeologist Reader,* II (1964), 265-74=*BA,* XX (Feb., 1957); Norman W. Porteous, "Actualization and the Prophetic Criticism of the Cult" in *Tradition und Situation* (*Weiser Festschrift*) (1963), p. 100. Note also the unpublished dissertation of Walter J. Harrelson, Union Theological Seminary, *The City of Shechem: Its History and Importance* (1953).

[25] So Alt, Noth, von Rad, G. E. Wright, Kraus, Brinker, B. Anderson, Harrelson, Murray Newman, Porteous. See also Otto Procksch, *Theologie des alten Testaments* (1950), pp. 250 f.; G. E. Mendenhall, *Law and Covenant in Israel and the Ancient Near East* (1955), p. 47; E. Neilsen, *Shechem,* pp. 35 f.; pp. 347-57, esp. p. 352; H. Graf Reventlow, "Kultisches Recht im Alten Testament," *ZTK,* LX (1963), 269 f.; W. Beyerlin, *Herkunft und Geschichte der ältesten Sinaitraditionen* (1961), pp. 136 f. and *passim;* J. J. Stamm, *Der Dekalog im Lichte der neueren Forschung;* H. Ringgren, *Israelitische Religion* (1964), p. 46. This view was anticipated as long ago as 1924 by Ernst Sellin in *Geschichte des israelitisch-jüdisches Volkes,* I, 98 ff.; also in *Oriental Studies Dedicated to Paul Haupt,* "Seit welcher Zeit verehrten die israelitischen Stämme Jahwe?" pp. 124-34. Also to be observed is Mowinckel's identification of the *Sitz im Leben* of the decalog with the autumnal festival (*Le décalogue* (1927), pp. 120 ff.).

[26] Von Rad understands the Sinaitic traditions of Exod. 19—24 as representing the content of the ancient Shechemite covenant festival and discerns the same general structure in Deuteronomy (*Das formgeschichtliche Problem des Hexateuchs,* pp. 34 f., 47). For a more detailed and impressive analysis of the *Festlegende* of Exod. 19—24, both in its Yahwistic and Elohist forms, see Murray Newman, *The People of the Covenant,* ch. 2, pp. 39-71, though Newman adheres to the Sinaitic provenance of the passage. For other attempts to reconstruct the Shechemite liturgies, see Harrelson, *Shechem,* ch. XII, pp. 545-65; E. Nielsen, ch. I, pp. 39-85. Compare Muilenburg, "The Form and Structure of the Covenantal Formulations," *VT,* IX (1959), 347-65.

different forms not only reflect a Shechemite provenance, but also the cultic ceremonies and celebrations that took place at Shechem and later at Shiloh, Gilgal, and Jerusalem.[27] Be that as it may, an early date of the Deuteronomic sacral traditions is widely held.[28] The upshot of our discussion is to bring the Elohist and the early traditions of *Urdeuteronomium* close together. When one undertakes to examine the Elohist source as a whole, fragmentary though it may be, and then turn to the Deuteronomic traditions, he can scarcely resist the impression that we are dealing with one and the same stream of sacral traditions, traditions which by and large center in the covenant and the complex of traditions associated with it. But there is more. The prevailingly prophetic character of the Deuteronomic traditions is directly related to the prophetic traditions of the Elohist.[29] Differences there are to be sure, but

[27] M. Noth, "Das Amt des Richters Israels" in *Festschrift für A. Bertholet;* H. J. Kraus, *Die prophetische Verkündigung des Rechts in Israel,* Heft 51 (1957); Artur Weiser, *Die Psalmen,* 3rd ed. (1959), English tr., 1962; Norman W. Porteous, "Actualization and the Prophetic Criticism of the Cult," in *Tradition und Situation (Weiser Festschrift)*, pp. 96 ff.

[28] Edward Robertson, *The Old Testament Problem: a Re-Investigation* (1950), pp. 44 ff., 52 (=*BJRL,* XXVI (1941-42), pp. 183-205); R. Brinker, *The Influence of Sanctuaries in Early Israel,* pp. 205 ff.; Lester Kuyper, "The Book of Deuteronomy," *Interpretation,* VI (1952), 321-40, esp. p. 324 date the book in the time of Samuel; Eissfeldt, W. F. Albright, and Beyerlin place Deut. 32 in the same period (see *infra,* p. 84). T. Oestreicher, "Das deuteronomische Grundgesetz," (1923) and A. C. Welch, *The Code of Deuteronomy* (1924), and *Deuteronomy: the Framework to the Code* (1932), assign the book in its original form to a slightly later period. W. F. Albright at one time suggested the ninth century as the appropriate date and derived it from the region of Shechem, *The Archaeology of Palestine and the Bible* (1932), p. 155; more recently he seems to support an even earlier date in The Goldenson Lecture for 1961, "Samuel and the Beginnings of the Prophetic Movement," p. 10. Albrecht Alt, "Die Heimat des Deuteronomiums," *Kleine Schriften,* II (1953), 250-75 locates it in the period immediately following the fall of the northern kingdom in 722/1; K. Galling, "Das Gemeindegesetz im Deuteronomium," *Festschrift für A. Bertholet* (1950), pp. 176-91 places it during the last period of northern Israel; W. O. E. Oesterley and T. H. Robinson, *An Introduction to the Books of the Old Testament* (1934), p. 58 apparently take a similar view as does Leonard Rost, "Sinaibund und Davidsbund," *TLZ,* LXXII (1947), 130-34. S. W. Yeivin, "Jerusalem under the Davidic Dynasty," *VT,* III (1953), 153 upholds a time towards the end of the reign of Solomon. See also his article in Hebrew in the Dinaburg Jubilee volume (inaccessible to me).

[29] J. Estlin Carpenter, *The Composition of the Hexateuch* (1902), p. 217; J. A. Bewer, *The Literature of the Old Testament* (1938), 6th ed., p. 74; K. Budde, *op. cit.,* pp. 220 ff.; J. Hempel, *Die althebräische Literatur und ihr hellenistisch-jüdisches Nachleben,* p. 139; W. O. E. Oesterley and T. H. Robinson, *op. cit.,* p. 58; O. Procksch, *Die Theologie des alten Testaments,* pp. 225 ff.; 561 ff.; G. Mendenhall, *op. cit.,* pp. 46 f.; G. von Rad, *Old Testament Theology,* I, 293 f.; T. Vriezen, *de literatur van oud-Israel,* 2nd ed. (1961), p. 127; A. Weiser, *The Old Testament: its Formation and De-*

no greater, perhaps, than one would expect during the course of the history of transmission.[30] Contemporary criticism of the Gospels offers, perhaps, a relevant parallel. But the point where the two streams of tradition reach their culmination is in the representation of Moses as the covenant mediator and prophet.[31] Here again, and most impressively, the Deuteronomic traditions attach themselves directly with those of the Elohist.

The book of Deuteronomy is the covenant book *kat' exochēn*. The three pillars of Mosaic faith undergird and support the entire work: the exodus from Egypt, referred to no fewer than fifty times; the covenant at Horeb about thirty times; and the giving of the Law at least twenty-two times. The motifs of the Sinaitic theophany are recalled again and again, and are elaborated at considerable length: the terror of the divine appearing,[32] the summons to self-witness ("your eyes have seen"),[33] the *'am qadosh*[34] and the *'am segullah*,[35] the call to obedience, and the mediation of Moses.[36] An inspection of the *Gattungen* will reveal how intimately they are related to covenant types: the casuistic and especially the various types of apodictic law, which have been fruitfully studied by von Rad[37] and more especially by Karlheinz Rabast[38]; the covenant

velopment, p. 135; Dennis J. McCarthy, *Treaty and Covenant*, Analecta Biblica 21 (1963), pp. 118 f. See also nn. 3 and 19.

[30] See n. 18.

[31] H. H. Rowley, "The Nature of Old Testament Prophecy in the Light of Recent Study," in *The Servant of the Lord and Other Essays on the Old Testament* (1952), p. 113. The article was first published in *HTR*, XXVIII (1948), 1-38. O. Procksch, *op. cit.*, pp. 78-81, 225 ff.; W. Eichrodt, *Theology of the Old Testament*, I, 289 ff.; W. Beyerlin, *Herkunft und Geschichte der ältesten Sinaitraditionen*, pp. 119, 169 f., 187; Y. Kaufmann, *Religion of Israel* (1960), pp. 222 ff.; H. Graf Reventlow, "Kultisches Recht im alten Testament," *ZTK*, LX (1963), 300: J. Scharbert, *Heilsmittler im alten Testament und im alten Orient* (1964), pp. 91-95. Cf. also von Rad, *Old Testament Theology*, pp. 293 f. where the contrast between the Elohistic and Deuteronomic representations of Moses as prophet is stressed. Note again the contrast drawn by Eissfeldt between the Covenant Code (Exod. 20:23—23:33) and the Deuteronomic Code of laws.

[32] Deut. 4:11-12, 32-36; 5:4-5, 22-26; 9:10; 10:4; 18:18.

[33] Deut. 4:3, 9, 34 ff.; 7:18-19; 10:21; 11:7; 29:2; 34:12. See Muilenburg, "The Form and Structure of the Covenantal Formulations," p. 354; also H. Wildberger, *Jahwes Eigentumsvolk*, p. 11 and pp. 55 ff.

[34] Deut. 7:6; 14:2, 21; 26:19. Cf. 28:9.

[35] Deut. 7:6; 14:2; 26:18.

[36] The mediatorial work of Moses is stressed by many scholars, *inter alios*, W. Beyerlin, W. Eichrodt, Y. Kaufmann, H. J. Kraus, M. Newman, O. Procksch, von Rad, H. Graf Reventlow, J. Scharbert, H. Wildberger.

[37] *Studies in Deuteronomy*.

[38] *Das apodiktische Recht im Deuteronomium und im Heiligkeitsgesetz* (1949).

sermons which have been influenced by the "royal speech" of Exod. 19:3*b*-6 [39]; the covenantal *rib* or lawsuit of Deut. 32, which has been examined in one way or another by many scholars.[40] Of the first importance, however, is the presence of the many conditionals, above all those which appear at the conclusion of the code in Deut. 28.[41] It is these conditionals which in reality dominate the work, a consideration which would seem to qualify to a degree at least von Rad's contention that Deuteronomy is to be understood as the composition of the so-called "false prophets." [42] It is the conditionals which lie behind many of the later formulations: the oracles of judgment as well as the lawsuits.[43] Fortunately, our understanding of the covenantal character of Deuteronomy has now been greatly enhanced by the recovery of the ancient treaties from the Near East. The contributions of almost a score of scholars have helped us to see ever more clearly the degree to which the treaty

[39] H. Wildberger, *Jahwes Eigentumsvolk,* also Muilenburg, "The Form and Structure of the Covenantal Formulations."

[40] U. Cassuto in *Atti del XIX Congresso Internationale degli Orientalisti Roma* 23-29, Settembre, 1935 (1938), pp. 480-84. I have not seen this article; the reference is G. E. Wright's. O. Eissfeldt, *Das Lied Moses Deut. 32:1-43 und das Lehrgedicht Asaphs Psalm 78 samt einer Analyse der Umgebung des Mose-Liedes* in *Berichte über die Verhandlungen der sächsischen Akademie der Wissenschaften zu Leipzig.* Philologisch-historische Klasse, Bd. 104, Heft 5 (1959); W. F. Albright, "Some Remarks on the Song of Moses in Deuteronomy XXXII," *VT* IX (1959), 339-46; Patrick W. Skehan, "The Structure of the Song of Moses in Deuteronomy," *CBQ,* XIII (1951), 153-63; G. E. Wright, "The Lawsuit of God: a Form-Critical Study of Deuteronomy 32," in *Israel's Prophetic Heritage* (1962), pp. 26-67; Julien Harvey, S.J., "Le 'Ribpattern,' réquisitoire prophétique sur le rupture de l'alliance," *Biblica,* XLV (1962), 172-96; W. Beyerlin, "Gattung und Herkunft des Rahmens im Richterbuch," *Weiser Festschrift,* pp. 17-27. Cf. also H. B. Huffmon, "The Covenant Lawsuit in the Prophets," *JBL,* LXXVIII (1959), 285-95.

[41] See "Form and Structure of the Covenantal Formulations," pp. 354-57 for details; note especially the parallels to the treaties of the ancient Near East. To these should now be added the Sefire treaty. See M. Andre Dupont-Sommer, *Les Inscriptions Arameénnes de Sifré* (*Stèles I et II*) (1958); J. A. Fitzmyer, S.J., "The Aramaic Suzerainty Treaty from Sefire in the Museum of Beirut," *CBQ* XX (1958), 444-76; *idem,* "The Aramaic Inscriptions of Sefire I and II," *JAOS,* LXXXI (1961), 178-221. Delbert R. Hillers, *Treaty Curses and the Old Testament Prophets* in *Biblica et Orientalia,* XVI (1964) does ample justice to the curse forms in Deut. 28 but fails to recognize that they are placed in a context of conditionals and thus conform to what we have both in the OT and the treaties. Note esp. the characteristic openings in 28:1 and 15.

[42] "Die falschen Propheten," *ZAW,* LI (1933), 109-20.

[43] Observe the characteristic *because . . . therefore* style of the indictments, for example, in such contexts as Deut. 28:47 ff. Observe too that the imagery of the conditionals with their blessings and curses is perpetuated in some of the prophets.

formulations have left their impress not only upon the structure, formulation, and terminology of the covenant, but also, to some degree, upon the substance or thought.[44] *Yahweh is the suzerain, Israel the vassal.* But Yahweh is no earthly monarch, and so the presence of the mediator is surely required. It has been contended that the Hittite treaties also have a mediator, but of this I am not sure.[45] At any rate, the mediator is the messenger, the one sent with a word from the divine suzerain.[46] The Mari archives provide striking parallels in terminology and phraseology to the announcements and proclamations of the prophets, who also have been sent with a commission to speak in behalf of the sovereign.[47]

Finally, throughout the book of Deuteronomy it is the design of the transmitter of the traditions to bring the age of Moses and the figure of Moses into the context of contemporaneity. I do not refer solely to the frequent repetition of the urgent *today,* or the emphatic use of the second person pronoun (whether singular or plural), or the recurring *wᵉʿattâ.*

[44] V. Kurosec, *Hethitische Staatsverträge* in *Leipziger rechtswissenschaftliche Studien,* 1931; G. E. Mendenhall, *op. cit.;* D. J. Wiseman, *The Vassal-Treaties of Esarhaddon* (1958); Klaus Baltzar, *Das Bundesformular. Wissenschaftliche Monographien zum alten Testament* (1960); Julien Harvey, *op. cit.;* Meredith G. Kline, *Treaty of the Great King* (1963); Dennis J. McCarthy, *op. cit.;* William L. Moran, "The Ancient Near Eastern Background of the Love of God in Deuteronomy," *CBQ,* XXV (1963); W. Beyerlin, *Herkunft und Geschichte der ältesten Sinaitraditionen,* pp. 60 ff.; *idem,* "Gattung und Herkunft des Rahmens im Richterbuch" in *Weiser Festschrift,* pp. 1-28; H. Graf Reventlow, "Kultisches Recht im Alten Testament"; Murray Newman, *People of the Covenant, passim.* For a full bibliography on the treaties, see McCarthy, *op. cit.,* pp. xiii-xxiv.

[45] I have not been able to see the work of Morstad who defends this view.

[46] Ludwig Köhler, *Deuterojesaja stilkritisch untersucht* (1923), pp. 102-9; *idem, Kleine Lichter* (1945), pp. 11-17; Johannes Lindblom, *Die literarische Gattung der prophetischen Literatur* (1924), pp. 97 ff.; H. Wildberger, *Jahwewort und prophetische Rede* (1942), pp. 42-77; M. Noth, "History and Word of God in the Old Testament," *BJRL,* XXXII (1950); Y. Kaufmann, *The Religion of Israel,* pp. 212-16; Claus Westermann, *Grundformen prophetischer Rede,* pp. 66-91; James Ross, "The Prophet as Yahweh's Messenger," in *Israel's Prophetic Heritage,* pp. 98-107. See also the critical comments of Rolf Rendtorff, "Botenformel und Botenspruch," *ZAW* LXXIV (1962), 165-77 and C. Westermann, *Forschung am alten Testament* in *Neudrucke und Berichte aus dem 20. Jahrhundert,* XXIV (1964), 171 ff.

[47] W. von Soden, "Verkündung des Gotteswillens durch prophetisches Wort in den altbabylonischen Briefen aus Mari," *Die Welt des Orients* (1950), 397-403; A. Lods, "Une tablette inédite de Mari," in *Studies in Old Testament Prophecy, Festschrift for T. H. Robinson,* ed. H. H. Rowley (1956), pp. 103-10; F. M. Th. de Liagre Böhl, "Profetisme en plaatsvervangend Lijden in Assyrie en Israel," *Nederlands Theologisch Tijdschrift* (1949), pp. 81-91; M. Noth (see foregoing note); C. Westermann, *Grundformen prophetischer Rede,* pp. 82-91; *idem,* "Die Mari-Briefe und die Prophetie in Israel," in *Forschung zum alten Testament,* pp. 171-88.

Rather it is the collocation, the strategic position, in which these words are used and the urgency they have in their contexts. The concern to make the Mosaic figure and the Mosaic age immediate and contemporary is consistent with our understanding of the original oral character of the traditions which lie at the base of the book. So the question of the speaker again becomes pressing. Who is this Moses of whom the traditionists speak? How are we to understand the role of Moses who is preaching to us here? For an answer to this question we turn to the *locus classicus* of the covenant mediator, the aetiology of the prophet like Moses (Deut. 18:15 ff.).

The literary complex to which our pericope belongs has as its common subject the office-bearers of ancient Israel: judge, king, priest, and prophet (Deut. 17:8–18:22).[48] That the "office" of the prophet is designed by the collector of the sacral traditions to be climactic is apparent not only from the context in which our pericope (Deut. 18:15-22) appears, but also from the important transition between the other offices and that of the prophet (Deut. 18:9-14). Here we have to all intents and purposes a Deuteronomic rendering of two apodictic commands (9*b*-10, 13) followed by two impressive motivations, each introduced by the characteristic climactic particle *kî* (12, 14). Israel is not to learn to follow the *tô'ēbôt* of the nations, the various modes and techniques of evoking revelation, or to resort to diviners, soothsayers, augurs, sorcerers, charmers, necromancers *etc.,* because these are all an abomination to Yahweh. Israel is to be blameless (*tāmîm*) before Yahweh her God: "For these nations which you are about to dispossess, listen to soothsayers and to diviners; but as for you, Yahweh your God has not permitted you to do so" (Deut. 18:14). It is precisely in this strategic context that the impressive words about the prophet appear. Prophecy stands over against all these alien practices, and the revelation which the prophet receives in Israel is of a radically different order from that of the nations. It is the Word of Yahweh which surpasses all other ways of revealing. But I think we may go farther to suggest that the passage about the prophet occupies a crucial place in the structure of the whole book, for here the office of the Mosaic speaker is described with a succinctness and compression, a formality of style and a profusion of prophetic and covenantal

[48] M. Noth, *Amt und Berufung im Alten Testament,* pp. 23-26; H. J. Kraus, *Die prophetische Verkündigung des Rechts in Israel,* pp. 12-20.

motifs and terms unmatched elsewhere. The three divisions of the composition are dominated by the word *nabi'*:

15*a* נביא מקרבך מאחיך כמני יקים לך יהוה אלהיך
18*a* נביא אקים להם מקרב: אחיהם כמוך
20*a* אך הנביא אשר יזיד לדבר דבר בשמי . . .

The first is Moses' defense or legitimation of his office, a kind of *apologia pro officio suo;* the second a sacramental ordination in the divine first person,[49] the third a pronouncement and interdict against the speaker who speaks falsely. Controlling all three parts is the centrality of the *dabar* and the command to hear and obey, the very heart of covenantal allegiance.[50]

Moses is surely speaking here as mediator of the covenant, and, what is more, he is identifying the office of the mediator with that of the prophet (15-16). That the word *nabi'* is meant collectively and not individually is generally admitted. Certainly there is no eschatological allusion here. It is precisely at the point of the *apologia* that the *locus classicus* of the covenant mediator in the event at Sinai-Horeb is remembered and quoted, the place where the people implore Moses to mediate between them and Yahweh: "Let me not again hear the voice of Yahweh my God or see this great fire any more, lest I die" (cf. Exod. 20:18-20, and Deut. 5:2-5, 22 ff.). This is the prophet of the Elohist traditions, whom Yahweh knew face to face, *pānîm 'el pānîm* (Deut. 34: 10), with whom he spoke mouth to mouth, *peh 'el peh* (Num. 12:8). Moses is here understood as the supreme prophet, the archetypal prophet, the first of the prophetic order, and it is he who is here passing on his office to speak and proclaim the Word of Yahweh. But is the succession handed down from prophet to succeeding prophet in an *unbroken* chain, the one following the other in lineal order? This is frequently assumed in much of the literature on the subject today. But the text surely

[49] Compare above all Jer. 1:9, but see also Num. 22:38; 23:5, 12; Isa. 6:7; 51:16; 59:21. For detailed discussion, see H. G. Reventlow, *Liturgie und prophetisches Ich bei Jeremia* (1963), pp. 64 ff. To be observed, too, is the motif of the mouth in the Elohist traditions of Moses.

[50] The noun appears some six times, the corresponding verb form eight times, the verb "to hear" three times. On the nature of the word spoken here, cf. Kraus, *ibid.*, p. 15, n. 16. See also E. Jacob, *Theology of the Old Testament* (1958), pp. 129 ff.

does not make this at all clear. It is just as possible and perhaps probable that the meaning is that Yahweh will raise up prophets "from time to time" or "as occasion may demand" [51] or "as need arises" (G. Ernest Wright). If this is the true meaning, then the whole vexing problem of the tensions between charisma and office is somewhat relieved. If the meaning should be an unbroken chain of prophets, as many hold, then we would have, to be sure, another instance of the Deuteronomic proclivity to structuralize the sequences of history by accompanying it with prophetic messengers, as in the Deuteronomic history of the kings.[52] What is clear, however, is that Deut. 18:15 ff. is giving an account of the prophetic office, a characterization, too, perhaps of the institution of prophecy, and an assurance that Yahweh will ever and again raise up prophets like Moses for the proclamation of his Word. The Yahwist account of the covenant mediator provides a good parallel: "Lo, I am coming to you in a thick cloud, that the people may hear when I speak with you, and may also believe you for ever" (Exod. 19:9). In a striking passage in his *Studies in Deuteronomy,* von Rad denies that the prophetic element in Deuteronomy represents a stream of tradition, that there is any prophetic tradition behind it. The prophetic, he says, is merely a form, and is not to be taken seriously (p. 69). On the contrary, I should contend that our pericope is in reality bringing to a culmination the prophetic motifs of the old traditions, especially those of the Elohist. Similarly, Noth greatly minimizes the importance of the pericope, contending that the prophet does not represent an office at all, that in the very nature of the case the charismatic speaker called to Yahweh's service could not fulfill an office.[53] But this is to ignore the context of our passage, and, as will become apparent, the whole of the subsequent stream of prophetic traditions which have their source in the traditions associated with Moses. This is not meant to argue for the historicity of the latter—though I do think there is a nucleus of material which has a legitimate claim to historicity. Rather, I believe that already at a fairly early period, say at the time of the early amphictyonies (Shechem, Shiloh, Gilgal), we already

[51] S. R. Driver, *Deuteronomy, International Critical Commentary* (1895), p. 227. Driver aptly refers to Judg. 6:16, 18 as a parallel.

[52] Von Rad, *Studies in Deuteronomy,* pp. 74-91. The numerous striking parallels between Moses and Joshua in the book of Joshua are probably to be explained by the same Deuteronomic propensity. Joshua serves as the Mosaic figure throughout the book.

[53] *Amt und Berufung im alten Testament,* p. 25.

have a substantial quantity of traditions centering in the Mosaic figure.

In passing from a consideration of Moses, the prophet and covenant mediator, to the succession of prophets who follow him, we are confronted at once with the old problem of continuity and discontinuity in the history of Israel's faith. The Wellhausen school tended to view the prophets as isolated, solitary figures, monolithic men rising precipitately into their times, breaking into history as sudden mutations. The situation is, of course, quite otherwise today. We recognize clearly how the prophets rise out of the past, how the traditions of the Mosaic age or associated with it condition much of what they have to say. What was once viewed as unique and unprecedented is now seen as typical and representative. Form criticism and traditio-historical criticism as well as the recovery of the texts from the ancient Near East tend to a considerable degree to confirm such a position. But in certain quarters the stress upon the typical has become so great that the historical contexts in which the prophets speak and the individuality of the particular prophet are dismissed almost completely. While it is certainly true that the prophets employ conventional types and forms of speaking, *the forms and types are never mere stereotypes.* One has only to compare the accounts of the prophetic calls or the various *Gattungen* which they employ to observe the *distinctive* elements and, indeed, the distinctive styles too. Failure to recognize what is distinctive in the context of the conventional characterizes the work of many of our younger scholars today, notably the work of such a stimulating and often discerning scholar as H. G. Reventlow.[54] Thus the prophets, we are told, have nothing at all new to say, that they do not reflect or speak out of their own times, but merely repeat traditional words, familiar clichés drawn from the cult. Now it is just as precarious to minimize the importance of the cult in the life of ancient Israel and to ignore its profound influence upon many of the prophetic formulations as it is to find a liturgy lurking in every prophetic corner. If there is continuity and indeed the degree of continuity which the prophetic records plainly reveal, then it is essential that we face the question of the matrix or structure which will best explain it. To this question the most plausible answer is cult or worship, but it must not be permitted to

[54] *Das Amt des Propheten Amos; Wächter über Israel; Liturgie und Prophetisches Ich bei Jeremia.* See also Gerstenberger, "The Woe-Oracles of the Prophets," *JBL,* LXXXI (1962), 249-63.

subsume everything within its sphere. Conventionality is certainly not to be restricted to the cultic sphere alone.

To speak more concretely, in dealing with the motif of Moses and the prophet like Moses, we must take into account the early traditions associated with the amphictyonic centers, such as Shechem, Shiloh, Gilgal, Bethel, and other sanctuaries. What is more, we must scrutinize these traditions very closely in order to discern their nature and form, the terminology and the keywords, the rhetoric or the way thought is articulated into speech, and not least of all their interior structures. I refer, for example, to one type of such investigation in the studies of many contemporary scholars of the Hittite and other suzerainty treaties and their striking affinities to the covenant formulations.[55] Or one could mention almost a score of works dealing with the influence of the legal *Gattungen* upon the prophetic proclamations.[56] Or one could refer to the detailed analysis of such crucial covenantal expressions as the divine first-person self-asseveration, "I am Yahweh," [57] or the classical covenant formula, "You shall be my people, and I will be your God,[58] or to the messenger's speech.[59] The conclusions to which all of these and many other similar studies point are incontestable: far from drawing a firm line of demarcation between the law and the prophets, we are now compelled by the evidence to recognize a prevailing continuity.

Now it is essential to recognize that the issue of continuity must not be too simply stated. One could argue plausibly and perhaps convincingly that continuity is by no means unilinear or that our contention by no means holds for all the prophets or, as we have already noted, that there

[55] Mendenhall, Huffmon, Baltzar, Newman, Harvey, McCarthy, Kline, Beyerlin, Hillers. See n. 44.

[56] Note, for example, E. Würtwein, "Amos-Studien," *ZAW* (1949-50), pp. 10-52; H. G. Reventlow, *Das Amt des Propheten bei Amos;* Robert Bach, "Gottesrecht und weltliches Recht in der Verkündigung des Propheten Amos," in *Festschrift für Gunther Dehn* (1957), pp. 23-54 on the affinities of the Covenant Code and other laws with the prophet Amos. Note also the studies of the *rib* Gattung by Huffmon, G. E. Wright, Beyerlin, Harvey, and others. Also Reventlow on the connections of the Holiness Code with the prophecies of Ezekiel, in *Wächter über Israel;* Claus Westermann *Grundformen prophetischer Rede* (1962) on the *Gerichtsrede,* and especially Julien Harvey on the breach of covenant. Cf. the discussion of the covenant conditionals in the writer's "Covenantal Formulations."

[57] Walther Zimmerli, "Ich bin Jahwe," in the *Alt-Festschrift, Geschichte und Altes Testament* (1953), pp. 179-210.

[58] Rudolph Smend, *Die Bundesformel.*

[59] See n. 46.

is diversity in the way that traditional types are appropriated. This is surely true. But I think we may say with some degree of confidence that we can clearly discern a continuous stream of tradition in those records which come to us from the northern kingdom of Israel, notably in the Elohist, Samuel, the Deuteronomic speakers, Elijah, Hosea, Jeremiah, and, to a degree, Second Isaiah. If we were to press our inquiry, we should be compelled to turn to the rituals and thanksgiving hymns of the covenant community at Qumran and to assess the influence of the age of Moses upon the eschatological community of the Essenes or the role played by Moses in the figure of the Teacher of Righteousness. But let us confine our attention to only two of the prophets: Samuel and Hosea.

The traditions which gather about Samuel are of a varied kind and in all probability reflect varying provenances and points of view. He is portrayed in ways which seem contradictory, and it is clear that each stratum of tradition betrays its own *Tendenz.* It is nevertheless questionable that the Deuteronomist has greatly altered the traditions concerning him. The affinities with the Elohist seem much clearer, as has been well argued and documented by Joseph Bourke, S. J., in an illuminating article.[60] Like Joshua, Samuel comes from the tribe of Ephraim, and if we could trust the striking reference of Josh. 18:1, then his association with the sanctuary at Shiloh would connect him with Joshua. Be that as it may, Samuel receives his call in the presence of the ark of the covenant, "the tangible symbol of the Sinai covenant." The imperious summons, "Samuel, Samuel" and the response reminds one of the call of Moses (cf. I Sam. 3:4, 8, 10 and Exod. 3:4), and the strong stress upon hearing is very characteristic both of the Elohist and the Deuteronomist. Similarly, the manner in which the *dabar* of Yahweh determines the structure and dominates the accounts is characteristic of the northern traditions of the Elohist, Elijah, Deuteronomy, and Jeremiah (cf., for example, I Sam. 3:1*b,* 7, 20 and I Kings 17:2, 8, 24). Samuel delivers a covenant speech (I Sam. 12), much in the manner and style of the royal covenant speech to Moses (Exod. 19:3*b*-6) and the speech of Joshua on the occasion of the establishment of the twelve-tribe federation at Shechem (Josh. 24). We listen again to the great asseveration of the divine deliverance, this time with the messenger's formula, "Thus says

[60] Joseph Bourke, S. J., "Samuel and the Ark, A Study in Contrasts," *Dominican Studies,* VII (1954), 73-103.

Yahweh, the God of Israel," to the breach of covenant motif (I Sam. 10: 18-19), and especially to the climactic conditionals of the treaties and covenants (12:14-15, cf. 7:3). Samuel is endowed like Moses with the charisma, and he stands at the head of the group of ecstatic prophets at Naioth. We have, too, what appear to be the remnants of the covenant lawsuit (I Sam. 8:7-9, 19-22), reminiscent of the lawsuits which Beyerlin has uncovered in the frameworks to the book of Judges. Surprisingly, in a laconic observation Samuel is said to have told the people the *mishpat* of the kingdom, "and he wrote it in a book and placed it before Yahweh," a passage which bears the marks of an early provenance (I Sam. 10:25). In an illuminating essay, Murray Newman contends that the call of Samuel is the aetiology of the office of the prophet; if this is right, then the connection with Deut. 18:15 ff. becomes very interesting.[61] At any rate, the man who was the maker of a king can have been no mean figure. Eissfeldt and Albright assign the lawsuit of Deut. 32 to the time of Samuel, and Beyerlin supports their position.[62] While it is difficult to think of the present composition as emanating from so early a period, the role of Samuel in the traditions associated with his name is apparently that of the mediator of the covenant as is the figure of Moses in the lawsuit of Deut. 32. Moreover, Samuel is perpetuating the theology of the Shechem federation. He is both prophet and covenant mediator,[63] Yah-

[61] "The Prophetic Call of Samuel," *Israel's Prophetic Heritage,* pp. 86-97.

[62] See especially Albright's stimulating discussion in "Samuel and the Beginnings of the Prophetic Movement," pp. 21-26. Note p. 26: "We can, at all events, use *Ha'azīnū* to illustrate the great religious reform which Samuel brought about and without which Elijah and Jeremiah could not have fulfilled their place in history." Beyerlin relates his discussion of Deut. 32 to the *rib* patterns which he finds in the frameworks of Judges.

[63] Among the many scholars who would support this position, see most recently J. Scharbert, *Heilsmittler im Alten Testament und im Alten Orient:* "Samuel ist der letzte der grossen Gottesmänner aus Israels Vorzeit, der *alle Bundesmittler-funktionen in einer Person vereint.* Die Tradition, die der Deuteronomist im wesentlichen unverändert wiedergibt, schildert ihn geradezu als einen zweiten Mose," p. 116. "Als Prophet ist er *Übermittler des Gottesworts und Gotteswillens,"* p. 117. "Aber Samuel ist wie Moses und Josue nicht nur Übermittler des Wünsche des Volkes an Gott, sondern aus Liebe und inniger Verbundenheit mit Israel auch *Fürbitter* und *Sühnemittler,"* p. 118. The italics are the author's. See also H. Wildberger, "Samuel und die Errichtung des israelitischen Königtums," *Theol. Zeitschrift,* XIII (1957), 442-69: A. Weiser, *Samuel, FRLANT,* LXXXI (1962), 82-93; Rudolph Smend, *Jahwekrieg und Stämmebund, FRLANT,* LXXXIV (1962); J. Kraus, *Die prophetische Verkündigung des Rechts in Israel,* pp. 23 ff.; M. Noth, "Das Amt des 'Richters Israels,'" pp. 404-17.

weh's messenger in a time of transition and change, "the faithful guardian of the Mosaic heritage" as Volz puts it, "the first great religious reformer after Moses," as Albright says. Again and again from the time of Wellhausen on scholars have called him the second Moses.

The prophet Hosea ben Beeri, probably from the tribe of Ephraim, stands midway in the history of the covenant traditions of ancient Israel as they were preserved by the northern traditionists. He is intimately acquainted, for example, with the Elohist narratives and legal formulations;[64] and his prophecy teems with parallels, both linguistic and theological, to the sacral traditions in Deuteronomy.[65] The major motifs of the age of Moses are so closely woven into the texture of his thought and the forms of his speaking, often drawn from the amphictyonic celebrations, come so congenially and naturally to him that it cannot be doubted that he conceived his prophetic office in relation to them. This is all the more significant because the coventional *Botenformel* is often wanting where we should most expect it. Again we discern the echoes from the ancient Near Eastern treaties, above all that of the breach of treaty. While the covenant conditionals are all but absent, the indictments and sentences have their source in these formulations. It is not too much to say that the time of Moses was normative for Hosea. Israel must return to the desert again, there to recover her ancient election-covenant

[64] On Hosea's familiarity with the Elohist, there is, so far as I am aware, universal agreement. So Steuernagel, Budde, Procksch, Sellin, von Rad, H. W. Wolff, and many others.

[65] See above all the commentary of H. W. Wolff in the *Biblischer Kommentar* series. Note his words in the introduction to his commentary, p. xxvi: "Alle drei Überlieferungskomplexe des Hoseabuches stellen insofern Parallelen dar, als jeder von ihnen den Weg von der Anklage und Strafdrohung bis zur Heilsverkündigung durchschreitet. Sie mögen auf verschiedene Hände zurückgehen, gehören aber doch alle in den gleichen Kreis zeitgenössischer Freunde des Propheten (s. S. XIV), der identisch ist mit den Vorläufern der deuteronomischer Bewegung.

"Darauf weisen die im Kommentar auf Schritt und Tritt aufzudeckenden Beziehungen der Hosea-Überlieferung zu Sprache und Theologie des Deuteronomiums hin. Ganze Denkbewegungen, die für die deuteronomische Paränese kennzeichnend sind, finden wir erstmals bei Hosea, so die Kombination der Erinnerung an den Auszug aus Ägypten, an die Leitung durch die Wüste und die Hineinführung ins Kulturland mit den Folgen: Sattwerden, Überheblichwerden, Jahwe vergessen (s. S. 48, 294); ferner den Kampf gegen Bündnispolitik (s. S. 273), die Art, von *tôrâ* zu sprechen (s. S. 176 f.), von Jahwe als 'Erzieher' (s. S. 125), von 'Liebe' Jahwes (s. S. 255), von 'Erlösung' (s. S. 162), vom Leben des rechten Propheten 'mit Gott' (s. S. 203), von Bruderschaft (s. S. 33), von Mazzeben der Kanaanäer (s. S. 225), von 'Korn, Most und Olivensaft' (s. S. 44)."

heritage.[66] Hosea recalls Yahweh's great theophanic words of self-revelation, "I am Yahweh from the land of Egypt" (12:9; 13:4); more than once he repeats the formal pronouncement by which the covenant was concluded, "You shall be my people, and I will be your God" (1:9; 2:23); like the Elohist before him he speaks of Israel as Yahweh's son (11:1 ff.; cf. Exod. 4:22-23). Israel's flouting of the first of all the commands in the Elohistic decalog sounds again and again throughout his prophecy; it is the breach of treaty *kat' exochēn*. Hosea knows the apodictic laws, both in his direct citation of them and in his indirect allusions to them. He employs the characteristic imperatives calling upon Israel to hear and the vocatives associated with them. He has apparently listened to the legal encounters of the litigants before the elders at the gates. Hans Walter Wolff suggests plausibly that most of his utterances have their *Sitz im Leben* in this context.[67] The prophet Moses stands at the head of the succession of prophets, the messengers called to speak for Yahweh to the people, and there can be no question that Hosea considered himself to belong to that succession (6:5; 9:7; 12:11, 14). His attitude toward the establishment of the kingdom is close to that of the law for the king in Deuteronomy and to the traditions associated with Samuel.[68] Hosea perpetuates the forms of speech and not infrequently the terminology of the old amphictyonic traditions; one thinks of the apodictic laws, the covenant lawsuits, the historical confessions of the Credos, the indictments and sentences, the exhortations and the speeches of the messengers. He is the proclaimer of the law, the announcer of judgment, the watchman of Ephraim, the prophet whose memories are rooted in the *magnalia Dei,* the mediator of the covenant in inchoate times. He summons his people to *da'ath elohim,* and in this he is again close to the Deuteronomic traditionists (Hos. 4:1, 6; 5:4; 6:6; 14:10. Cf. Deut. 4:39; 7:9 ff.; 8:5; 9:3).[69] Like them he appeals to the love of God

[66] Note, for example, O. Procksch, *Theologie des Alten Testaments,* p. 588: "Schon Hosea sieht die Mosezeit als ein Vorspiel der Zukunft an; wie zu Moses Zeit soll Israel auch in Zukunft noch einmal durch die Wüste wandern (Hos. 12:10) wie ehedem, als Mose es hütete (v. 14), der ausdrücklich hier als Prophet bezeichnet ist."

[67] *Hosea* in Biblischer Kommentar series, pp. xv, 83, and *passim.*

[68] Albrecht Alt, "Die Heimat des Deuteronomiums," *Kleine Schriften,* II (1953), 267 f.

[69] H. W. Wolff, "'Wissen um Gott' bei Hosea als Urform von Theologie," *EvT,* XII (1952/53), 533-54. See also Porteous' judicious criticism in *Tradition und Situation* (*Weiser Festschrift*), p. 97.

with intimate nuances, and here again we recognize a parallel with the treaties. In this connection it is well to note his polemic against the treaty politics of Israel, another Deuteronomic motif (5:13; 7:11; 8:9; 10:4; 12:2; 14:4. Cf. Deut. 7:2; 17:16; 20:16). In the prophecies of Hosea we listen to echoes from the great covenant lawsuit of Deut. 32.[70]

How are we to explain this extraordinary familiarity of the prophet Hosea with the traditions and the formal and covenantal patterns of speech? Wolff sees the prophet as a member of Levitical circles, and this may well be, but it must always be remembered that according to an important tradition it was Moses who transmitted the law to the Levites (Deut. 33:10).[71] And this may account for his reference to Moses and for the relation of his prophecy to the Mosaic traditions.

We may now attempt to state some of the conclusions which would seem to follow from our discussion. It has been apparent that we have had to deal with many issues in a rather sketchy fashion. This is perhaps unfortunate since the force of the argument depends in no small part upon the detailed scrutiny of numerous literary contexts in the light of form and traditio-historical criticism.

1. There were many prophets in ancient Israel, and it is probable that the canon has preserved the memory of only a relatively small number of them. But there were also different kinds of prophets too, and it is precarious to undertake to understand them in the light of a single background or cultural provenance.[72] While it has been our intention to speak of those who preserve the northern traditions, it must be remembered that the southern prophets not infrequently avail themselves of the same traditions, notably Amos and Micah.[73]

2. The traditions which we have examined have as their common matrix the covenant of Yahweh with Israel at Sinai-Horeb. Not only the literary forms and types but also the treaties from the ancient Near

[70] E. Baumann, "Das Lied Mose's (Dt. xxxii. 1-43)," *VT*, VI (1956), 421 f.

[71] H. W. Wolff, "Hoseas geistige Heimat," *TLZ*, LXXXI (1956), 83-94.

[72] H. H. Rowley, "The Nature of Old Testament Prophecy in the Light of Recent Study," in *The Servant of the Lord and Other Essays on the Old Testament* (1952), pp. 91-128; A. Jepsen, *Nabi. Soziologische Studien zur alttestamentlichen Literatur und Religionsgeschichte*, 1934.

[73] E. Würtwein, "Amos-Studien," *ZAW*, LXII (1949), 10-52; W. Beyerlin, *Die Kulttraditionen Israels in der Verkündigung des Propheten Micha. FRLANT*, LXXII (1959).

East now show how the prophets from the north were speaking within a covenantal framework.

3. That there were prophets who understood themselves as having participated in the decisions and announcements of the divine council is certainly true, but it is doubtful if we can say this of all of them, especially those from the north. As Huffmon has demonstrated, there were at least two major types of lawsuit, one of them centering in the Sinaitic covenant.

4. In early traditions Moses is viewed as the mediator of the covenant and as prophet. Among the types of traditions associated with his name are the messenger's speech, the royal covenant speech, the apodictic and casuistic laws with their striking motivations, the lawsuit, and the great conditionals, which we understand to be the basis of the indictments and sentences, on the one hand, and the assurances of felicity, on the other. What is important to observe here is that the prophets avail themselves of the same types of material and thus are continuous with Moses or the Mosaic figure.

5. The question of the *Sitz im Leben* of the *Gattungen* is difficult, but there is a substantial number of contexts which suggest the existence of an annual festival in which the covenant memories of Israel were reactivated into the present, perhaps the autumnal festival. But it is unnecessary to hold that all the kinds of speaking we have mentioned were associated exclusively with that celebration. Inevitably one raises the question of how our "literary" materials were employed in the life of the people. They certainly were not designed to be read as literature.

6. This raises the vexing question of the relationship of the prophets to the cult. On the one hand, they seem to stand over against it in their bitter criticisms of it, but on the other hand there are not a few contexts which more than suggest that they bore some relation to it. One thinks of Amos at Bethel or of Jeremiah in the Temple, or in an earlier period, of Samuel at Gilgal. Moreover, one cannot well ignore the presence of cultic formulations in the prophets. One thinks, for example, of the liturgy (Isa. 33; Mic. 7:9-20; Jer. 14:1—15:3, and others).

7. Who, then, is Moses and who are the prophetic figures who follow him? First of all they are *messengers.* This understanding of the prophetic function has long been recognized by scholars (Ludwig Köhler, Johannes Lindblom, Claus Westermann, H. W. Wolff, M. Noth, Reventlow, and

others).[74] In the second place, they are *speakers for Yahweh, proclaimers of the law, apostles sent to particular times to speak particular words.* They do more than repeat inherited and traditional cliches; they seek to make the Word of God immediate and relevant and contemporary. They are politicians, to use the word G. Mendenhall and G. E. Wright have taught us—Yahweh's politicians proclaiming covenantal proclamations. But more, they are charismatically endowed by Yahweh to perform their fateful missions. The succession of prophets is a succession of charismatic persons, and we must remind ourselves once more that there were many more such persons in Israel than those of whom the OT tells us. Yehezkel Kaufmann does not go too far in maintaining that there was a long succession of apostles in Israel.

What then shall we say of the prophets of whom we have been speaking? In the light of our general survey of one major strand of tradition in the OT it does not seem to me to be out-running the evidence to say that they were indeed prophets like Moses, Yahweh's messengers, his covenant mediators, intercessors for the people, speakers for God. They are sent from the divine King, the suzerain of the treaties, to reprove and to pronounce judgment upon Israel for breach of covenant. The work of Mendenhall, Baltzar, G. E. Wright, Julien Harvey, S. J., Kline, and others have made this very clear.

But, more than all else, Moses comes and the prophets come to speak the Word of Yahweh, and it is the power of his Word which lies behind their various pronouncements. This stress upon the Word of Yahweh in the northern traditions is not the same as that of the prophets from the south. From beginning to end in the north the Word assumes a central role.

So today we no longer speak of Moses *or* the prophets, or of the law *or* prophecy, but rather of Moses *and* the prophets.

[74] Note especially James F. Ross, "The Prophet as Yahweh's Messenger," in *Israel's Prophetic Heritage,* pp. 98-107, but also the criticisms of R. Rendtorff and C. Westermann. See n. 46.

STANLEY BRICE
FROST

Apocalyptic and History

It may, perhaps, be considered not inappropriate if on this historic occasion in the life of our Society I take the occasion to deal not only with the assigned subject of apocalyptic, but also with that of history. My title, if spelt out in fuller detail, is the apocalyptic contribution to the biblical consideration of history.

Much has indeed been claimed for the apocalyptic school of writers with regard to their view of history. Thus, for example, R. H. Charles wrote in the Introduction to his *Commentary on Daniel:* "Apocalyptic was a Semitic philosophy of religion and concerned itself with the questions of whence? wherefore? whither? It sketched in outline the history of the universe, and of the angelic and human worlds, the origin of evil, its course and ultimate overthrow. It was thus apocalyptic and not prophecy that was the first to grasp the great idea that all history, human, cosmological and spiritual, is a unity—a unity that follows inevitably as a corollary to the unity of God as enforced by the O.T. Prophets." [1] Similarly I myself twelve years ago wrote of the apocalyptists: "If their task was a theodicy, then their answer must be made good in the one sure medium of revelation—and that for the Hebrew was *history,* the story of what God had done in creation and providence . . . in their own strange way they were trying to view all history *sub specie aeternitatis,* and if they did not always get their facts clear, they were at least the first men to essay a philosophy of history." [2] D. S. Russell has recently expressed a more moderate view. He writes: "Such a claim, however, does less than justice to the Old Testament prophets and enhances the reputation of the apocalyptists in a way they hardly deserve. It is more accurate to regard the apocalyptists as middle men than as pioneers in this regard. What they did was to carry still further the sense of divine purpose, which was already to be found in the prophets, as the unifying

[1] *Commentary on Daniel,* Oxford, 1929, p. xxv.
[2] S. B. Frost, *Old Testament Apocalyptic,* London, 1952, p. 8.

principle of all human history." [3] The purpose of the present paper is to suggest that apocalyptic is best described neither as pioneering a philosophy of history nor as acting as interpreter of the view of history which had been expressed by the prophets, but rather as departing from that view as untenable, and turning to an expression of religious reality which, indeed, draws upon historical thinking but also upon prehistorical thinking, and offers a new and distinctive synthesis. We are well accustomed to calling the latter kind of thought myth, and the element derived from historical thinking we often call eschatology.[4] Thus from the time of Gunkel apocalyptic has been freely described as eschatologized myth. The tag ran *Urzeit wird Endzeit*. That apocalyptic thus identified represents within the complex of biblical thought a rejection of history as the medium in which religious truth is to be sought and expressed, has not, I believe, been so widely recognized.[5]

I

To give substance to this view we must see the apocalyptists in the perspective of the Bible as a whole and particularly in relation to some aspects of the biblical treatment of history, and so we begin by commenting on the nature of historiography in the OT. E. H. Carr has recently reminded us that: "It used to be said that the facts speak for themselves. This is of course untrue. The facts speak only when the historian calls on them: it is he who decides to which facts to give the floor, and in what order and in what context," and reminds us that as long ago as 1894 James Anthony Froude remarked that history is "a child's box of letters with which we can spell any word we please." [6] The word which the Hebrews chose to spell was they believed the Word of God, but it is im-

[3] *The Method and Message of Jewish Apocalyptic,* Philadelphia, 1964, p. 218.

[4] Eschatology is in fact a misnomer as applied to preapocalyptic writers; teleology is the more correct term, seeing that an end was envisaged *in* history rather than *of* history. See further below, p. 109.

[5] The matter is not, I venture to suggest, one of small importance. The so-called "biblical theology" movement would not perhaps have trusted the idea of revelation through biblical history so unquestioningly if it had been realized that not only eminent secular historians but also some biblical writers themselves were clearly warning us: "Put not your trust in history." For an extreme example of such overconfidence, cf. *Offenbarung als Geschichte,* ed. W. Pannenberg, Goettingen, 2nd ed., 1963.

[6] *What Is History?* London, 1961, p. 5. He cites on p. 21 J. A. Froude, *Short Studies in Great Subjects,* I, 1894, p. 21 (see also p. 7 in 1871 ed.).

portant to recognize that this was, from the human point of view, consciously or unconsciously, a matter of choice.[7] Further, we have to break down that "Word of God" into its constituent ideas, and in this way to inquire what were the ideas which the Hebrew history writers chose that their history should express.

It can be shown, I suggest, that Israel took over (as one would expect) the ideas of religion as they were familiar to her in the myths of the ancient Near East and reclothed those same fundamental notions in the dress of her own history. As a result of the work of Gunkel, Hooke, Frankfort, Engnell, Mowinckel, and others, we have been able to recognize that the dominant themes of ancient mythology were six-fold: the divine conflict with and victory over the forces of chaotic evil, the divine creation of the existing order, the kingly relation of the divine to the creation, the worship which is the creation's proper response to that sovereignty, the vitality of the divine as expressed in the death and resurrection motif, and the divine fertility expressed in the sacred marriage. It is fundamentally these same ideas which Israel's history is made to express, by the early biblical historiographical tradition, though, of course, there is much modification, redistribution of emphasis, and an all-important selectivity.[8] The result is a fresh, highly characteristic Hebrew version of the basic complex of religious ideas which evolved in the ancient Near East. Thus the conflict of Marduk and Tiamat (to use the terminology of the Babylonian variant) becomes the conflicts of Yahweh and the successive enemies of Israel.[9] The creation of the world is paralleled by the creation of Israel,[10] and the kingly relationship is expressed very

[7] This does not of course rule out a doctrine of inspiration, except in the extreme form that the writers were wholly dominated by the Holy Spirit.

[8] The attempt to express the age-old religious ideas of mankind in terms of Israel's history can first be traced in the sagas which we know as the Pentateuchal sources J and E, though it probably antedates them. It appears more characteristically in the works of the Deuteronomic tradition. For the attitude of the Priestly school writers, see the citation from von Rad, pp. 104-5.

[9] This is particularly well illustrated in the case of Yahweh's conflict with Egypt by the cycle called "The Ten Plagues."

[10] Later, however, the history-period is extrapolated back into the past, so that the creation of the world itself can become an event in time, and thus become an event in Israel's history. This has the result that it becomes unclear whether the memorial of creation, the weekly sabbath, is to celebrate the creation of Israel or the creation of the world. Cf. the Deuteronomic and Priestly recensions of the Fourth Commandment, Deut. 5:15; Exod. 20:11.

appropriately in terms of covenant.[11] The motif of worship appears in the mythology as the need for Marduk to have built for him *esagila,* the ziggurat of Babylon; or again as the need for Baal, fresh from the conquest of Prince Yamm, to have a house built for him by 'El's command. This is expressed in Hebrew historiography as the need to provide a tabernacle or house for Yahweh after his victory—especially the success of Israel under David over the Canaanites, the last and greatest in the series of victories such as were recorded no doubt in the "Book of the Wars of Yahweh." [12] Israel was, however, hesitant as to how to express the vitality of God as testified by the dying and rising myth. Her teachers shifted the relationship of the motif from Yahweh to a number of surrogates closely allied to him and yet separate from him. Thus the story of the defeat of Israel and the capture of the ark, its descent into the House of Dagon and its triumphant return from thence, has been recognized as one of the Hebrew expressions of this theme; and A. R. Johnson has found reason to think that the theme also expressed itself in the role of the king in the Jerusalem cultus. Again, the dying and rising role is transferred from the divinity not only to his ark, or to his Messiah, but also later to his people, Israel, who undergo death at the exile and are resurrected to life in the return.[13] Perhaps the most striking feature of Hebrew religion is its almost total rejection of the fertility motif. True, it provided the metaphor of the marriage relationship of Yahweh and Israel and its converse, the adultery metaphor which referred to the worship of other gods, but otherwise the divine sexuality was the one major theme of ancient Near Eastern mythology which Israel refused.[14] In the early days, this resulted in a divorce between Yahweh and the natural order, but it was later corrected by a vigorous doctrine of world

[11] The relationship of Hebrew covenant forms to second millennium treaty-structures setting out kingly relationships has been discussed by G. E. Mendenhall, "Law and Covenant in Israel and the Ancient Near East," *BA,* XVII, No. 2, May, 1954, 26-46, and No. 3, September, 1954, 49-76.

[12] Num. 21:14.

[13] Cf. J. R. Porter, "The Interpretation of II Sam. 4-6 and Ps. 132," *JTS,* N.S. V, 1954, 161-73; A. R. Johnson, "The Rôle of the King in the Jerusalem Cultus," in *The Labyrinth,* ed. S. H. Hooke, London, 1935, pp. 73-111; Ezek. 37:1-14.

[14] The divinity of the reigning king was another idea which Israel by and large refused, but while it has been the subject of much modern study it was a relatively minor theme of ancient religion.

creation and world providence, as distinct from Israel creation and Israel providence.[15]

The history was made to convey these ideas by means of a teleological interpretation. The patriarchal traditions, the descent into Egypt, the exodus, the wanderings in the desert, the conquest, were built into a saga wherein Israel was the chosen people of Yahweh and wherein his activity could be plainly discerned as bringing the tribes through many crises to the splendid goal of being a people, with a god, an identity, a law, a land of their own. No doubt the *telos* to which the history led was not a wholly static concept, and by the time *Heilsgeschichte* first achieved something like literary form at the hands of the Yahwist, it had become the Davidic Kingdom, with the reigning Judean king as Yahweh's Messiah. A little later, when the division of the kingdom and the resultant political weakness made the present seem less than wholly desirable, the goal was no longer thought of as attained, but was put off into the future as something yet to come. The *Yom Yahweh,* the *telos* in which *Heilsgeschichte* must finally fulfill itself, became in the teaching of the prophets the sustaining hope of Israel. It was an end which had indeed once been achieved, in the time of David and Solomon,[16] and would assuredly be given to a loyal Israel once again. But it is important to notice that this Golden Age was to come within history, and as a result of Yahweh's control of history.

II

History, then, and not myth, was the medium in which Israel's religious understanding found expression. A change of medium, however, inevitably affected profoundly the character of the ideas themselves. Notably, the covenant relationship became more prominent and with it the Torah in which the Hebrew's obligations to his god were set forth. In the hands of the prophets, however, this appeal to history was given a natural but dangerous turn. If Israel was asked to read her past history in terms of a revelation of her God, his nature, his power, his will, it was only to be expected that this same divine activity should also be looked for in current events. This task the prophets undertook, but whereas it had been

[15] Hos. 2:8-9; cf. also Ps. 65 and the evidence for rain-making ceremonies at the Feast of Tabernacles in N. H. Snaith, *The Jewish New Year Festival,* London, 1947, p. 62 f. Also, Ps. 104, itself modeled upon the nature-hymn attributed to Ikhn-aten (Pritchard, *Ancient Near Eastern Texts,* 2nd ed., 1955, pp. 369 f.).

[16] Cf. I Kings 4:20-34.

comparatively easy to impose a standard interpretation upon past history, it was by no means so easy to do so with regard to contemporary history. First, there was the problem that the interpreters disagreed among themselves. The disagreement came to a head at the time of the great crisis of Israel's existence, the Babylonian attack upon the Judean state at the beginning of the sixth century B.C. How deep was the cleavage and how bitter the quarrel between the adherents of the two interpretations the book of Jeremiah reveals in numerous passages.[17] This inability of her experts to agree upon the interpretation of those all-important events dealt a severe blow to the belief that history could convey a revelation of the divine mind, a blow from which that belief never fully recovered. Secondly, while it was possible in the early post-exilic period to make a massive effort to interpret the disaster which had befallen Israel as the punitive will of Yahweh, the long Persian domination and its immediate sequel, the prolonged Greek domination, made a similar explanation of contemporary history more and more unconvincing. The burden laid upon credulity is well expressed by the seer in II Esdras, a comparatively late work in which this dissatisfaction is given overt expression: "Then I answered and said, 'I beseech you, my lord, why have I been empowered with the power of understanding? For I did not wish to enquire about the ways above but about those things which we experience daily: why Israel has been given over to the Gentiles as a reproach; why the people whom you loved have been given over to godless tribes, and the law of our fathers has been made of no effect and the written covenants no longer exist; and why we pass from the world like locusts and our life is like a mist.' "[18] Another aspect of the increasing difficulty of belief in a revelation of God in history was that if the purpose of God thus revealed was the salvation of Israel, why then was the scale of history so unnecessarily large? What was to become of all the Gentiles? And indeed, what was to become of all the Jews who were not "wise," i.e. members of the apocalyptic movement? It is again the seer of II Esdras who puts

[17] Cf. I Kings 22:1-28; Isa. 9:15-16, 29:10; Deut. 18:15-22; Jer. 4:9-10, 14:11-15, 23:16-17, 18-22, 23-32, and especially Jer. 27—29.

[18] II Esdras 4:22-24. Wilfred Cantwell Smith draws attention to the fact that this same dilemma, arising out of a reading of history which is controverted by hard facts, is the major problem of modern Islam. Cf. *Islam in Modern History*, Princeton, 1957, p. 41: "The fundamental *malaise* of modern Islam is a sense that something has gone wrong with Islamic history."

these thoughts into words. He can at a pinch, though with obvious reluctance, summon up sufficient orthodoxy to dismiss the Gentiles as of no moment: "As for the other nations which have descended from Adam, thou hast said that they are nothing, and that they are like spittle; and thou hast compared their abundance to a drop from a bucket." [19] He can also make his angelic interlocutor say: "The Most High made this world for the sake of many, but the world to come for the sake of few . . . many have been created, but few shall be saved," [20] but the problem remains in his heart unanswered. The frame of history was, in fact, too large for the *Heilsgeschichte* it was supposed to contain, and earnest minds were increasingly aware of the incongruity.

History thus lost favor as the great medium for the expression of religious ideas. The only motive Israel had had in writing her history had been thereby to demonstrate her faith and to use that history as a medium for its expression. Once that motive was preempted, Israel lost interest in the writing of history and (apart from a tendentious reworking of earlier writing by the Chronicler) history writing ceased in Israel. When it recommenced in the Maccabean period, it was a very difficult thing, no longer *Heilsgeschichte* but rather history as the Greeks understood it.[21]

The apocalyptists came therefore at a critical period in the development of Israel. At the turn of the first millennium B.C., myth had been outgrown and abandoned, and faith-expressive historiography had taken its place. But in the fourth and third centuries B.C. the limitations of history as the medium in which religious ideas might be expressed, had become woefully apparent. How were believing men to meet this challenge?

III

Gerhard von Rad recognizes that history had already been effectively abandoned by the Priestly school, in their case for law. He writes: "In understanding the law in this way, Israel parted company with history,

[19] II Esdras 6:56.

[20] II Esdras 8:1-2.

[21] The difference is so marked that R. G. Collingwood, taking the Greek style of historiography as the norm, will not concede that the Hebrews wrote any history before the Maccabean period: "These two forms of quasi-history, theocratic history and myth, dominated the whole of the Near East until the rise of Greece." *The Idea of History*, Oxford, 1946, p. 16.

that is, with the history which she had hitherto experienced with Jahweh. She did not part company with her relationship to Jahweh. But once she began to look upon the will of Jahweh in such a timeless and absolute way, the saving history necessarily ceased moving on. This Israel no longer had a history, at least a history with Jahweh. From now on she lived and served her God, in, as it were, an enigmatic 'beyond history.' " [22] This was the response of what might be called normative Judaism to the question "What to do with history?" but it is clearly not so much an answer to the question as an evasion of it. The apocalyptic movement at least did not ignore history, but earnestly tried to come to terms with it. Their response was to revert to mythological ways of thought, but just as, when Israel left myth for history she could not make a clean break with her past, and her history in fact includes much myth and considerable legend, so when the apocalyptists reverted to myth they could not wholly leave behind the habits of thought engendered by almost a millennium of thinking in terms of history. They tended therefore on the one hand to historicize myth and on the other to mythologize history, and in fact very effectively blurred the distinction between the two. But a review of their work in the light of our greatly increased understanding of the role of myth in the ancient Near East (an advantage which has accrued to us almost wholly since Charles's death in 1931) will enable us I believe to see that basically their thought is neither "historiological" nor mythological but a new blend of the two for which the term "eschatological" should be strictly reserved.

At this point we have to attempt to isolate the major characteristics of mythological thought and, following the guidance of Henri and H. A. Frankfort,[23] I suggest that it was characterized by three major elements. First it was aetiological, in that it attempted to make comprehensible the

[22] *O. T. Theology,* New York, 1962, I, 91-92. The notion of *Heilsgeschichte* was not, of course, wholly rejected; it was rather relegated to a sacred, unassailable past. To continue the comment made in n. 5 above, we may observe that the question now raises itself (and on none does it press more hardly than on von Rad himself) : if the idea of *Heilsgeschichte* proved inadequate for the men of the post-exilic period, are we right in making it the all-important, interpretative principle of the whole of the Old Testament? (Cf. the introduction to von Rad's deservedly acclaimed book.) Even more pertinent is the question whether such a "biblical theology" should then be made the basis for a systematic theology in which a "theology of history" is assumed to be intrinsically superior to a "theology of nature."

[23] Cf. H. and H. A. Frankfort, "Myth and Reality" in *The Intellectual Adventure of Man,* ed. Frankfort, Chicago, 1946, pp. 23 f.

human situation. Man had to come to terms with his environment and even more importantly he had to come to terms with the strange contradictions of his own nature.[24] The second characteristic is that the events which myth described are located in a world related to but not identical with this present order. It is as it were a mirror-image world, but like Alice's world *Through the Looking-Glass* it has its own reality, its own flow of events, its own patterns of behavior, which impinge very effectively, at times even determinately, upon this world. The third characteristic is that the world of myth is in another order of time—what Frankfort calls "absolute time." The mythical past never recedes any further into the distance, and the Annus Magnus in its revolution never brings the future Golden Age any nearer.[25]

In turning again to mythological ways of thinking the apocalyptists did not, however, simply put the clock back a whole millennium. The historiological period left its mark, and we find the new style of apocalyptical thinking repeating these three characteristics of mythological thought with subtle but unmistakable differences. Thus the burden of the aetiological task of myth had been transferred by Israel to the broad back of historiography, but with this difference, that the task was no longer to accommodate man to his environment and to himself; this could be taken fairly unreflectively from the earlier period. The contemporary task was to explain what Israel was, and how Israel was to relate herself to her situation and to her God. Similarly, the apocalyptic movement did not go back to the concerns of the Israelite period. The new aetiological task was two-fold. Consequent upon the work of Jeremiah and Ezekiel in particular, and the atomizing effect upon Israel of its *diaspora* experience, the first need was to meet the concern of the individual believer for personal reassurance. As early as the book of Daniel the "wise," that is, the members of the apocalyptic movement, are in fact being thus reassured: "And those among the people who are wise shall make many understand, though they shall fall by sword and flame, by captivity and

[24] While a word based on so philosophical a concept as the Greek *aitia* is perhaps too intellectual a term for the process of mental accommodation we are describing, nevertheless it serves to indicate that the myths of the ancient world enabled man to relate to his own environment and to his own self-awareness. This as we have seen was achieved by the use of the six dominant themes of mythology described above.

[25] It is because the cycle of the Annus Magnus is associated with the "absolute time" of the mirror image world that the ancient Near East could believe in a future Golden Age without achieving teleology or eschatology.

plunder, for some days . . . and some of those who are wise shall fall, to refine and cleanse them, to make them white . . . and many of those who sleep in the dust of the earth shall awake, some to everlasting life, and some to shame and contempt. And those who are wise shall shine like the brightness of the firmament; and those who turn many to righteousness, like the stars for ever and ever." [26] Thus the role played by aetiology in the pre-Israelite mythology is played by soteriology in the post-Israelite mythology.

But not by soteriology alone. As the long centuries of Persian and Greek rule creep past, so the historiological idea that God's nature may be discerned in current events gives rise to the unwelcome thought that the only God an honest mind can discern in these unhappy years is an ineffectual deity, a deity indifferent to the experience of his people.[27] To defend God against such impious thoughts, the apocalyptists drew on the ancient myths to say that this world was governed, or rather misgoverned, by the angels into whose hands God had consigned it for a stated term. The disorders of man's terrestrial experiences are due to the celestial disobedience of the angels. In Ethiopic Enoch God says "Observe and mark everything that the shepherds (i.e. angels) will do to those sheep (i.e. Israel) ; for they will destroy more of them than I have commanded them." [28] Because God can never go back on his word, he cannot intervene to rescue the "wise" and to punish the angels, until the predetermined time has come. This is not a very effective theodicy, but it does fill out the role previously played by aetiology.

Turning to the second of the three features of myth, we are reminded that the most familiar characteristic of apocalyptic is its doctrine of the

[26] Dan. 11:33, 35; 12:2-3. The same concern shows itself in the Ethiopic book of Enoch, in all its major components, and, as we have seen, while the seer of II Esdras accepted the divine justice as impeccable, he was greatly concerned that of all created humankind only a favored few were to be saved. The salvation of the individual looms large in the *Apocalypse of Baruch* and in the *Secrets of Enoch,* while in the great Christian apocalypse, *The Revelation to John,* the concern becomes central: "To him who conquers I will grant to eat of the tree of life. . . . He who conquers shall not be hurt by the second death. . . . He who conquers shall be clad thus in white garments and I will not blot his name out of the book of life." (Rev. 2:7, 11; 3:5. Cf. 20:11-12; 21:7, 27; 22:14.)

[27] Just such charges lie barely concealed beneath the surface of Ps. 44. Similarly the problem of the book of Job is basically the question: "Is God good?" a question which could not have arisen before the disillusionment with the idea of salvation-history. Job, it should be remarked, is both an individual and also the righteous sufferer, Israel.

[28] Eth. Enoch. 89:61.

two ages, the time of this present age and the time of the age to come. This is indeed the mirror-world of myth brought back into Jewish thought, after it had been largely banished for the historiological Israelite period. It is true that during that period there is a lingering tradition from the mythological period, whereby the Hebrew seer could conceive of Yahweh "in heaven," surrounded by his *sôd,* conducting the affairs of heaven and earth, but the characteristic concept of the Israelite period is of Yahweh resident on Zion and conducting the business of his people from his holy hill. He is thought of as active and operative in this world, not as removed and distant in some other, parallel existence. The apocalyptists, however, picked up the older tradition, and for them the realm of God was a transcendent order, perfect, ideal, removed, having its communication with this world only by means of its ambassadors and plenipotentiaries, that is, the angelic interlocutors who play such a large role in all the apocalyptic works.

The third feature which we remarked of myth was that it located the other world in absolute time, while in this world it conceived of time in a cyclic fashion. The Hebrews, on the other hand, in inventing history had at the same time invented teleology; that is, they conceived the historical process as moving to a climax, in time, on earth, called the Day of Yahweh. The apocalyptists took over this teleological or progressive thrust of the historiological period and applied it to the transcendent order of the kingdom of God. Thus, they reversed their previous practice, and instead of mythologizing history, they historicized myth. They took the timeless myth of the other world and, identifying it with the Golden Age of historiological thought, they brought it down on to the stage of human affairs. That is, they conceived of the other, mirror-image world as breaking into this world, at a particular moment in time. In so doing, they created the idea of the Fifth Kingdom, the future Rule of the Saints, the coming kingdom of God.[29]

There was, however, almost as it were inevitably, a corresponding development whereby myth was made part not only of future history but also of past history. As the two worlds were to become one in the future, so it was reasonable to think they might have been originally one, and

[29] The relation of this-worldly teleology to other-wordly absolutism was not, however, easy to achieve, and the device of "the Days of the Messiah," or "the Millennial Reign of Christ," had to be invented before the new eschatology and the old teleology could be rightly accommodated each to the other.

had been divorced only by great wickedness. This moment of divorce was, in the apocalyptic tradition, the flood.[30] Those who lived prior to the flood, then, obviously had greater access to that other world and to its secrets, so that men like Enoch, Lamech, Noah, or even Adam himself, could be expected to have left traditions of arcana behind them for the guidance and information of later generations. This meant that the flood became very definitely an historical event, and as an historical event, the critical event of all this-worldly time. Thus for the apocalyptists, neither the exodus nor the return is the climactic of time; for them it is the flood. As the judgment day, the day of Yahweh, lies in the future, so the judgment day, the day of the flood, lies in the past. In both directions, as it were, past and future, myth is historicized and made part of the chronological process. But the effect of blending the teleological approach to time, and the mythological absolute character of time produces a new concept. It is the idea of that other order of time, often called eternity, as that from which this present order is divorced and to which this present order nevertheless properly belongs, and to which it is one day to be re-related. It is this concept which we rightly call eschatology.

In this process of historicizing myth and mythologizing history, the apocalyptists have thus reached eschatological concepts. At the same time, however, they have effectively robbed mundane history of its significance. For these writers it is the other world which is the real world. It is there that events on earth are initiated and there that their outcome is determined. In the book of Daniel, for example, we hear of the mysterious "prince of the Kingdom of Persia" and of "the prince of Greece" and of "Michael the great prince who has charge of your people." It is these powers who are deciding Israel's fortunes. In Ethiopic Enoch it is the angelic Watchers and "Shepherds" whose activities decide the destinies of earth. Moreover the time schedule is fixed by divine decree and nothing can interfere with its fulfillment. This indeed gives the seers an opportunity to display their knowledge of the foreordained chronology. Thus Daniel produces seventy weeks of years as his schedule of pre-

[30] It was only in later apocalyptic, e.g. II Esdras and Apoc. Bar., that the divorce was attached to the Adam and Eve myth. Cf. N. P. Williams, *The Ideas of the Fall and of Original Sin:* "The Ezra-Apocalypse [II Esdras] which dates from the last quarter of the first century A.D. seems to mark the complete disappearance of the Watcher-story and the triumph of the Adam-narrative as the generally accepted Fall-story" (p. 30; cf. also p. 75 f.).

determined time. The "Dream-Visions" of Enoch have similarly seventy shepherds, and the Apocalypse of Weeks has ten "weeks" into which the history, past and future, of the whole world is schematized. Almost every work has its own variant scheme.[31] The classic comment is that of II Esdras: "For he has weighed the age in the balance, and measured the times by measure, and numbered the times by number; and he will not move or arouse them until that measure is fulfilled." [32] But a world in which what happens on earth is predetermined by a heavenly timetable, and where the outcome of events is not dependent upon the balance and interrelationship of forces and personalities on earth, but rather on the outcome of struggles on another plane of existence, is a world in which mundane history has been deprived of any meaning. Such a world is far removed from the world of Amos, for example, who was confident that in history Yahweh did nothing without informing his prophets; or of Jeremiah, who conceived his role to be that of a prophet to the nations, and by his divinely inspired word to build them up or to tear them down; or again of Deutero-Isaiah, who confidently predicted the rise of Cyrus, because it was Yahweh's purpose through him to release Israel. For the prophets history was the sphere in which Yahweh worked out his purposes, but for the apocalyptists it was a mere succession of events with which God would not, indeed could not, interfere until the ordained moment arrived. History, so far from being the medium in which religious ideas could be expressed, had become literally a marking time until the *eschaton* should come.[33] The apocalyptists in this way released men from the overburdening task of trying to find any meaning or significance in the succession of mundane events. For them only the final event is significant.

IV

There are four comments to be made. First, while mundane history has become insignificant in the eyes of the apocalyptists, time has not.

[31] D. S. Russell (see n. 3 above) gives many instances of these schemes, pp. 224 f.
[32] II Esdras 4:36-37.
[33] Cf. J. A. T. Robinson's comment: "It is a transition from an understanding of time as *kairos* to an understanding of it as *chronos* that perhaps more than anything else distinguishes the prophetic from the apocalyptic outlook." *In the End God,* London, 1950, p. 47. Given the general validity of the distinction between *kairos* and *chronos* (despite James Barr, *The Biblical Words for Time,* London, 1962) the comment is perceptive.

All man's existence is proceeding according to a predetermined plan. Mundane events are thus, paradoxically, both determined and insignificant. But human existence is not insignificant. It is full of hope. He that endures to the end shall be saved! The time of the kingdom is at hand! When Daniel calculated that from the setting up of the "abomination of desolation" to the end was a mere period of three and a half years, he was speaking for all his fellow apocalyptists. For all of them, the time of the end is very soon, it is *now*. It is only those who do not share in the positive convictions of the apocalyptists that time is predetermined and that the end is now, who find their outlook negative.

Secondly, it is their attitude to history which explains the notorious historical inaccuracies of the apocalyptic writers. Actually, they are more notorious than numerous. Nevertheless they are significant. History has in fact become so unimportant that the apocalyptists do not hesitate to make it fit into their numerical and other schemes, even at the cost of somewhat rearranging the past. Thus in Daniel, Belshazzar the Chaldean becomes the son of Nebuchadrezzar, and Darius the Mede and his Empire interpose between the Babylonian and the Persian kingdoms in a most unhistorical manner.

Thirdly, just as in the myths gods and goddesses blend and merge, borrowing each other's traits and exchanging personalities, so too in the Enoch literature the central figure is more than a little confused with Lamech and with Noah in the earlier strata, and in the Similitudes he is enigmatically identified with the Son of Man himself. In the hands of the apocalyptists, history itself takes on an unhistorical character.[34]

The fourth observation is that the reason for the apocalyptists acquiring such a high but undeserved reputation as historians and philosophers of history was their frequent use of historical surveys and retrospects. Their purpose, however, was to gain credence for their prognostications of the future by putting them into the mouth of some long dead seer, whose "prophecies" were thus seen to have been proved so far amazingly correct,

[34] D. S. Russell (see n. 3 above) comments that two incidents having similar "psychological" content or two persons partaking of a similar "psychological" character were readily given a "psychological identity" or "contemporaneity" and so the givenness of history is overruled (p. 211). He also argues that history remains meaningful for the apocalyptists because they allowed for the exercise of free will by individuals. Cf. pp. 230 f. But so long as the major movements of mundane time are predetermined, individual free will cannot restore significance to world history.

and therefore might confidently be trusted with regard to what was yet to come. The really important point is that whether the history of the four empires is being sketched in Dan. 2 or 7, or the wearisome marching to and fro of the kings of the north and of the kings of the south is being mapped in ch. 11, the *eschaton* interrupts the history; it is not something which the history prepares for, or in any way causes to occur. Similarly, in II Esdras, after much confused coverage of many events, the eagle finally achieves unitary rule of the earth; then the lion of the Most High announces its doom, not because of this achievement, but because "the Most High has looked upon his times and behold they are ended and his ages are completed."[35] Thus apocalyptic, while using history surveys freely, nevertheless did not, indeed could not, take mundane history seriously.

We may conclude then, that, so far from being the first philosophers of history, the apocalyptists are in fact a school of biblical writers who recognized that the burden which Hebrew religion had laid upon history was greater than it could bear. They therefore returned from history to myth, myth in a new amalgam with history, which we have learned to call eschatology. In so doing, however, they abandoned the teleological view of history and with it the attempt to justify in mundane events the ways of God to man.

It is worthy of remark that none of the NT writers resumed the task. St. Augustine indeed sought to undertake it in the fifth century A.D. with his *Civitas Dei,* and since his day theologians have struggled to preserve for the Christian account of mundane history that element of purposiveness of which a thoroughgoing apocalyptic would deprive it.[36]

[35] II Esdras 11:44.

[36] Not, however, all Christian theologians. Karl Löwith, for example, appears to embrace a negative view of history with considerable enthusiasm. His summary of the matter runs: "Historical processes as such do not bear the least evidence of a comprehensive and ultimate meaning. History as such has no outcome. There never has been and never will be an immanent solution of the problem of history, for man's historical experience is one of steady failure. Christianity, too, as a historical *world* religion, is a complete failure. The world is still as it was in the time of Alaric; only our means of oppression and destruction (as well as of reconstruction) are considerably improved and are adorned with hypocrisy." (*Meaning in History,* Chicago, 1949, p. 191). But can we be content with such a heartless view of human endeavor? Does it not, to adapt the memorable phrase of Dionysius of Alexandria, "slander our most merciful God as merciless"? As the Israelites abandoned myth, and the apocalyptists abandoned history, in order to embrace new concepts, may not we, too, be called, not

The difficulties they have encountered, and the modesty of their success, lead us to recognize that the apocalyptists were not imagining or creating difficulties. Rather they were men who found the thought-forms of their religious tradition inadequate for the age in which they lived, and while in looking for a new medium of expression they may not have found a full answer, they at least arrived at a sufficient one, whereby faith could still be cogently affirmed. It may be that a sense of fellow feeling will lead us to be not unappreciative both of their sincerity and of their achievement.

---

only to establish how our fathers thought, but also how, in a new age, we ourselves should think? A more perceptive approach is that of R. L. Shinn (*Christianity and the Meaning of History,* New York, 1953). He finds the Christian view of history to be compounded of the ideas of the church, purposiveness and eschatology. This may still leave many questions to be answered, but it has the virtue of recognizing that no view of history which does not give a man a reason for entering into it can ever be satisfactory.

4

JAMES M.
ROBINSON

Kerygma and History in the New Testament

I

I have been invited to address you on the topic: Kergyma and History in the New Testament. Our first task is to seek in the language of this topic the subject matter intended. Hence I begin by dismantling the topic to lay bare its subject matter, and from this analysis to derive the structures of the subject matter in terms of which the more detailed investigation will be ordered.

This preliminary analysis is intended as an exemplification of the *Grundlagenkrise,* the crisis with regard to our basic categories, in which biblical scholarship finds itself today. The general categories with which we of necessity have been operating, such as normative Judaism, Hellenistic Judaism, apocalyptic, gnostic, cultic, existential, history, kerygma—such categories *are* the capsules in which the heritage of scholarly achievement is transmitted from generation to generation. But they are also the blinds that cut out fresh light and help perpetuate the preconceptions and limitations of the past. The synthetic achievements of the past *do* provide the working hypotheses out of which our research grows. Yet the advancement of research calls for a critical analysis of inherited categories, their dismantling and reassembling in new synthetic efforts that grow out of the present grasp of the subject matter.

What is behind the title's pairing of the two terms "kerygma" and "history"? In the literature in the field there is one important issue often designated with a phrase juxtaposing just these terms. In 1960 a 710-page collection of essays debating the new quest of the historical Jesus appeared in German under the title *The Historical Jesus and the Keryg-*

matic Christ,[1] and in 1964 an English collection of essays on the same topic has appeared with the same title.[2] Indeed a standard international bibliographical tool in the NT field introduced for the years 1961-62 and 1962-63 [3] a new subdivision with much the same title. Rudolf Bultmann's Heidelberg address criticizing the new quest was entitled in a somewhat similar way *The Relation of the Primitive Christian Message about Christ to the Historical Jesus,*[4] and Gerhard Ebeling answered Bultmann's criticism with an extended essay entitled "Kerygma and Historical Jesus." [5]

If the phrase "kergyma and history" thus has its primary focus for NT scholarship in "Christ Jesus," then it is apparent that the innocent-sounding connective "and" is a euphemism, covering a problem, to put it mildly. For "Christ Jesus" was a primitive Christian confession not only implying the copula "is," "Jesus is Christ," but also calling forth the variant: "Jesus be damned" (I Cor. 12:3). And one may in our century note that the positive correlation currently being sought between kerygma and historical Jesus has in its background other alternatives expressing themselves in more tense connectives. The emphasis between the two World Wars can be summarized in such formulae as: *"Not* the historical Jesus *but* the Easter kergyma is the foundation of Christianity." "The Gospels are kerygma, *not* history." Such antithetic formulations stand polemically over against alternatives at the turn of the century, where the signals were reversed and the terminology somewhat different, though

[1] *Der historische Jesus und der kerygmatische Christus: Beiträge zum Christusverständis in Forschung und Verkündigung,* ed. Helmut Ristow and Karl Matthiae (Berlin: Evangelische Verlagsanstalt, 1960).

[2] *The Historical Jesus and the Kerygmatic Christ: Essays on the New Quest of the Historical Jesus,* tr. and ed. Carl E. Braaten and Roy A. Harrisville (Nashville: Abingdon Press, 1964).

[3] *Internationale Zeitschriftenschau für Bibelwissenschaft und Grenzgebiete,* VIII (1961-62), 14 f.: "Kerygma und historischer Jesus"; IX (1962-63), 18-22: "Historischer Jesus und kerygmatischer Christus."

[4] "Das Verhältnis der urchristlichen Christusbotschaft zum historischen Jesus," *Sitzungsberichte der Heidelberger Akademie der Wissenschaften, Philos.-hist. Klasse, Jg.* 1960, 3 *Abh.* (Heidelberg: Carl Winter Universitätsverlag, 1960).

[5] *Theologie und Verkündigung* (*Tübingen:* J. C. B. Mohr [Paul Siebeck]; *Hermeneutische Untersuchungen zur Theologie,* I, 1962), Part III: "Kergyma und historischer Jesus," 19-82. The title of the German translation of *A New Quest of the Historical Jesus* in 1960 was also *Kerygma und historischer Jesus* (Zürich: Zwingli-Verlag). This is a reversion to the original title of the address at the Congress on "The Four Gospels in 1957" at Christ Church, Oxford, August, 1957: "The Kerygma and the Quest of the Historical Jesus."

the same issue was involved: "Jesus preached the kingdom *but* Paul preached Christ." "*Either* Jesus *or* Paul." "*Back* (from Paul) *to* Jesus." Put in more recent terms, it is the issue of how and with what degree of legitimacy the proclaimer became the proclaimed.

It is then the topic that half a century ago was referred to as "faith and history" which is now designated "kerygma and history." If there are reasons why the seemingly more subjective term "faith" was replaced by "kerygma," a synonym for the "word of God," there may also be reasons why the terminology current today may itself be less than final.

1 Both "kerygma" and "history" are first of all quite ambiguous terms. "Kerygma" refers both to the content of preaching, in which sense Dodd primarily used it, and to the act of proclamation, in which sense Bultmann primarily used it. In the one sense the resurrection of Jesus is in the kerygma and hence a necessary Christian belief; in the other sense Jesus rose into the kerygma, lives as what happens in preaching. "History" is equally ambivalent. It means both *Historie* and *Geschichte,* loan words that can hardly be translated "history" and "story," since the latter term is too weak. (The adjectival forms historical and historic may come nearer to some of the distinctions intended by the German terminology.) Even the simple English term "history" has the complexity of referring both to research and to the subject matter of research. Since each of the members in the correlation "history and kerygma" has at least two clearly distinct *foci* of meaning, the seemingly simple correlation comes to involve at least four distinct correlations, plus various combinations of these four, and any of these alternatives can be implied by the supposedly simple phrase.

In the second place, the terms kerygma and history do not actually fit 2 the intended distinction of Jesus from the Easter faith. For the term kerygma emerges only at two points in the primitive Christian literature, in I Cor. 1:21; 2:4 to designate Paul's word of the cross and in Q (Luke 11:32; Matt. 12:41) to designate Jonah's preaching to the Ninevites and hence by implication *Jesus'* message. Furthermore, Jesus and the Easter faith certainly cannot be distinguished in terms of one being historical, the result of reconstruction on the part of the critical historian, and the other not. For anything we know about the primitive Christian kerygma is known by means of historical reconstruction, be it by disengaging kerygmatic hymns and confessions imbedded in the NT literature, be it by analyzing the explication of the kerygma by a given NT writer, or be it by tracing the progressive kerygmatizing of Jesus in the Gospels by means of form criticism and *Redaktionsgeschichte.* Thus both Jesus' message and the apostolic preaching were called kerygma, and both are known to scholarship only in terms of historical research, as the historical Jesus and as the historical reconstruction of the primitive church's kerygma. The current modern categories have foisted upon us a distinction which is neither in the language of the sources nor in our relation to the sources.

Our inherited categories, ambiguous at best, thus maintain a distinction which on critical reflection turns out not to exist. This is what is meant by saying we are in a *Grundlagenkrise,* a crisis consisting in the recognition that our categories are less our heritage than our fate. "Fate" means literally "what is spoken"—not what we speak but what is spoken upon us so as to predetermine our future by blocking our free access to the reality with which we have to do. An unreal distinction has been built into our language—in this case the categories kerygma and history —which consequently still speaks out of them but which on reflection we can no longer affirm to be real. Precisely because of our unawareness of this structuring of the problem it has not been subject to our critical control but has rather been a power over us, a word spoken upon us through our language that all the more predetermines the lines upon which our research will run and hence controls our results. Thus our categories have indeed become our fate.

In view of this subliminal role inherited categories usually play in our research, it is significant to note in the assigned title what seems to be a not insignificant, indeed perhaps an intended modification. For rather than it being the phrase "historical Jesus" that is correlated with the term "kerygma," it is merely the word "history," as if the problem usually focused in terms of Jesus were symptomatic of a broader problem. Furthermore the title goes on to specify: in the NT. To be sure this could be taken to refer us simply to the historical Jesus and the primitive Easter kerygma, in that both of these, though antedating the NT by a generation or more, are to be reconstructed from NT material and hence are an important aspect of NT scholarship. Yet the title seems to be calling for a confrontation with the problem in the NT texts themselves, and I propose to take seriously this hint heard in the title. This does not mean to turn one's back on the debate going on about the kerygma and the historical Jesus within contemporary theology. Indeed one reason that debate is becoming repetitious may be that it is spinning without getting geared in adequately with reality. Hence an analysis of what "kerygma" and "historical Jesus" actually were and how they were actually related to each other in a segment of past history could serve to implement a restructuring of categories in terms of which the contemporary debate could profitably be refocused, if it be that the contemporary debate is simply the current stage of the movement to be analyzed here in terms of early Christianity.

There seems to be no problem in regarding "kerygma" as a term applicable to what we find in the NT, for kerygmatic theology has taught us that the NT itself is to be understood as an explication of the kerygma. But what then is the history with which this NT explication of the kerygma has to do? Not simply the historical Jesus! For the historical Jesus had been undergoing kerygmatization for a generation before the NT writings began. Wrede was mistaken when he derived the messianic secret in Mark from an effort to reconcile a kerygma proclaiming Jesus as Messiah with the historical fact that Jesus was not messianic. The history with which the NT kerygma had directly to do was not the historical Jesus but rather the "history of the transmission of the traditions"[6] about Jesus. And our access to that history is via the method itself called *Traditionsgeschichte,* the tracing of the traditions with their changing use, shape, and meaning. In such an investigation it becomes clear that a lot more was happening to the traditions about Jesus than simply a straight-line development such as the term "kerygmatizing" might seem to suggest. This is not only because other influences than the kerygma were at work upon the tradition. It is also because the kerygma pointed the tradition in various directions. That is to say, the kerygma itself was subject to a plurality of understandings.

This variation of the kerygma itself was due to the fact that the kerygma had still another relation to history than its relation to the history of the transmission of traditions about Jesus. For the kerygma was related to the series of historical situations in which it was proclaimed and heard.

[6] It takes this whole phrase to produce a hermeneutically responsible translation of *Traditionsgeschichte*. Cf. the discussion of this point in the introductory essay to *Theology as History* (*New Frontiers in Theology* 3; New York: Harper and Row, 1966).

The very language in which the kerygma happened was historically determined—and not simply because the kerygma was talking about historical events. It was talking about them in historically conditioned categories, just as such terms as preexistence, incarnation, resurrection, exaltation, ascension do not simply refer to historical occurrence, but are also themselves historically conditioned language. Rather than the saving event simply being described as it happened, to some extent it happened as it was described. For whatever happened happened among people living within languages. Man's being is not logically prior to his language, but is constituted in terms of his linguistic world. Hence whatever happened, to whatever extent it was an event in the lives of man, happened as a linguistic event. The event itself included a process of understanding in terms of given categories. To this extent the saving event cannot be shelled out as a brute fact behind the language witnessing to it.

Yet language is not simply verbalizing. It conveys a point that can be heard by careful listening. And then that point can be scored in another language, and indeed must be scored in a different language if it is to be scored in a different historical situation where the original language is hardly intelligible or has begun to shift its meaning. Even though the kerygma takes place in *different* language in *different* situations for the sake of scoring the *equivalent* point, still such hermeneutical translation will to some extent involve alteration of meaning. This is not simply because the equivalent point scored in different situations cannot be identically the same point, in that the live options in the new situation were not the options in the prior situation. It is also because here is the constant possibility of mistranslation. Nor can this danger be eliminated by simply not translating. In a new situation the old language itself means something different.

Thus the rapid changes in the kerygma's historical setting—from Palestine to the Diaspora, from Jew to Gentile, from the context of imminent expectation to that of the delay of the parousia, from an apocalyptic to a gnostic environment, from the social and political role of a Jewish sect to that of a world religion—all these contextual alterations necessitated a rapid series of translations of the kerygma. And thus we are confronted with a second relation to history that inheres in the kerygma as kerygma. For the kerygma not only by its very nature kerygmatized Jesus; it also by definition kerygmatized the situation in which it spoke by pronouncing upon it the Lordship of Christ. Proclaiming Jesus as Lord meant laying his claim on the concrete situation; the proclamation in word and deed was itself the carrying out of the saving event, the event's own future. Thus the saving event goes on as a language event that names God in our world, identifies him in performatory language in which reality is cast in the mode of creation. This on-going linguistic transaction in which the kerygmatic point is successively scored in ever-changing historical contexts is thus a central dimension in which kerygma and history are related in the NT.

We have analyzed the topic "Kerygma and History in the New Testament" into the translation of the point of the "kerygma" so that it strikes home in each new situation and into the "history" of the transmission of traditions. Thus we have carried through a transmutation of Bultmann's kerygmatic categories with which we began into the categories of hermeneutic and *Traditionsgeschichte,* categories being used for alternate structurings in the new theologies of Ebeling and Pannenberg, or, nearer home, in theology directed to the secular meaning of the gospel for a culture in which the consciousness of God is dead, and in process theology. Hence I would suggest that the restructuring of basic categories, set out here in a preliminary way, could point the way to a real relevance of biblical research for contemporary theology. Such a relevance was real in the early years of our Society when the spread of critical historical method played a major role in liberalism's dismantling of the dogmatic systems, and it has been real in German biblical scholarship in more recent times in the orientations provided for example by Bultmann and von Rad. But such a real relevance has been lacking to large measure in American biblical research of late, and I am convinced this is in considerable measure the cause for the apparent lack of vigor with which creative NT research has been carried on in America since the retirement of Goodspeed and Cadbury. A crisis in the basic categories of a discipline is a crisis at its very foundations. Such a crisis can unleash creative powers and introduce an epoch of vigorous research, if it leads to new structures more commensurate with the subject matter and with the categories in which our age understands reality to be actually ordered. It is my hope that the analysis of the categories of kerygmatic theology into those of hermeneutic and *Traditionsgeschichte* may serve such a purpose.

The following exegetical analyses are hardly more than a pair of rough sketches, two trial runs into an uncharted future. They are intended to investigate in turn "kerygma" and "historical Jesus" in the NT in terms of the reformulation of those categories along the lines of hermeneutic and *Traditionsgeschichte* as we have proposed.

The investigation of the "kerygma" in Part II will be primarily in terms of hermeneutical translation in varying situations, although one may sense that this is simply a focus in terms of hermeneutic for what is also a history of the transmission of traditions. For not only was there such a thing as the transmission of the Easter kerygma as a tradition, but also the history of the transmission of traditions about Jesus was to a large extent the history of a kerygmatizing process, so that varying understandings of the kerygma variously affected traditions about Jesus. Our sample will be largely confined to the interpretation of the resurrection in the kerygma, with incidental observation of its bearing upon the transmission of sayings of Jesus.

The investigation of the "historical Jesus" in part III will be primarily in terms of the history of the transmission of traditions about Jesus, although one may sense that this is simply a focus in terms of *Traditionsgeschichte* for what is also a process of hermeneutical translation. For not only were stories about Jesus themselves kerygmatic in intention, but also the Easter kerygma was correlative to an understanding of the traditions about Jesus, so that varying understandings of these traditions variously affected the interpretation of the kerygma of Jesus' death and resurrection. Our sample will be largely confined to the history of the transmission of the miracle stories, with incidental observation of their bearing upon the understanding of the Easter kerygma.

II

First, the kerygma. What more obvious place to begin than I Cor. 15: 3-5? Paul says it is the gospel, the word he preached to them. Furthermore the succinct and strictly parallelized affirmations about Jesus' death and resurrection betray the hand of careful codification, so that the passage stands out as an ancient crystal imbedded in a later composition. And Paul not only puts the formula in quotation marks (better known as *hóti recitativum*), but even introduces it with the concession that it is something for which he is dependent on the tradition. For our purposes it is important also to note that it is introduced as what the Corinthians had received from Paul, and hence as common ground between Paul and the Corinthian clique he is combatting, or at least a common point of departure. For Paul's Corinthian opponents seem to have taken Paul's kerygma and promptly departed from Paul's understanding of it.

The opponents' misunderstanding of the Pauline kerygma could derive from the very baptismal instruction Paul gave, if we may judge by such a Pauline *locus classicus* on baptism as Rom. 6, where baptism is described kerygmatically as dying and rising with Christ. Or is it? We have usually assumed so, namely that in baptism our experiencing of Jesus' resurrection is quite parallel to our experiencing of his death, just as in I Cor. 15:3-5 Jesus' death and resurrection are themselves so rigorously paralleled. But when one looks more carefully one notes that although Paul speaks in the perfect of our having experienced baptismally Jesus' death, he speaks in the future of our *going to* experience his resurrection, vss. 5 and 8, with eternal life the *goal,* vs. 22. Indeed, according to vs. 12 we are still in *mortal* bodies, so that we have hardly completed our dying and entered already into resurrection, unless it be that the body is just a mortal coil that does not participate in the resurrection but is simply to be shuffled off. Thus Paul can speak in the indicative of our having died with Christ as a basis for the imperative to put to death sin in our lives, but he does not speak in the indicative of our having risen with Christ as a basis for the imperative to walk in newness of life.

This omission has been largely overlooked or regarded as purely accidental until Ernst Käsemann drew our attention to it recently to exemplify what he calls the "eschatological reservation" in Pauline theology, the theologically relevant role that futuristic eschatology plays for Paul. The following instance may serve to illustrate the modern oversight, which may be somewhat analogous to that in Corinth. Along with missing the eschatological reservation in Rom. 6 that Käsemann was subsequently to emphasize, Erich Dinkler, in an article of 1952,[7] summarized the Pauline position on eschatology as follows:

Hence one may say that for Paul mythological eschatology is not the basis but [only] a form of expression for the eschatological consciousness of existence, not a

[7] "Zum Problem der Ethik bei Paulus; Rechtsnahme und Rechtsverzicht bei Paulus (1. Kor. 6, 1-11)," *ZTK,* XLIX (1952), 167-200. Quotation is from pp. 187 f.

[constitutive] motif but [only] a [non-essential] inference. But this means simply that it is an existentialist eschatology that is expressing itself in the cosmological eschatology and that the real intention of Paul is preserved when we interpret as follows: The eschatological promise pointing into the future has already [!] created the eschatological existence of the Christian here and now. With regard to the world the Christian already [!] *has eleutheria* (Gal. 5:13; I Cor. 10:29; II Cor. 3:17), among the *adikoi* the Christian is already [!] *kainē ktisis* (II Cor. 5:17).

Thus we have an illustration of the way one can begin with Paul's kerygmatic interpretation of baptism, overlook the eschatological reservation, and end up with a triumphant emphasis upon salvation as already achieved. The eschatological reservation hardly survives even in demythologized form, since the "already" is about as undialectical as we conjecture it to have been in Corinth. If it can happen today on the part of an outstanding Pauline interpreter, it could probably happen then, and indeed II Tim. 2:18 indicates that a generation or so after Paul's time it did happen: Hymenaeus and Philetus "have gone astray with regard to the truth, by affirming: The resurrection has taken place already [!], and they are upsetting the faith of some." To this the Deutero-Paulinist counters with the "safe formula": "If we have died with him, we shall [!] also live with him; if we endure, we shall [!] also reign with him" (II Tim. 2:11-12, RSV).

Recent scholarship has made it clear that the fanatical form of belief in the resurrection combatted in the Pastorals was already rampant in Corinth in Paul's own time. The form of expression used in the names of the factions in Corinth, to "belong to" someone (I Cor. 1:12), was the form of expression normally used to designate people as Christians when they were baptized (cf. Gal. 3:27-9). And Paul's way of disassociating himself from the Pauline party is to play down his role as a baptizer in order to show that it was not he who had done the saving act for the Corinthians (I Cor. 1:13-17), that is to say he disassociates himself from the role of mystagogue or mediator of salvation. All this would suggest the Corinthians saw in baptism not simply their union with Christ, whose resurrection was the breaking of the grip of evil over all men so that *his* resurrection is the indicative on the basis of which the Christian imperative is built, but also as the final consummation itself, so that their own dying had been gotten over quickly and they were now already [!] in the rest of the blessed.

This can be inferred also from Paul's corrective in I Cor. 15:23, which is in substance saying: Hold on! Not so fast! "Each in his own order: Christ the first-fruits, then those who belong to [!] Christ at his parousia [and only then!]." [8] Death is the last enemy to be destroyed (15:26). Hence when Paul criticizes "some of you" for asserting that "there is no resurrection of the dead" (I Cor. 15:12), one now[9] assumes he is alluding to a position that is not to be taken as the enlightened rationalism of the Greek philosophic mind but rather as the turgid fanaticism of those who have already risen and are living it up in glory. For although the word "already" is lacking in 15:12, it is present with all its heretical overtones in Paul's description of his opponents in I Cor. 4:8: "Already you have feasted to the full; already you have reached wealth; without us you have taken over the reign."

It would seem to be this heretical interpretation of the kerygma in terms of an already consummated eschaton for the initiated that is behind the various Corinthian excesses to which Paul addresses himself in I Corinthians. They are literally above concern with such mundane matters as what their bodies do or how their secular affairs are carried on or whether at the holy sacrament everybody gets a square meal; they are in mystic sweet communion with realms above, and indeed speak with the voice of angels, as 13:1 seems to interpret speaking in tongues. They "know all mysteries and all knowledge" (13:2), so that at the *gnosis* level Paul also has to emphasize the eschatological reservation: *"Now* we know [only] in part; *then* [and only then] will we have the full knowledge on a level with heavenly knowledge" (13:12). The opponents' attitude toward their weaker brothers in the matter of meat offered to idols expressed in their doctrinaire, unsympathetic slogan "We all have knowledge," is met with the Pauline rejoinder: *"Gnosis* puffs up; love builds up" (I Cor. 8:1). And yet these hard-hearted proto-gnostic fanatics be-

[8] For this interpretation of the verse cf. Werner Georg Kümmel in the *Anhang* to Lietzmann's commentary (*HNT,* 9; Tübingen: J. C. B. Mohr [Paul Siebeck], 4th. ed., 1949), pp. 192 f. Cf. the debate about this passage as an interpretation I Cor. 15:3-5 in the Bultmann school: Hans Conzelmann, "Zur Analyse der Bekenntnisformel 1. Kor. 15, 3-5," *EvTh,* XXV (1965), 1-11, and Ernst Käsemann, "Konsequente Traditionsgeschichte?" *ZTK,* LXII (1965).

[9] Since Julius Schniewind's essay "Die Leugner der Auferstetung in Korinth," *Nachgelassene Reden und Aufsätze* (Berlin: Alfred Töpelmann, 1952), pp. 110-39.

lieved the primitive Christian kerygma Paul had proclaimed in Corinth. Their heresy must hence be acknowledged to be an interpretation of the kerygma.

One can to some extent trace the missing links in such a development, missing because writings from the opposing side have not survived, by noting how such views gradually worked their way into that part of the Pauline school that gained admission into the canon. Already the interpretation of baptism in Col. 2:12-13 has brought the believer's rising into line with his dying by omitting the eschatological reservation: ". . . having been buried with him in baptism, in which you were also raised with [him] through faith in the working of God who raised him from the dead. . . . He made you alive with him." That this is a growing edge in the Pauline school is indicated by Eph. 2:5-6, where even our enthronement in heaven is already accomplished: "He made us alive with Christ—by grace you have been saved—and he raised us with [him] and seated us with [him] in the heavenly places in Christ Jesus." In view of this growing edge of Pauline interpretation in the Deutero-Pauline period it is not too surprising when the same Paul who had opposed baptismal resurrection in Corinth came to be claimed by precisely those gnostic movements that held to this heresy, such as the Valentinians; indeed Paul was hailed by them as "apostle of resurrection." [10] Nag Hammadi has filled in one missing link, by turning up a gnostic document that affirms explicitly, "Already you have the resurrection," [11] and quotes Paul for precisely the Deutero-Pauline development moving toward that heresy: "But then the apostle said: We suffered with him and we arose with him and we went to heaven with him" (45, 24-28). Thus we have at the opening of the second century a clean split in the understanding of Paul: Gnostics appeal to him for support of baptismal resurrection, while the Pastorals reject that view as heresy (II Tim. 2:18), though indeed expressing a not dissimilar understanding of baptism in the language of regeneration (Tit. 3:5), a safer formulation in that it does not seem to jeopardize the future resurrection.

Bishop Polycarp of Smyrna attacks the same heresy of baptismal resur-

[10] Tertullian, *De praescriptione haereticorum* 33, 7; *Excerpta ex Theodoto* 23, 2. Both are cited by the editors of *De resurrectione* (cf. next note), pp. xi and 27.

[11] *De resurrectione* (*Epistula ad Rheginum*) from the Jung Codex, ed M. Malinine, H.-Ch. Puech, G. Quispel, and W. Till, 1963, 49, 15 f.

rection at the opening of the second century, and here we catch sight of another ingredient in the heresy that has not been mentioned thus far. Polycarp 7:1 asserts: "Whoever distorts the sayings of the Lord (τὰ λόγια τοῦ κυρίου) to his own lusts and says there is neither resurrection nor judgment, he is the first-born of Satan." The Pastorals, so kin in various ways to Polycarp, and in II Tim. 2:18 our basic source for the heresy of baptismal resurrection, seem also to combat this second ingredient in the heresy. I Tim. 6:3 condemns someone who "teaches heterodoxly and does not agree with the sound words of our Lord Jesus Christ (ὑγιαίνουντες λόγοι οἱ τοῦ κυρίου ἡμῶν Ἰησοῦ Χριστοῦ)." [12] And indeed it would not be too surprising for gnostics considering themselves already resurrected to claim a higher grasp of the hidden meaning of the Lord's sayings than the common Christian understanding, a viewpoint rather like the gnostic claim to be in possession of sayings of the resurrected Lord that are of higher authority than the sayings of the earthly Jesus claimed by orthodoxy. Thus the debate about the meaning of the resurrection in the kerygma within the lives of the believers may have run parallel to a debate in the history of the transmission of the traditions about Jesus, specifically with regard to the sayings of Jesus.

Such a view would seem to be confirmed when one examines sayings of the Lord in a gnosticizing environment. Although the Gospel of Thomas does not refer to the resurrection as such, it certainly has the gnostic concept of having attained the goal of the higher life, and it associates with this achievement a higher understanding of the sayings of Jesus.[13] Saying 51 states: "His disciples said to him: On what day will rest for the dead occur, and on what day does the new world come? He said to them: That [rest] for which you are waiting has come, but you do not recognize it." Here the reader is clearly urged to discover the eschaton to be already actualized, and the very first saying of the Gospel of Thomas relates this discovery to the gnostic interpretation of Jesus' sayings: "He who finds the explanation of these words will not taste

[12] Dibelius-Conzelmann, *HNT*, 3rd ed., 1955, pp. 21 f. and 64, take the phrase to refer to the church's message as is the case with ὑγιαίνουσα διδασκάλια I Tim. 1:10; II Tim. 4:3; Tit. 1:9; 2:1, and ὑγιαίνουντες λόγοι II Tim. 1:13; cf. also Tit. 1:13; 2:2, 8. But then one would have to do with a tautology in I Tim. 6:3.

[13] Cf. Philipp Vielhauer, "ANAPAUSIS; Zum gnostischen Hintergrund des Thomasevangeliums," *Apophoreta* (Haenchen-*Festschrift, Beiheft* 30 to *ZNW*, 1964), pp. 281-99.

death." The Gospel of Philip is quite explicit in advocating baptismal resurrection: "Those who claim: One first dies and [then] rises, is in error. If one does not first receive the resurrection while one is still alive one will receive nothing at death" (121:1-5).

The Gospel of John also suggests that after Jesus' earthly life there will be a higher understanding of his sayings through the Spirit. And it is precisely this one of the four canonical Gospels that speaks of resurrection in this life: "Truly, truly, I say to you, the hour is coming, and now is, when the dead will hear the voice of the Son of God, and those who hear will live," 5:25 RSV. To this verse Ernst Haenchen says, "From the viewpoint of the earthly Jesus the hour is still to come, for the Spirit has not yet been poured out. But from the viewpoint of the church this hour is now." [14] Hence one higher understanding following Jesus' exaltation would seem to be the understanding that one is already resurrected. "Whoever lives and believes in me shall never die," 11:26, RSV. To be sure it may not be without significance that John seems to avoid the category of baptismal resurrection, as if it were suspect, and introduces a different category, baptismal regeneration: "Unless a person is born anew from above, he cannot see the kingdom of God," 3:3 (cf. 3:5). But the protection of 5:25 from a suspicion of heresy by the emphasis on futuristic eschatology in 5:28-29 may be the work of an ecclesiastical redactor, as Bultmann suspects. To be sure John stands in some tension to his proto-gnostic environment, and yet, even if in a broken way, he provides information about that environment. For John tends to confirm the picture derived from gnostic sources to the effect that the advocates of baptismal resurrection were engaged in the deeper or higher interpretation of sayings of the Lord.

It has become apparent that the gnosticizing interpretation of the primitive Christian kerygma of the resurrection came to be involved in a gnosticizing interpretation of the sayings of the Lord, and hence that the debate about the translation of the kerygma involved also a debate in the history of the transmission of these traditions about Jesus. Now if this heretical interpretation of the kerygma was already the subject of debate in I Corinthians, one may well wonder whether at this early a time the corresponding debate about sayings of the Lord was not also going on. I do not think such a thing can be conclusively proven, but

[14] "'Der Vater, der mich gesandt hat,'" *NTS*, IX (1962-63), 214.

there are a few factors that point in that direction. Rather than pursue them here, it may be sufficient merely to note the possibility, and to suggest that it would not be as surprising as we had assumed should it prove to be the case. For I Corinthians stands in contrast to the general Pauline pattern of making practically no use of sayings of the Lord. Of the four instances in which Paul explicitly cites sayings of the Lord, three occur in I Corinthians: on divorce, 7:10-11; on paying the preacher, 9:14; and the institution of the Lord's Supper, 11:23-5. Now it is significant that apart from the last instance derived from the eucharistic liturgy, Paul does not actually quote the saying in question, but only makes its point in his own language. For example, compare Q (Matt. 10: 10; Luke 10: 7): "For the worker is worthy of his food (or: pay)," with Paul: "Thus the Lord gave orders for those who proclaim the gospel to live from the gospel." On divorce Paul even uses a different term for divorce from Mark and Q. It is equally difficult to find in the only other citation, I Thess. 4:15-16, any specific terms shared with the synoptic gospels.

If simply scoring the point of a saying was Paul's way of using it, it would be difficult in cases where a quotation formula is lacking to say whether Paul intends to allude to a saying of the Lord or not. Such an allusion may be intended in 13:2, the reference to faith that removes mountains, for which there are parallels in Q and Mark.[15] In that case Paul's allusion to the saying would be remarkable, in that the word of the Lord is not used as final authority settling the issue. Rather Paul criticizes it, or, more exactly, he criticizes the use made of it, much as in the case of speaking in tongues, where Paul recognizes a factor as a divine gift and still criticizes its misuse. I Cor. 13:2 would then tend to suggest the Corinthians were misusing sayings of the Lord.

An area in the debate between Paul and his Corinthian opponents in which sayings of the Lord may have played a role is that of the wisdom of which the Corinthians are so proud. The so-called Johannine pericope of Q (Matt. 11:25; Luke 10:21), in spite of its roots in Wisdom Literature,

[15] Matt. 17:20; Luke 17:6; Mark 11:22-23; Matt. 21:21. Cf. Bultmann, *RGG*, 2nd ed., IV (1930), 1028: "It is also possible that in Paul's parenesis sayings of the Lord are echoed, e.g. Rom. 12:4; 13:9-10; 16:19; I Cor. 13:2. But it is precisely such parenesis as originates for Jesus and for Paul alike from Jewish tradition or Jewish spirit." Strack-Billerbeck, I (1922), 759, give parallels for "uprooting mountains" as an idiom for doing the impossible; but the association of this power with faith is not there attested.

is critical of that wisdom context: "Thou hast hidden these things from the wise and understanding and revealed them to babes." Paul begins his criticism of the Corinthian wisdom in much the same vein, by asserting the gospel to be "foolishness," i.e. hidden, to those who perish (1:18), who are identified as the "wise" and "understanding" (1:19), but to be God's power to the "saved," the "babes in Christ" (3:1). Ulrich Wilckens has shown that most of the material in I Cor. 1:18 ff. can be explained on the basis of the Wisdom Literature.[16] Yet one item finds no explanation there: Why in vs. 22 does Paul widen his attack to brand a two-pronged opposition, "Jews demand signs and Greeks seek wisdom," when his interest here is just in combatting the Corinthian wisdom? Perhaps simply because the initial listing of a series of parties in 1:12 is still in mind. Yet it is rather striking that this association of "signs," "wisdom," and "kerygma" crops up in only one other place in primitive Christianity, in Q (Matt. 12:38-42; Luke 11:29-32): Here the demand of the Jewish leaders for a sign is connected with Jonah's kerygma and Solomon's wisdom. Indeed these are the only two places in first-century Christianity where the term kerygma occurs at all. And for it to occur in these two cases in precisely the same associations does tend to suggest some common tradition.

If thus Paul's criticism of the wisdom of the Corinthians has parallels in Q, the Corinthians themselves could have found other parts of Q quite congenial to their position. Indeed the very *Gattung* of "Sayings of the Sages" of which Q is an instance was moving through a trajectory that lead from Wisdom Literature to gnosticism.[17] And hence it is not surprising that it is Q that presents Jesus as wisdom's spokesman: Luke 11:49 introduces a saying as spoken by wisdom, and another Q saying (Matt. 11:19; Luke 7:35) refers to John and Jesus in terms of wisdom: "Wisdom is vindicated by its works (or: children)." Thus we have in Q one of the connecting links between the hypostasizing of Sophia in Jewish Wisdom Literature and the gnostic redeemer myth attested in the second-century systems. I Corinthians and Q have in common then the issue of Jesus and wisdom. It is hence possible that the Q material may in part have had such a *Sitz im Leben* as the conflict in Corinth; that is to say,

[16] *Weisheit und Torheit; Eine exegetisch-religionsgeschichtliche Untersuchung zu 1 Kor. 1 und 2* (*Beiträge zur historischen Theologie,* 26), 1959.

[17] Cf. my article, "ΓΟΛΟΙ ΣΟΦΩΝ; Zur Gattung der Spruchquelle Q," *Zeit und Geschichte* (Bultmann-*Festschrift*), 1964, pp. 77-96.

our initial assumption that the sayings of the Lord are not likely to play a role in Pauline Christianity might not be as obvious as it has seemed on the basis of the sparse use by Paul of sayings of the Lord.

There is one collection of sayings that occurs in free variation frequently enough[18] in the early church to suggest it must have been some common catechetical cluster. It is at the core of the Sermon on the Mount/Plain in Q, is introduced into the Two Ways in Didache 1:3-5, and recurs in I Clement 13:2 and Polycarp, Phil. 2:2-3. Hence when one finds in I Cor. 4:5-13 similar material in somewhat the same context,[19] though without quotation formula or verbal quotation, one may at least wonder whether a debate about this cluster of sayings is in the background. Paul's critical description of his opponents in I Cor. 4:8 suggests the woes of the Sermon on the Plain (Luke 6:24-25). This could well be Paul's response to such a distorting use of the beatitudes to eliminate the eschatological reservation and make the initiates already at the goal of life as one finds in the Gospel of Thomas, saying 58: "Blessed is the man who has suffered; he has found life." Over against such a subjectivistic and spiritualistic interpretation of suffering as is here to be presupposed,[20] Paul would then reassert the earthly literalness of suffering, as in the beatitudes of Q, with the eschatological reservation as the inevitable concomitant of that earthiness (I Cor. 4:11-13). Not only do we have in these verses something rather like the beatitudes of the Sermon on the Plain, but imbedded in the middle are three parallel lines,

When reviled, we bless,
When persecuted, we endure,
When slandered, we conciliate

that are very much like what immediately follows the beatitudes and woes in the Sermon on the Plain (Luke 6:27; cf. vs. 35, RSV):

Love your enemies,
Do good to those who hate you,
Bless those who curse you,
Pray for those who abuse you.

[18] Cf. the page of parallels cited by Aland, *Synopsis Quattuor Evangeliorum*, p. 106.

[19] In I Clement there is a similar attack upon the wise who boasts in his wisdom as one has in I Cor. 1–4; in Polycarp the passage is related to the future resurrection that his—and Paul's—heretical opponents deny.

[20] Cf. saying 69: "Blessed are those who have been persecuted in their hearts; these are they who have known the Father in truth."

And, perhaps in analogy to the following section in the Sermon on the Plain against judging (Luke 6:37 ff.), Paul in 4:5 expressed his eschatological reservation against judging "before the time, until the Lord comes." None of these parallels is compelling, and even a cluster of imprecise parallels is far from convincing. As Bultmann says of similar cases: "All at most possibilities!" [21] Yet it is striking that just this cluster of sayings is used by Polycarp (2:2-3), whom we have seen to be involved in a debate against the heresy of baptismal resurrection. If this remains only a striking coincidence, then to say the least we can by Polycarp's time, if not already in Paul's, see the way in which the debate about the kerygma involved a debate about sayings of the Lord.

Our first trial run towards relating the hermeneutical translation of the kerygma and the transmission of the traditions about Jesus in the NT has sought to trace the debate about the meaning of the resurrection in the life of the Christian, and to see it influencing the transmission of the sayings of the Lord. We have seen both undergoing parallel distortions and corrections as they move into a gnosticizing environment. The simple factors kerygma and historical Jesus have thus been seen to be quite complex factors, as the translation of the kerygma necessitated by the changing historical situations sweeps with it, whichever way it goes, the history of the transmission of the sayings of the Lord. Yet the causation is not simple or unilateral. Both factors are under the influence of the same historical situations. And a development within the history of the transmission of the traditions about Jesus could just as well influence the translation of the kerygma as the reverse. We turn now to a second trajectory moving through primitive Christianity where indeed it seems to be the transmission of traditions about Jesus that is the primary source of the difficulties.

III

The second trial run begins not with the kerygma, but with the historical Jesus. If what had seemed such a simple and unambiguous thing as "the kerygma" in I Cor. 15:3-5 became complex and ambiguous as soon as one considered how it was understood and translated, we must also recognize that "the historical Jesus" was less "common ground"

[21] *Glauben und Verstehen,* I, 191.

than a common point of departure, when one thinks in terms of the history of the transmission of traditions about Jesus.

In his criticism of the new quest of the historical Jesus Bultmann said: "If one inquires as to the material continuity between Jesus and the kerygma, then surely one does not inquire as to Jesus' personal faith, but at most as to whether the understanding of existence encountered in Jesus' activity as a possibility and requirement involves believing *in* him." [22] Yet how ambiguous such a historical fact would be as a point of departure for primitive Christianity, even if it could be established, is evident from the presentation by those pupils of Bultmann who are here most positive. Günther Bornkamm asserts: "With all due attention to the critical examination of tradition, we saw no reason to contest that Jesus actually awakened Messianic expectations by his coming and by his ministry, and that he encountered the faith which believed him to be the promised Savior. The faith which is expressed by the two disciples at Emmaus: 'But we hoped that he was the one to redeem Israel' (Luke 24:21) seems to express quite accurately the conviction of the followers of Jesus before his death." [23] And Erich Dinkler has recently argued that Peter's confession to Jesus as Christ is a historical fact that took place during the public ministry.[24] Yet even if this were a certain conclusion, it would hardly be an unambiguous common ground. Indeed Dinkler goes on to argue that Jesus' rebuke to Peter: "Get behind me, Satan," did not originally follow the first prediction of the passion, but rather followed directly upon Peter's confession. That is to say, Dinkler thinks the historical Jesus flatly rejected the title Messiah. Bornkamm himself goes on to speak "of a movement of broken Messianic hopes, and of one who was hoped to be the Messiah, but who not only at the moment of failure, but in his entire message and ministry, disappointed the hopes which were placed in him." Of course Bornkamm means this quite positively, in that he is appealing to the historical Jesus over against falsely understood messianic hopes. He also speaks of "a faith which first had to break down at the cross of Jesus, only to be rebuilt upon his cross and resurrection." In other words, Bornkamm appeals finally to the kerygma

[22] *Das Verhältnis der urchristlichen Christusbotschaft zum historischen Jesus,* p. 19.
[23] *Jesus of Nazareth,* 1960, p. 172.
[24] "Petrusbekenntnis und Satanswort. Das Problem der Messianität Jesu," *Zeit und Geschichte,* pp. 127-53.

to establish the right interpretation of Jesus. And this is also what Bultmann appeals to in order to clarify the ambiguity of a possible pre-Easter faith in Jesus, for he immediately adds to his original statement: "Hence one can ask: Is, or to what extent is, the disciples' understanding even before Easter to be designated as believing in Jesus Christ, the crucified and resurrected?" All this serves to indicate that primitive Christianity had a common, but not an unequivocal point of departure for its christology in the pre-Easter period. For either there was a christology at best implicit in Jesus' self-understanding prior to Easter, which could then be made explicit in various ways, or there was a quite ambiguous or wrong-headed messianic view about Jesus that stood in potential tension to the kerygma.

We wish to face this problem here not in terms of *our* reconstructions of the historical Jesus, but in terms of the NT church, that is to say in terms of the history of the transmission of traditions about Jesus. If our first trial run beginning with the kerygma pulled into its wake the transmission of the sayings of the Lord, we wish on this second trial run to begin with the stories about Jesus, primarily the miracle stories, and we will have occasion to observe that the traditions about Jesus, in turn, tend to affect the understanding of the kerygma.

The emergence of the Gospel as a literary form has been defined kerygmatically by Martin Kähler as the prefixing of a long introduction to the kerygmatic passion narrative. We wish here to focus upon that long introduction, which in the case of Mark consists primarily in a collection of miracle stories, whose importance is only accentuated by the *Sammelberichte* and by the emphasis upon miracle working in the mission of the twelve.[25] This cycle of miracle stories presents Jesus sufficiently in the role of a glorious *theios anēr* that it can culminate in what would otherwise be comprehensible as a resurrection story,[26] but which is here simply the culmination of the cycle of miracle stories: the transfiguration. Mark has hooked this cycle to the passion narrative in a rather jarring manner by overlapping the first prediction of the passion with Peter's

[25] Cf. Dieter Georgi, *Die Gegner des Paulus im 2. Korintherbrief; Studien zur religiösen Propaganda in der Spätantike* (*Wissenschaftliche Monographien z. Alten u. Neuen Testament,* 11), 1964, pp. 210 ff.

[26] Cf. Charles Edwin Carlston, "Transfiguration and Resurrection," *JBL,* LXXX (1961), 233-40; *RGG,* 3rd ed., VI (1962), 1835, Ernst Käsemann's article "Wunder IV. Im NT."

confession and thus with a messianology pointing in the direction of making Jesus king (John 6:15); as a result the "confession" becomes in Mark "Jesus' temptation by Peter, Satan's tool," [27] and the glorification of Jesus at the transfiguration which follows upon the confession becomes paradoxical in its Marcan setting in view of its proximity to the passion motif. The evangelist has then given a veneer of overall unity to the Gospel by means of the messianic secret, which undercuts the direct demonstration of Jesus' messiahship originally intended by the miracle stories. Thus we can to some extent sense in Mark a tension between traditions about Jesus, in this case primarily the miracle stories of the first half of the Gospel, and the kerygma, in this case represented by the passion narrative around which the last half of the Gospel is organized.

This state of affairs has led Harald Riesenfeld to detect the redactional hand of Mark in the last half, but, in view of the absence of the church's kerygma in the first half, to sense here more nearly a direct report of the historical Jesus.[28] Yet Dibelius posited preaching, taken in a broad sense to include the various kinds of Christian witnessing, as the *Sitz im Leben* even of the miracle stories, as indeed the role of exorcisms and healings in the mission of the twelve would suggest that miracle stories were a

[27] Oscar Cullmann, "L'Apôtre Pierre instrument du Diable et instrument de Dieu. La place de Matt. 16:16-19 dans la tradition primitive," *New Testament Essays* (T. W. Manson-*Festschrift*), 1959, p. 96: "For at the same moment when Peter made the declaration, 'You are the Messiah,' he must already have had, according to the narrative of Mark, the diabolical conception of the political role of the Messiah, the view that the majority of the Jews shared and which excluded his suffering."

[28] Riesenfeld, "Tradition und Redaktion im Markusevangelium," *Neutestamentliche Studien für Rudolf Bultmann* (*Beiheft* 21 to *ZNW*), 1964, p. 162. Hans Conzelmann, in a lecture on "Das Selbstbewusstsein Jesu" in Uppsala on Sept. 24, 1963, a lecture that is to be published only in Swedish, agrees with Riesenfeld to the extent "that we can recognize within the Gospel of Mark a certain shift, in style and content, of what is reported. Until Mark 8:26, Jesus is portrayed as a teacher in Galilee. But no specific content of this teaching is given. From Mark 8:27 on, the content of the teaching is described: messiahship and suffering. Here the structuring reflection of the evangelist is at work. Hence a tension between tradition and redaction becomes visible." However Conzelmann does not agree with Riesenfeld's inference that the first part of Mark goes back directly to Jesus: "Yet doubts are to be registered against his inferences. The philological analysis of the text shows that not only *two* layers are to be distinguished (tradition and the evangelist's reflection), but rather that there is a layer between Jesus and the evangelist that already contains important elements of reflection. Precisely the comments about Jesus as teacher belong not to the oldest layer, but rather are often literarily wooden and hence clearly secondary, interpolated into the oldest layer." Conzelmann had already (*ZTK*, LIV (1957), 293 ff.) called attention to the fact that the messianic secret is imposed not on historical pre-messianic material, but on material that was already all too messianic.

part of early Christian missionary propaganda. Thus we must investigate the history of the transmission of the traditions about Jesus as itself a kind of kerygma, to see what that kerygma had to say and how it stood in relation to the kerygma of cross and resurrection. Julius Wellhausen seemed to be right about Mark when, on the one hand, he affirmed that "the gospel is imbedded in the nest between Peter's confession and the passion," [29] but on the other hand, goes on to say of the first half: "The miracles and exorcisms, the recognizing of Jesus by the demons, fitted popular taste, and perhaps even, as 'signs' of the messiahship, they possessed the most force as publicity in the missionary preaching of the gospel in those circles in which Christianity did most of its recruiting." [30] Paul himself seems to concede much the same thing, though he states it somewhat sarcastically: "Tongues are a sign not for believers but for unbelievers" (I Cor. 14:22). And indeed miracle working was listed prominently by Paul among the spiritual gifts in I Cor. 12:9, where there is a significant cluster of "gifts and healing," "working of powers," i.e. miracles, and, in first place in this cluster, the odd gift of "faith," odd because normally for Paul "faith" is the response of every Christian to God and not a special gift of God reserved for a select few. But in this case we clearly have to do with a technical term of miracle workers, namely the faith that moves mountains (13:2). The miracle workers were faith healers, and in the two synoptic gospels most dependent on them, Mark and Luke, these faith healers have left their characteristic slogan in the miracle stories of Jesus they transmitted: "Your faith has healed you," Mark 5:34 and parallels; 10:52 (Luke 18:42); Luke 7:50; 17:19.[31]

It is a pity that recent research on Mark has not, in a way comparable to that on Matthew and Luke, produced a basic breakthrough to insight into what Mark intended to do. Hence, rather than pursuing the question of the transmission of traditions about Jesus in terms of the miracle stories in the first half of Mark (which may find its answer in the unpublished manuscript by Morton Smith on "The Aretology Used by Mark"), I wish to shift to what seems to be a rather striking parallel, which will serve our purposes here and perhaps indirectly be of relevance for the study

[29] *Einleitung in die drei ersten Evangelien,* 1905, p. 82.
[30] *Ibid.,* p. 53.
[31] Ernst Käsemann, *RGG,* 3rd ed., II, 995.

of Mark. I refer to the Signs Source used by the Fourth Gospel.[32] This source was first detected by Alexander Faure,[33] was picked up by Bultmann,[34] and has become the one of his sources for John that has withstood best the current trend toward discounting Johannine sources in the light of the pervasive unity of style in the Gospel. Both Käsemann [35] and Haenchen,[36] while quite skeptical about the Discourses Source, do assume the Evangelist used, though freely, the Signs Source, and Kümmel concedes that the places where typically Johannine stylistic traits are most lacking fit rather well the places where the Signs Source seems to be most faithfully followed.[37] Hence the most recent survey of the lit-

[32] Helmut Köster, "Häretiker im Urchristentum," *RGG,* 3rd ed., III (1959), 19, has already associated the heresy of II Corinthians with the Signs Source as well as with Mark and parts of Acts.

[33] "Die alttestamentlichen Zitate im 4. Evangelium und die Quellenscheidungs-hypothese," *ZNW,* XXI (1922), 99-121, esp. pp. 107-12.

[34] *Das Evangelium des Johannes* (*Meyer-Kommentar*), 10th (1941) through 17th (1962) eds., esp. p. 78.

[35] Review of Bultmann's commentary, *Verkündigung und Forschung; Theologischer Jahresbericht,* 1942-46, 1947, 186-89; *RGG,* 3rd ed., VI (1962), 1836. Käsemann rejects the Discourses Source in *ZTK,* LIV (1957), 16.

[36] "Aus der Literatur zum Johannesevangelium 1929-1956," *ThR,* XXIII (1955), 303; "Johanneische Probleme," *ZTK,* LVI (1959), 19-54; "'Der Vater, der mich gesandt hat,'" *NTS,* IX (1963), 208 f. The criticism of Haenchen's work on the Signs Source by Wilhelm Wilckens, "Evangelist und Redaktion im Johannes-evangelium," *Theologische Zeitschrift,* XVI (1960), 81-90 is valid only on the assumption of the validity of his own theory about the origin of John set forth in his dissertation *Die Entstehungsgeschichte des vierten Evangeliums,* 1958, which theory is however untenable. For apart from the implausibility of his reconstructions (cf. my review article, "Recent Research in the Fourth Gospel," *JBL,* LXXVIII (1959), 242-46), his attributing of an original Book of Seven Signs to the same (apostolic) author as composed the succeeding stages overlooks the basic theological tension between the Signs Source and the Fourth Gospel. D. Moody Smith, Jr., *The Composition and Order of the Fourth Gospel; Bultmann's Literary Theory* (New Haven and London: Yale University Press, 1965), p. 110, n. 181, asserts "Haenchen rejects Bultmann's semeia-source hypothesis," but adds: "His [Haenchen's] own understanding of the way in which the evangelist employs narrative material is, after all, not so different from Bultmann's." It is the latter statement that is the focus of Haenchen's work, who envisages a written source used in the Fourth Evangelist's home congregation and hence cited freely, a source containing more of the Synoptic-type materials than just the miracle stories. It gives something of a wrong impression of Haenchen's assessment of Bultmann's analysis to refer to this as a "rejection."

[37] *Einleitung in das Neue Testament,* 12th ed. of Feine-Behm, 1963, pp. 146 f.: "On the other hand it has also become apparent that in individual pericopes the characteristics distinctive of John are so clearly lacking that one must assume that here traditions have been incorporated (. . . especially 2:1-10, 13-19; 4:46-53; 12:1-8, 12-15)." Eduard Schweizer, "Die Heilung des Königlichen: Joh. 4, 46-54," *EvTh,* XI (1951), 64-71, esp. p. 65, n. 5, gives the details on 4:46-54. To be sure Kümmel does not himself draw the positive inference, but rather continues: "But this does not at all lead to a written 'Signs Source' used by the Evangelist."

erature on the problem of Johannine sources by D. Moody Smith, Jr. concludes: "The prima facie possibility of something approximating Bultmann's semeia-source is to be granted, although the characterization and delineation of that source remain doubtful." [38]

What makes this Signs Source stand out in the Fourth Gospel are precisely those traits that characterize it as a collection of miracle stories by a faith healer designed for missionary purposes. At least in the early chapters of John the Signs Source also stands out because of literary seams, the wooden redactional style one would rather expect in the Synoptics. The second sign, the healing of the centurion's son (4:46-54), occurs in the same setting of "coming from Judea to Galilee" (4:43, 45, 54) as does the first sign, the wedding in Cana (2:1-11); the Evangelist even takes Jesus back to Cana for the second sign (4:46), thus reflecting the broken connection to the wedding in Cana (just as 2:12 reflects the broken connection to 4:46).[39] It is also striking, not only from the point of view of literary criticism, but now also from the point of view of *Sachkritik,* that the first two signs are numbered: In 2:11 the wedding in Cana is called the "beginning of the signs," and in 4:54 the centurion's son is called the "second sign." Not only is this counting of signs not continued and indeed seems without point in John's presentation, but it is even contradicted by the intervening Johannine material, which speaks in 2:23 (cf. also 4:45) of a plurality of signs having been done, a clash between source and redaction only faintly covered over by the fact that it is in fact the second Galilean sign.[40] Yet from the point of view of the source itself the numbering of the signs fits in well with the apologetic emphasis on the number of signs. "When the Christ appears, will he do *more signs* than this man has done?" (7:31, RSV). "What are we to do? For this man performs *many signs!*" (11:47, RSV). *"So many signs* he

[38] *The Composition and Order of the Fourth Gospel; Bultmann's Literary Theory* (New Haven and London: Yale University Press, 1965), p. 113. Cf. also "The Sources of the Gospel of John: An Assessment of the Present State of the Problem," *NTS,* X (1964), 336-51, esp. p. 345.

[39] Eduard Schweizer, "Die Heilung des Königlichen: Joh. 4, 46-54," *EvTh,* XI (1951), 65, n. 7, shows that the allusions to Jesus' brothers and to Capernaum in 2:12 make sense only as a transition to 4:44 ff., and that 4:43 and 4:46*a* are here recalling the original context of the first sign.

[40] Schweizer, *ibid.,* p. 65, n. 4, shows how this numbering makes sense only on the assumption that the two miracles belong together following upon one same trip from Judea to Galilee.

had done before them, and yet they did not believe in him" (12:37). Apparently this verse led up directly to the conclusion of the Signs Source, whose ending was separated off and put at 20:30-31: "Now Jesus did *many other signs* before his disciples, which are not written in this book." And now comes the apologetic, missionary scope or *Sitz im Leben* of the Signs Source: "But these were written down that you may believe that Jesus is the Christ, the Son of God." It is the very quantity of such miracle stories that produces faith, and the narrator had assured the reader he could just go on and on.

Thus there is a direct, unambiguous, non-paradoxical causal relation between the signs that demonstrate Jesus to be a *theios anēr* and the resultant faith (or credulity) in him as such a miracle worker. It is the same reasoning that Nicodemus uses: "Rabbi, we know that you are a teacher come from God; for no one can do these signs that you do, unless God is with him," 3:3. But it is also the reasoning of primitive Christian missionaries, at least as Luke conceives of Peter commending Jesus to the Jews as "a man attested to you by God with mighty works and wonders and signs which God did through him in your midst" (Acts 2:22).

The Fourth Evangelist himself maintains that the true form of faith is faith in Jesus' word.[41] "He who hears my word and believes him who sent me, has eternal life; he does not come into judgment, but has passed from death to life," 5:24, RSV—which happens to be precisely the section cited earlier as the nearest Johannine approach to the heresy of baptismal resurrection. It is as if in backing away from the false interpretation of the earthly Jesus represented by the Signs Source the Fourth Evangelist backs into a position dangerously near the converse error. Thus the position of orthodoxy tends to be a mathematical point, or hardly a position at all, or at best a dialectical position, or perhaps even better a direction: "Orthodox" were not the traditions or conceptualizations one used, but the direction one went with them, the point one was scoring.

By focusing attention upon the general orientation of the Signs Source we have come to hear the point being scored as it transmits traditions about Jesus, specifically miracle stories, and we have conjectured that such a point may have been commonly heard in such stories in oral

[41] Already Faure, *ZNW*, XXI (1922), 111 f., makes this contrast.

transmission. Yet the very fact that such a point is subjected to some criticism by the Fourth Evangelist, who also transmits these stories, would tend to indicate that the missionary purpose, the point, intended by such transmission of traditions could vary, just as the understanding of faith varies between the Johannine redactor and the traditions transmitted to him. If in the case of the kerygma we conceptualized this process in terms of hermeneutical translation, we wish in this case to see the debate taking place in terms of the history of the transmission of traditions about Jesus. That is to say, listening to the way the tradition grows and is altered, hearkening to the way the stories are told, should betray the point they were intended to convey, the faith to which they witness and for which they call.

This can be illustrated by the story of the healing of the centurion's son, a story that occurs both in Q (Matt. 8:5-13; Luke 7:1-10) and in the Signs Source (John 4:46-54). In Q this miracle story has always posed a problem, since Q is not supposed to have narrative, and this story is the main exception to that rule. As a matter of fact it does not really contradict the general understanding of Q as a source focused on Jesus' word. For, to begin with, very little of the narrative material in the story is common to Matthew and Luke. Hence the part clearly attributable to Q is mostly dialogue. There is really no more narrative in the part clearly attributable to Q than is absolutely necessary to make sense of the dialogue, just as we find in a few places in the Gospel of Thomas. But even more relevant with regard to Q's orientation to Jesus' word is the fact that this is precisely the one story about Jesus in which the very point is faith in his word. The centurion says Jesus does not even need to come home with him. "Just speak the word and my servant will be healed" (Matt. 8:8 and parallel). The centurion goes on to state that as an officer he is quite familiar with the authority of commands that effect what they say. And it is this faith in Jesus' word that is elevated to the point of the whole story. "With no one in Israel have I found such faith" (Matt. 8:10 and parallel). What more perfect story to follow upon the contrast between the stability of those who "hear my words and do them" (Matt. 7:24 and parallel) and the shaky status of those who do not! It is not even clear that Q went to the trouble to tell whether the miracle actually happened, and indeed such a continuation of the narration would seem anticlimactic.

Quite the reverse is the case in the Signs Source! For at the point the story ends in Q, in the Signs Source it has hardly begun. We follow the father on the way home, where his servants come to meet him, and tell of the miraculous cure, which is shown to have happened at exactly the same hour that Jesus had spoken. Then the father and all his house believed—now that they see the evidence, the miracle itself. Where does this leave the faith the father had when Jesus gave his word? It seems forgotten, as in Jesus' word itself. Rather we are told that the story is the second *sign* Jesus worked (4:54). That is to say, the story that Q oriented to faith in Jesus' word is oriented in the Signs Source to faith in Jesus as a miracle worker. This is too much really for the Fourth Evangelist, who interpolates the biting remark, vs. 48: "Unless you see signs and wonders, you will not believe." [42] And Q also criticizes by implication the emphasis of the Signs Source, by rejecting the miracle-worker interpretation of Jesus' divine sonship by means of the three temptations, significantly absent from the Signs Source and Mark but put prominently near the opening of Q.

If John's backing away from a rather primitive kind of primitive Christian faith imbedded in traditions about Jesus as a miracle worker on behalf of a more profound and spiritual Christianity almost pushed him into the camp of the spiritualists, something not dissimilar seems to have been the outcome for Paul when such traditions arrived in Corinth. We may assume that the arrival of I Corinthians in Corinth collapsed the radical, gnosticizing left wing of the congregation, which was perhaps the Apollos party. This Pauline victory not only pulled the congregation together, but to some extent strengthened the other wing of the congregation, the weaker brethren with Jewish leanings. They agreed heartily that one was not already completely in the eschaton, for they were so convinced of their unbroken continuity with the past that they could not free themselves from their former taboos. This side may have been represented by the Cephas party (of the Christ party, cf. II Cor. 10:7, if such a party existed). They had been relatively spared in the attacks of I Corinthians, being mentioned critically only in the general listing of parties at the opening and the general listing of spiritual gifts at the conclusion, whereas in the central section on meat

[42] For this comparison of the varying forms of this story cf. especially Haenchen, *ZTK*, LVI (1959), 23-31.

offered to idols Paul had come to their defense. Thus it happened that the congregation was ripe for wandering missionaries, who had meanwhile arrived in town (II Cor. 11:4) and emphasized their continuity with Israel's glorious past (II Cor. 11:22). Apparently they saw this past in terms of the potency of a *theios anēr* transmitted in the divine tradition, reaching from Moses' signs in the court of Pharaoh to Jesus' equally numerous miracles, and embracing the no less impressive faith healings of the missionaries themselves, who like Moses and Jesus are "transfigured from glory to glory" (II Cor. 3:18). For these wandering missionaries came equipped with letters of recommendation (II Cor. 3:1) that must have listed their glorious deeds, as did the many lurid acts of various apostles later; and they also boasted of having to their credit the "signs of an apostle," namely the ability to work "signs and wonders and miracles" (II Cor. 12:12). It is no wonder the Corinthians now "demand proof that Christ is speaking" in Paul (II Cor. 13:3); the word of Christ—whether in terms of sayings of the Lord or whatever—is not itself convincing revelation, but needs to be supplemented by the confirming miracle, a requirement that recalls the shift in emphasis in the story of the centurion's son from the Q version, with its focus upon faith in the authority of Jesus' word, to the Signs Source, where real faith takes place when one sees the miracle performed.

Paul pokes fun at the self-esteem of these wandering miracle workers by referring to them (II Cor. 11:5; 12:11) as "super-apostles," and he presents a takeoff on their self-commendations in the way he presents his autobiography in 11:23-33. For Anton Fridrichsen has recognized here the stylistic traits of what is known as a *peristasis* catalogue, the listing of a potentate's glorious triumphs over all kinds of hardships, "such as one finds in the inscriptions of oriental kings, in the *res gestae* of Roman Caesars and in Greek novels. From this stylistic tradition are to be explained the asyndeta, the numbering, the occurrence of *pollákis,* the alternation of lists and narratives, the chronicle-like addition in 11:32-33, and the like. To be sure, the fact that the praise of the apostle consists only in suffering turns the use of this stylistic form into a clearly intended paradox."[43]

[43] So Werner Georg Kümmel, *HNT,* IX 4th ed. (1949), 211, in his summary of Fridrichsen's work, of which only part has been accessible to me.

This debate between Paul and the "super-apostles" concerning which way of life legitimizes the apostle, the life of ignominious suffering or the life of glorious triumph over every impediment, is also carried on in terms of traditions about Jesus. It may be no coincidence that the name Jesus occurs so frequently in II Corinthians unadorned with an accompanying title "Lord" or "Christ." [44] Paul accuses his opponents of preaching "another Jesus" (II Cor. 11:4), and the evidence seems to indicate that this other Jesus is a power-laden glorious miracle worker, much as in the Signs Source, whose earthly ministry could well be epitomized by comparing his glory with that of Moses, as in II Cor. 3,[45] and in the cycle of miracle stories dominating the first half of Mark and culminating in the transfiguration alongside of Moses and Elijah.[46] Hence Dieter Georgi can assert:

So it is not true that Paul developed his christology in complete ignorance of the contents and tendencies of the developing tradition about Jesus. Rather he knew about them and hence clearly rejected a motivation that at least at times clearly asserts itself, namely the objective of using a certain form of presentation to make of the life of Jesus an unambiguous manifestation of the divine, to cover over the offense of the cross and the humanness of Jesus in general and to replace the eschatological revelation of God with historically ascertainable "proofs of God." [47]

Perhaps the most dramatic confirmation of the fact that the historical Jesus—in the form of a certain segment in the history of the transmission of traditions about Jesus—is claimed by the opponents in II Corinthians is II Cor. 5:16, where Paul emphasizes the irrelevance of knowing Christ according to the flesh. This is strikingly reminiscent of the cry of the gnosticizing party in I Corinthians, "Jesus be anathema," that Paul condemned in I Cor. 12:3, but which could have been directed against much the same portrayal of Jesus as Paul himself now rejects. That is

[44] Georgi, pp. 282 ff.

[45] Georgi, pp. 265-82. In John 2:11 Jesus' signs "manifest his glory."

[46] Here too the concept of Jesus' "glory" emerges in Luke 9:31-32; II Pet. 1:17; cf. Mark 8:38.

[47] P. 289, note 3. This stands in contrast to Bultmann, e.g. *RGG,* 2nd ed., IV (1930), 1028: "For no matter whether Paul knew much or little of that tradition [sc. about Jesus]; for his preaching of salvation the content of Jesus' life as that of the teacher, the prophet, the miracle worker, the one crowned with thorns, plays absolutely no role."

to say, we again find Paul in opposing one heresy making use of formulations that are so hard to distinguish from the other heresy that Walter Schmithals has (wrongly) argued that II Cor. 5:16 was a gnostic gloss.[48] And what is equally striking is that in opposing the emphasis on continuity with the past Paul so emphasizes realized eschatology (II Cor. 5:16-17; 6:2) as to sound reminiscent of the heresy of baptismal resurrection he himself combatted in I Corinthians.[49] Again we see that primitive Christian statements cannot be understood, much less evaluated, as doctrinal assertions in and of themselves, in isolation from the situation into which they spoke and hence apart from the way they cut. Orthodoxy and heresy have not only not yet separated into different ecclesiastical organizations, they have not even yet separated their theological conceptualizations. Rather, from a common body of traditions, ambiguous in their concrete meaning, each side transmits in terms of understandings that only gradually came to objectify themselves into fixed positions that could be branded as right or wrong in and of themselves. By that time the tagged theological vocabulary was already dead or dying, and the real issues, out of which the heresy and orthodoxy of a later age would emerge, were already being debated in not yet dogmatically defined areas where freedom and ambiguity still prevailed.

In I Corinthians Paul was primarily confronted by a mistranslation of the kerygma in terms of baptismal resurrection, and he replied with a corrective interpretation of the kerygma, emphasizing: the eschatological reservation; love and the upbuilding of the congregation as the point of the action to which the Christian is empowered; the power of the resurrection as the power to endure; and hence the limiting of the kerygma to the focus of Christ crucified. This debate about the valid translation of the kerygma colored the transmission of the sayings of Jesus as soon as that debate came in contact with this tradition. In II Corinthians Paul was primarily confronted by a distorting transmission of traditions about Jesus as a glorious miracle worker, and he replied

[48] "Zwei gnostische Glossen im 2. Korintherbrief," *EvTh,* XVIII (1958), 552-73, esp. pp. 552-64.

[49] Note Dinkler's appeal to II Cor. 5:17, *ZTK,* XLIX (1962), 188, cited above, in attributing to Paul in I Corinthians what would be more in analogy to than a corrective of the position of his opponents there. His appeal to Galatians is also hardly valid, in that here as in II Corinthians Paul is facing the converse front to that in I Corinthians; neither II Corinthians nor Galatians can be used as the hermeneutical principle for interpreting Paul's stance in 1 Corinthians.

with an ironic presentation of himself within that succession to document the invalidity of that scope for the traditions, and by repudiating such knowledge of Jesus. However, we might expect him to argue his case in II Corinthians not only in terms of such traditions, but also in terms of the kerygma of cross and resurrection. And one might indeed wonder whether that kerygma would not color his view of the traditions about Jesus. There are some indications which point in this direction.

The pattern of the kerygma to which Paul appeals is provided by II Cor. 13:4: "For he was crucified in weakness, but lives from the power of God." Here divine power is precisely not attributed to the earthly Jesus, but to the resurrected. That is to say, we have here a parallel to early kerygmatic texts such as Rom. 1:3-4 and Phil. 2:6-11 that accord Jesus first at the exaltation honorific titles, in the sense of enthroning him in an office he had not previously had, the investing of him with "all authority in heaven and earth" (Matt. 28:18),[50] "the receiving from God the Father honor and glory" at the transfiguration (II Pet. 1: 17), which transaction would however for Paul (as for II Peter?) be at the resurrection, not during the earthly ministry. Hence the relation of the apostle's ministry to Jesus is not that of continuing a power he had on earth, but rather that of submission in service to the rule he has received in heaven. "For we preach not ourselves but Christ Jesus as Lord, but ourselves as your servants because of Jesus" (II Cor. 4:5). The apostle's relation to the Lord is that of earth to heaven, servant to Lord, and that service takes the form of serving his body the church.

Paul's addition that this service is not only subjection to the Lord reigning in heaven but also takes place because of Jesus suggests to Georgi [51] that the apostle's earthly service is the true parallel to the earthly Jesus, whom Paul would interpret by seeing the public ministry in a scope provided by the phrase "crucified in weakness." That is to say, Paul would conceive of the earthly Jesus as a long introduction to and of a piece with the passion narrative. This scope given to Jesus' life and the believer's life by the cross is made explicit in II Cor. 4:10-11: "We always carry in the body the killing of Jesus. . . . For in this life we are always being given up to death because of Jesus." Here Christian

[50] Cf. Günther Bornkamm, "Der Auferstandene und der Irdische. Matt. 28:16-20," *Zeit und Geschichte* (Bultmann-*Festschrift*), 1964, pp. 171-91.

[51] On this passage cf. pp. 285 f.

existence defined by, i.e. "because of," Jesus means living in acceptance of death, or, as the kerygma puts it of Jesus, "obedient unto death," Phil. 2:8. That is to say, the Christian life is not understood as a resurrected life that has finished its dying and needs merely at the end of life to return to the sun from which it came, nor as standing in the glorious tradition of a miracle-working earthly Jesus whose power one continues to exercise, but as life freed from the demonic sway of the fear of death, so that the apostle may persist in obedience, in service.

It is this freedom from the grip of evil, the power of death, to a life of suffering and service that is the paradoxical presence of the resurrection in this life. For Paul takes the phrase "life of Jesus," which Georgi suspects is derived from Paul's opponents who used it to refer to the miracle-working earthly Jesus, and puts it in the position where the kerygma has the resurrection life. Thus life, in the sense of higher or divine life, is, like the terms power and glory, shifted from the earthly Jesus to the resurrected, and hence is only paradoxically related to this life for the believer.

This analysis of Paul's position in II Corinthians began with the argument that the situation he confronted in Corinth had to a large extent reversed itself between I Corinthians and II Corinthians, and that Paul accordingly shifted the categories in which he argued, and to this extent shifted his position. For not only was the one argument primarily about the right translation of the kerygma, and at most only secondarily a debate about the right transmission of traditions about Jesus, whereas in the other case the primary focus was the tradition; furthermore the position Paul had assumed in the first debate to some extent prepared the ground for the heresy that blossomed between I Corinthians and II Corinthians, and the position he assumed in II Corinthians was to some extent parallel to that of his opponents in I Corinthians. Thus a great fluidity in the use of concepts and traditions could be observed, and Pauline theologizing has turned out to be not simply the citation of relevant materials from an abstractly conceived generalized system, but rather the development of materials to fit one situation, and a different development to fit another. And yet one can sense, in where he comes out in the two structures of thought related to the two situations, an analogous point being scored.

Paul's opponents in the two cases could emerge in a Pauline congregation with the claim to be rightly translating the kerygma and transmitting the traditions, in part by appealing to Pauline structures of thought to implement a divergent point. To the extent such structures were themselves taken as Pauline theology, it would be easy to shift a Pauline congregation from one point to the other, as long as the modification of structure remained minimal. And Pauline pupils could readily emerge to complete one or the other instance of a Pauline "system," with widely fluctuating points; perhaps their expansions were also at times more nearly dull and pointless, too weak to withstand unintended points latent in the language itself.

We are forced to conclude that any meaningful discussion of Pauline theology on our part would have to move beyond the common body of concepts and traditions he shared with other Christians, beyond the particular structurings of such materials he developed in any concrete situation, to a listening for the points scored, and in their continuity with each other—though not without the language in which they were scored—attempt to attain a more nuanced and comprehensive understanding of the historical phenomenon "Pauline theology" than that which characterized the Deutero-Pauline period and much Pauline study still today.

IV

Two "trial runs" have traced trajectories through primitive Christianity that are significant in and of themselves. Yet they were intended to be illustrative of certain broader matters, which may now be summarized.

1. The use of current categories in the assigned topic provided an occasion for calling to attention the crisis in the basic categories of our discipline in which we find ourselves today. This crisis has emerged partly because of the careful detailed research of our day that has, in spite of contrary categories, established facts calling for a revision of inherited categories. Yet the inadequate categories persist and in many cases continue to provide guide lines that mislead the direction of research, so that results of even carefully detailed research may be less relevant than would have been the case had the *Fragestellung* been more accurately focused. This could have been exemplified in various areas. For example, at a time when the study of early gnosticism is calling attention to the important role that the interpretation of the OT within heterodox Judaism played in that development, the older pattern of argu-

ment persists to the effect that a text can be disassociated from the gnostic problem by showing its OT or Jewish rootage. The inherited conceptualization in terms of mutual exclusivity, built upon the antithesis between normative Judaism and advanced gnosticism in past generations of scholarship, has been carried over into a period where the development from heterodox Judaism to early gnosticism, from Qumran to Nag Hammadi, calls for a new conceptualization, more like a continuous progression, through a period of contiguous centuries and cultures. The present paper has intended to carry through such a restructuring of categories in the case of the inherited pair "kerygma and history," from which emerged more adequate conceptualizations in terms of the hermeneutically understood process of translating language's point and of the transmission of traditions. Such illustrations of a *Grundlagenkrise* are designed to sharpen our awareness of the fact that we confront our sources through the mediation of the inherited language of scholarship, and that we are to alert our critical sensitivity to this medium or prism in which we have access to the sources. This should not be taken as an invitation to a kind of primitivism, according to which outsiders free of the ballast of scholarship could see what the scholars had not. It is from those who have worked their way through the history of scholarship to its growing edge that further advances are to be expected. It is to them that this paper is addressed, in the hope that they can be encouraged to be more explicit as to the basic inferences for the structuring of research that can be drawn from their present insight into the state of things in the sources.

2. Both "the kerygma" and "the historical Jesus" turned out to be abstractions, when confronted with the realities of the church of NT times. We have found instead a process of understanding and translating the kerygma, without there being any instance of the kerygma, however carefully codified, that was itself not another instance of that hermeneutical linguistic process. And we have found instead of instances in which the historical Jesus was directly a factor in the time of the church, as memorized sayings or unaltered memories, rather a process of the growth, deletion, and shifting involved in the meaningful transmission of traditions. The "kerygmatizing" of the "historical Jesus" turned out on examination to be a series of conflicting influences on the transmission of traditions about Jesus, in terms of varying understandings of the

kerygmatic meaning of Jesus. On the other hand these traditions were seen to have "kerygmatic" implications of their own, so that it became increasingly difficult for the Pauline development to ignore them or to leave them unrevised in terms of understandings of the kerygma. In some instances the kerygmatic overtones involved in such traditions could have imposed themselves on the kerygma of Jesus' death and resurrection, so that the process of influences between "kerygma" and "historical Jesus" could have been mutual, a process of interaction. And indeed such an interaction seems to go back to the beginning, in that Jesus' word had kerygmatic relevance and the Easter kerygma translated into the new situation created by Jesus' death the christology implicit in that word. Thus the clear distinction, not to say antithetical relationship, characteristic of the terms kerygma and history, can be recognized as derived from the pendulum swings in the last century of scholarship, as the historical Jesus replaced dogmatic christology and then the kerygma replaced the historical Jesus, rather than being derived from the situation in the sources themselves, where a much more nuanced and complicated series of relationships calls for recognition.

3. The relation of heresy and orthodoxy in the primitive church becomes a topic in need of further investigation. For the situation would seem to be neither that of a pristine purity in which the tensions can either be dismissed as purely personal or removed from historical investigation by attributing them to Satan leading the faithful astray, nor that of a later day in which an unambiguous separation at least in doctrine and eventually organization could be assumed. For the reading back of such clear distinctions into the beginnings on the part of subsequent orthodoxy is as unreal a procedure as Hollywood's neat separation between the "good guys" and the "bad guys." We have seen Paul in facing one front make use of conceptualizations analogous to those of the other front, and on turning against the second front using such as are reminiscent of the first front. There seems not yet to be a central body of orthodox doctrine distinguished from heretical doctrine to the right and the left, but rather a common body of beliefs variously understood and translated or transmitted. In such a fluid situation one must ask not simply what was said, but rather which way what was said cut, what happened when the language was used. To this extent the terms "heresy" and "orthodoxy" are anachronistic. To be sure, such a recognition does

not lead to the complete relativism suggested by the emphasis upon the variety of theolog*ies* in the NT, which common emphasis may be just as much replacing the historical reality of recognizable continuity within primitive Christianity by mirroring a modern pluralistic society with a denominationally organized Christianity as was the other assumption of one system of doctrine in the NT an unhistorical reflection of a monolithic understanding of Christianity in the preecumenical age. One has been able to sense convergences in Paul's points in spite of the different positions he assumed in differing situations, and one may suspect some underlying continuities between the differing "heresies" of I and II Corinthians facilitating the efforts of the wandering "super-apostles" opposed in II Corinthians to gain control not only of the party most congenial to them, but also of the "opposite" party that Paul had temporarily brought back into line by writing I Corinthians. And at the level of intention, connections with other bodies of primitive Christian literature have been sensed, so that something like ongoing streams of orientation have been detected, although they may not conform to the streams of interpretation and transmission of given conceptualizations or traditions, where indeed conflicting intentions have been observed within the same conceptualization or tradition.

4. The dismantling and reassembling of the categories "kerygma" and "history" in terms of hermeneutic and *Traditionsgeschichte* involved by implication both a restructuring of the subdivisions within NT scholarship, such as NT theology and early Christian history, and also a reassessment of the relations among the various theological disciplines, as biblical studies leads via the history of doctrine and church history to contemporary theology, ethics, and various forms of practical theology. It has been difficult of late for some to find a theologically relevant place for historical research, the matters handled in NT introduction, now that the basic critical revision of the traditional picture has been carried through with such a high degree of success as to present much less of a challenge than was the case a generation or so ago. This is no doubt responsible for the quick generalization, the skimming of the cream, the harmonized unity of the Bible, that has made of "biblical theology" a discipline hardly more respectable academically than its predecessor "English Bible." The present paper has advocated the thesis that only the most penetrating analysis of the specific historical situation in which

the source was written is able to make possible a penetration *through* the conceptualizations and traditions used *to* the point being scored, which is really what should be referred to as the theology of the text. Indeed von Dobschütz's call for "an individual hermeneutical for every New Testament writing," left unheeded some forty years ago,[52] may be the way in which the discipline of NT introduction could be more relevantly integrated into the ongoing enterprise, thus acknowledging to responsible historical research the importance it deserves and according to critical NT theology the scholarly respectability it deserves. Such a restructuring of NT scholarship would then find itself at the growing edge of neighboring disciplines, from literature (the "new criticism"; Emil Staiger) and philosophy (Whitehead; Gadamer) to contemporary theology translated for a world come of age and contextual ethics.

[52] *Vom Auslegen des Neuen Testaments* (Göttingen: Vandenhoeck und Ruprecht, 1927), p. 16.

DAVID M. STANLEY, S.J.

RESPONSE TO JAMES M. ROBINSON'S "Kerygma and History in the New Testament"

Professor Robinson's most original discussion of kerygma and history in the NT has provided us with much food for reflection, and we are all indebted to him for his thought-provoking communication. In the brief time at my disposal, I can do no more than formulate some of the questions which it has raised in my own mind.

I

In the first place, I cannot help but wonder whether the dichotomy between kerygma and history, which the assigned title of the paper appears to set up, does not tend to create a false problem. It is certainly true that kerygma should not be confused with "history," an unmistakably modern conception. History concerns itself with the remembered past as such: kerygma deals with the remembered past, indeed, but with the past *re-presented* as an *ever recurring actuality*. At the same time, it is clear that kerygma as understood here cannot rightly be viewed as adequately distinct from history, as if its axis inclined towards a totally mythological presentation. Yet again, we cannot lose sight of one sense of myth, which is pertinent in the present discussion. The term can, as my former colleague R. A. F. MacKenzie, S.J., has correctly observed, denote a "narrative about the past which is meaningful and operative in the present. It symbolizes and constitutes, for those who listen to it or narrate it or act it out, a lived experience of the significant past reality." [1]

Robinson has addressed himself to two specific aspects of the general question of the very complex relationships between kerygma and history. In what he modestly refers to as the "first trial run" he "has sought to trace the interaction of the debate about the existential meaning of the resurrection with the sayings of the Lord." If I understand him aright, his investigation leads him to the conclusion that, as the understanding

[1] *Faith and History in the Old Testament* (Minneapolis: University of Minnesota Press, 1963), p. 65.

of the resurrection moves in the direction of an heretical gnosticism, the sayings of Jesus are given an increasingly gnostic interpretation. In the second part of his inquiry, he finds that "a development within the history of the transmission of the traditions about Jesus could just as well influence the translation of the kerygma."

For his "first trial run," Robinson has chosen to reexamine the difficulty experienced by certain members of the Corinthian community with regard to the glorious resurrection of the just. I must confess that I find it difficult to accept his interpretation of the erroneous view of these Corinthian Christians, particularly in the light of certain data in I Cor. 15. On Robinson's view, these Greek-speaking converts to Christianity were forerunners of Hymenaeus and Philetus, who are reproved in II Tim. 2:18 for "saying that our resurrection has already taken place."

We may begin our review of the evidence adduced with the passage in I Cor. 1:10-17. While it is doubtless true that Paul's intention here is "to play down his role as a baptizer in order to show that it was not he who had done the saving act for the Corinthians," yet surely the apostle adopts this position to remind his addressees that their baptism at the hands of Apollos or Cephas or himself has made them disciples of no one but Christ himself, the one crucified for them, in whose name they were baptized (vs. 13). Frankly, I cannot see how this argument "suggests the Corinthians were seeing in baptism not simply their union with Christ . . . [but] primarily the experience of one's own death and resurrection, so that one's own agonizing dying had been gotten over quickly and one is now already [!] in the rest of the blessed."

When we turn to a reconsideration of I Cor. 15, which contains Paul's criticism of the assertion by some Corinthian Christians that "there is no resurrection of the dead" (vs. 12), can this possibly be taken to imply that these men are persuaded that their own resurrection has already occurred? (1) What possible force can one find in the argument in vss. 12-19 on such an hypothesis? "If there be no resurrection, then Christ was not raised," or, "It follows also that those who have died in Christ are utterly lost" (vs. 18). (2) Moreover, is not Paul's mysterious reference to baptism for the dead (vs. 29) made all the more unintelligible on the supposition that the Corinthians already feel they have personally experienced resurrection? (3) Paul's argument from his own sufferings in the course of the apostolate appears almost incomprehensible: "If the dead are not raised to life, 'let us eat and drink, for tomorrow we die'" (vs. 32). (4) Finally, in vss. 33 ff. we appear to be given the principal reason for the Corinthian difficulty about the future glorious resurrection: they cannot imagine *how* it is to be accomplished. We are not given any indication that they think they have now experienced resurrection.

With regard to what Käsemann has aptly called Paul's "eschatological reservation," it must be admitted that this is always present, not only in Paul, but even in the Fourth Gospel, whose author inclines to insist more upon an eschatology which may be described as largely "realized" (John 3:18; 5:24; 12:31). The passage in 5:24 which Robinson has cited (". . . the hour is coming, and now is, when the dead will hear the voice of the Son of God, and those who hear will live") does indeed witness to the truth that the process of resurrection has already been begun in this life. Yet it seems clear that this expresses only one aspect of the Johannine description of the Christian *Heilsereignis*, which is completed by vss. 28-29: "Do not wonder at this; for the Hour *is coming* in which all who are in the grave *will hear* the voice of God's Son. And those who have done right *will rise* to life; those who have done wrong will rise to condemnation." This futurist eschatology is found elsewhere in the Fourth Gospel: "It is my Father's will that everyone who looks upon the Son and puts his faith in him shall possess eternal life; and I will raise him up on the last day" (John 6:40). The scene between Jesus and Martha in the story of the resurrection of Lazarus illustrates the author's awareness of the twofold aspect of Christian eschatology. To Martha's affirmation of faith (which Jesus does not contradict, but merely attempts to amplify), "I know that he will rise at the resurrection on the last day," Jesus replies, "I am the resurrection: he who believes in me, even if he die, shall live; and whoever lives and believes in me shall never die" (John 11:24-26).

Moreover, this same ambivalent character can also be discovered in Pauline eschatology, even if the Apostle does not perhaps emphasize its realized aspect as much as the Johannine writings. I believe that Käsemann is correct in finding the "eschatological reservation" in the baptismal passage in Rom. 6:3-8. Yet, as I have stated elsewhere,[2] the passage implies the Christian's participation *in some real sense,* in the resurrection of Christ. For the imperative in vs. 11 would appear to demand this: "So you likewise must consider yourselves dead with reference to sin, but alive with respect to God in Christ Jesus." It is this reality, or indicative, which founds the imperative expressed in vss. 12 ff.

Certainly it is a part of Paul's characteristic theological viewpoint to regard the resurrection process as already commenced in the Christian life here below. It is indeed true that this conception does not appear in what I at least regard as the earliest Pauline letters (I-II Thessalonians, Philippians). It is however found in passages in II Corinthians. It is expressed first on the psychological level: "Just as the sufferings of Christ pour over into us, so through Christ our consolation also flows over" (II Cor. 1:5). Paul does actually describe the Christian apostolate as a sharing in Christ's resurrection as well as in his death: "[We are] continually bearing the dying of Jesus in our body, in order that the life of Jesus also may be manifested in our body. For always we the living are being handed over to death for Jesus' sake, in order that Jesus' life also be manifested in our *mortal* flesh" (II Cor. 4:10-11). That Paul conceives the risen life of Jesus as affecting the Christian already in his present condition is not only indicated by the term "mortal flesh," employed here, but this has been asserted less ambiguously in an earlier statement in this same letter: "Yet all of us, while with unveiled face we reflect, as in a mirror, the glory of the Lord, are being transformed into the same image with ever-increasing glory, as by the Lord [who is] Spirit" (II Cor. 3:18). A passage in Galatians, which I believe to have been written about the same period, also draws attention to the Christian's present participation in the risen life of Christ: "And thus I live no longer my own life, but in me Christ lives. As regards my present life in the flesh, it is a life of faith I live in the Son of God, who loved me and handed himself over for my sake" (Gal. 2:20).

This same ambivalence is to be discovered also in certain other typically Pauline concepts which attempt to express these same realities. One of these is *huiothesia,* which in Gal. 4:5; Rom. 8:15 is regarded as the present possession of the Christian, but which in Rom. 8:23 is presented

[2] *Christ's Resurrection in Pauline Soteriology* (Rome: Pontificio Istituto Biblico, 1961), p. 185.

in terms of futurist eschatology. The same seems true of *apolytrōsis,* already bestowed on the Christian "in union with Christ Jesus" (I Cor. 1:30; Rom. 3:24), yet awaiting consummation in the future (Rom. 8: 23). The process of salvation, while always incomplete in this present existence (I Cor. 5:5; Rom. 5:9) is nonetheless inaugurated (I Cor. 1:18; 15:2; II Cor. 6:2) in the present era.

These somewhat sporadic reflections would seem to lead to the conclusion that one can hardly do justice to the Pauline and Johannine understanding of the resurrection in the kerygma, unless one takes cognizance of its effect upon the present status of the Christian as well as upon the future state of those who will experience salvation in its totality. As regards the statements in Col. 2:12-13 and Eph. 2:5-6, which Robinson regards as Deutero-Pauline, it is difficult to see them as gnostic in tendency. Are they not rather the attempt by a writer imbued with the Semitic mentality to assert the present possession by the Christian of certain realities already actualized by the death and resurrection of Christ? From the biblical point of view, salvation can scarcely be comprehended except in terms of its effect upon the whole man, even on the material side of his being. Accordingly, in order to describe what the Christian enjoys even in this life of the eschatological goods proclaimed in the kerygma, these authors—as indeed also the author of Revelation (20:4)—felt compelled to postulate a "first" resurrection.

II

I should like now to turn my attention to the question of Pauline citations of or allusions to the sayings of Jesus. In an article published a few years ago,[3] I attempted to assemble a collection of Pauline texts which appeared to depend upon the logia preserved in the common evangelical tradition. While a number of them do occur in I Corinthians, I was impressed by the fact that they seemed to be present throughout the Pauline corpus more consistently than is generally judged to be the case. Accordingly I should hesitate to assert that any significant conclusion could be drawn from the use of such sayings of the Lord in I Corinthians. I should like to draw your attention to some logia whose point Paul makes in his own language in Romans. "I know this (I have it on the

[3] "Pauline Allusions to the Sayings of Jesus," *CBQ,* XXIII (1961), 26-39.

word of the Lord Jesus): nothing is unclean of itself" (Rom. 14:14; cf. Matt. 15:11, 20; Mark 7:1 ff.). Paul's apostrophe of his Jewish contemporaries, "You are convinced you are a leader of the blind" (Rom. 2:19), is reminiscent of a phrase employed by Jesus (Matt. 15:14; 23:16, 24). The Pauline statement, "Christ is the fulfilment of the Law" (Rom. 10:4), recalls Matt. 5:17. The picture of creation as "suffering birthpangs" in preparation for the eschatological glory (Rom. 8:22) recalls Jesus' apocalyptic description of the ruin of Jerusalem (Matt. 24:9). The apostle's assertion that "love is the fulfilment of the law" (Rom. 13: 8-10) is a restatement of the "new commandment" recorded in the Fourth Gospel (John 13:34; 15:12, 17). Paul's "Bless those who persecute you. Bless them; do not curse them" (Rom. 12:14) echoes Luke 6:27-28, while his remarks on judging others (Rom. 2:1) recall the similar warning in the sermon on the mount (Matt. 7:1-2). Perhaps even the Pauline command, "Give to all men what is due them . . . taxes to whom taxes are due" (Rom. 13:7) may well be a repetition of the logion, "Give to the Emperor what belongs to the Emperor" (Matt. 22:21).

III

I should like to offer some remarks upon the nature of the kerygma itself, which have been inspired by Robinson's perceptive remarks in the earlier section of his paper. Surely one of the very fascinating questions in NT studies is the problem of the relation of the traditions regarding Jesus, both his "works" and his teaching, to the apostolic kerygma.

Perhaps the most striking feature of the attitudes evinced by all the NT authors towards these traditions is the very free way in which they employ them. The evangelists do not hesitate to set the logia of Jesus in quite new contexts, and thus give them a new or an extended meaning. They are no less free frequently in their handling of the narratives concerning the Master's public life, which they received in tradition. At the same time, they all display a superlative regard for these traditions concerning Christ. Paul displays the same attitude in an even more remarkable way. His letters bear witness to the fact that he was always conscious of being a *pneumatikos,* of possessing what he calls the *"nous Christou"* (I Cor. 2:16). He does not hesitate to command that his letter be read out to the assembled Thessalonian community "in the Lord's name" (I Thess: 5:27). He always appears to be aware that in carrying out his apostolic work he is furthering Christ's mission by adding to the teaching of the Lord. He can refer to the kerygma as "the Gospel of Christ" (Gal. 1:7), "the Gospel of God" (Rom. 1:2), or simply "my Gospel" (Rom. 2:16). This apostolic freedom and complete confidence reposes upon his unshakable conviction that "I too have the Spirit of God" (I Cor. 7:40). Paul appears at all times as a man endowed by the Spirit with authority and thus entitled to speak in his own name—and not as one who relied for his authority upon his mere recollection of what Jesus said or did.

The evangelists in their turn show their awareness of the inadequacy, for the kerygma, of mere recall; for they constantly bear witness to the fact that the words Jesus uttered to his disciples *during his earthly life* were frequently misunderstood, only imperfectly comprehended, indeed never grasped in their full significance even by the twelve. One of the principal weaknesses of the hypothesis set forth by Harald Riesenfeld in "The Gospel Tradition and Its Beginnings" [4] is, in my judgment, the fact that the authority of the Gospel record is made to depend upon the apostolic memory rather than upon the apostolic possession of the Spirit. The evidence of the NT urges the conclusion that the writers of the primitive church were never able to forget that they were dealing with a living tradition, rather than with a dead letter.

This consideration serves, I believe, to underscore Robinson's statement that, "Rather than the saving event simply being described as it happened, to some extent it happened as it was described. To this extent the saving event cannot be shelled out as a brute fact behind the language witnessing to it."

There is another aspect to the kerygma, not explicitly adverted to by Robinson, which also serves to remind us of the relationship of the kerygma to the historical situation. The proclamation of the Word is an historical event, which occurs in the midst of the worshiping community to which it is announced. Yet this historical happening merely subsumes the historical reality of the earlier events which form its content, viz. the "words and works" of Jesus himself. Of this, the words of Institution of the Lord's Supper are the most dramatic example which the NT contains.

[4] Published in pamphlet form by Mowbray and Co., London, 1957.

The recent *Instruction on the Historical Truth of the Gospels,*[5] issued by the Pontifical Biblical Commission on April 21, 1964, gives an illustration of the manner in which this process of subsumption of the kerygma passed through three successive stages. There is first of all the phase of Jesus' public ministry, then that of the creation of the apostolic preaching, finally that of the literary production of the written Gospels. As the document points out, what necessitates the continual reformulation of these traditions is principally the variation in the audience to which at each stage the kerygma was addressed. It is a truism that any audience always assists in a very real way in the formulation of any message addressed to it. Moreover, salvation history *de natura sua* is a continually growing reality, which evolves and re-presents itself with each new proclamation of the kerygma before each new audience. The historical reality of the original event persists through all its subsequent reformulations—a fact of paramount importance which cannot be ignored without running the risk of disrupting the continuum, the historico-kerygmatic tradition which constitutes the basis of Christian faith.

One final query must be added, which may serve as a conclusion to these observations. It concerns the nature of the "Signs Source" which the author of the Fourth Gospel, in the opinion of Robinson and many modern exegetes, employed in composing his book. If this hypothesis be accepted—and Robinson has provided us with a reasonable basis for accepting it—then the question must be raised concerning the theological reasons for the author's consistent and almost exclusive use of the term *sēmeion* to designate the miracles attributed to Jesus. The Synoptic tradition employed the word relatively rarely in this sense (Matt. 12: 38-39; 16:1, 4 and parallels; Luke 21:11, 25; 23:8). But the tradition recorded by the author of the Fourth Gospel insisted upon the symbolic or pedagogical meaning of Jesus' miracles. The important thing for Christian faith is the seeing of the "sign" in the bread (John 6:26). The encounter between Nicodemus and Jesus shows that the purpose of such "signs" is not merely the construction of a scholastic apologetic (John 3:2). It is rather to enable the Christian to see the Lord's Anointed and the Son of God in Jesus (John 20:21). Accordingly, I find it difficult to accept the view that "it is the very quantity of such miracle

[5] For the Latin text of this document with the official English tr., cf. *CBQ,* XXVI (1964), 299-312.

stories that produces faith" as the real opinion of the author of the "Signs Source." His insight and religious spirit is too sophisticated, theologically speaking. Whatever one may think of the "wooden redactional style" of the writer who employed such a source to compose the Fourth Gospel, he too is no theological *ingénue* but one of the great religious thinkers of the apostolic age.

FLOYD V. FILSON

RESPONSE TO JAMES M. ROBINSON'S "Kerygma and History in the New Testament"

Professor Robinson has written an instructive, stimulating, and provocative paper. His attempt to restructure the categories used in his assigned subject is legitimate. Such an attempt makes contact with certain current trends in NT study; it thus may throw new light on the subject; and the categories "kerygma" and "history" are not prominent or basic in NT terminology. The word history, we should note, is not a NT word at all. The word kerygma is not the usual NT word for the gospel message, although it does occur in one Q saying (Matt. 12:41; Luke 11:32), in two letters of Paul (Rom. 16:25, which quite possibly is an addition to the original letter of Paul, and I Cor. 1:21; 2:4; 15:14), and in two of the Pastoral Letters (II Tim. 4:17; Tit. 1:3), which probably are expanded letters of Paul.[1] The categories of history and kerygma Robinson proposes to replace by *Traditionsgeschichte* and hermeneutic. He does not mean that these two terms are the exact equivalents of the terms history and kerygma, but rather that in our present state of knowledge and concern these new terms will enable us better to grasp and state the content and concern of the NT.

Robinson is correct in saying that in the NT period the saving event to which the NT bears witness was continually restated. At times in recent decades the kerygma has been described as though it were a rather rigidly fixed proclamation, always presented in the same set pattern. It is more accurate to say that the kerygma did have a solid constant core—it spoke of the saving action of God in Jesus Christ to provide for erring men a redemption they could never win for themselves—but that there was a healthy variety in the way the early preachers stated that core. In other words, the varied form of witness to the saving event was a fact in the

[1] The verb *kērússō*, "preach," "proclaim," occurs much more frequently, being found thirty times in the Synoptic Gospels, eight times in Acts, eighteen times in nine letters of the Pauline corpus (two of the nine being Pastoral Letters), and once each in I Peter and Revelation.

NT period, and a similar variety is legitimate in our day, provided the "once for all" note of the NT kerygma is respected. The fact of process and restatement must respect the fact of basic identity.

The peel-off-the-husk-and-discover-the-kernel method of getting at the historical Jesus is rejected by Robinson. He rightly maintains that the saving event cannot thus be shelled out as a brute fact. It is doubtful, to say the least, whether it is possible to speak of any significant event without interpretation. Certainly the NT never tries to do so; it presents events as a blend of happening and meaning, evidently with the conviction that the two cannot be separated. When we ask what happened, the NT speaks not only of God's action but also of man's involvement and of the necessity of participation in order really to know what did happen. In other words, if the kerygma is true, what happened in Jesus made a claim on people, and no neutral presentation of his life and work gives a true translation of what happened. This in itself, however, does not validate in detail any specific reconstruction of the early stages of the kerygma.

One of the striking features of Robinson's paper is the reconstruction of the situation at Corinth when Paul was writing letters to the church there. We have more definite information about this church than about any other local church of the Apostolic Age except possibly Jerusalem. Such information comes to us from Paul, the founder and pioneer supervisor of the Corinthian church. In view of the extent and acknowledged authenticity of the material, it appears that if we avoid the assumption that what happened in Corinth was what happened in all the other churches of Paul's day, his dealings with Corinth may be the best place to begin a reconstruction of the Christian mission and message of the Apostolic Age.

Even more important, and probably the most important feature of Robinson's paper, is his fresh study of the interaction between the kerygma and the gospel tradition. The kerygma has usually been dealt with on the basis of The Acts and the Letters of Paul, with no real attempt to bring the material of the Synoptic Gospels into effective connection with the Apostolic preaching. Yet if the position taken by form criticism is true, that the gospel material, before it found permanent form in our Synoptic Gospels, was in constant use in the church's worship, teaching, controversies, and problem solving, then one of two things must be true: either (1) the gospel tradition was being preserved, used, and shaped in a teaching ministry that was parallel to but separate from the kerygma preaching; or (2) the early kerygma itself included at least some of such Synoptic material in its earliest form, and there was constant interaction between the evangelistic preaching and the transmission of the gospel tradition. It is essentially this latter position which Robinson assumes as a working hypothesis and explores fruitfully in the second main section of his paper, and in a somewhat different manner in the third main section. He finds parallels between Paul and Q, and notes the strain of wisdom tradition in both Q and I Corinthians. The conflict at Corinth thus becomes one part of the *Sitz im Leben* of the Q material. This means that the Q material was in prominent use in Pauline churches in the fifties of the first century, and this active use implies, as form criticism has really implied, that such Q material was in active use for years prior to the Corinthian Letters. And as Robinson also notes, with inferences that I cannot accept, considerable use of the miracle stories is implied at Corinth and elsewhere.

A careful consideration of Robinson's paper leads us to point up certain other questions or objections:

(1). The idea of continual restatement of the kerygma, as we have noted, is not in itself objectionable. A question may be raised, however, concerning the idea of progressive kerygmatization of the tradition. This need not mean that the church gradually developed a form of the kerygma that ignored the original historical content and lost from view the basic events of the gospel story. Robinson does not say that the process moved toward such a final result, and the writing, use, and ultimate canonization of the Synoptic Gospels show that the church did not permit such an outcome. But the reference to progressive kerygmatization may suggest that at the earliest stage of development the kerygma was not interlaced in a vital unity with its historical base in the original historical events. The words may suggest an essentially non-kerygmatic beginning, an inference which Robinson does not intend. Indeed, he notes that both Jesus' preaching and the Apostolic message were called kerygma, and that the transmission of the traditions concerning Jesus was a kind of kerygma. My concern here is simply to urge clear recognition of the fact that this kerygmatic note was present in an appropriate form in the message and ministry of Jesus and was likewise present from the start in the Apostolic preaching.

(2). Another point which needs clarification is the role of miracle stories in the Gospels of Mark and John. I would not say that Mark 1—13 is dominantly a collection of miracle stories; over half of the material of these chapters does not deal with miracles. Nor do I feel that such stories clash with the preresurrection situation. Robinson rightly emphasizes the importance, in Jesus and the church, of faith and of humble and active love, but there is no adequate evidence that this vital accent excluded a constructive place for the miracles in the kerygma and teaching of the church. The miracle stories were not presented merely as acts of compassion, nor were they regarded essentially as objective and indubitable proofs of God's working in Jesus; to people of faith they were signs of God's presence and power in and through Jesus, and so were clues to the coming already in a real though partial way of the kingdom of God. It does not seem that the writer of the Fourth Gospel was sharply critical and negative towards the miracles or "signs" of Jesus; otherwise it is hard to see how he could have made such a favorable reference to these signs in the climactic statement of his purpose which he presents in his gospel conclusion (John 20:30-31).

(3). More discussion is also needed concerning the relation of the passion and resurrection narratives to the preceding chapters in each Gospel. Robinson recalls with some favor the view of Martin Kähler, that the Gospels are passion narratives with extended introductions. This view underlines justifiably the prominent and climactic role of the passion narrative (and resurrection narrative) in all four of our Gospels. It also rightly notes that what precedes cannot be cut off from the passion and resurrection narrative without departing from the gospel writer's outlook and purpose. But it does not do justice to the blunt fact that Mark uses only three of the sixteen chapters to present the passion and resurrection account; Matthew uses only three of twenty-eight chapters; Luke, only three of twenty-four; the original John, only three of twenty. It also fails to do justice to the significance of the parables and the other teaching of Jesus; to the highly probable existence of Q; and to the large role which the Gospels give to the kingdom message of Jesus and to his active representation in his ministry of the claim and offer of God. When these points are taken into consideration, as Robinson does in others of his writings, Kähler's provocative description of a Gospel appears inadequate to represent the full scope of Jesus' ministry as the Synoptists conceived it.

(4). My final question is whether the paper says as much as can be said about the historical Jesus. Obviously one paper cannot deal with all aspects of the total problem, and the historical Jesus of Nazareth was not the focus of the paper which Robinson has presented. Indeed, it is no doubt part of his view that this quest will remain unfinished, and we others must agree that we do not expect to answer all of our own questions. What the paper seeks to do is to restructure the basic categories and on the basis of two trial runs indicate how such a restructuring opens the way of solid progress. It should also be noted clearly that Robinson is contending for the historical reality of Jesus of Nazareth in a way that will keep the kerygma from fading out into Docetism or myth; he is maintaining that when, in the light of the new historical methods and hermeneutic, we understand the message and impact of Jesus, we will see that there was a real basis in this historical person for the proclaimer to become the proclaimed, and that there was a real kinship between the passion and resurrection narrative and Jesus' ministry and message. I would add that the indirect approach taken in the paper in the two trial runs was fruitful and holds promise of further usefulness.

Part of what I want to suggest is that neither of the two categories of *Traditionsgeschichte* and hermeneutic speaks directly of Jesus of Nazareth; they both deal primarily with transmission and translation of the tradition. There is still a place for more direct grappling with the question of what Jesus said and did as he expressed his understanding of his existence. The purpose of such direct study is not to provide a chronology, a psychological understanding of Jesus, nor an objective proof of the claim that may be made for Jesus. It is rather to provide as definite a grasp as possible of what Jesus proclaimed in word and represented in life, and this cannot be done without dealing with specific sayings and events which throw light on his understanding of life. Without returning to the untenable presuppositions of the old quest of the historical Jesus, there is more that can be derived from the narrative material of the Gospels, and while any reconstruction of a narrative framework must be attempted with caution, it should be possible to sketch an admittedly very meager chronological framework.

When we have done our best along these lines, we will not have proved the truth of the kerygma. Literary and historical questions will leave us with problems we cannot decisively solve. But the new historiography and the recognition that we know Jesus of Nazareth through his place in the kerygma still leave a place for serious historical study, and this Robinson has fully recognized in his book entitled *Kerygma und Historischer Jesus.*[2]

It is a serious question whether the existentialist philosophy, which has considerable capacity to translate the kerygma into a form meaningful to modern man, will prove adequate to translate and transmit adequately the content and power of the kerygma, with its message of the sovereign and redeeming God's decisive action and gift to men. In any case, it must not blur the need to determine with the maximum probability what Jesus said and did in the first century as he undertook to bring his message and appeal home to men.

[2] This book, published in 1960, is a translation, revision, and expansion of his earlier English work entitled *A New Quest of the Historical Jesus* (1959).

5

JOHANNES
MUNCK*

Pauline Research Since Schweitzer

The Society of Biblical Literature has done me the great honor of inviting me to give the major address on Paul on this solemn occasion, and the title of my paper is defined as "Pauline Research Since Schweitzer." In this way surrounded by the august name of Albert Schweitzer and by my excellent colleagues, W. D. Davies and Helmut Koester, who are to speak on Pauline problems, I feel myself in an embarrassing situation. First of all, the book of Schweitzer which should mark the starting point of my remarks, *Geschichte der Paulinischen Forschung* . . . etc., 1911, in English: *Paul and His Interpreters* . . . etc., 1951, is only a review of Pauline research in Germany, as if there existed no other countries with Pauline research, no international research on Paul, where French and Anglo-Saxon, German and Scandinavian books were studied and discussed. Albert Schweitzer, who was born on the borderline between French and German culture, is only one of numerous examples. Many of the later reviews of Pauline research from Germany show the same opinion on Pauline research. With the better linguistic equipment of our modern German colleagues, they have read books from other countries, but this does not change the character of their research as a pure German investigation. So this is a fact in Pauline research as in most other parts of biblical scholarship. There is a German research and an international research.

Feeling the difficulty of my task I read with great relief what was

* Editor's Note: Professor Munck died on February 22, 1965, soon after returning to Denmark from the United States, where he had served as a guest professor in Princeton Theological Seminary. His widow, Dr. Elisabeth Munck, has generously given permission for the publication of his paper and has assisted with the proofreading.

written to me about it. I quote: "We hope that you will not get so stuck in the past two generations that you will not have time to take a look also into the probable future." And again in another letter, I quote: "Please feel that we have given you large liberty in the manner you choose for discharging the obligation you have assumed." Encouraged by these gracious remarks I plan here to speak of the problems and difficulties of Pauline research.

I

The first difficulty of Pauline research is the treatment of the Jesus-problem in the last forty or fifty years. What is needed for fruitful Pauline research is the work of placing the apostle in connection with Jesus, the twelve apostles and the church after his time. This cannot be done when scholars think there is no historical Jesus, no connection with the twelve apostles and with the first generations after Paul. The apostle can only be understood in the historical context of the past, his own time and the following decades. There is no short cut to be taken through philosophy or systematic theology which could bring anybody to an understanding of Paul without serious and unprejudiced historical investigation.

Now the temporary suspension of the problem of the historical Jesus has hindered Pauline research. If you make of the immediate past a dogmatic formula you are not able to understand the time following, that is: Paul and the whole of primitive Christianity. It is necessary, in my opinion, for international Pauline research to take up again all the problems of the historical Jesus. But it must be said very seriously that this must be done without the general aim of substituting for the Christ of the church a Jesus who is understandable for "modern man," which is a systematical theological and not a historical concern. On the contrary, what we shall try to find is a historical Jesus who can explain the Christ of the church, so that the historical connection between the man Jesus and the Christ, Son of God, in the belief of the church is understandable. And it is not our task to follow some of our predecessors in finding the explanation of this process in fraud by the apostles and the later church. Fraud is not a historical explanation, but only an expression of a different religious belief. And if some of the liberal colleagues have been or are inclined to be intolerant, it is our task to be historians and to give everybody an unprejudiced hearing, even the church.

We can in modern times speak about a very dogmatic treatment of the Jesus-problem; "dogmatic" means here substituting for the Christian understanding of Jesus any other religious, non-Christian opinion. This "historical" Jesus has had its consequences for NT studies. I think that you all know that outside the church generally Paul is a very unpopular person. In the literature and the general history of culture you can find many expressions of this unpopularity of his. I have the impression that this unpopularity is a sign that we have not misunderstood him completely. Paul was a Christian, a church Christian, a missionary, and an indefatigable preacher. No wonder that he must be unpopular outside the church in which he also may meet some censure. I remember from my own time a Danish pastor who was a personal enemy of Paul and who on his own initiative stopped reading the Epistle texts in the service which were written by Paul, and replaced them with texts from the OT.

Now it is different with Jesus. There is not only in his case the veneration for him which is understandable in countries which for centuries have been called Christian, but there is too an eagerness for having Jesus as one belonging to your own party and representing the same viewpoint as yourself. "Jesus was the first socialist," we have heard from workers of a former generation, and in our times we read with surprise that Jesus as a Galilean was blue-eyed and an Aryan. In this way it too often happens that Jesus belongs now to one side, now to the other. There could probably be no better proof that we have as yet not given a clear and decisive solution to the Jesus-problem. The reason is, as far as I can see, that the classical "historical" Jesus has had so blurred outlines and has been so mild and harmless that nobody could help respecting and venerating him. But the story of Jesus, not the mild teacher of ethical truth, but the man who was persecuted and crucified and after his death was worshiped by his disciples and persecuted by other men in his disciples, cannot be the basis of this unanimous veneration of all those who do not worship him. By a better understanding he ought, it seems, to have had the same fate as Paul, his disciple and his apostle.

II

In what in a stricter sense can be called modern Pauline research, the most notable difficulty has been that the old Tübingen school has not been radically rejected. Although the arguments for it have long since been recognized as absolutely valueless, many of the viewpoints of that school are still generally accepted. I think that I have proved this in my book, *Paul and the Salvation of Mankind.*[1] In dividing up primitive Christianity into Jewish Christianity on the one hand and Paul and Gentile Christianity on the other hand, it has been made nearly impossible to understand the early church in Palestine and Paul. If you want an example, I can tell you that in writing a book on Rom. 9—11 (*Christus and Israel* [2]) I found by my use of every commentary I could lay hand on, only two commentaries on Romans which mentioned that the problems treated by Paul in these chapters were to be found in the Gospels. Thus the different parts of the NT are like completely watertight compartments thanks to a school which no one believes to be of interest for our modern research, but whose points of view are used without the knowledge that they are being used.

This splitting up of the NT into watertight compartments has had another consequence. As there was no connection between the different parts, texts outside the NT were felt to be nearer and more important for NT studies than the other NT documents, the sources of early Christian religion. This trend, which was understandable and to be defended at the beginning of the so-called religio-historical school, can today only be regarded as terribly bad method. We certainly are to study the Nag-Hammadi texts and the Qumran manuscripts as well as the Mandaean literature, but our primary concern must be to read and study the NT as a whole which can explain itself much better than it can be explained by farfetched parallels which have their day, but will be forgotten tomorrow.

To try to find the relations between primitive Christianity to which Paul belongs, and the church in the later decades of the first century is an extremely difficult task, because the later NT writings and the early Christian literature are of different times and different countries in a church which is now expanding to many parts of the Roman empire. Most of this literature is of a sort of timelessness; you can move some of

[1] Tr. Frank Clarke from *Paulus und die Heilsgeschichte* (Copenhagen, 1954), London: SCM Press, 1959.

[2] *Christus und Israel. Eine Auslegung von Röm. 9—11* (Acta Jutlandica, Aarsskrift for Aarhus Universitet, XXVIII. 3, Teologisk Serie 7), Copenhagen: Ejnar Munksgaard, 1956. An English edition is in preparation.

these writings ten or twenty years up or down without feeling any embarrassment. And yet it is a most important task to try to find out how the history of the church in the post-apostolic age really marched. We cannot do like Rudolf Bultmann and put all these writings and their testimony in one chapter, covering one hundred years, as he did in his *Theology of the New Testament* (I, 1951) in the chapter called "The Kerygma of the Hellenistic Church aside from Paul." Seen from a historical point of view no Gentile Christianity could exist at the beginning of the history of the church. As later History of Missions has showed, there must go generations before a new characteristic Christianity can originate on the mission field. There can be many Gentile Christians in the sense of Gentiles who have become Christians, but not a Gentile Christianity as a special kind of Christianity.

But just as the connection between Jesus and the Judaism of his time is of the greatest importance for our understanding of the beginnings of Christianity so is the connection between the primitive Christianity and the later Christianity which we must do our utmost to perceive. If we cannot get a reasonable picture of this connection it is in many cases because our picture of primitive Christianity is wrong, more a construction of our modern ideas than a real historical fact.

III

What I have said here may need some comments. I have given a picture of NT research where old philosophical and systematic theological doctrines have furnished the arguments for so-called historical conceptions even in later times, and I will try to demonstrate that a little further. The first thing we ought to acknowledge is that such philosophical and systematic theological doctrines which are involved in NT studies of exegetical and historical character some day are abandoned; they are in their original field felt to be obsolete, and you will find them neither in the philosophical nor in the systematic theological discussions; often they are not to be found in the textbooks any longer. But these obsolete ideas—and that is extremely interesting—are still having a sort of afterlife in the NT discipline as the anonymous arguments for what is considered historical conceptions, believed to be based on historical arguments.

The philosophical doctrine behind the Tübingen school led Ferdinand

Christian Baur to find in the four so-called parties in the church of Corinth two parties representing Gentile Christianity and two representing Jewish Christianity. The main argument for the construction of early church history in the Tübingen school was the literary conception that all NT writings had been written in the first and second centuries expressing the original contrast between Jewish and Gentile Christianity. This contrast grew gradually weaker in the course of time, as the later NT writings show, so that primitive church history ended with a compromise between them in the form of the so-called Old Catholic Church.

When the scholars in the second half of the nineteenth century had proved that the dates of composition proposed by the scholars of the Tübingen school were wrong, the literary conceptions of the school were abandoned, but what we could call its historical conceptions went on living until our days, although the whole development of the first and the second century according to the Tübingen school now had to have taken place in the three decades between the death of Jesus and the death of Paul.

In our times we have seen how theological views have led scholars to create what they think are historical facts—I think that most of us would say: what they substitute for historical facts. The trend was in our time introduced by Martin Dibelius with respect to the Acts of the Apostles, he being of the opinion that in the case of Acts no tradition existed corresponding to the gospel tradition behind the gospels. Thus Luke does not in the Acts appear as a transmitter of tradition, but as an author, and for this reason one cannot pursue so-called "form historical" studies in the Acts, but only critical investigations of style. This trend in research on Acts, introduced by Dibelius, has culminated in Haenchen's commentary on Acts in the Meyer series. The aim of Haenchen's commentary is to explain Acts as a work of Luke the author, who deals with the material he has found in a high-handed way, or invents new tales which he tells for the edification of the congregation. But against Dibelius and Haenchen it must be said that the primitive church preached *on* the apostles, as the letters of Paul preach *on* himself, *on* the origin of his churches and their life and work, as the Norwegian scholar Jacob Jervell has so excellently proved.[3]

[3] "Zur Frage der Traditionsgrundlage der Apostelgeschichte," *Studia Theologica*, XVI (1962), 25-41.

Here again we have presumably historical points of view, built on another philosophy in Germany than that of Baur's from the first half of the 19th century, but giving the same effect. Again Acts is regarded as a piece of propaganda where the purpose distorts history or replaces it with free invention. The period in the nineteenth century and the beginning of the twentieth century where Acts was understood as history and Luke as a historian, and where many historical arguments for the reliability of Acts were produced, is forgotten. With a few theological ideas all the historical work on Acts has been set aside as non-existent.

This confusion between philosophical and systematic theological ideas and historical facts explains why the NT discipline is so conservative. The word "conservative" has for a long time been a name for certain viewpoints in contrast to "liberal" viewpoints. So if you, for example, meant that the Pastoral letters were written by Paul you were conservative, but if you did not think so you were liberal. This is not the meaning of the word "conservative" here. I use this word in the original sense, for conserving viewpoints from the older generations. To be "conservative" therefore after a generation or two of liberal theology means to conserve viewpoints from former liberal generations which now have lost their importance and in no way can count as progressive and broad-minded, and leading scholarship into new and fruitful ways. This liberal conservatism has in our days, I am sorry to say, sometimes shown intolerance, because its adherents have not always been able to understand new and shocking views which were not old-fashioned liberal, but have understood them as conservative conservatism, and with religious fervor they have fought against them. In this way our venerable NT discipline is in danger of ending as a conservatism, an orthodoxy of liberal origin, hindering any progress of the study of the NT and the origin of Christianity.

Personally I feel this danger as an immense threat against our scholarly work. I have met it for years. I remember in the twenties saying to a liberal professor: I should like to work on the parables of Jesus, and his answer: but all that Jülicher settled in the eighties. I think that this spirit is a general phenomenon in our time. It may be that today the books which count are not as old as Jülicher's, but these new books may only be new in date, not in content. They give the old conservative liberal views, and are accepted by those who do not seem to like to think new thoughts. We are, I fear, on the way to a sort of Byzantinism where we repeat the wisdom of the fathers, our liberal predecessors, but do not dare to try to be as wise as those fathers.

I think we ought to choose between following our liberal predecessors in their spirit or in their results. If we choose their spirit we must be courageous, open-minded and without fear, not only of the church, but also of our colleagues. If we choose to stick to their results we will, I imagine, have a free and easy life until we hear our students whispering: he is probably the last man believing in the Tübingen school. In choosing the spirit of courageous and free research I think that we honor most the liberal theologians of the period of liberal theology in the past, that important epoch of our scholarship. In not regarding the great liberal theologians as authorities, but taking up their work where they left it and doing our research in a new and fruitful way, we whom the orthodox liberal call conservative or neo-orthodox are the real heirs of the best of liberalism.

Very often what are called "the general opinion of scholars" or "the assured results of scholarship," what are now opposed to new and interesting points of view, have lost their value in the course of time. These old views have been repeated through generations, but not been taken up for new discussion and new demonstration. Their classical character is an immense danger for our discipline, for how can a new view ever sound as convincing as these other views which we have heard and repeated since our first years as theological students? We have seen that in other kinds of scholarship revolutionary changes have occurred; the classical physics has been given up and a new physics has been founded. Why should it not be possible for us to leave the classical NT doctrines, and start a new scholarship with conceptions proved by arguments in our own generation? Everything in our discipline ought to be taken up to new investigation, and only what we can accept in our generation should be able to survive.

As modern physics has had an enormous importance for our modern world, so would a modern NT scholarship have an enormous importance for our modern world. Every time has the right to its own interpretation of the Bible and thereby to its own preaching. I am here not thinking of "modern man," with whom far too many are concerned these days. The modern conception of "modern man" is in most cases combined with an interest for obsolete viewpoints. But I am thinking of the big, very often patient, but not very progressive people of the church in all countries. They meet the problems of our days and they want help to understand them and to cope with them. If we continue to solve the NT problems with obsolete solutions, or with answers based on philosophical ideas from the time of the fathers or grandfathers of contemporary church members, we are not able to help them with a preaching corresponding to this exegesis, as their problems and difficulties are of today, but our solutions are from a time which did not know these problems and difficulties. Not only as scholars is it our task to renew our scholarship, but for the church and its members it is of importance that we interpret the Bible for men and women of today, and thus not remain hindered by obsolete philosophical or theological doctrines. And we must never forget that the life of so-called modern man is very short; in less than thirty years modern man has become unmodern.

IV

Looking back on Pauline research in the last decades there is one trend which is generally accepted in international scholarship, namely, that Paul is a Jew, and that he must be understood on the background of Judaism and the OT. Here many different scholars agree; I only mention W. D. Davies, Munck, and Schoeps. I think that this is a very valuable change which one can only wish to be continued in future scholarship. In Germany, and mostly in the school of Bultmann, some have tried to return to a Hellenistic explanation of Paul, trying to find him connected with Gnostic ideas. This is one of those trends I spoke of, where scholars will explain some part of the NT not by other parts of the NT, but by religio-historical material from another time and another place.

On the contrary, what we need is the giving up of the last traces of the ideas of the Tübingen school and the placing of Paul where he belongs, in the midst of primitive Christianity. We will have to see him in his connection with the Palestinian apostles and their mission to Israel, and their recognition of him. Then we need to understand the Jesus tradition known by Paul and the Gentile Christians. And also to understand the general continuity and the very limited rupture between Jewish Christianity and its tradition, and those who will later become Gentile Christians. For Christianity had its origin in Judaism, and it is

Jesus who recreated Israel's religion in the form in which it became a religion of Gentiles all over the world. This development without parallel —a reform of Judaism, which became a religion for Gentiles—makes the origin of Christianity difficult to understand. In the beginning it was Jewish Christianity, but it developed into Gentile Christianity. The NT material shows us that Christianity was something new from the start, not covered by contemporary Judaism and its conception of Israel's religion, and that this new element, which is due to Jesus, is the cause of the later division between Jew and Jewish Christian, between Jew and Gentile Christian. According to the NT the development might have been different. It was the unbelief of the Jews that altered the course of Christianity. In its way, Christianity, you could say, gained the whole world, but it lost its connection with the Jewish people, God's own people. To Jesus, to primitive Jewish Christianity, and to Paul the first and essential thing was God's never forgotten election of Israel after the flesh.

As far as regards the Pauline theology, I think that our studies would improve extraordinarily if we brought the methods of what we call NT theology under investigation and sought appropriate revisions. In many cases our inability to find or to acknowledge new points of view depends on our old-fashioned methods and our traditional categories. It is very often true that we in the discipline of NT theology crossexamine the NT authors on the basis of a modern philosophy or a modern dogmatics. In many cases it is possible to get answers from the interrogated authors, but it is not clear if they really have ever thought of the subjects which we want them to talk about. And we do not get the slight differences of meaning which are so important in the NT, showing us how the first Christian generation tried to express its Semitic religion in Greek words and thoughts. And by not catching their words in their inner coherence, we fail to understand what they really said and wanted to say. There is here a difference between those scholars who want to know what the NT authors said *to us,* or probably we should say *to them,* and those scholars who grasp that this question can only be a later concern. Our first question must be about the words and the meaning of the NT authors and figures which cannot *a priori* be the same as our meaning today. If this distinction is overlooked, we will put some modern thoughts into the NT texts and get a sort of confirmation of these our own thoughts from the Bible, but not learn anything about what Christianity is from the beginning. This is not only a question of bad scholarship, but our NT scholarship should also serve the church by investigating the Bible without sticking to the tradition of the church, and here I think especially of the tradition of the church of today. There can be no scrutiny of the church of today and its tradition by the help of the Scripture, if we already know our results before we start our research. We must have the freedom to work and to understand, which is not alone the necessary condition of all scholarship, but at the same time the necessary condition through which we can serve the church of today. By our work the church is helped to go back to the beginning and find out if it really continues what was given in Jesus and the apostolic age, or has its starting point in a later theology or philosophy with a doubtful connection with the original revelation. And by this work any tradition of the church of today, be it a more traditional church doctrine or a philosophical interpretation of Christianity, is a hindrance for the freedom of scholarly work.

Coming from these more general viewpoints back to the discipline of NT theology and Pauline theology, it would be a healthy change if we tried to find and express the thoughts of the NT authors without the help of a modern dogmatics or a popular philosophy. In that case we should try to find the key to the life and work of the man whose thoughts we would investigate. In the case of Paul we would find that he was an apostle. We should then start to find out what he thought of his apostleship and the missionary work it involved, Israel and the Gentiles, or in other words the salvation of mankind. This would in a new way express a very much used formula: we should then ask questions about Paul's existence as an apostle, and about all the existential acts and thoughts which are the foundation of his life as an apostle. In that way we would be able to start with the essential and go on to the less important. We would know what was the center of his life and his thought, and what did not interest him so much as it does modern philosophers or writers of modern dogmatics. We should see Paul in his difference from us, and we would see ourselves in our difference from him, and in that way our understanding of Paul and, I hope, our learning from him, could take its beginning.

A last point in this short survey has not only importance for Pauline research but for all parts of the NT discipline. In modern times the OT discipline has in the Protestant faculties attained an exceptional position. Without any discussion going to the last questions of what theology is, the OT has been placed at the borderline of theology and there is much more freedom for OT scholars than for their NT colleagues. It is here not the question if we like this development or not, but I think that we in the NT ought to take advantage of the fact and learn from our OT colleagues. In their greater freedom they have developed many different historical methods and used them on their part of the Bible, methods which could be important for historical biblical scholarship as a whole. We have already taken up some of their methods and acquired results in that way. We can mention examples like form history and earlier source criticism, where they in the OT certainly had the advantage of founding their source criticism on a clear picture of the development of the OT religion, whereas we in the NT had and have much less distinct criteria to use for the sources behind the gospels.

If you have not seen this difference between us and the better position of the OT scholars I can give you an example. It is a thing which for many years has puzzled me. Namely, that in the NT discipline a prophecy of Jesus about, let us say, the destruction of Jerusalem must be a *vaticinium ex eventu,* a prophecy invented after the event. When Jerusalem had been destroyed these words were attributed to Jesus by the church. But in the OT discipline when a prophet has predicted the destruction of Jerusalem then our OT colleagues will say: as Jerusalem was destroyed the year so and so, this prophecy must have been spoken some years before.

In this paper I have only been able to give you some light on a few of the questions of Pauline research today. I think that in general this research is rich and varied. But the problem is if there will be a real discussion of the views which have been set forth in the last twenty years, or if the already mentioned liberal conservatism will hinder the, in my opinion, obvious progress which these new views could bring. Will there be any discussion or only a happy return to opinions of former days? The answer to this question I cannot give you, but it will depend very much upon you in this great country if we will go forward or we shall not get anywhere.

W. D. DAVIES

Paul and Judaism

The theme divides itself naturally into two parts with each of which we shall deal in turn.[1]

I

Judaism as the Background of Paul

In the first place, the theme can be made to refer to the background of Saul of Tarsus. To what world did he most belong? Out of what current or currents in Judaism did he emerge? It is to the changes in our understanding of Paul's Jewish background since Schweitzer that we turn first. These changes have been radical and enriching. They can be clarified in the light of two main assumptions that governed the work of Schweitzer both on the Gospels and on Paul.

The first of these assumptions was made by most scholars and informed most treatments of the background of the NT in Schweitzer's day. The assumption was that it is possible to make a clear distinction between what was Semitic or Palestinian Judaism and Hellenistic or Diaspora Judaism in the first century. On the basis of this distinction Schweitzer set Paul, who was dominated by Palestinian categories, over against John, who was dominated by Hellenistic ones.[2] On the other hand, the same assumption led Montefiore to interpret Paul as a Diaspora Jew, who, had he known the superior Judaism of Palestine, would never have embraced the gospel.[3] The dichotomy between Palestinian and Diaspora

[1] For surveys of Paulinism, see A. Schweitzer, *Paul and His Interpreters,* tr. W. Montgomery (London, 1912); B. Rigaux, "L'interprétation du paulinisme dans l'exégèse récente," *Litterature et Theologie Pauliniennes, Recherches Bibliques,* V (Bruges, 1960), 17-46; E. Earle Ellis, *Paul and His Recent Interpreters* (Grand Rapids, Michigan, 1961); Hans Joachim Schoeps, *Paulus: Die Theologie des Apostels im Lichte der jüdischen Religionsgeschichte* (Tübingen, 1959), pp. 1-42. On methodology, see Samuel Sandmel, "Judaism, Jesus and Paul: Some Problems of Method in Scholarly Research," in R. C. Beatty, J. P. Hyatt, and M. K. Spears, eds., *Vanderbilt Studies in the Humanities,* I (Nashville, 1951), pp. 220-50.

[2] See his *The Mysticism of Paul the Apostle,* tr. W. Montgomery (London, 1931).

[3] C. J. G. Montefiore, *Judaism and St. Paul* (London, 1914); the position is also represented by Joseph Klausner, *From Jesus to Paul,* tr. W. F. Stinespring (London,

Judaism made it possible to localize Paul conveniently, according to one's approach, either within or without Palestinian Judaism. This dichotomy, while not universal (Schürer had long voiced a caveat against it [4]), was widely accepted when Schweitzer wrote. Its vitality is still evident. It informs, for example, the program of the Society in its centennial meeting. Professor Koester and I have been assigned to deal with what are, subconsciously at least, presumed to be separate, perhaps watertight compartments, Hellenism and Judaism in their relation to Paul.

But it is precisely this sharp separation which so much work since Schweitzer has made increasingly impossible. Historical probability alone should have warned against it. Judaism for a long period before the first century had been open to Hellenizing forces of an aggressive kind. These forces impinged upon it both from within and from without the borders of Palestine. And what historical probability suggests has been confirmed from Jewish literary sources and archaeological discoveries. Rabbinic sources have been more and more revealed to reflect Hellenistic influences in both their vocabulary and ideology.[5] Conversely, Hellenistic sources have often betrayed the influence of Semitic concepts and even documents.[6] Daube [7] suggested, with much probability, that even the methods of rabbinic exegesis, which at first encounter seem so peculiarly Jewish, were inspired by Greek models: Aristotle begat Akiba. On the archaeological side, the evidence has been overwhelming that Judaism was open to and receptive of Hellenistic influences on all sides.[8] It is

---

1942); S. Sandmel, *A Jewish Understanding of the New Testament* (New York, 1956), pp. 37-51, *et alia.*

[4] E. Schürer, *The Jewish People in the Time of Jesus Christ,* tr. Sophia Taylor and Peter Christie (5 vols. and Index; Edinburgh, 1885); see Vol. I, Division II, pp. 29-50, (The 4th German ed. should be consulted.) For a brief survey of the problem, A. D. Nock, *Early Gentile Christianity and Its Hellenistic Background* (Harper Torchbook; New York, 1964), pp. ix-x and the whole introduction, pp. vii-xxi, including a bibliography.

[5] See my *Paul and Rabbinic Judaism* (2nd ed.; London, 1955), ch. I.

[6] See C. H. Dodd on the *Hermetica* in *The Bible and the Greeks* (London, 1935).

[7] *HUCA,* XXII (1949), 239 ff.; in *Festschrift Hans Lewald* (Basle, 1953), pp. 27 ff. on "Alexandrian Methods of Interpretation and the Rabbis." Cf. W. F. Albright, *From the Stone Age to Christianity* (Baltimore, 1946), pp. 274 f., 337, n. 26.

[8] See especially the monumental work of E. R. Goodenough, *Jewish Symbols in the Greco-Roman Period* (New York, 1953-65). (As an example of Hellenistic penetration, see Benjamin Mazar, "Excavations at the Oasis of Engedi," in *Archaeology,* XVI [1963], 99-107.) Goodenough postulates a widespread Hellenistic Judaism, represented particularly by Philo, which he sets over against rabbinic Judaism, which sought at first

not necessary to labor the obvious. The old dichotomy between Palestinian and Diaspora Hellenistic Judaism is no longer tenable. At this point American scholarship in particular deserves the greatest credit. The work of Morton Smith [9] and Liebermann [10] on documents deserves our grateful recognition. But, above all, the monumental works of E. R. Goodenough on Jewish symbols in the Greco-Roman world claim attention. It would be an impertinence to praise these works: their full significance for the study of Christian origins has still to be recognized.

The area in which Schweitzer particularly drew a contrast between Hellenistic and Semitic concepts was that of mysticism, which is closely related to *gnosis*. But since the publication of *The Mysticism of Paul the Apostle* (English translation, 1931) the understanding of so-called mystical elements in first-century Judaism has been largely transformed. The work of Gershom Scholem [11] in particular has compelled the recognition of mystical and proto-Gnostic currents within Palestinian Judaism, so that Schweitzer's confidence in drawing rigid distinctions between Pauline and Johannine forms of mysticism can no longer be justified. Here the Dead Sea Scrolls are highly significant: they con-

to control all Jewry. But it failed to do so. The Judaism of the rabbis did not become normative for all Jews. It would be impertinent to discuss Goodenough's work here; we may be permitted a few comments. First, we should go further than Goodenough in recognizing that first-century "legalistic" or Pharisaic Judaism was itself Hellenized, so that the gulf between Hellenism and Judaism of a rabbinic kind is not so sharp as he proposes. Secondly, whatever the variety of Judaism in the first century and subsequently (and this Goodenough and others have established beyond doubt) the historically significant force in first-century Judaism was the Pharisaic. And it was this force that the church, and especially Matthew, had to oppose. That the extent and depth of Pharisaic-rabbinic authority has been exaggerated, we may admit, but that it asserted itself we must also admit. For discussions of Goodenough's work, see the following: Morton Smith, "The Image of God: Notes on the Hellenization of Judaism, with Especial Reference to Goodenough's Work on Jewish Symbols," *BJRL,* XL (1958), 473-512; Cecil Roth, *Judaism,* III (1954), 129-35; *ibid.,* 179-82; S. S. Kayser, *Review of Religion,* XXI (1956), 54-60; A. D. Nock reviewed vols. I-IV and vols. V-VI in *Gnomon,* XXVII (1955), 558-72 and XXIX (1957), 524-33; E. J. Bickerman, *HTR,* LVIII (1965), on "Symbolism in the Dura Synagogue," 127 ff.

[9] Most conveniently in *Israel,* ed. M. Davis (New York, 1956), pp. 74 ff. on "Palestinian Judaism in the First Century."

[10] *Greek in Jewish Palestine* (New York, 1942); and an article, "How Much Greek in Jewish Palestine," in *Studies and Texts,* Vol. I: *Biblical and Other Studies,* ed. A. Altmann (Cambridge, 1963), pp. 123-41.

[11] G. G. Scholem, *Major Trends in Jewish Mysticism* (Jerusalem, 1941); *Jewish Gnosticism, Merkabah Mysticism, and Talmudic Tradition* (New York, 1960). See also his article on "Religious Authority and Mysticism," *Commentary,* (November, 1964), pp. 31 ff.

firmed the awareness which was already growing before their discovery that pre-Christian Judaism, although it does not reveal a fully developed Gnosticism, did emphasize *da'ath* and exhibit incipient tendencies towards later Gnosticism: they have made it luminously clear that much that has often been labeled Hellenistic may well have been Palestinian and Semitic.[12]

To sum up. While there is an unmistakable difference between figures such as Hillel and Philo, this difference must not be made absolute.[13] The lines between Hellenism and Judaism, by the first century, were very fluid. Consider how difficult it is to define what forces mold a figure such as President Lyndon Johnson. Is he a Southerner with a northern veneer, or is he a northern liberal who happens to have been born in the South, or is he a Southern Texan? To define what went into the making of a Paul is infinitely harder. In Paul Athens and Jerusalem are strangely mixed, not because he was a Tarsian (if Van Unnik be

[12] W. D. Davies, "'Knowledge' in the Dead Sea Scrolls and Matthew 11:25-30," in *Christian Origins and Judaism* (Philadelphia, 1962), pp. 119 ff.; Bo Reicke, "Traces of Gnosticism in the Dead Sea Scrolls?" *NTS,* I (1954), 137-41; K. G. Kuhn, "Die in Palästina gefundenen hebräischen Texte und das Neue Testament," *ZTK,* XLVII (1950), 192 ff.; Helmer Ringgren, *The Faith of Qumran* (Philadelphia, 1963), pp. 114 ff. On "Gnostic Themes in Rabbinic Cosmology," see A. Altmann in *Essays in Honour of J. H. Hertz* (London, 1942), pp. 19 ff. "The early stages of Tannaitic thought are already under the spell of Gnostic ideas" (p. 20). On Mysteries and Judaism, see A. D. Nock in *Mnemosune,* S. 4, V (1952), 190 ff.; R. E. Brown, "The Pre-Christian Semitic Concept of 'Mystery,'" *CBQ,* XX (1958), 417-33; see also W. C. van Unnik, *Die jüdische Komponente in der Entstehung der Gnosis, Vortrag im katholisch-philosophischen Seminar der Universität Frankfurt am Main, 4-2-1960,* pp. 65-82. On Gnosticism, see F. C. Burkitt, *The Church and Gnosis* (Cambridge, 1932); R. P. Casey on "Gnosis, Gnosticism and the New Testament," in *The Background of the New Testament and Its Eschatology: Studies in Honour of C. H. Dodd,* W. D. Davies and D. Daube, eds. (Cambridge, 1956), pp. 27 ff.; Hans Jonas, *The Gnostic Religion* (Boston, 1958); R. McL. Wilson, *The Gnostic Problem* (London, 1958); J. Dupont, *Gnosis* (Louvain, 1949); C. Colpe, *Die religionsgeschichtliche Schule* (Göttingen, 1961).

[13] See the suggestive statement of this in Richard N. Longenecker, *Paul, Apostle of Liberty* (New York, 1964), p. 28. The geographic span of Judaism must be given due weight and within this span variety. After the New York meetings, Professor Koester urged the importance of geographic differences. With this I fully agree; see, for example, *The Setting of the Sermon on the Mount* (Cambridge, 1964), appendix VII, "Galilean and Judaean Judaism," pp. 450 ff. I may be permitted to mention that I often warn beginning American students against thinking in an American—that is, in this context, a "continental" manner—about the world of the NT, a manner which tends to ignore the almost "infinite" variety which is possible in older cultures within a little space. I can recall a time, for example, when I could detect not only from what county certain of my fellow countrymen came merely by their use of idioms and accents, but from what valleys in their various counties.

right, Tarsus can have influenced him very little[14]), but because the Judaism within which he grew up, even in Jerusalem, was largely Hellenized, and the Hellenism he encountered in his travels largely Judaized.

But Schweitzer made a second assumption which had important implications for his own work and has colored most interpretations of Paul. Within Judaism itself he drew a sharp distinction between apocalyptic and Pharisaism and other aspects of Judaism. In his work *Von Reimarus zu Wrede* (English translation as *The Quest of the Historical Jesus*), Schweitzer insisted that Jesus is "simply the culminating manifestation of Jewish apocalyptic thought.[15] But this apocalyptic thought is to be utterly divorced from that of the Rabbis: it was the product of popular circles opposed to the learning of the Scribes. Rudolf Otto carried the matter further by connecting apocalyptic especially with Galilee from whose religious aberrations official Judaism had turned away.[16]

From this point of view Schweitzer was able to isolate Paul, as he had previously isolated Jesus, and place him in a purely eschatological context, divorced from Pharisaism and other first-century currents.

But this assumption of Schweitzer's has again been questioned and must now be most emphatically rejected. Studies and discoveries since Schweitzer's work have made it clear that apocalyptic and Pharisaism—differing as they did in emphases—were not alien to each other but often, if not always, enjoyed a congenial coexistence. Such a figure as Akiba alone should have warned us that this was the case, and now the Dead Sea Scrolls, which reveal a people fiercely dedicated to the Law and yet ardent in their eschatological hopes, have put the matter beyond any possible doubt.[17]

[14] *Tarsus or Jerusalem* (London, 1952); for a summary of this, see G. Ogg, *Scottish Journal of Theology,* VIII (1955), 94-97.

[15] *The Quest of the Historical Jesus* (London, 1910), pp. 365 ff.

[16] *The Kingdom of God and the Son of Man,* tr. F. V. Filson and B. L. Woolf (London, 1938), pp. 13 ff.

[17] See my *Christian Origins and Judaism,* on "Apocalyptic and Pharisaism," pp. 19-30; J. Bloch, *On the Apocalyptic in Judaism* (Philadelphia, 1953); E. Stauffer, *Die Theologie des Neuen Testaments* (4th ed.; Stuttgart, 1948), pp. 3 ff.; D. S. Russell, *The Method and Message of Jewish Apocalyptic, 200* B.C.-*400* A.D. (Philadelphia, 1964); for the penetration of Greek ideas into apocalyptic, see T. F. Glasson, *Greek Influence in Jewish Eschatology* (London, 1961).

But the dominance of Schweitzer in Pauline studies has been such that the old dichotomy between apocalyptic and Pharisaism upon which he insisted still invades this field. The approach to Paul along almost exclusively apocalyptic lines and the rigidity of Schweitzer's dogmatic Paul reemerges again and again. We note the two most recent significant, large-scale treatments of the apostle. Our late distinguished guest, Professor Johannes Munck, whose passing we all mourn, has forcefully, and with a disarming and insidious charm, done for Paul what Schweitzer did for Jesus—that is, placed him in an eschatological straitjacket or an eschatological isolation, even though we now realize that the pre-conditions for such an isolation did not exist.[18] With Schoeps we move forward, because, although he still emphasizes the eschatological framework of Paulinism chiefly in the manner of Schweitzer, he does insist that Rabbinism and other factors have to be exploited for the interpretation of Paul.[19] And his work forms a convenient bridge to the next section of this Pauline report. Before we go on to it, let us sum up the problem of Paul's background. What has happened since Schweitzer is that the simple picture of a normative Pharisaic Judaism standing over against apocalyptic and Hellenism has vanished. Its fast colors have become blurred and mixed. Judaism has emerged as more varied, changing, and complicated than Schweitzer could have appreciated. In particular, the Dead Sea Scrolls have triumphantly confirmed the suspicions of those who had already suspected Schweitzer's neat dichotomies.[20]

II

Judaism in the Theology of Paul

But let us move on to the second section of this report. Our subject has another aspect: it relates not only to Judaism, as his background, but to Paul's treatment of Judaism as a man "in Christ." How did the apostle interpret Judaism in the light of the gospel? In his great work *The Mysticism of Paul the Apostle,* true to his eschatological emphasis,

[18] See my critique of Munck in *Christian Origins and Judaism,* pp. 179-98, on "A New View of Paul—J. Munck *Paulus und die Heilsgeschichte,*" reprinted from *NTS,* II (1955), 60-72.

[19] See my review in *NTS,* X (1964), 295-305.

[20] The literature on the Scrolls and the NT is immense: to set the matter in perspective, see the volume edited by K. Stendahl, *The Scrolls and the New Testament* (New York, 1957) and articles by Herbert Braun, *ThR,* N. F., XXIX (1963), 142 ff., XXX (1964), 89 ff., "Qumran und das Neue Testament."

Schweitzer found the heart of Paul in a quasi-physical solidarity of the baptized believer with Christ. To support this view he appealed exclusively to the concept of the solidarity of the elect with the Messiah, a concept frequently found in apocalyptic sources. It is this that lies at the root of his interpretation of Paul in terms of a cosmic mysticism "in Christ." [21] This eschatological approach is Schweitzer's permanent contribution to Pauline studies and, as we saw, it has informed the work of all who followed him. To recognize the eschatological character of Jesus Christ in the full light of Jewish eschatological expectations and to pursue this insight with a ruthless logic has been the hallmark of Schweitzer's work and it has been immensely enriching.

But it has also raised many questions. Two are pertinent to this report.

First, in the light of Pauline eschatology and the cosmic mysticism "in Christ," which Schweitzer declared to be the heart of Paulinism, in what relation does Paulinism stand to Judaism? Before Schweitzer, Protestant scholarship, by and large, had given a clear answer to this question. Under the influence of Luther, it had found the heart of Paul and, indeed, of all the NT in justification by faith. And as long as this doctrine was regarded as the essence of Paulinism, in the last resort, the relation of Paul to Judaism could only be one of opposition or antithesis. But Schweitzer relegated justification by faith to a secondary position.[22] By insisting in a thoroughgoing way on the eschatological context and content of Paul's thought, he inevitably introduced a new perspective. He opened the way for the interpretation of Paul's understanding of Judaism in terms, not of opposition, but of fulfillment or finality. To root Paul seriously in Jewish eschatology, as did Schweitzer, was to remove the center of gravity of Paulinism from justification by faith to a cosmic act involving the destiny of the totality of nature and of man: it was to shift the essential direction of the Pauline salvation from being primarily the alleviation of the pangs of conscience (a term not found in the OT and borrowed in the NT from popular Hellenistic "philosophy") [23] to being the redirection of the cosmos. The Pauline concept of salvation included, but was not exhausted by, a new self-

[21] *The Mysticism of Paul the Apostle,* pp. 101 f.; *Paul and His Interpreters,* p. 225.

[22] *The Mysticism of Faul the Apostle,* p. 225. "The doctrine of righteousnessness by faith is therefore a subsidiary crater . . . ." See *Paul and Rabbinic Judaism,* 2nd ed., pp. 221 ff.

[23] See my article on "Conscience" in *IDB.*

understanding. Indeed, it has recently been urged by Käsemann [24] and Stendahl [25] that even the doctrine of justification by faith itself has to do, not so much with the individual conscience, as with the inclusion of Gentiles in the true Israel. What Käsemann and Stendahl affirm is, in my judgment, right; what they deny is not so altogether convincing. Did the inclusion of the Gentiles in "Israel" so shake the very "foundations" of Paul that his moral awareness was spurred into a new sensitivity, just as the current struggle for civil rights in this country has "awakened" many who previously "slept." [26] There are, in any case, many—perhaps they are the majority of scholars—who still find the essence of Paulinism in justification by faith, interpreted in terms of self-understanding. Bultmann has stated this position with moving brilliance in his treatment of Paul—surely the richest portion of his *Theology*. But it is significant that Bultmann, unlike Schweitzer, has emphasized Paul's affinities with the Hellenistic world, not with Judaism. The debate continues. But it was Schweitzer who radically reopened it, and in doing so he has, in the mind of some, helped to deliver us from Protestant and Western provincialism.

But this leads to the second question raised by Schweitzer's work. He enlarged our perspectives and delivered us from provincialisms, but did he also introduce into his interpretation of eschatology mechanical and even magical categories which deprive it of full moral seriousness? For example, does not baptism, the act whereby the believer already has participated in the cosmic redemption, become a magical rite for Schweitzer? [27] As Professor Louis Martyn suggested to me, Schweitzer's description of Paulinism is often reminiscent of the thought of those whom the Paul of the NT opposed, that is, those who felt that they had already been enriched and had already attained. The fact is that

[24] "Gottesgerichtigkeit bei Paulus," *ZTK*, LVIII (1961), 367-78.

[25] "The Apostle Paul and the Introspective Conscience of the West," *HTR*, LVI (1963), 199-215, reprinted in S. H. Miller and G. Ernest Wright, eds., *Ecumenical Dialogue at Harvard* (Cambridge, 1964), pp. 236-56. In our view, for Paul what was a crisis of eschatology became a crisis of conscience.

[26] On sociological influences on Paul, see Ernest Benz, "Das Paulus-Verständis in der morgenländischen und abendländischen Kirche," *Zeitschrift für Religions- und Geistesgeschichte*, IV (1951), 289-309.

[27] See *Paul and Rabbinic Judaism*, pp. 98 ff., where I quote V. Taylor, *Forgiveness and Reconciliation* (London, 1941), p. 138: "What is described by Schweitzer is not personal communion conditioned by faith, but a mode of being effected by eschatological rites."

Schweitzer's Paul is so exclusively eschatological that he cannot participate in the full richness of Judaism. Schweitzer so isolated apocalyptic from other currents in Judaism that he deprived Paul of much of his Jewish heritage, even while insisting on his Jewishness. The nemesis of Schweitzer's approach was that it became difficult for him to do justice to other than strictly eschatological aspects of the apostle's thought. For example, the whole Pharisaic dimension in Paul could be neglected. In my own work (*Paul and Rabbinic Judaism,* 1948; 2nd ed., 1955), I sought to do justice to elements in the apostle that are derived from Pharisaism. I ventured to suggest that the Paul revealed in the epistles was far more complicated than can be exhausted in purely eschatological categories. The Judaism which Schweitzer found fulfilled "in Christ" was an emasculated, apocalyptic Judaism, not the varied Judaism of Pharisaism, Qumran, and other currents. From the essential emphasis of Schweitzer there is no possibility of escape. But his emphasis must be related to aspects of Judaism which he ignored.[28] It is this process that is now going on—the exploitation of the fullness of Judaism, Hellenistic, Pharisaic, Essene (Qumran), Septuagintal and classically Hebraic, in the interests of a deeper understanding of Paulinism. In short, the rooting of Paul not only in apocalyptic but in the whole complex of Judaism as an integral part of the ancient Greco-Roman-oriental world is the way of advance beyond a Schweitzer, who in his rightful concern to emphasize the "strangeness" of primitive Christianity endangered its relations with the continuities of history. Recent scholarship is already revealing that the relation between Paul and Judaism cannot adequately be expressed in terms of the simple antitheses so long customary in Pauline scholarship. If Schweitzer rightly revolted against the "liberal" psychological concentration of the nineteenth-century scholars, the time is now ripe for a revolt against the "dogmatic" eschatological concentration of their twentieth-century successors.

[28] An interesting, forcefully argued example of this came to my notice after the above comment was communicated to the Society, in James Kallas, *The Significance of the Synoptic Miracles* (London, 1961), pp. 103 ff. His words apply *mutatis mutandis* to Paulinism.

HELMUT H. KOESTER

Paul and Hellenism

There is no doubt that the question of the Hellenistic background of Paul's thought and theology has become more and more of a puzzle, if not a conundrum. Hypotheses of Hellenistic parallels to Pauline thought, which were given high probability one generation ago, have become rather unpopular today. The discovery of new material to illuminate the Jewish background of the NT and, at the same time, a deplorable decay of students' knowledge of the Greek language have only served to enhance the process through which the Hellenistic background of Paul has been brought into ill repute. All this, however, is no more than the external sign of a more serious methodological crisis in scholarship, a crisis that concerns the question of the Jewish background as well. Thus, I want to discuss in this paper: the history-of-religions question, and the methodological impasse.

I

The history-of-religions question

With respect to the Greek philosophical tradition it is beyond question that Paul, in the style of his preaching and in the method of his arguing, is dependent upon the Cynic-Stoic diatribe.[1] On the whole, his rhetorical education is Greek, rather than that of a Jew from Palestine. But if Paul had any real knowledge of Greek philosophy, it certainly did not influence his theology materially, nor does he ever concern himself critically with any subject matter of the Greek philosophical tradition.[2]

With respect to a possible influence of Greek and Hellenistic religion upon Paul, in the recent history of Pauline research the following major hypotheses have been advanced:

[1] See Rudolf Bultmann, *Der Stil der paulinischen Predigt und die kynisch-stoische Diatribe* (FRLANT 13), Goettingen, 1910.

[2] Adolf Bonnhöffer, *Epiktet und das Neue Testament,* 1911; Max Pohlenz, "Paulus und die Stoa," *ZNW,* XLII (1949), 69-104; Werner Jaeger, *Early Christianity and Greek Paideia,* 1961, especially pp. 105 f.

1. As in the so-called mystery religions Paul understands salvation in terms of a participation in the fate of the cult deity. Thus, in the Christian sacrament of baptism, according to Paul's understanding (Rom. 6:1 ff), the Christian is initiated into his new faith by the experience of the fate of Christ, dying and rising with him into a new otherworldly existence.[3] To be sure, Paul himself seems to depart somewhat from the basic mystery religion model. The rising with Christ is expected to take place only in the eschatological future at the *parousia,* while the present is understood as the time in which the Spirit leads into a new ethical conduct as it is governed also by an ethical imperative. But this peculiar deviation only appears to underscore the existence of such an underlying pattern. A more serious criticism has been raised by questioning the assumed mystery religion model itself. Questions have been raised as to the form in which it existed and the method by which it could have been introduced into pre-Pauline Christianity.[4] It is not impossible that this presupposed model had long since been separated from its original environment and survived only as a widespread figure of speech. Consequently, whoever uses such a pattern cannot be understood as a student of the Greek mysteries. However, the occurrence of this and other mystery religion formulae in Paul's writings cannot be denied and calls for an explanation.

2. The question of the background and significance of the christological usage of the title "Kyrios" has led to the assumption of strong influences from the world of Hellenistic-Roman religion. The attempt, however, to relate this title, as well as other aspects of Paul's theology (such as the term "Gospel" and the title "Savior"), to the Roman Emperor cult,[5] has failed completely, simply because the Emperor cult did not have any serious religious implications throughout the first and second Christian centuries.

Another more persuasive hypothesis seeks to explain the Kyrios title

[3] Similarly such concepts as "transformation," the doctrine of the Spirit, and certain aspects of Pauline ethics are seen in parallelism to mystery religion patterns; see especially R. Reitzenstein, *Die hellenistischen Mysterienreligionen,* 3rd ed., 1927 (1956).

[4] A. D. Nock, *Early Gentile Christianity and Its Hellenistic Background,* 1964 (first published 1928), *passim;* G. Wagner, *Das religionsgeschichtliche Problem von Römer 6, 1—11,* (Abhandlungen zur Theol. d. A. u. N.T., 39), 1962.

[5] E. Lohmeyer, *Christuskult und Kaiserkult,* 1919; E. Stauffer, *Christ and the Caesars,* 1955; J. Schniewind, *Euangelion, Ursprung und erste Gestalt des Begriffs Evangelium,* 1927.

as analogous to the usage of the same title for the cult heroes in Hellenistic religion.[6] Yet it has become evident that Paul's usage, on the whole, has different roots: the use of Kyrios in the Septuagint and the earlier Christian designation of Jesus as the eschatological (not cultic) Kyrios —Maran. On the other hand, the "Hellenistic" thesis cannot be dismissed completely here, since this Jewish Christian background in itself shows various signs of a typical syncretistic development that is part of the Hellenistic world. Furthermore, Paul himself can on occasion use the title Kyrios in a way that is more closely akin to oriental and Hellenistic mysteries than to Septuagint usage, e.g. Phil. 2:8, and Paul's opponents in Corinth (see I Corinthians) apparently understood the title Kyrios with reference to the presence of Christ in the sacrament, i.e. in a non-eschatological fashion.

3. Influences from Hellenistic mysticism have been discovered primarily in the Pauline formula "in Christ." [7] This has become a most successful hypothesis. Unfortunately, there is very little in Paul's writings to support this assumption. In some cases the Greek *en* is to be translated by "through" (instrumentally), and otherwise, as especially R. Bultmann has shown,[8] "'in Christ,' far from being a formula for mystic union, is primarily an *ecclesiological* formula." [9] Consequently, this formula for Paul has social, ethical, and ecclesiological connotations rather than mystical implications. Two open questions, however, remain: a) Is there a pre-Pauline usage of the formula "in Christ" that signifies the mythical concept of a cosmic body of the redeemer? b) Are there any mystical tendencies among Paul's opponents, especially in II Corinthians? It seems to me that the answers to these two questions have to be in the affirmative to a certain degree. But, at the same time, we will not be confronted with a purely Hellenistic background in this matter. On the contrary, any attempt at an answer inevitably leads into certain aspects of the theology of Hellenistic Judaism—which in turn is not a purely "Jewish" phenomenon either, but a product of Hellenistic syncretism.

[6] W. Bousset, *Kyrios Christos*, 2nd ed., 1921.

[7] A. Deissmann, *Die neutestamentliche Formel "in Christo Jesu,"* 1892; *idem: Paul, a Study in Social and Religious History,* 1926 (tr. from the 2nd German ed. of 1925).

[8] R. Bultmann, *Theology of the New Testament,* Tr. Kendrick Grobel, I (1951), p. 311; cf. also pp. 327-29.

[9] *Ibid.*, p. 311.

4. Very widely discussed in the last decades has been the question of Gnostic motives in Paul's theology. Especially the studies of R. Bultmann and of some of his students have stressed the importance of this problem.[10] More recently this has led to the development of two equally absurd positions: on the one hand, to the claim of an almost exclusively Gnostic influence upon Paul and, even more so, on his opponents everywhere;[11] and on the other hand to the absolute denial of the existence of any Christian or pagan Gnosticism before Valentinus.[12] Two tasks seem to be most urgent here: (a) A new and careful definition of the phenomenon of Gnosticism. Such definition should avoid the clichés used heretofore on both sides of the issue, such as "Gnostic redeemer myth." To line up certain typical mythological concepts in a positivistic fashion can only obscure our understanding of the Gnostic religion. The criteria should rather result from an analysis of Gnostic self-understanding and religious world view, following the lines of Hans Jonas' studies of the phenomenon of Gnosticism.[13] (b) The suggestion that Gnosticism actually is of Jewish origin rather than of oriental or Hellenistic provenance has to be qualified. If there are close relations between Gnosticism on the one hand, and Jewish mysticism and wisdom theology on the other, it is necessary to determine and to localize with more precision the decisive turning point in the line that leads from such Jewish predecessors into Christian and pagan Gnosticism. The category "development" is certainly of little use, and it is questionable whether the supposed Jewish background provided the essentials for the emerging Gnostic religion. If allegorical interpretations of the first chapters of Genesis

[10] *Ibid.*, pp. 164-83; instead of giving a full bibliography here, I just want to mention as a representative work: E. Käsemann, *Leib und Leib Christi* (1933). A thorough discussion of the whole issue was presented by C. Colpe, *Die religionsgeschichtliche Schule* (1961). Decisive methodological directives came from H. Jonas' brilliant analysis of the Gnostic Religion in *Gnosis und spätantiker Geist,* I (1934).

[11] Out of the many works of W. Schmithals, who has been the most outspoken advocate of this view, I only refer here to his book *Die Gnosis in Korinth,* 1956, and his article "Zur Abfassung und ältesten Sammlung der paulinischen Hauptbriefe," *ZNW,* LI (1960), 225-45; for fuller bibliographical references see my article "ΓΝΩΜΑΙ ΔΙΑΦΟΡΟΙ," *HTR,* LVIII (1965), 279-318, espec. 283.

[12] R. M. Grant, *Gnosticism and Early Christianity,* 1959.

[13] See the reference in n. 10 above; the first part of the 2nd vol. was published in 1954; vol. 1 is now available in a 3rd rev. ed. 1964; these two German vols. are particularly important for the question of method. But see also Hans Jonas, *The Gnostic Religion,* 2nd ed., 1963.

have what can be called a "gnostic proclivity,"[14] this would not yet be enough to produce Gnosticism as long as such tendencies are controlled by the Jewish belief that God created world and men. Gnosticism apparently results only when such Jewish inheritance, in the process of Hellenization, is exposed to the fascination of a novel and original religious experience: that man is a foreigner in this world, that he is of divine origin, and that this world (and whoever created it) is inferior or even hostile to man's ultimate destiny. It is possible that this novel experience was dependent upon certain theological developments in Jewish thought, and that it also presupposes a considerable influence of Judaism upon the Greco-Roman world. But in its essence, Gnosticism is a typical phenomenon of Hellenism—both in spite of and because of its Jewish elements.

For the historical dating of the emergence of Gnosticism I would maintain that it cannot be dated later than Simon Magus, that it is a presupposition of Philo's philosophy, and that many aspects of Pauline theology (not to speak of Paul's opponents in I Corinthians) cannot be explained, unless we recognize that a considerable formation of Gnostic thought had already taken place before Paul.

As a result of this brief review, the most important task seems to be: to describe more precisely the major factors in the development of the religion of Hellenistic Judaism and Judaized Hellenism, such as Jewish apologetics, the theology of the Jewish mission and propaganda, the Hellenistic-Jewish wisdom movement, the formation of the religious and cultic life of the Synagogue as well as the development of schools of scriptural interpretation, especially outside of Palestine.[15] Another related point is equally important: it is necessary to abandon the unhistorical evaluation of the evidence from our sources, such as the mere lining up of parallels, motifs, myths, and themes. This procedure usually neglects the *Sitz im Leben* of such elements and overlooks the fact that they are part of the history of Hellenistic Judaism, a syncretistic religion; it, finally, obscures the character of religious language in a syncretistic environment. The essential desideratum is the interpretation

[14] James M. Robinson with reference to certain tendencies in the Synoptic sayings tradition, in "The Problem of History in Mark, Reconsidered," *Union Sem. Quarterly*, XX (1965), 135.

[15] Such a fresh approach was presented recently by D. Georgi, *Die Gegner des Paulus im 2. Korintherbrief*, 1964.

of the religious self–understanding in the particular historical setting, rather than the clever arrangement of history-of-religions parallels in a non-historical fashion.

This necessitates further discussion of the methodological impasse.

II

The methodological impasse

The various attempts to relate certain aspects of Paul's thought to a particular feature of his religious background usually tend to overemphasize one single element of his theology at the expense of others. This is the case with Bousset's thesis of the Kyrios-cult as the center of Paul's religion, Deissmann's emphasis upon the Christ mysticism as the place where Paul's religious heart really beats, and also the grand design of Albert Schweitzer who presents Paul as an apocalypticist, as well as Johannes Munck's recent hypothesis of the conversion-of-the-Gentiles theology as the core of Paul's thought. It is quite significant that all these fresh attempts in the interpretation of Paul's theology try to expel his doctrine of justification by faith from its commanding position. This has become so widespread that scholars are looking for a particular polemical situation in which Paul, prompted by opponents, was enticed to discuss theories so alien to his thought as those proposed in the epistle to the Romans.

Resulting from a similar confusion is the resignation which insists that Paul had no theological integrity, but was only inventing arguments *ad hoc* for particular purposes as it was demanded by each situation. Equally suspect, however, is the creation of a system of doctrines into which one could possibly fit harmoniously the diversified elements from various backgrounds as they occur in Paul's epistles (often including the Deutero-Pauline writings of the NT).

At the root of all this, I believe, is the uncertainty with respect to the history-of-religions question. What is evident here is the lack of historical understanding of the syncretistic character of the theology of Paul and of his environment. It is useful to recall the procedure which Paul follows in order to express his own point of view in an environment of syncretistic religious language. Adapting certain terms, concepts, and forms of speech—whether from his own tradition or from the theological vocabulary of his opponents—Paul alters and modifies these vehicles of religious language according to his own theological criteria. Thus, his own opinion is usually not present in the occurrence of a certain term or concept as such, but only in the specific modifications which Paul introduces in his own usage and which differ from the usage of his opponents. It is, for example, not relevant for Paul's own thought that the Jewish Law in his writings is interpreted in the dimensions of a cosmic validity (as elsewhere in Hellenistic Judaism). This feature is also found among Paul's opponents in Galatia. Paul's particular emphasis is upon the historical limitation of the Law, since it is fulfilled through Jesus' crucifixion. Or, the view that Jesus is present in the cult meal of the church as the Lord and as the supranatural medium of salvation, is not particularly Pauline. It is rather the concept of his Corinthian opponents, although Paul does not dispute this thesis of a sacramental theology as such; his emphasis, however, is evident in his insistence that, with the celebration of the Eucharist, the church proclaims the death of the Lord and his future coming which render impossible the present boasting over otherworldly possessions.

It is not the occurrence of such terms, concepts, myths, and theological doctrines, but only the movement of interpretation of such traditional language, together with the quest for the criteria and for the direction of Paul's interpretation, that will inform us about Paul's thought and about his understanding of Christian existence, even if he shares the theological terminology of his opponents. The task of our scholarship will be to devote ourselves to the most precise definition of the background of Paul's theological vocabulary in order to describe most precisely and most adequately *in our own words* the particular differences between Paul and his opponents, rather than to repeat in Paul's words his theological vocabulary (with parallels, of course) and thereby blur the important distinctions in Paul's theological controversies with his adversaries.

In fact, in all Pauline epistles, except Romans (and by all means Philemon), Paul's theological vocabulary is not that of his own theology, but is intimately related to the controversies with his opponents. They are in all cases exponents of various theologies which the early church developed (and Paul himself, to be sure, contributed to this development) in the religious environment of Hellenistic Judaism. In all instances, this Hellenism was a particular form of syncretistic development that Greek-speaking Judaism had undergone for many centuries, before it was absorbed in part by Christianity, rejected by rabbinic Judaism, and finally disappeared altogether—often leaving no more traces than the Qumran community before the year 1945.

That Paul shares the language of Judaized Greek mystery religions and the terminology and concepts of Hellenized Jewish wisdom theology does not, however, explain satisfactorily the origin and character of his theological vocabulary. There is one feature, which does not fit into this formula: in the discussions with his opponents, particularly in Philippians and in II Corinthians, Paul reveals peculiar elements of a theological vocabulary which seem to be of different provenance—the theology of justification by faith. Only once, in Galatians, this language is more closely related to a polemical situation. In this language, related to Paul's peculiar concept of justification, we are confronted directly with Paul's own and self-reliant theological terminology, since it is the center of his argument in the one and only case where he propounds his theology apart from a polemical situation, in Romans. At the same time, this epistle reveals how much Paul has learned for his theology from the controversies which he has fought out before.

This is relevant for our question, insofar as the language of Romans is much less Hellenistic, i.e. Jewish-Hellenistic, than the language of Paul's other epistles. Contrary to the further Hellenistic elaboration of Paul's theology by his students in Colossians and Ephesians (cf. also Ignatius of Antioch), Paul himself in his last letter [16] turns to a more traditionally Jewish structure of thought and argumentation when he tries to present his final and only systematic summary of his theological efforts.

But even if Qumran and the rabbinic literature provide us with more parallels to Romans than to any other Pauline epistle, it should not be forgotten that also such background is deeply influenced through the process of Hellenization. It would be a mistake, if one wanted to introduce at this point once again the misleading distinction between "Jewish" on the one hand and "Hellenistic" on the other. But there are different types of the syncretistic development of Judaism in the post-

[16] If Philippians and Philemon were written during an earlier Ephesian imprisonment and Colossians and Ephesians are un-Pauline, Romans would be Paul's last letter.

exilic period, and Paul's "own" theological language seems to be related more closely to Palestine than to theological developments in the diaspora. It is not possible to isolate Paul's theological vocabulary in Romans, since the roots of these final theological conclusions are to be sought in the thoroughly Hellenistic Jewish controversies of his earlier epistles. Also in this respect, Romans cannot be understood against the background of an ideally reconstructed Judaism that is uncontaminated by Hellenistic influences. As a whole, the epistle to the Romans, together with the other Pauline epistles, seeks to solve the problems of a church that arose out of the religion of Hellenistic Judaism, which was the environment of the Christian church after Stephen and after the foundation of the congregation at Antioch. The developments and the controversies in the various theologies of this truly "Hellenistic" Judeo-Christian community and the interpretation of the thoroughly Hellenistic religious self-understanding of its Jewish background provide the key to Paul's theology.

6

KRISTER
STENDAHL

Method in the Study of Biblical Theology

In its comprehensive coverage of our different disciplines, the program for this Hundredth General Meeting of our Society singles out the concern for method only twice: in the study of early Hebrew history and in the study of biblical theology. No one would deny that questions of method are as pertinent to the other areas covered. The more or less unconscious formulations indicate, nevertheless, that here are two areas where the present discussion has reached a point where an analysis and awareness of the methodological presuppositions and alternatives are a *sine qua progredi non possumus*. Such a concern for method makes us conscious of the fact that two major alternatives are hidden already in the genitive construction of our assigned title. Is biblical theology the object of the study so as to urge us to consider the methods called for by such an object of inquiry? Or are we concerned with a type of study which consists of the acts of doing theology, and if so, a special kind of theology which could claim to be biblical in some sense? Much depends on how one reacts to these alternatives or to what extent one accepts these alternatives as valid ones, or to what extent one attempts to apply methods which transcend these two alternatives. We are not unaware of the fact that answers in these areas are related to one's understanding of the theological enterprise at large.[1] We would, however, rather begin by giving attention to the adjectival component of the term biblical

[1] The student of the Bible and of early Christianity finds the ancient beginnings of "theology" especially interesting, see, e.g. F. Kattenbusch, "Die Entstehung einer christlichen Theologie. Zur Geschichte der Ausdrücke θεολογία, θεολογεῖν, θεολόγος," *ZTK,* XI (1930), 161-205 [Libellus 69, Wissensch. Buchges., 1962]; cf. also. W. Jaeger, *Theology of the Early Greek Philosophers* (1947).

theology. What is involved in speaking about a *biblical* theology?

There is no Bible without a community of faith, no "Old Testament" [2] without an Israel, no Old [3] and New Testament without the church. This is of course true in terms of the origins of these collections of writings, in most cases both individual books and sources, and in all cases the collections as we now know them. This is a historical truism, but a truism which is worth pondering from a theological point of view. Thus there would have been no Bible were it not for the communities of faith within which these documents came into being.

It is equally true that there would be no Bible now, were there not the communities of faith which today hail these collections as their Holy Scriptures. This is also a truism, but one which is even more overlooked than the historical one. There would be certain collections of more or less—sometimes really less—religious documents. In the case of the so-called OT these documents span a long period of history, and they can be studied as evidences of religious and social conditions in the time of their respective origins, or they can be studied as evidences for the attitudes of those who recognized the Torah, later with the Prophets, and even later with the Writings, as their Holy Scriptures. In the case of the NT we have by and large the earliest surviving literary remains of the nascent Christian movement; but that is not true in any absolute sense, since the First Epistle of Clement may well be older than the latest NT writings. Nor can we consider the NT the most clearly revelatory writings of that early period, since neither the book of Acts nor Paul's epistle to Philemon would in themselves raise such claims.[4] As a matter of fact, there is only one book of the NT which presents itself with an explicit revelatory claim, "The Revelation of Jesus Christ which God gave him (Jesus Christ) in order to show to his servants what must soon happen;

[2] On the canonization of the Jewish Scriptures see now J. P. Lewis, "What do we mean by Jabneh?" *JBR,* XXXII (1964), 125-32.

[3] It should be noted that the Christian churches carried out their own canonization, see A. C. Sundberg, *The Old Testament of the Early Church* (1964) [Harvard Theological Studies 20].

[4] There is, of course, something anachronistic in such a reference to "writings." The revelatory authority may express itself otherwise. We could point to two radically different elements here by mentioning on the one hand E. Käsemann's article "Sätze heiligen Rechtes im Neuen Testament," *NTS,* I (1954-55), 248-60 [=*Exegetische Versuche und Besinnungen,* II (1964), 69-82], and, on the other, B. Gerhardsson, *Memory and Manuscript* (1961); cf. also *idem, Tradition and Transmission in Early Christianity* (1964) [Coniectanea Neotestamentica 20].

and by sending his angel he indicated it beforehand to his servant John, who testified to the word of God and to the witness of Jesus Christ, all that he saw" (Rev. 1:1). Through what has been called higher criticism we are able to evaluate the biblical material in our use of the Bible as part of the legacy of early Christianity. In such a study there is no intrinsic difference between the canonical and the extracanonical. The gospel traditions which appear in a somewhat transformed shape in the Gospel of Thomas or in the Agrapha may point toward traditions which are as valid as those in the NT. For the student of early Christian history the limitation to the "biblical" is an act of textual laziness or a methodological sin.[5]

In short, there is no other principle to be found, which accounts for the choice and limitations of the Bible, than the actual fact of canonization.[6] He who says Bible says church.[7] He who says "my Bible" identifies himself with that church, which even today hails these writings as its Holy Scriptures. Any reference to biblical theology requires a clear awareness of this fact. Not only would there have been no Bible were it not for the church, there is no Bible now unless the claim of the church be recognized as to the authority of this specific collection of writings.

I

Considerations of this kind lead me to the conviction that in the study of biblical theology we must make a definite distinction between the

[5] On the Agrapha see Joachim Jeremias, *Unknown Sayings of Jesus* (1957), and H. Koester, "Die ausserkanonischen Herrenworte," *ZNW*, XLVIII (1957), 220-37. On the place of non-canonical material in the panorama of early Christianity, with special attention to the Gospel of Thomas, see H. Koester, "ΓΝΩΜΑΙ ΔΙΑΦΟΡΟΙ," *HTR*, LVIII (1965), pp. 279-318; cf. also below, n. 17.

[6] It is important to see this fact apart from the question of "inspiration." Everything canonical is "inspired," but much "inspired" is not canonical. See D. Stanley, "The Concept of Biblical Inspiration," *Proceedings of the Twelfth Annual Convention of the Catholic Theological Society of America* (1959), pp. 65-89; and Ellen Flessemann-van Leer, "Prinzipien der Sammlung und Ausscheidung bei der Bildung des Kanons," *ZTK*, LXI (1964), 404-20.

[7] Since my thinking naturally centers around the NT, I shall discuss the problem of biblical theology from the point of view of Christianity and the NT. In so doing I am nevertheless convinced that my argument is equally relevant to the Jewish tradition in its relation to its Scriptures. I would even claim that the question of the Christian interpretation of the OT is "only" a special and drastic form of the ongoing interpretation of the Scriptures which is a common phenomenon in all scripture-minded traditions. For that reason all our references to Bible (=OT+NT) and church, could apply to the Tanak and the Synagogue as well; cf. below, n. 14.

descriptive study of the actual theology and theologies to be found in the Bible, and any attempt at a normative and systematic theology which could be called "biblical." [8] We would have to make very clear that the descriptive task has no claim or intention toward the normative. This is of utmost importance, since anything called "biblical" has a tendency to participate in the authority assigned to the Bible in Christian churches. It is this problem of authority which confuses the distinction between the descriptive "what it meant" and the normative-systematic "what it means." It is this problem of authority which plays into the historical romanticism of much so-called biblical theology, when a Semitic way of thinking is dubbed "biblical" and when "Greek" or "Hellenistic" have become words with negative connotations.[9] It is the question of authority which contributes to a modern type of evolutionism in reverse, where the primitive is superior to the more reflected and developed.[10] The authority of the words of Jesus, the omniscient Son of God, and of the Holy Spirit speaking through the apostolic authors, has been transferred to the thought pattern and concepts of the early church. The authoritative and timeless Word of God lends its authority somehow to the *Sprachereignis,* the "word event," in early church history.

Were it not for this problem of authority and for a preoccupation with the normative, the situation would be rather simple, and the descriptive approach would be greatly clarified as a properly historical discipline. We would ask what a certain writer meant, what for example, Paul thought that he meant. We could go on to ask what his different readers

[8] For a fuller statement of the views which I defend and elaborate in this paper see my article "Biblical Theology, Contemporary" in *IDB,* I (1962), 418-32.

[9] It is, I think, a well founded uneasiness with this tendency in so much modern "biblical theology" which gives the spark and timeliness to James Barr's attack in *The Semantics of Biblical Language* (1961). His plea for the "translatability" of the biblical material tallies well with the sentiment of the early Christian centuries. The fathers had little concern for retaining the Semitic patterns of thought. The truth they saw and lived by was not confined to such biblicality. But if we recognize with them that the "Semitic" has no higher authority, then we may be more willing than is Barr to admit that interesting changes take place in the transfer from one linguistic framework to another.

[10] See R. M. Grant, "'Development' in Early Christian Doctrine: A Review Article," *Journal of Religion,* XXXIX (1959), 120-28; not least his references to O. Chadwick, *From Bossuet to Newman: The Idea of Doctrinal Development* (1957). It is in this context that the questions raised by Tillich (*Biblical Religion and the Search for Ultimate Reality* [1955]) should be considered, and much can be learned from J. Hessen, *Griechische oder biblische Theologie?* (1956).

understood him to mean. Thus the history of interpretation begins already within the study of the Bible itself. And the line between the reactions of the Corinthian recipients and that of later readers like Ignatius, the writer of *de Resurrectione*,[11] Origen, Theodore of Mopsuestia,[12] Augustine, Thomas Aquinas, Luther, Calvin, Barth, and Bultmann, would be a continuous line of interpretations, of "meanings." They would not yield answers to the question, "what does this statement of Paul's mean?" The question of meaning would always require a subject (for whom?) and a framework, a *Sitz im Leben* (when and in relation to what question or questions?). We would be constantly reminded of the fact that a community of faith and individuals in that community have listened to the words of Paul as an authoritative word, speaking to their own conditions. They are all—also the more contemporary ones—answers to the question what it means *to someone* who finds Paul worthy of authority in matters of faith and order. They are not answers to the normative question "what it means" in a timeless and absolute sense.

I think one can demonstrate how this same shadow of the authoritative and normative falls over the contemporary hermeneutical discussion when we use terms like *historisch* and *geschichtlich*. The fact that these terms cannot easily find their correspondence in English is in itself no reason for rejection, but it may well force us to think harder about what is really achieved by such a distinction. It is my suspicion that this pair of terms has come to function as a welcome device for an apologetic purpose, for the purpose forced upon biblical studies by the problem of authority and the normative.

If the *historische* Jesus is what is usually meant by "the historical Jesus," i.e. the picture we can reconstruct from sources of diverse kinds about when and where he was born, what he did and said, what he thought he was doing and meaning, and what happened to him, then the *geschichtliche* Jesus is what he became in the subsequent history, in the minds of his followers or in the antagonism of his opponents. In

[11] Ed. M. Malinine, H.-Ch. Puech, G. Quispel, and W. Till (1963). I single out this part of the Codex Jung since it demonstrates a distinct understanding of Paul as "the Apostle of the Resurrection"; cf. *Excerpta ex Theodoto* 23:2 (see the introduction to *de Resurrectione*, p. xiii).

[12] See now U. Wickert, *Studien zu den Pauluskommentaren Theodors von Mopsuestia*. Beiheft 27 z. *ZNW* (1962), and *idem*, "Die Persönlichkeit des Paulus in den Pauluskommentaren Theodors von Mopsuestia," *ZNW*, LIII (1962), 51-66.

this sense *Geschichte* is *Nach-Geschichte,* subsequent history. *Der geschichtliche Jesus* is the Jesus tradition as it came to play a meaningful role in the life of the church and in history at large. Both kinds of "history" can be studied by the same historical methods. We can observe this process of interpretation and response at work. In so doing we are dealing with historical data pure and simple, and not with any special kind of history, requiring a special method. I doubt that we need two words for "historical" in order to understand the *historische* Socrates as compared with the *geschichtliche* Socrates of the Platonic tradition, although it is clear that it is mainly the latter who influenced our culture. Or do we need two words for "history" in the study of the relation between the words and deeds of the historical Abraham Lincoln and the equally historical phenomenon of the image of Lincoln and its influence upon United States history?

It is supposedly a very significant insight that we have the "kerygma" in which and through which Jesus must be understood under the sign of *Geschichte,* not *Historie.* And we have heard and said for a long time that the Gospels do not lend themselves to become building blocks for an inner or outer biography of Jesus. These insights about the nature of our sources are valuable and should make us sensitive to the way in which we can use them for historical information other than the one they intend to give. But there is nothing new in this. Historians usually deal with tendentious or incidental material, and they try their best to control such tendencies and factors. It is true that the nature of the Gospel material raises serious obstacles for the investigation of the events and the dicta in the actual Jesus history in Galilee and Judea. Some of these obstacles are insurmountable and leave us in ignorance about things we would like to know. That impasse is a fact which the terms *historisch* and *geschichtlich* tend to transpose into a virtue, when they suggest that what really matters is *Geschichte,* i.e. the subsequent history of meaningful interpretations in the kerygma.

Thus this two-partite language becomes an apologetic device—I would say, a gimmick—called for by a faith which is related to the past —in this case to Jesus Christ, true man—in an organic tradition of ever ongoing interpretation. This linguistic convention, the *geschichte*-language, threatens to conceal this factor of subsequent interpretation in the church by juggling impressively with two words for history. It conceals the fact that the problem of the historical Jesus in such a discussion is a problem for the believing community or the believing reader of the Bible, not a historical problem. It conceals the fact that the continuum of subsequent interpretations can be studied by the same historical methods as apply to the study of the historical Jesus. The problem to which the *geschichte*-language speaks occurs first when one asks for an essential connection, which can contribute to the quest for the normative. It may well be that this method of relating faith to history has its merits. If so, they can only be evaluated and assessed within the disciplines of metaphysics or systematic theology. For they presuppose a specific theological stance, as do all attempts at answering the question "what it means" in an essential and normative manner.

II

It must sound to some as if we were exalting the glories of descriptive historical work and piling up nothing but suspicion against faith and theology.

To the extent that we give that impression, we are anxious to stress first that we are not thinking of the descriptive historian as a man capable of some kind of absolute objectivity. Such is not to be had. But much work done in the biblical fields indicates that we can achieve a common discourse among different kinds of believers and non-believers as long as we define the descriptive task clearly. The increasingly ecumenical nature of our deliberations in this Society and in our sister organizations, and of the journals in our field, witness clearly to this fact. This is —I am afraid—not so much due to a suddenly increased respect for scientific truth among so-called believers, nor—I trust—to a lack of serious convictions among the contemporary performers of our craft. It is because we have found it possible and profitable to distinguish the question "what it meant" from the question "what it means." It is a methodological device—some will call it a gimmick, and why not? The relative progress in the area of descriptive biblical theology depends upon a rigorous control of our presuppositions, also the presuppositions which such a method carries with it. We have to know exactly what we are doing and what we are not doing, lest we extend the significance of our results beyond the limits imposed by our method. We must know that we are doing something different from what theologians and preachers and believers have done before us. In describing the message of Paul or the kerygma of Hellenistic Christianity in Antioch, we are also doing something totally different than did Paul or those Christians in Antioch. They theologized, proclaimed, confessed, interpreted—we describe. We want to understand them; they "understood" God in Jesus Christ.[13]

This limitation of descriptive biblical theology must be imposed rigorously. We remember that everything called "biblical" easily becomes adorned by the authority of the Scriptures.[14] Now we must stress this fact in the interest of theology. And we want to show that the chief beneficiary of our argumentation is not "history" but "theology." The origin of the term biblical theology shows clearly that the church did quite well for seventeen centuries without that term.[15] Before the controversies between Orthodoxy and Pietism no one had had the idea to speak about such a special kind of theology. Neither Origen nor Luther, formidable biblical scholars as they were, thought they were doing bibli-

[13] These differences and the ensuing limitations of the descriptive task have been stressed by B. Childs, "Interpretation in Faith: The Theological Responsibility of an Old Testament Commentary," *Interpretation,* XVIII (1964), 432-49. The observation, however, leads Childs to think that the descriptive task cannot be seen as a "neutral" preparatory stage to exegesis. This, he says, destroys from the outset the possibility of genuine theological exegesis (p. 437). He gives three reasons: the text must be seen "as a witness beyond itself to the divine purpose of God" (p. 440); "the analogy between the two [OT and NT] is to be sought on the ontological [as over against a historical] level" (pp. 440 f.); and there must be "the movement from the level of the witness to the reality itself" (p. 444). I fail to see any of these reasons, which are useful formulations of the step from the descriptive to the normative and theological, capable of substantiating his main point, i.e. the fallacy in isolating the descriptive task. In that task we are *both* able to describe scriptural texts as aiming beyond themselves, as ontological and theological in their intention and in their function through the ages, *and* we are able to guard ourselves against having our description assume the normative role of defining "in advance the nature of biblical reality" (p. 439). Childs' discussion focuses on the relation between the Old and New Testament, an issue well covered in the recent collection edited by B. W. Anderson, *The Old Testament and Christian Faith: A Theological Discussion* (1963).

[14] It should be noted that this authoritative bent is not confined to "believers." Also in the secular setting of the humanities at our universities there is a lingering "King James Version piety," which has some striking similarities with that of the Sadducees in the times of Jesus. The Sadducees with their respect for the hallowed and unadulterated Scriptures of the fathers, stand out in sharp contrast to the Pharisees who were the progressives in their concern for innovation and for application of the Scriptures to radically new situations. Thus there is among the Pharisees a recognition of the necessary interplay between ancient meanings and now-meanings. On "Change and Adaptation in Judaism," see J. Goldin, *History of Religion,* IV (1965), 269-94.

[15] See G. Ebeling, "The Meaning of 'Biblical Theology'," *JTS,* VI (1955), 210-25; and O. Betz, "Biblical Theology, History of," *IDB,* I (1962), 432-37.

cal theology. They thought they were doing theology. Their theologies were informed by the Bible in certain specific ways, as other theologians were so informed in similar or different ways. But they never got the idea of a biblical theology as a special discipline over against some other kind of theology. I must confess that I think they were right, and I am convinced that a rigorous practice of descriptive biblical theology will lead us to a state of affairs in accordance with their correct instincts in this matter. The reasons for this are implicit in what we have said already. I would stress and explicate two of them as follows.

1) If biblical theology claimed to be more than a first chapter of a descriptive, non-normative historical theology, how would we understand the relation between such a biblical theology and systematic theology, what I would call theology proper? If we had a truly biblical theology which thought of itself as a viable contemporary theology, what else would we need? Or, we could ask, how are we to understand a systematic theology within the context of the Christian church which did not claim itself to be truly biblical, i.e. informed by and in accordance with the Scriptures? Our emphasis upon the descriptive limitation of biblical theology is designed to rescue the church from the arrogant imperialism of biblical theology. It is aimed at defending the freedom and the creativity of systematic theology as it expresses itself both in the more academic form of system building and reflection, and in the more familiar form of preaching and application to the multiformed contemporary issues of each and every member of the church.

It is true that we can speak of different kinds of theology in the sense of Thomist, or Lutheran, or Calvinist theology, but by such terms we do not mean a mere systematization of the thoughts of Thomas, or Luther, or Calvin. A Lutheran theologian is informed in a certain way by Luther, but he does not practice a contemporary "Lutheran theology" in one chapter, after which he proceeds to "theology" in the next. His theology *is* "Lutheran." It is important for us to see that in this sense *all* Christian theology *is* biblical in its intention. To be sure, there are different ways to understand the relation between Scripture and theology, and some theologies are more conscious of their relation to the Scriptures, but the assessment of that very relationship is a fundamental part of the enterprise of all systematic theology.

2) When we limit the term biblical theology to the descriptive, non-

normative task and consider it to be nothing more than a first chapter of historical theology, we must be aware of the fact that the term "first chapter" does not define the role of authority which the Scriptures may claim, or which has been claimed for them. Nor do we define the way in which this "first chapter" should stand as the Word of God over against the church. To be sure, in our work as descriptive biblical theologians, we have many opportunities to show how such features and claims are at work in these texts from the early times, and we can describe both the various understandings of the authority of the OT and the complex process of canonization of the NT. We can discern the authority of the Words of the Lord both in contrast to and in confluence with that of the Apostles, e.g. I Cor. 7:10, 12, and 40, etc., etc. This is part of the descriptive task. It is just part of sound historical awareness of the nature of our material always to have such functions in mind.

Nevertheless, we are anxious to leave the assessment of these matters to the systematic theologian, lest we abuse our unfair advantage of being more "biblical" in the eyes of the church. For it is, and it has always been, the task of theology to define these matters in the total context of the life and thought of the church. It should also be admitted amongst us here in our Society of Biblical Literature, that most of us have not the proper training in the disciplines of philosophy and theology which such a task calls for. Some may have it, but that does not invalidate the necessity of our distinction from a methodological point of view. We must protect the church against the imperialism implicit in our ability to read the Bible in the original.

III

Two or three generations ago the great word was "eschatology." Then it was by rightly using the word "kerygma" that we proved ourselves educated. Now it is "hermeneutics." [16] The rediscovery of eschatology could well stand as a symbol for the way in which descriptive biblical theology draws attention to material which has been suppressed or at least covered over in the process of continuous interpretation. "Kerygma" could well serve as a catchword for an increased awareness of the nature of biblical material and of the organic beginnings of

[16] While this word was not an entry in earlier editions, the 3rd ed. of *RGG* devotes 20 columns to the subject, III (1959), 242-62.

the theology of the church, as the first step in that very same continuous interpretation. And now "hermeneutics" is of primary importance since the content and nature of the biblical material call for a more conscious awareness of different senses of the word "meaning." The primary hermeneutical question is not "what it means," not even "what it meant" to men in the past. The primary hermeneutical question is "why assign any 'meaning' to these events or texts at all?" In that ultimate sense the hermeneutical question can only be answered within the community of faith, which recognizes these writings and these events as meaningful, as authoritative, as normative. In that sense the hermeneutical question is a theological question. In that sense the hermeneutical question is dependent on canonicity and the contemporary affirmation of the same. He who says Bible says church.[17]

It is within such a hermeneutical cycle that descriptive biblical theology can function as a power toward renewal of theology and preaching. Set free from the pressure to furnish contemporary interpretations with the claim to contemporary truth and relevancy, such a biblical theology heightens the impact of the Scriptures upon the life and thought and preaching of the church. It is actually nothing else than a purified and intensified form of that function which the Scriptures always have had in the life of the church. The question of the meaning of these Scriptures *hic et nunc,* the existential question of meaning, finds its answer in a theological act which should not be called "biblical,"

[17] It is obvious that many theologians have argued for a biblical theology which is not dependent on the canon in the sense of sixty-six books. It would perhaps be pedantic to say that such theologians should refrain from letting "the Bible" lend authority to their enterprise. And there remains the problem of the hierarchy of importance within the canonical books, not only in the balance between the OT and NT, but also within the NT itself. Nevertheless, this question leads us back to the distinction between a "biblical" (or a NT) theology and an early Christian theology which somehow participates in the "biblical" authority. A good illustration of this problem is the section on Ignatius in R. Bultmann's *New Testament Theology* (§ 58:3; cf. "Ignatius and Paul," in *Existence and Faith: Shorter Writings of Rudolf Bultmann,* ed. S. M. Ogden [1960], pp. 267-77). Here the thought of Ignatius is described in all its drastic difference from Pauline Christianity, which for Bultmann is the decisive standard for the best in NT theology. And yet the Apostolic Father becomes one of the truly significant witnesses for the same, and that for one specific reason. "Nevertheless, for Ignatius, the paradoxical presence of the future salvation is understood in a much more radical way than anywhere else, with the exception of Paul and John—namely, not as a new chance to achieve salvation, but as actually at work in the existence of the faithful" (*Existence and Faith,* p. 272).

although it is informed by the Scriptures. The informative and suggestive function of the Scriptures is best achieved when these Scriptures are liberated from the heavy layers of interpretations accumulated over the centuries.

Much of the enthusiasm engendered by biblical theology stems exactly from this suggestive function of a more or less conscious descriptive approach. It rescues the forgotten, it speaks up in a timely fashion for elements considered untimely in the contemporary theologies. An impressive example of this can be found in the recent writings of Ernst Käsemann, when he finds himself compelled to speak up for the apocalyptic and even for the positive dimensions of "Frühkatholizismus," while his own framework of now-meaning remains relatively unchanged.[18]

In times of radical questioning of what Christianity is about anyway,[19] the glories of the accumulated tradition shine less attractively, and the search for more original intentions and expressions may become more than museum pieces for nostalgic pilgrimages. What Christianity looked like in the first century is not only shocking but sometimes suggestive in its differences and diversities. Also for that inner theological reason

[18] "Die Anfänge christlicher Theologie," *ZTK*, LVII (1960), 162-85; and "Zum Thema der urchristlichen Apokalyptik," *ibid.*, LIX (1962), 257-84. Käsemann's presentations have been sharply criticized by G. Ebeling, *ibid.*, LVIII (1961), 227-44, by E. Fuchs, *ibid.*, 245-67, and now also by R. Bultmann, in *Apophoreta, Festschr. E. Haenchen,* Beiheft 30 z. *ZNW* (1964), pp. 64-69. This discussion is of significance since it demonstrates the pressure of the descriptive approach within Käsemann's own work. At the same time Jesus is somehow rescued into a limbo of uniqueness and the final outcome as to a now-meaning for the church and its preaching is strangely unaffected by Käsemann's emphasis on the apocalyptic. The same tension can be seen in his article "Paulus und der Frühkatholizismus," *ZTK,* LX (1963), 75-89, in which the thesis is that there is a positive and not only an antagonistic relation between Paul and "Frühkatholizismus." Nevertheless, in the final pages of the article, we are back to the traditional contrast between the decisive elements in Paul as over against the phenomena of *Frühkatholizismus,* the latter now used as a model for what is wrong also with Protestant Christianity. In short, the power of the descriptive approach manifests itself impressively even within a framework where the concern for now-meaning still asserts itself in the language of the theology which is in for criticism. It will be interesting to follow the future development of this drama. The three articles by Käsemann to which we have referred are reprinted in his *Exegetische Versuche und Besinnungen,* II (1964), 82-104, 105-30, and 239-52.

[19] There can be little doubt that such is the import of the Honest-to-God debate, but the question has been vexing theology ever since Barth. The impact of the descriptive approach to the Bible should be recognized both as a contributing factor and a potential source to creative new attempts at answering the questions which agitate theology today.

it is important to be well prepared by the careful studies of a descriptive biblical theology.

Its voice belongs nevertheless within the full hermeneutic circle. It is a voice in a dialogue, it is only one element in a teamwork. Even the more adequate description of Paul's thought about Jews and Gentiles or about the resurrection or about Wisdom and all the rest, is not to be equated with the Word of God for the church today. And even if one tries to find the inner core in Paul's words in what relates to existential human questions, both Augustine and Luther knew that their existence was different from Paul's. It was the awareness of the difference as well as of the similarity that gave them freedom to respond creatively when they interpreted the words of Paul as speaking to their own existence. In so doing they were not "biblical" theologians. They were "theologians" spanning the whole hermeneutical cycle. It is correct that we today find them treated and studied not in our field, but in other departments and disciplines. In our libraries their commentaries on the biblical books are shelved elsewhere than under "Bible." And it is no doubt correct when the same usually applies to great theological works such as Barth's treatise on Paul's Epistle to the Romans.

Or let us take a more secular example. There has been much consideration of the so-called Monroe Doctrine in relation to Castro's Cuba. Some argue that such a doctrine means that the Communists have no business in Cuba, while others would argue that the real intention of the doctrine was to protect young revolutions from the interference of well established major powers. This is a parallel and parable for hermeneutical purposes. First there is the question whether this doctrine has any "meaning" at all in the present. Then there is the descriptive task of what actually was meant by the Monroe Doctrine in its own setting. Then there is the question of what this may mean here and now—if one grants it such meaning—and that requires as much knowledge of the here and now, as it demands access to the result of the descriptive historical analysis. The point of this parable is only one—in an orthodox Jülicher fashion. The interplay between these three questions concerning "meaning" does not obviate, but necessitates the distinction which we have proposed.

Such an interplay takes place more or less unconsciously every time a Christian reads his Bible, every time a preacher delivers a sermon.

So much is here fused in one, that the church does not think of this only as an interplay but as something requiring the assistance of the Holy Spirit. But in the exacting task of theological scholarship there is wisdom in stressing the distinctions, and that for the reasons we have tried to give. Within that task we, the members of this Society, are fulfilling a limited role; a role which we fulfill whether we like our work to be so used by the church or not; whether we care for the church or not; whether we share its faith or not; a role which has theological meaning not by our attempts at being theologians, but by our faithful adherence to the canons of descriptive historical work.

AVERY DULLES, S.J.

RESPONSE TO KRISTER STENDAHL'S "Method in the Study of Biblical Theology"

With his usual freshness of approach and style, backed up by uncommon erudition, Professor Stendahl has given us an intriguing statement on the nature of biblical theology. In responding I speak not as a biblical theologian or exegete, but rather as one primarily engaged in dogmatics or systematics, or more accurately in "fundamental theology," which is a kind of mediating discipline.

Stendahl's analysis of biblical theology depends very much on his distinction between descriptive and normative theology, which he explains as corresponding respectively to "what it meant" and "what it means." This distinction appears to me to be a variant on the familiar German distinction between *Historie* and *Geschichte,* with which it shares much the same strengths and weaknesses. As applied to the Bible, he acknowledges both a descriptive approach, which seeks to unveil the past as past, and a normative approach, which deals with what we may paradoxically call—the phrase is mine—the past as present. So far as I know, Stendahl does not designate this normative approach by the term "biblical theology."

As regards method, Stendahl maintains that conventional scientific history is suitable for descriptive biblical theology, whereas normative theology, availing itself of ecclesiastical directives and suitable hermeneutical principles, must make the Bible speak to the contemporary situation.

In my capacity as commentator, I must express uneasiness at the radical separation which Stendahl makes between what the Bible meant and what it means. For the believing Jew or Christian, the question what the text meant, especially at the time when it came to be accepted as canonical, is not a harmless question of merely historical interest. What the text meant to the inspired author and as taken up in the inspired tradition, is still normative. While the church's understanding of Scripture is far from static, it is not so fluid that the meaning in biblical times has lost all binding force. If the original meaning is in any sense normative, the basis of Stendahl's dichotomy is seriously impaired.

It might seem as if, by giving normative value to what the Bible meant, I am denying the possibility of an "objective" or non-committed descriptive approach, and thus doing away with one of the most attractive features of Stendahl's position. To clarify my own position, I should like to appeal at this point to the three levels of biblical work described by Père Roland de Vaux in his talk to this group on Monday.[1] Biblical work, he said, can be done on the level of factual history, on that of the history of religions (*Religionsgeschichte*), or finally on the level of theology. The first two of these levels are "objective" in the sense that the Bible is treated like any other historical or religious literature of ancient times. This type of approach will be of primary importance in tracing the profane and religious history of the biblical peoples, including the history of their religious ideas. It corresponds closely, but not precisely, with what Stendahl would call the descriptive task of biblical theology. The main difference would be that for Père de Vaux religiously committed theology would concern itself with the original meaning of the Bible, and not simply with some modern adaptation.

On the level of objective scientific history, therefore, there are enormous possibilities of fruitful collaboration between Protestant and Catholic, Christian and Jew, believer and agnostic. Working side by side, they can correct each other's biases. The believer will no doubt have the advantage of greater empathy with the sacred writers, but he will also labor under the liability of tending to read back his own more developed faith into the minds of the pre-Christian and proto-Christian authors. The rigorous demands of historical method, which can be practiced by men of all shades of belief and disbelief, help one and all to enter more authentically into what Karl Barth has aptly termed "the strange new world of the Bible."

Stendahl takes the view that the objective, non-normative approach to the Bible is theology, i.e., descriptive biblical theology. De Vaux, however, seems to deny this, and I find myself preferring the latter position. Theology in its modern meaning usually signifies a discipline informed by faith. It is discourse about God and divine things from the

[1] See pp. 15-17 above.

point of view of revelation, accepted in faith. Personally I should deny that an agnostic could really be a theologian; but I am certain that he can do valid descriptive work on the Bible. This descriptive work, done without appeal to faith, is not theology properly so called, but belongs rather to the non-theological discipline traditionally known as the history of religions. The mere fact that there is theology in the Bible does not make the study of that theology—I am here using the objective genitive—itself theology. Perhaps one could say of such biblical study, as Fr. Bernard Lonergan has said of positive theology as a whole, that it is "theology in indirect discourse," i.e. not my theology but my understanding of the theology of another, such as the Deuteronomist, the Chronicler, Paul, or John.

If objectively descriptive work on the Bible derives its theological character from the fact that some of the biblical authors were theologians, we must raise the further question whether it is proper to use the term "biblical theology" in the singular. Would it not be better to say that there are biblical theologies which can be studied in the history of religions? Stendahl would no doubt answer that the Bible is not a miscellany of unrelated theologies, that there is a basic harmony or even an organic unity among them. But this implies only that a unified account or history of the biblical theologies is possible, not that there is a single biblical theology.

Let me now pass from the descriptive to the normative use of Scripture, as I myself would conceive it. In using the Bible normatively, the exegete or theologian seeks in it the word of God, not merely for us today but for men of every age. He takes it for granted that the Bible is a canonical set of books, permanently authoritative. He also presupposes that the teaching of the Bible does not contradict, but positively agrees with, that of the living church. He wishes to find in the Bible what he can and should accept as a believing Christian—to enrich, not to overthrow, the content of his faith. If any biblical passage seems to contradict what he knows to be true on other grounds, he will seek indications in the Bible that it is not really the teaching of Scripture. This religiously committed exegesis may appear dishonest to some, but I believe that a man should in all honesty seek a unified faith in which the apparent tensions between the Bible, the contemporary teaching of the church, and secular knowledge are brought into some kind of tolerable compatibility.

In admitting such a confessional biblical theology I might seem to be advocating a return to an unecumenical and tendentious type of biblical scholarship. But I should reject this charge. A religiously committed approach to Scripture would be unecumenical only on the supposition that ecumenism consists in nothing but a search for agreed texts, common translations, and non-denominational commentaries. While this search has its value, we ought not to ignore the importance of listening attentively to one another in the areas where our confessional patrimonies lead us to differ. Such a dialogue can help us to understand better that our own positions are not self-evident, and that the Bible, when viewed from other angles than our own, has dimensions we never suspected. In the long run such theologically responsible confrontation among exegetes of different traditions may do more to advance the cause of ecumenism than a tacit agreement on the part of all to put their confessional positions in parentheses.

Normative theology, then, is theology in direct discourse. It is the theologian's own effort to set forth the contents and implications of God's revelation, as he himself understands it within the tradition of the church to which he belongs. But can such normative theology be legitimately divided into distinct disciplines such as, in our context, biblical and systematic? Is there any room to insert a normative or confessional biblical theology between the history of religions on the one hand and systematic, or dogmatic, theology on the other?

After some vacillation, I have come to lean toward admitting the legitimacy of such a discipline. It differs from modern systematic theology insofar as, in biblical theology, the very principles of systematization are themselves drawn from, or at least suggested by, the Bible, rather than by church documents or by scholastic or modern philosophy.

In our century many theologians have become convinced that the rather static and abstract categories of standard Western philosophy are not apt vehicles for conveying what the Bible has to say. They therefore propose to synthesize its message with primary reliance upon terms and categories developed by the inspired theologians who composed the Bible. To be sure, the contemporary biblical theologian cannot fully clothe his own synthesis with biblical authority. He must take personal responsibility for selecting some biblical notions rather than others as his operative terms. One biblical theologian may construct a synthesis in terms of the word of God, a second in terms of the acts of God, a third in terms of election, covenant, etc. But each of these theologies will be in its way biblical. If the biblical terms are not simply repeated but investigated and reflected upon, this manner of constructing the biblical message, achieved totally within the situation of faith, can be a genuinely theological discipline.

There are a number of limitations and hazards in this type of biblical theology, and no one has pointed them out more clearly than Stendahl, who would apparently reject the whole enterprise as unsound.

There is a danger, for instance, that such theology will exert a kind of tyranny over all other types of systematization and will even brand them "unbiblical" and hence unfaithful to the word of God. Such a dismissal of patristic, scholastic, and modern forms of speculative theology would be wholly unjustified. The proper understanding and presentation of the faith requires that it be formulated not simply in biblical terms but also in other frames of reference, which may make it possible to discern new connections, coherences, and relevancies in the contents of the Bible itself.

A second danger, as Stendahl and James Barr have pointed out, is that the biblical theologian will fall victim to a kind of romanticism or primitivism, in which he canonizes the mythopoeic mode of thinking characteristic of the early Semitic peoples. Contemporary Western man cannot, except by an effort of imagination, think like an ancient Palestinian. The theologian, in particular, cannot be content to rest in the language of metaphor, even though it be inspired metaphor. He must strive to use precisely honed concepts and to define the content of revelation as exactly as the mysterious nature of the matter itself allows.

A third peril in biblical theology is that, under the guise of biblical thinking, it will surreptitiously introduce a heavy dose of contemporary philosophy. Karl Barth and Rudolf Bultmann have often been accused—with some justification—of finding too many of their own favorite philosophical ideas in the Bible. Any number of supposedly biblical theologies in our day are so heavily infected with contemporary personalist, existential, or historical thinking as to render their biblical basis highly suspect. This deficiency is the less tolerable when the author naively imagines himself to be repeating the unadulterated message of the Bible itself.

For reasons such as these we should be on our guard against too high an estimate of biblical theology. But I think that Stendahl goes to the other extreme by apparently denying that biblical theology, in this normative or confessional sense, has any legitimate place among the theological disciplines. I believe that one of the important tasks of theology is to meditate profoundly, in a spirit of faith, on the key words and central themes of the Bible, not simply in isolation from each other, but in their mutual connections, in such a way that a synthesis is achieved which is recognizably biblical in character. Through a more careful exploration and judicious use of the biblical notions of revelation, sin, redemption, and the like we can revitalize our contemporary theology and make it less inadequate to the awesome task of restating in human language the inexhaustible treasures of divine revelation. Would not our christology, for instance, be greatly enriched, as Cullmann has suggested, by a fuller appropriation of the biblical notion of the "Son of Man"?

I am not of course advocating a return to an exclusively biblical theology in the place of patristic, dogmatic, and systematic theology. On the contrary, I believe that all these types of theology are of value in helping us to assimilate in a human and rational way the word of God. Systematic theology has the advantage of being able to make the word of God more accessible and intelligible to reflective men of our day. But systematics is not without its own vocational hazards. Too often the systematizer succumbs to the temptation of reducing the word of God to what he can handle by means of his "clear and distinct ideas." The biblical categories, less clear and less distinct, are usually more dynamic and more suggestive of the deep mystery of God. Theology is at its best when systematic and biblical theologians work side by side, constantly criticizing, and profiting from, each other's work.

Because the biblical and the systematic theologian must listen to each other, it should be evident that they do not work in completely separate fields. In the last analysis, no theology is purely biblical or purely systematic. The biblicist, if he wishes to be a theologian at all, must become somewhat systematic. By his personal reflection and synthesis he inevitably modifies the meaning of the biblical terms he employs. And the dogmatician, conversely, cannot isolate himself within the castle of a closed system. If he wishes to be a truly Christian theologian, he must ever and again return to the Bible, to ask it questions and let it put its questions to him. In confronting the biblical word the systematic theologian will have to be something of a biblicist. Even his speculative categories will have to be inwardly transformed by the biblical message in order that they may better present it.

In summary, then, I may say that while there is indeed such a thing as biblical theology it is not rigorously, or specifically, distinct from systematics. The opposition between the two disciplines is polar rather than contradictory; they differ in degree rather than in kind. All theology is in a measure biblical, but some is more highly biblical and therefore deserves to be termed biblical *a parte potiori*. Theology in its completeness is an undivided whole, in which biblical and systematic elements are inextricably intertwined.

7
The First Christian Century

HANS G. CONZELMANN

As Christian History

I
Prolegomena

According to Acts 17:21, the Athenians spent their time telling or hearing something new. But when Paul came to Athens with "good news," some said: "What would this babbler say?"

Unlike Paul, the present speaker has neither new material nor a new topic. He has only some problems: Why do we speak at all about the "first Christian century"? Does this suggest a dividing line in real history? The difficulty of this concept becomes clear when we consider an important work such as Luke-Acts: When was it written? Does it belong to the first century? The same question concerns other important sources. The controlling concept must not be a matter of fixed time limit, but of a real transition in history. Now, we have no new sources. The only new texts, the texts of Qumran, shed some light upon the *backgrounds* of early Christianity, but not upon its *history*. And our well-known sources, Acts above all, are sharply criticized in modern research.[1] Is it—on the basis of this criticism—possible to form, not a picture, but at least a sketch of early Christian history?

Let us consider some steps of modern research. The Tübingen school

[1] J. Knox, *Marcion and the New Testament*, Chicago, 1942; J. Munck, *Paulus und die Heilsgeschichte*, Kopenhagen, 1954; E. Haenchen, *Die Apostelgeschichte* (in the Meyer series),[13] Göttingen, 1961; J. C. O'Neill, *The Theology of Acts in Its Historical Setting*, London, 1961.

understood the development of the church in terms of Hegelian philosophy, namely, as determined by thesis, antithesis, and synthesis, i.e. by the struggle between Jewish-Christian nomism and Gentile-Christian antinomism during the apostolic age, until a synthesis was worked out in the post-apostolic church. This picture of history is—partly unconsciously—in many minds till today. It is criticized especially by Johannes Munck. He states that modern scholars even read back the Tübingen hypothesis from the second into the first century, and that this is worse than the original Tübingen reconstruction. This criticism is substantially correct.

The Tübingen school was followed by the school of history of religions with its emphasis on eschatology on the one hand and Hellenistic mysticism on the other. The fundamental categories of description are no longer the dogmatic ones: law and freedom, etc., but they are historical: Jews and Greeks, apocalyptic and pneumatism, and so on. The understanding of history is on the one hand *sociological,* interested in the community, in analysis of the social and religious environment. It is on the other hand *psychological,* interested in the great personalities, especially in Paul and his inner experience. The result of this era of research is: Christianity is a product of various influences, a syncretistic religion. From the previous Tübingen epoch, the scholars of history of religions took over the idea of a synthesis of two early streams in the post-apostolic age: the result of this synthesis was a universalistic Christianity which was strongly influenced by the Judaism of the diaspora, more strongly even than by the original ideas of Jesus or Paul.

Of special interest is the research on Gnosticism during this epoch. The previous view was: Gnosticism is a heretical movement in the post-apostolic church. But now, Gnosticism has been discovered outside the church and within the church of the apostolic age, e.g., in the theology of Paul, of his disciples, and of the Fourth Gospel.

By such discoveries, a fundamental problem was stated: What was there that was *normative?* However, the historical school did not go on to deal with this question. It was interested in forms of piety, religious feeling, not in faith and dogmatics. Its program was to understand history as objectively as natural scientists understood nature. Was this an adequate understanding of history?

No, said the dialectical theologians. Christianity, as every phenomenon in history, is more than the product of external influences and internal feelings. It is a phenomenon in its own right and must be interpreted as *such* a phenomenon of its own. The dialectical theologians maintained that it was methodologically wrong to leave out of account theological factors and criteria, when it was obvious that the phenomenon being studied was inclusive of such factors. It is insufficient to describe Christian history as a history of influences, motifs, streams, etc. It has to be described as the history of the *church.* We cannot leave out of account the self-understanding of this community. And the core of its self-understanding is the conviction that they are God's people at the end of time, that its message concerns the salvation of mankind, and that it is possible to perceive the purposes of God only by faith.

Now the question is: What are the factors which are constitutive and normative for the existence of the Christian community? Is it possible to describe *in historical terms* its essence—both in history and in its self-consciousness?

If we ask this question, we are carried to a further problem: What was the historic function of the *creedal formulations* of the early church? [2] Is it possible to obtain through an analysis of these early formulae a better understanding of the first century as *Christian* history?

II
The Creedal Formulae in History

In many early Christian writings we find a fixed scheme of confessions of the faith, a type of formulae which one may characterize as definitions of "the faith," of what is faith in its essence. Now, it is important to see that these definitions are not, so to say, timeless. In the formulae, faith is understood as a relation to historical events: resurrection, appearances of the risen Lord, etc. The constitutive element of the "confessions" is not an abstract definition, but the historical content.[3] The formulae are not themselves "the faith," but they are the *confession* of faith and are the criteria to *understand* salvation and faith. An understanding of the *church* and its history is implicit in them. This can be shown by certain

[2] Such formulae can be found in nearly all NT documents. O. Cullmann, *The Earliest Christian Confessions,* Tr. J. K. S. Reid, London, 1949; J. N. D. Kelly, *Early Christian Creeds,* London, 1950.

[3] H. Köster, "Häretiker im Urchristentum als theologisches Problem," *Zeit und Geschichte (Festschrift R. Bultmann)*, Tübingen, 1964, pp. 61-76.

expansions and additions. A short type is: God raised Christ from the dead. An expanded type (found as pre-Pauline tradition in I Cor. 15:3–5) names not only the resurrection, but also the appearances of the risen one and the witnesses of this event: Peter and the twelve. Paul has added further witnesses: James, the apostles, more than five hundred brothers, and himself.

By naming the witnesses, the church points not only to an event in the past, but also to the consistent tradition of the salvific event, to the church itself as a factor of the *Heilsgeschichte.* Its self-consciousness is a historical one from the beginning. This can be demonstrated by the function of the formulae: In the formula, "God raised Christ from the dead," a specific idea of history is implicit. For, who is this "God"? The God of Israel, of a people and its history. It is not by chance that the central Jewish creedal formula is taken over by Christianity: "One God!" It is true that some scholars state that this One-God-formula is used only in the church of the Gentiles. But I think that J. N. D. Kelly in his book, *Early Christian Creeds* (London, 1950), pp. 25 ff., is right in insisting that the "One God" is used in the church as early as the christological formulae.

By observing this, we come to a clearer understanding of the *attitude of the church toward the Jews* not only through the first, but also through the second and later centuries. The external facts are well known to all of us and must not be repeated here: the events before and during the Jewish War A.D. 66–70, the disappearance of the Christian *Urgemeinde,* etc. Now we can observe an internal scheme of history: There are certain rules according to which these Jewish-Christian relations developed in the course of the first century: In the beginning, all Christians are Jews, and the discussions about the Christian faith are not discussions between two different religious groups, but between Israelites and Israelites, in the common framework given by Israel and the OT. Both groups, the Jews of the old and the Jews of the new faith (the latter ones sharing the convictions of the former ones), state that they are the true people of God, the true Israel.

But soon the style changes; the church is disappointed because the majority of the Jews refuse the Christian faith. The consequence is that the church more and more ceases to speak with the non-converted Israel: instead, it speaks with itself as the true Israel. A specific type of

Christian literature is concerned with this topic: Acts 7, Ephesians, Hebrews, Barnabas, and Justin Martyr. In these writings, a theoretical system on church and Judaism, on *Heilsgeschichte,* is worked out by means of the OT and the creedal formulae. Take for example Eph. 4:4-5. Here the basic formula is quoted and expanded. The starting point is: "One God." It is now set into the framework of the christological creed and of the idea of the church: "Eager to maintain the unity of the spirit in the bond of peace. There is one body and one spirit, just as you were called to the one hope that belongs to your call, one Lord, one faith, one baptism, *one God* and Father of us all, who is above all and through all and in all. But grace was given to each of us according to the measure of *Christ's* gift." [4]

It is exactly this common base, the use of Israel's tradition by the church that in later times provoked the terrible eruptions of Christians against the Jews. In the first century, however, the situation was a different one. There are the Christians who are the weak party and feel themselves persecuted (see I Thessalonians, Luke-Acts). The situation becomes more severe by the consequences of the Jewish War: in the course of the inner reconstruction of Judaism after the war, the Jews begin to ban the heretics (*minim*). We remember that W. D. Davies states that the Sermon on the Mount is a Jewish-Christian answer, a reaction against these Jewish proceedings: "Blessed are those who are persecuted," and "Pray for those who persecute you." [5]

However, the major work on this topic—church and Israel—was done outside Palestine. And the theory on *Heilsgeschichte* was a stronger factor for the attitude of the Christians against the Jews than historical events were. We can recognize some steps of development: the creedal formula is expanded according to the following scheme, which is, naturally, a scheme, not an exact historical sequence:

1) Christ died and was raised.

2) Jesus (or the Son of Man) must (suffer and) die (Mark 9:31 and parallels). The meaning of "must" is explained:

3) He died according to the definite plan of God (Acts 2:22-23).

[4] Heb. 6:1, etc.

[5] *The Setting of the Sermon on the Mount,* Cambridge, 1964; cf. A. Harr, *The Theme of Jewish Persecution of Christians in the Gospel According to Matthew,* Diss. Union Theol. Sem., 1963.

4) The key word "must" and its explanation point to the OT: "Thus it is written that the Christ should suffer and on the third day rise from the dead (Luke 24:46, cf. 24:26-27: "And beginning with Moses and all [!] the prophets, he interpreted to them in all [!] the Scriptures the things concerning himself").

5) This evidence from the Scriptures can be directed against the men who murdered Jesus: he died by the hands of lawless men (Acts 2:23). This topic is developed further in two different directions: the one points to a statement which is primarily *heilsgeschichtlich:*

6) Jews and Gentiles came together against him (Acts 4:23 ff. with explicit evidence from the Scriptures). The goal of this development is given by the reception of the name of Pilate into the Apostles' Creed.

7) But there is another tendency, a primarily polemical one: The Jews have murdered him. It is found as early as I Thess. 2:14-15 and elaborated in later writings, e.g. in Luke-Acts (especially in his rewriting of the passion story), or, in the second century, by Justin Martyr.[6]

We are all aware of the immense historical consequences of this charge against the Jews and the sufferings of the Jewish people caused by a perverted understanding of the creedal formulations. There is no excuse for the crimes Christians committed against Jews. We should see, however, that in the beginning the point of the formulations against the Jews was not charge but blessing, and that the formulae got their meaning by their framework—by the understanding of the church as the "little flock."

III

The Formulae in the Internal History of the Church

We come to another field where the formulae had a decisive function as a normative criterion: in the relations between Jewish and Gentile Christianity. I agree with the critics of the Tübingen school (e.g. J. Munck, see above): in the beginnings of the church there was no real nomism in it, although all its members were devout Jews. *Why* no nomism? Because Christian life and thinking was regulated by faith in a strict sense, i.e. not by feelings, but by normative definitions of faith.

[6] He addresses an "Apology" to the Romans, and publishes a "Dialogue" with a Jew (Trypho).

These are the constitutive elements not only of early Christian life, but also of theology. To be sure, the Christians continued living according to the customs of their people. But the Mosaic Law was no longer the basis of salvation, and therefore it was no longer the center of life and thinking. It was surpassed by faith and hope. So it was possible that Jewish-Christian circles grew up who abrogated the Mosaic Law: the Hellenists around Stephen are the one we know of by the report of Acts. But there must have been a wide spread of such movements beyond the boundaries of Palestine. For Paul struggled against Jewish-Christian communities in which the law was abrogated, as he indicates in Gal. 1. And now we must emphasize: the Lord encountered Paul when he persecuted free Jewish Christians (namely, free from the Mosaic law, at least in a certain degree). So the appearance of the Lord justified the abrogation of the law by Paul, in his missionary work as well as in his theology.

When Paul started on his work amongst the Gentiles, there were existing already mixed (Jewish-Christian and Gentile-Christian) communities, and it seems that there were no serious internal conflicts in their midst. And when a conflict grew up in Antioch, it was not very difficult to come to an agreement, at the famous Apostles' Council in Jerusalem (Gal. 2; Acts 15), a gentleman's agreement against some hotspurs.

One may object: but where is a creedal formula? It is not found in the reports on the Apostles' Council, neither in Galatians nor in Acts. Indeed, but we must remember: all the letters of Paul we possess are written after this council, and in all these letters the formulae are stated

a) as the principle of unity of the church;

b) as the basis of mission amongst the Gentiles; and

c) as a regulation of Christian thinking and of Christian life.

Evidence can be given by an analysis of every letter of Paul, e.g. Credo and unity, Rom. 1:3-4; Credo and mission, Rom. 3:30; Credo as a regulation of theology, Rom. 3:24-25; 4:25, etc.

There is another major field of function of the Credo: It is the criterion for discerning between *orthodoxy and heresy*. Walter Bauer[7] has shown that the concepts of orthodoxy and heresy do not fit with the

[7] *Rechtgläubigkeit und Ketzerei im ältesten Christentum,*[2] Tübingen, 1964.

facts of early church history. These concepts did not exist from the beginnings on; they were elaborated in lengthy internal crises. Helmut Köster is therefore right in asking for criteria which can explain the historical facts as well as the systematic phenomenon of orthodoxy and heresy.[8] Take as an example the sharp controversy between Paul and some circles in the community of Corinth. In spite of different positions there is a common base of argumentation: the creedal formula, as can be seen in I Cor. 15:3 ff. Some scholars explain the controversy in this way: the Corinthians were Gnostics or enthusiastic mystics; Paul states orthodoxy against enthusiastic heresy.

Such a view of the Corinthian discussion is neither a correct historical description of the facts nor a sound theological analysis of them. For Paul himself shares Gnostic or at least pre-Gnostic terms and ideas. On the other hand the Corinthians adhere to the orthodox Credo: there is no discussion between Paul and them about the validity of this formula. But they develop faith in the risen Lord further to an enthusiastic type of self-understanding, and this is the point of Paul's criticism. He reminds them, not that "The Lord is risen," but that "Christ died," and of the consequences of the cross for thinking and life.

We could continue by analyzing later documents where the Credo is the principle of sound theology, e.g. I John. But we continue by considering another point in the course of church history which should not be overlooked.

IV

The Problem of the Concept of an "Apostolic Age"

We can start from one certain result of modern research: there never was an epoch of the church and its history which was dominated by the apostles. There *were* apostles, but we do not even know what was the essence of the ministry of the apostles. All research in this field has come to the final result: *non liquet.* All we know with certainty is: the twelve and the apostles are *different* groups. There never were "twelve apostles." The "twelve apostles" are not a reality in history, but an idea that grew up toward the end of the first century. This idea is closely connected with a specific understanding of *tradition* and salvation history, a type of

[8] See n. 3.

understanding we can detect about A.D. 100, plus or minus about twenty years. In this epoch there were Christian writers who defined their own place in history in this way:

We are the *third generation,* namely, the third after the generation of the apostles, and after the generation of the disciples of the apostles. We are, so to say, the transition generation, at the transition from the apostolic age to the post-"apostolic" church.

It is a strange phenomenon that this should be the task of the third, not—as we would assume—of the *second* generation. The reason for this is that the "Apostolic Age" is not a reality but an idea—an idea exactly of this generation which looked back to the *Urzeit* of the church: the Twelve have now the function of guaranteeing the authenticity of the tradition which is being passed on. The "second generation" (of the disciples of the apostles) had—according to this later view—the task of collecting the writings and the teachings of the "apostles." "We"—the new generation—have to form the tradition for all further Christian generations.

The outstanding document of this state of mind is the prologue of the Third Gospel. But this type of understanding of history is implicit in many other documents, e.g. I John, Jude, II Peter, and the writings of the "Apostolic Fathers": Didache, I Clement, Ignatius, Polycarp, and Papias. It is found till the end of the second century, namely in Irenaeus. Irenaeus states that he—towards the end of the second century!—is the third link in the chain of tradition, which is handed over from John the theologian to Polycarp; and he, Irenaeus, when he was a child, listened to old, old Polycarp. It is clear: this is not a record of real handing over of tradition, but the statement of a consistent idea. Here we see the offspring of a picture of the early church which is in many minds till today. We may describe it by quoting a passage from Eusebius in which he professes to summarize the view of an earlier author, Hegesippus. This Hegesippus was a very bad historian, and Eusebius has reformed Hegesippus' picture of the church and its history into an impressive sketch of the primeval church and of the transitions to the "present time." While the passage is clearly later than the "third generation," we may quote it as a summary and result of it:

In the first epoch of its history, the church was "a pure and uncorrupt virgin. If there were any who tried to corrupt the sound doctrine of the preaching of salvation, they still hid in a dark hiding place. But when the sacred chorus of the apostles in various ways departed from life, as well as the generation of those who were deemed worthy to hear their inspired wisdom, then also the faction of godless error arose by the deceit of teachers of another doctrine. These, since none of the apostles survived, henceforth attempted shamelessly to preach their 'knowledge falsely so-called' [I Tim. 6:20] against the preaching of the truth." [9]

This is a picture, an idea, not historical reality. In history there was error in the church from its beginning. There never was such a sacred chorus. There was faith and weakness, there was God's message and men's error—there was: church in history.

[9] Quoted from R. M. Grant, *Second-Century Christianity*, London, 1957, p. 61.

MARTIN A.
COHEN

As Jewish History

It was in the first century A.D. that Judaism as we know it today began to emerge.[1]

An old man living in the year A.D. 110 could not help but marvel at the changes that had swept over the heritage of his fathers during the span of his own lifetime. When he was born, Judaism was still primarily a sacrificial cult; now it was a religion of prayer. Then the majestic temple in Jerusalem, built by Herod, was the cynosure of Jewish life; now each of the synagogues throughout the world was an autonomous center, united to the others by a common tradition and a readiness to listen to the teachers of the Holy Land. Then the official leaders of Judaism were priests, born to the purple and trained in biblical ritual; now they were rabbis, often of humble beginnings, nurtured on law and lore and the knowledge of life. Then Judaism was a tradition of conflicting movements; now uniformity loomed where diversity had prevailed. Then a struggle for control between universalists and nationalists still raged in Judaism; now the struggle was suspended, but its outcome was clear: Judaism would be a universal faith, a faith whose new attitudes, new forms and new philosophy, barely adumbrated in the early years of the first century, had developed to the point where they could be fixed and recorded for posterity.[2]

[1] These notes are intended to serve as a guide for the student of first-century Jewish history. The comprehensive nature of this paper precludes exhaustive notes or detailed consideration of the numerous problems involved in research on this period. The selected secondary works mentioned here will, however, delineate these problems and lead the reader to further bibliography. It is important to recognize the variety of a prioris these works contain, and the fact that a thorough and cautious investigation of most of the problems yields probability more often than certainty.

[2] The only comprehensive work dealing fully and exclusively with this subject on the basis of a thorough analysis of primary source material is Solomon Zeitlin, *The Rise and Fall of the Jewish State,* now in the process of composition and publication. To date only Vol. I has appeared (Philadelphia, 1962). Other works, like J. Derenbourg, *Essai sur l'histoire et la géographie de la Palestine* (Paris, 1867) and Max Radin, *The Jews Among the Greeks and Romans* (Philadelphia, 1915) continue to have value, though they have been superseded. Much valuable data on this period

The Setting and the Methodology

Our knowledge of first-century Jewish history is growing constantly both as the result of the discovery of new evidence and the development of improved methods for appraising the old. The documents are rich and varied. They range from the philosophy of Philo to the histories of Josephus; from the apocalypses of the Pseudepigrapha to the manuals and commentaries of the Dead Sea Scrolls; from the book of Acts and the early writings in the Gospels to the first creations of the fathers of the church. They include above all the treasures of early rabbinic literature, compiled in works like the Mishna, the Tosefta, the homiletical and legal commentaries known as the Midrash, and the early strata of the Talmud. Although these works were redacted much later than the first century, they throw a flood of light on Judaism's earlier foundations and on those of Christianity as well.[3]

Yet, despite the quantity of these sources—perhaps because of them—the first century has lent itself to a wide variety of often conflicting interpretations. This has been due primarily to two factors: the surprising silence or laconism of the sources in many critical areas, and the prevalence of theological prejudice over dispassionate analysis in much of the Jewish and Christian historiography of the period. Happily an increasing number of scholars are approaching this vital era with a suspension of their theological predilections and a recognition that the

---

can still be gleaned from Heinrich Graetz's classical *Geschichte der Juden* (1853-1870) and Simon Dubnow's methodologically superior *General History of the Jewish People,* published originally in Russian (1901), translated into Hebrew as *Divre Yeme Am Olam* (Vols. 2 and 3), by Barukh Karu. Indispensable for studies on this period is Salo W. Baron, *A Social and Religious History of the Jews* (Vol. II, part 2, New York, 1952), with a stupendous bibliography.

[3] Occasionally Jewish scholars discredit the authenticity of texts in the literature of the early rabbis reputed to date back to the first century (analogous to tendencies in Christianity to discredit early material in the Gospels). Such studies operate on the principle current in much of the historiography on this period in the late nineteenth and early twentieth century, e.g., Wellhausen, that historical events recorded in documents of late composition are suspect or worthless. On the other hand, traditional Jewish accounts of the *res gestae* of the leading teachers of the period tend to accept uncritically nearly everything that tradition says about them. Thus the classical work by Zechariah Frankel, *Darkhe Ha-Mishnah* (Leipzig, 1859; the edition of Tel Aviv, 1959 is excellent); Isaac Hirsch Weiss, *Der Dor ve-Dorshav* I and II (Vienna, 1871, 1876); and Isaac Halevy, *Dorot Ha-Rishonim* (Pressburg, 1897 and Frankfort, 1913), written at least in part as a protest against Weiss's work, with frequent examples of unscholarly originality.

elements now established and important in their respective traditions were often non-existent, dormant or emergent in the first century and must be studied in contexts radically different from their own. They recognize further that historical analysis eschews the arbitrary conjunction of discrete data but seeks the reconstruction of events through the application of the refined techniques of current historical and sociological disciplines. Above all they are approaching the documents of the first century as they approach other documents of the past, *sub specie humanitatis,* as the products of human beings, struggling with basic human problems, working through man-made institutions and expressing themselves through language and ideas socially developed and to a large extent socially determined.[4] The first century as Jewish *history* therefore involves a consideration of the relationship of social circumstance to spiritual achievement.

Fundamental to this understanding is the realization that the life context of our hypothetical elder was not identical with our own. However similar his emotions and problems were to ours, the institutions and doctrines through which he sought their satisfaction were fundamentally different. We divide human thought and action into categories such as social, political, and religious. These divisions were foreign to him. For him all of life was dominated by the ideology we call religion. For him all life was governed by the Pentateuch, the Torah; he regarded the Torah as the Law, perfect, unamendable and revealed by God to Moses on Sinai. Actually the Pentateuch had been canonized in the fifth century B.C.; but since that time it had served as the constitution of Jewish society, and Jewish leadership was empowered to enforce its legislation. The Torah provided the ideological basis for all Judaism in the first century, but what the Torah meant in A.D. 100 was something quite different from what it meant a century before.

[4] While, as many have pointed out, the application by scholars not trained in history, sociology, or cognate disciplines of primary principles in these fields can lead to distorted views of the period under consideration, the importance of these disciplines, properly applied, for an understanding of this period, should not be underestimated. This realization has been repeated frequently, most recently and very eloquently by T. W. Manson, "The Life of Jesus: Some Tendencies in Present-Day Research," in *The Background of the New Testament and Its Eschatology,* ed. W. D. Davies and D. Daube (Cambridge, Eng., 1964), pp. 211-21.

For our hypothetical elder the seminal event in the first century occurred four decades after the ministry of Jesus. In A.D. 70 the temple in Jerusalem was destroyed by the Roman armies, and the sacrificial cult and the primacy of the priesthood were ended. Rome was the catalyst of these events. Its destruction of the temple marked the end of one era in Judaism and the beginning of another, and its activity helped to shape them both.

The Pre-Destruction Era

1. *The Rule of Rome.* Thanks largely to Josephus, the history of Roman control in Judea in the pre-Destruction era is widely known. Rome had not come to Judea as a tyrant; yet a tyrant it became. It had begun by confirming the Jews in their individual and corporate privileges; it ended by sowing frustration, insecurity, and rebellion under its puppets, procurators and publicans. Its unaltered aim was to insure stability in the land which served as a vital link in its three-continent empire; its achievement was the creation of a restiveness that could not be pent. Each successive decade of the first century saw the flames of rebellion flare with increasing frequency and violence until in the year 66 they conjoined in full-scale warfare against Rome.[5]

Rome exercised a tight control over the political life of Judea. And though directly or through its puppets it told the High Priest when he could don his sacred vestments,[6] it interfered little in the Jews' internal life. As long as the Roman Empire controlled Judea, the Torah remained the constitution of the land. Perhaps as much as a decade before Rome's coming in 63 B.C., certainly not many decades thereafter, the authority to interpret the Torah passed from the priestly aristocracy known as the Sadducees to the popular movement called the Pharisees.

2. *The Leadership of the Pharisees.*[7] The origins of the Pharisees are

[5] The standard works for this history are of course, Josephus' histories, the standard Jewish histories mentioned in n. 2 above, Emil Schürer's *Geschichte des jüdischen Volkes im Zeitalter Jesu Christi,* 3 vols. (Leipzig, 1898-1901) and Joseph Klausner's *Historia Shel Ha-Bayit Ha-Sheni,* 5 vols. (Jerusalem, 1958).

[6] See *Antiquities* XX, 1.2.

[7] The Pharisees, mentioned infrequently in Josephus, the NT, the church fathers, and the literature of the early rabbis in puzzling and often contradictory contexts, have been the subject of numerous articles and several full length studies. Outstanding among the latter are R. Travers Herford, *The Pharisees* (London, 1924), Louis Finkelstein, *The Pharisees,* 2 vols. (Philadelphia, 1938, 3rd ed., Philadelphia, 1962), and

shrouded in obscurity. They emerge from legend only after the Maccabean Revolution of 168-165 B.C., and their early history is a continual struggle with the Sadducees for control of Jewish life. They appear to have surged into power on the crest of the revolution, to have been nearly crushed in the reigns of John Hyrcanus (135-104) and Alexander Jannai (103-76), and to have returned to predominance with Salome Alexandra (76-67). Regrettably, little is known about the activities of the Pharisees in the first century B.C.; the earliest reliable data concerning their institutions and ideas date from the end of this century and the beginning of the first century A.D.

The Pharisees and Sadducees differed primarily in their approach to the Torah-constitution. The Sadducees were strict constructionists, cleaving to the letter of the Written Law. The Pharisees were loose constructionists, insisting that the Law's letter be subordinated to its spirit. Since they could not amend the Law, they developed a system for its interpretation, which they called the Oral Tradition or the Oral Law. They claimed that the Oral Law had been revealed to Moses along with the written Torah, that it had been used to interpret the Torah in all previous generations, and that by virtue of their knowledge of the twofold Law—Oral and Written—they were the legitimate spokesmen for their tradition. In their interpretations the early Pharisees manifest liberalism and egalitarianism; their policy seems to have been the subordination of law to human needs: their "regard for the public," [8] as Josephus puts it, was uppermost in their minds. This, perhaps more than any other factor, won them the allegiance of the vast majority of the people.[9]

3. *The Cardinal Doctrines of the Oral Tradition.* Three cardinal doctrines of the Oral Tradition and their corollaries—all opposed vigorously by the Sadducees—played a vital role in the thought and activity of first century Jews. These were first, the MITZVAH SYSTEM; second, the WORLD TO COME; third, the RESURRECTION OF THE DEAD. All of these included old ideas blended with new in distinctive forms.[10]

Ellis Rivkin, *The Pharisees,* presently in the process of publication. Like the plethora of articles dealing with the Pharisees, these books differ on crucial issues.

[8] *Wars* II, 8.14.

[9] *Antiquities* XIII, 10.6; XVIII, 1.3.

[10] A treatment of these beliefs (covering the entire Talmudic period, but containing references to many of the early rabbis) can be found in Kaufmann Kohler, *Jewish*

According to the early rabbis, every man was obligated to fulfill the commandments of the twofold Law: these were the *mitzvot*. Later tradition counted six hundred and thirteen *mitzvot* which man was daily to heed.[11] In a sense the leaders of the Oral Tradition regarded the *mitzvot* as sacraments; as Jesus knew and believed, all of them, great or small, were to be performed with equal fervor, for, said the teachers of the tradition, "You do not know what reward the performance of the *mitzvot* will bring." [12] The reward—or in case of default, the punishment—was to be meted out not on earth, but in an afterlife of the soul in a world to come (the *'olam ha-ba'*). The Pharisees had conceived the world to come as an answer to the problems of theodicy which the Pentateuch and the Sadducees had left unsolved, especially for the underprivileged. In addition, the Pharisees promised that the righteous—those with a high tally of *mitzvot* on the heavenly slate—would be favored with bodily resurrection at the end of days.

The goal of this system of thought was thus redemptive and eschatological, though we cannot ascertain what beliefs the Pharisees of the pre-Destruction era held concerning the end of days. The term "kingdom of heaven," so prominent in rabbinic literature, seems clearly to have formed part of their conceptual frame,[13] but how the Oral Tradition related to the messianic ideas that had been developing in Judea for several centuries cannot be determined. One thing seems certain: whatever the relationship, the position of the Pharisaic leadership prior to A.D. 70 precluded its emphasizing messianic ideals.

4. *The Divisions and Sects Among First-Century Jews.* The twofold Law was essentially an ideology for stable times, and the Pharisees and many of their followers enjoyed a stable life in the early decades of the first century. Entrusted with the Law, showered with prerogatives and privileged in taxation, the leadership of the Pharisees evolved into a powerful scholar-elite. Removed socially and intellectually from increas-

---

Theology (New York, 1918), Solomon Schechter, *Some Aspects of Rabbinic Theology* (New York, 1909), and articles on these subjects in *Jewish Encyclopedia* and *The Universal Jewish Encyclopedia.*

[11] See Rabbi Simlai's well-known statement in the Babylonian Talmud (henceforth referred to as "b.") Makkot 23*b*-24*a*. See however, Wilhelm Bacher, *Die Agada der Palästinensischen Amoraer* I (Strassburg, 1892), p. 558, n. 1.

[12] Abot II.1. Cf. *ibid.*, IV.2 and Matt. 5:19.

[13] See the works mentioned in n. 10 above and George Foot Moore, *Judaism* (Cambridge, Mass., 1927, 1958), *passim.*

ing numbers of its constituents, this elite became the defender of the status quo and the voice of subservience to Rome.

Yet during these very decades mounting oppression and insecurity turned life into an incubus for widening circles of the urban and rural population in Judea, and the spokesmen for status quo could not provide an adequate answer for the dilemma of the afflicted. When pain and hunger thieved their strength and obstructed their performance of the *mitzvot,* it was natural for them to withdraw from society or seek an explanation for their lot in the ideology of messianism, or both. Messianic tradition told of the trouble, injustice, and anguish that would precede the advent of the millennium, and by implication brought the lowly a message of hope: though oppressed, they were yet not rejected; they had been signaled that they might adequately prepare for the proximate glory. Rejected indeed, they could believe, were their complacent leaders—the Pharisees of the Synoptic Gospels, insouciant in their iniquity, and for whom the Messiah's untimely arrival would result in a cancellation of their privileges and prerogatives. The cleavage between the oppressed and the Pharisaic leaders is best seen in the case of the small-farmer class, the *'am ha-'aretz,* which had been one of the Pharisees' mainstays in their rise to power. By the beginning of the war with Rome, the word *'am ha-'aretz* had begun to connote "rustic" and "boor" for the Pharisaic leaders; and the antipathy between the two groups grew so violent that at the close of the century Rabbi Eliezer could gruesomely jest that it was permissible to slay a boor even on an Atonement Day that fell on a Sabbath.[14]

An ideology is only as stable as the society which supports it. Even in times of maximum stability, a society breeds centrifugal tendencies, directly related to human needs. In times of instability these tendencies well into movements. Almost concurrently various groups (some undoubtedly with earlier foundations) appear in the sources, all responding to the pressures of the times through the ideology of Torah, and many through the basic doctrines of Oral Tradition.[15]

[14] b. Pesaḥim 49*b*.

[15] One of the finest introductions to the first-century sects (with references to the primary sources) is to be found in R. K. Harrison's *The Dead Sea Scrolls* (London, 1961), pp. 72-101. It contains an excellent basic bibliography of works published on the subject. There is no work as yet which deals adequately with all these sects in terms of their social contexts and institutional alignments.

There were the groups that sought refuge from the sinking ship of society in a monastic life, secure and regulated, indifferent to the pursuit of gain and sensual gratification, and concerned with purity of body and soul, the practice of ethics, and a regimen of contemplation, prayer, and study of the Law. Groups such as the Essenes, the Damascus Covenanters, and the sect or sects of Qumran, are amazingly similar to one another, and also to the Therapeutae, who Philo tells us flourished in Egypt two centuries before. They differed from one another mostly in details, such as the extent of their asceticism, the length of their novitiate, and the nature of their rule. The Essenes included groups urban and rural, mostly celibate, yet some familial; other groups had no restrictions against women. The Essenes were pacifists; the Qumran sectaries appear militarily inclined. Most of these groups had a strong belief in the messianic coming. Our Jewish sources on the Essenes tell us of their belief in the immortality of the soul, but nothing of their eschatology. The Christian writer Hippolytus at the end of the second century or the beginning of the third tells us in *The Refutation of All Heresies* that the Essenes believed in the resurrection of the body and the coming of the Judgment Day.

Apocalypticism ran high in these groups and in others which had not withdrawn from the vertigo of society. Their implicit belief in the Torah was accompanied by the certainty that the writings of the prophets were intended for the contemporary scene. They were convinced that they were living in what the Mishnah was to call the "tracks of the Messiah," and looked eagerly for the advent of the new order. Their writings are filled with visions of vindication and fulfillment that compensate for, and hence betray, the grim reality of their lives.[16]

The doctrines of the apocalyptics are often similar to those of the Oral Tradition; the authors of some of the visions could well have been adherents of the twofold Law. The two traditions need not have been mutually exclusive, however inimical their respective leadership groups may have been. The same body of doctrine that served the Pharisees as a source of stability could have been tapped by the apocalyptists to serve

[16] See M. Sotah IX.15. On apocalyptic literature, see W. D. Davies, *Christian Origins and Judaism* (London, 1962), pp. 19 ff., and most recently D. S. Russell, *The Method and Message of Jewish Apocalyptic* (Philadelphia, 1964).

people in the throes of despair. Indeed, Jesus himself was in all probability an apocalyptic Pharisee.

The militancy of the Qumran community is evidenced in numerous other groups that sought to end oppression by a call to arms. Among them were the Fourth Philosophy, the Sicarii, and the Zealots. To regard any of these groups as purely political is to impose modern categories upon them. The element we call religion was essential to them all. The Fourth Philosophy is known to have shared Pharisaic ideas and to have fought under the slogan that God alone is Ruler and Lord; and similar platforms were doubtless held by the other groups.[17] Hippolytus even goes so far as to identify the Zealots and Sicarii with Essenes! [18]

However similar these groups responding to life's impositions were to one another, there is no basis to assume that they were institutionally connected. Their programs and platforms bear an unquestionable resemblance; yet a study of subgroups in all great movements of history (the Maccabean, French, and American revolutions, and the contemporary movement for civil rights in the United States being four of hundreds of available examples) demonstrates convincingly that affinity of belief and purpose does not necessarily result in identity of leadership.

This realization has become increasingly important since the discovery of the Dead Sea Scrolls.[19] If the Scrolls have done nothing else for the historian of Judaism, they have at least consoled him that the often recondite allusions of early rabbinic literature are not the *most* difficult to decipher. The Scrolls' cryptic references to personalities and events are highly resistant to disinterested historical reconstruction, and little that is certain can as yet be said about the history and institutional alignments that there appear. Indeed, however much we may like to date the Scrolls in the early rabbinic period, we cannot close our eyes to the

[17] *Antiquities* XVIII, 1.6. See also XX.5.1 and 8.6, where Josephus speaks of self-proclaimed prophets who appeared during the feverish pre-war days, phenomena which are understandable in the light of contemporary concepts.

[18] *The Refutation of All Heresies* Book IX, ch. 21 (in *The Ante-Nicene Fathers* V [New York, 1896], p. 136).

[19] A vast literature dealing with the Scrolls has been forming. For the texts, the student is referred to Abraham Meir Habermann, *Megillot Midbar Yehudah* (Tel Aviv, 1959); Theodor H. Gaster, *The Dead Sea Scriptures* (New York, 1956; rev. 1964); Geza Vermes, *The Dead Sea Scrolls in English* (Harmondsworth, 1962); Millar Burrows, *The Dead Sea Scrolls* (New York, 1955), and *More Light on The Dead Sea Scrolls* (New York, 1958) and n. 15. above.

perplexing fact that the *historical* evidence within these documents does not demand such dating.

If the Scrolls can be placed with certainty in the period of our interest, they will have contributed to two important areas: first, to our knowledge of the calendar,[20] practices, institutions, thought, and values of a group or groups that could have influenced emergent Christianity; and second, to our awareness of the complexity and diversity of sub-ideologies connected to the concept of Torah and the twofold Law in the pre-Destruction era. But the Scrolls that we presently possess are insufficient to lead a historian to a definitive identification of the Qumran community with the Essenes or any other group.

5. *The Basic Institutions of the Pre-Destruction Era.* Reflected in the literature of the spectrum of sects are the basic institutions of Judea in the pre-Destruction era.

First among these was the sacrificial temple in Jerusalem, served by the priesthood, but supervised in the first century by spokesmen for the twofold Law.[21]

The Pharisaic leaders added a new element to the service. The priesthood traditionally was divided into twenty-four courses, which alternated at the services, each officiating for a week. The Pharisees created twenty-four corresponding groups, each known as a *ma'amad,* or course, and each authorized to have observers at the sacrifices for an entire week. The rest of the *ma'amad* assembled daily in its community hall for appropriate readings and prayers.[22] This, rather than chance gatherings of

[20] The problem of the calendar, crucial for an understanding of the development of Judaism and Christianity, has long attracted scholarly attention. A bibliography of basic works in the field can be culled from the spate of excellent studies published since the discovery of the Scrolls. Prominent among these are Julian Morgenstern "The Calendar of the Book of Jubilees, Its Origin and Its Character," *VT,* V (1955), 34-76; Annie Jaubert, *La Date de la Cène* (Paris, 1957) and J. Van Goudever, *Biblical Calendars* (Leiden, 1959). There are still a number of basic problems regarding the Jewish calendar of the first century which merit consideration. I am in the process of completing a long study entitled "The Accession of Hillel," which deals with the importance of recent calendar information for the early literary tradition of rabbinic Judaism.

[21] See, for example, Mishna (henceforth "M") Yoma and Tosefta (henceforth "T") Yom Hakkipurim.

[22] M. Ta'anit IV. 2-4. Note that the Mishna attempts to move the origin of this institution back to the days of the "early prophets." According to later commentators (beginning with Rashi) the early prophets were none other than David and Solomon. See commentators *ad loc.*

previous ages, provided the most likely setting for the birth of an institution unknown to the literature as late as Ben Sira's day,[23] and in subsequent Judaism known as "the house of assembly" (*bet ha-knesset*), "the house of study" (*bet ha-midrash*), and "the house of prayer" (*bet ha-tefillah*), an institution which, through the Greek, is known to us as the synagogue. (It is probable that the word synagogue referred to a congregation for the purposes of worship before it referred to the building where it met.) In the first century synagogues were thriving throughout Judea and abroad: there was one even in the temple's Hall of Solomon.

Even before attaining power, the Pharisees seem to have developed organizations and schools for the transmission and development of the Oral Tradition and laid the foundation for a system of local and appellate courts. At the top of their structure stood the *bet-din ha-gadol,* the Great Legislature, which is often mistakenly likened to a supreme court and then further identified with the High Court or pre-70 Sanhedrin, headed by a Sadducee, the High Priest himself.[24] If the tradition in the Mishnah is correct, an officer known as the Prince (*nasi'*) presided over the Great Legislature. He represented the majority faction within the Pharisaic party; his surrogate, called the Father of the Legislature (*'av bet-din*), led the minority group. The Mishnah records the names of five such "Pairs" (*zugot*), as it calls the duumvirates, ending with the renowned Hillel and Shammai in the dawn of the first century. In the case of the first two pairs the chief officer appears to have been a conservative; beginning with the third—at the time of Salome Alexandra—the leader of the liberal wing seems to have headed the entire party. By the middle of the first century the title "rabbi" (originally "my teacher")

[23] See E. Rivkin, "Ben Sira and the Nonexistence of the Synagogue: A Study in Historical Methods," in *In the Time of Harvest, Essays in Honor of Abba Hillel Silver on the Occasion of His 70th Birthday* (New York, 1963), pp. 320-54. See also S. Zeitlin, "The Origin of the Synagogue," *Proceedings of the American Academy for Jewish Research* 1930-31, pp. 69-81, especially pp. 72 and 78.

[24] See Adolf Büchler, *Das Synedrion in Jerusalem und das grosse Beth-Din in der Quaderkammer des Jerusalemischen Tempels* (Vienna, 1902); S. Zeitlin, *Who Crucified Jesus?* (New York, 1964 [3rd ed.]), *passim,* esp. pp. 228 ff. Sidney B. Hoenig, *The Great Sanhedrin* (Philadelphia, 1953), especially pp. 42 f., and Hugo Mantel, *Studies in the History of the Sanhedrin* (Cambridge, Mass., 1961). See also S. Zeitlin, "The Political Synedrion and the Religious Sanhedrin," *Jewish Quarterly Review,* XXXVI (1945-46), 109-40. By way of contrast see the recent work of Asher Finkel, *The Pharisees and the Teacher of Nazareth* (Leiden, 1964), pp. 59 f.

appears to have become the official designation for scholars within the Legislature and doubtless outside; the Prince was designated as "rabban" (originally "our teacher").

6. *The "Halakha."* Out of the institutions of the Pharisees came the great ideological achievement of Judaism in the pre-Destruction era—the development of the Oral Law into bodies of procedure and practice. These procedures and practices are known as *halakha*.[25]

In Jewish circles today the word *halakha* has acquired the connotation of peremptory assertion or final law. This was not the connotation or function of *halakha* in the first century. *Halakha* represented the application of the dynamic and liberalizing Oral Tradition to the exigencies of daily life. Traditionally *halakha* is said to hark back to Sinai and certain practices, not ascribable to later teachers, are called "*halakhas* given to Moses from Mount Sinai."[26] Doubtless traditional explanations of the Written Law had existed during biblical times and the Hasmonean era. But these can be called *halakha* only in retrospect from the first century, for it was at that time that rabbinic practice, as we know it today, began its luxuriant growth.

Tentatively one can reduce the complex history of early *halakha* into four stages, each commencing before, yet coexisting with, its successor.[27]

First, beginning with the Hasmonean period, perhaps somewhat earlier, the Pharisees adopted previous *ad hoc* interpretations of Torah, enunciated others and began to transmit them through oral tradition (*kabbalah* in its pristine sense of "tradition," rather than in its acquired connotation of "mystical tradition").[28]

Second, beginning with the Roman period, the Pharisees developed new *halakha* from the Pentateuch through exegesis (or *midrash* in its

[25] A historically oriented, scientific analysis of the history of *halakha* is yet to be written. Traditional works such as those by Frankel, Weiss, and Halevy mentioned in n. 3 above, and an equally traditional but in many ways more scientific work like Chaim Tchernowitz, *Toledoth Ha-Halakah*, 4 vols. (New York, 1934-50) should form the basis for such a history. *Halakha* as used by the early rabbis must be distinguished from law or practice as found in earlier books. There is no question that customs and practices prior to, and often different from those of the early rabbis existed, but there is no basis to call these *halakha:* the technical term is simply not used.

[26] See the Palestinian Talmud Peah II.6; M. Peah II.6; Eduyot VIII.7, Yadaim IV.3.

[27] This reconstruction is my own. I hope to publish it in fuller form in the near future.

[28] On the "chain," or rather "chains" of tradition, see Abot I. 1, Yadaim IV.3; b. Rosh Ha-Shanah 7*a*, 19*a;* Ḥagigah 10*b;* Genesis Rabba S. 7, etc.

earliest sense). The first Pharisees known as exegetes were Shemayah and Abtalion, who flourished sometime around 50 B.C.[29] But the major impetus to exegetical activity was given by Hillel the Babylonian, Prince or *nasi'* from about 34 B.C. to A.D. 10. Hillel introduced the effective use of the first of the hermeneutic rules by which *halakha* evolved. The introduction of these principles made it possible to develop Oral Law by logic as well as tradition, even in preference to tradition, and the sources evidence the struggle between the traditionalists and the exegetes.[30]

Third, beginning in Hillel's latter days and continuing to the end of the pre-Destruction era came the proliferation of the *halakha* and the struggle for its control between the liberal and conservative wings of the Pharisaic party, the Hillelites and Shammaites respectively.[31] The literature preserves over three hundred of their controversies, whose thought, form, and occasionally even content bear an amazing resemblance to those of the Proculians and the Sabinians, the contemporary Roman schools of law. Prior to the first century few examples of *halakha* are recorded, and even fewer controversies. Tradition mentions only one controversy, a continuing one, between the Princes and the Fathers of the Legislature.

Fourth, shortly after the destruction of the temple, a program was begun to control the direction of *halakhic* growth by bringing the *halakha* under the new centralized authority which was developing in Judaism. This tendency culminated at the end of the second century in the compilation of the Mishna under the aegis of Judah the Prince.

The liberal Hillelites were universalists and ardent supporters of Rome; the conservative Shammaites were nationalists and at best ambivalent toward Rome. The Shammaites appear to have joined the revolution against Rome in the mid-sixties, and in the early heat of the rebellion, to have wrested power from the Hillelites. In a kind of Rump Parliament called by the Shammaite leader, Hananiah ben Hezekiah ben Gorion in

[29] b. Pasaḥim 70*b*. Shemayah and Abtalion are often identified with the Sammeas and Pollion of Josephus (*Antiquities* XV, 1.1.).

[30] I will deal with this important and heretofore insufficiently treated problem in my study on the accession of Hillel (see n. 20).

[31] On the Hillelites and Shammaites see Adolf Schwarz, *Die Controversen der Schammaiten und Hilleliten* (Vienna, 1893). See also Louis Ginzberg's attempt at a socio-economic appraisal of some of these controversies in his "The Significance of the Halacha," in *On Jewish Law and Lore* (Philadelphia, 1955), pp. 77-124, first published as *M'komah shel Halakhah B'Ḥokhmat Yisrael* (Jerusalem, 1931).

his "upper room" (which, I suppose, entitles it to be called the first Summit Conference), the Shammaites, outnumbering the Hillelites, promulgated eighteen decrees in their favor.[32]

The Post-Destruction Era

1. *The Rule of Rome.* Thanks again to Josephus, we know the details of the Great Revolt by Judea against Rome in A.D. 66-70. The Hillelites and the high priests strove in vain to avert it; the Jews' initial successes and the rout of the Roman Twelfth Legion fed it; the irrepressible offensive of Vespasian and Titus doomed it; and the internecine strife and bloodshed among the Jews destroyed it. In its wake the war brought destitution, devastation, and the puncturing of the popular illusion that God would suffer neither the temple nor his holy city to be harmed. The land was parched, the population cowed by decimation and thraldom. Yet life had to go on, and it was in the interest of both Rome and the Judean leaders that it be structured.[33]

When the smoke of battle cleared in the year 70, various groups were grappling for control of Jews and Judaism. Rome seems to have stepped early into the fray and made a choice of leadership. Their selection could have surprised no one. The Shammaites had joined the rebellion; how the Sadducees aligned themselves we do not know, for the evidence is inconclusive. On the other hand, the Hillelites had sought to avert the revolt; failing, they had moved to control it through their own generals; failing again, they had defected to the Romans or remained within rebel lines to agitate for an early truce. These the Romans made the undisputed leaders of Jewish life; Sadducees and Shammaites fought, failed, and faded from history.

The leader of the Hillelites at this time should have been Simeon, the son of Gamaliel I and the great-grandson of the founder of the Hillelites. Simeon seems to have joined the revolutionaries and then disappeared.[34]

[32] M. Shabbat I.4.

[33] There are few adequate monographs dealing with the post-destruction era. The basic texts mentioned above remain the best secondary sources for this period. To these should be added Gedaliah Alon's studies, published posthumously in book form by his students under the titles *Toledot Ha-Yehudim B'Eretz-Yisrael biT'kufat Ha-Mishnah v'Ha-Talmud* (Tel Aviv, 1952), and *Meḥkarim b'Toledot Yisrael bime Bayit Sheni* (Tel Aviv, 1956).

[34] Josephus, *Life*, SS. 38 f; *Wars* IV, 3.9. Abot 1.17 and a statement in Tosefta Sanhedrin 2.13 are attributed to him, the latter, in my estimation, incorrectly.

If Rome was angry at Hillel's dynasty,[35] it bore no lasting grudge: ten years after the war a descendant of Hillel again occupied the seat of power.

The mantle of leadership was cast by Rome on a man by the name of Johanan (John) ben Zakkai, one of the most colorful of the early rabbis.

John was a logical choice for the position.[36] He was a priest, a symbol of continuity, but not a Sadducee. Like many others of privileged birth, he had become a devout Pharisee, steeped in Oral Tradition and determined to reduce Sadducean prerogatives. He had been a leader of the Hillelites before the Destruction, a teacher of Oral Law in the shadow of the temple and an eloquent advocate of peace with Rome.

2. *The Age of Jamnia.* John ben Zakkai's moral virtues, halakhic proficiency, and adeptness in symbolism and allegory are extolled by legend; his political acumen is not always discernible. Yet a famous legend reveals his high political position and his entree with Rome's command. It has him stealing out of a besieged Jerusalem in the twilight of the war to promise Vespasian (or Titus) an end to hostilities in return for permission to build in Jamnia a school where he might perpetuate his heritage. It goes on to say that Vespasian (or Titus) granted this modest request and the school was established in the city near the Mediterranean coast.[37] In reality, however, Jamnia, populated by Jews and non-Jews who proved their loyalty to Rome early in the war,[38] became the administrative seat of Jewish life. The little school was the State House; its headmaster the Chief Justice and Executive Officer of the land. Its Legislature (or *bet-din*) assumed the importance of the Sanhedrin of old, and even its name. Jamnia was the new Jerusalem.

John ruled for a decade as head of the Legislature at Jamnia. Whether his title was Prince (*nasi'*) or Father of the Legislature (*'av bet-din*)

[35] See Semakhot VIII.8 (ed. Higger) and b. Taanith 29*a*, Gittin 56*b*.

[36] On John ben Zakkai, see J. Neusner, *A Life of Rabban Yohanan ben Zakkai* (Leiden, 1962) and Alon, *Toledot*, pp. 61 ff. Some basic primary texts on statements in this and the following paragraphs include M. Yadaim IV.6; T. Parah III.8; b. Yoma 71*b* and 39*b*; b. Pesaḥim 26*a* and Mekhilta, Baḥodesh, ed. Lauterbach XI.83. On John's knowledge of symbolism and allegory see for example T. Ḥagigah II.2 and b. Ḥagigah 14*b*; also Wilhelm Bacher, *Die Agada der Tannaiten* I (Strassburg, 1903), pp. 27 ff.

[37] b. Gittin 56*a-b*; *Abot d'Rabbi Nathan*, ch. 4.

[38] Josephus, *Wars* IV, 3.2 and IV, 8.1. See also Adolf Neubauer, *La géographie du Talmud* (Paris, 1868), pp. 73 ff.

in the absence of a descendant of Hillel is a moot question;[39] that he functioned as Prince is undeniable. Around the year 80, his work of reconstruction successfully begun, John retired to the academy at B'ror Hayil in the environs of Jamnia, and the scion of the House of Hillel, Gamaliel II (not to be confused with Gamaliel I,[40] who was apparently the teacher of Paul), moved into the position of leadership. John's coterie of advisers remained in Jamnia with Gamaliel but continued close to their old master, who could not have failed to rejoice in seeing his successor carry to fruition many of the policies which he had initiated.[41]

The combined administrations of John and Gamaliel constitute the Great Age of Jamnia. Covering over a third of a century, it embraced the period of Rome's Flavian Dynasty (A.D. 79-96), which limited Judea's autonomy, and the beginning of the era of the Five Good Emperors, when this autonomy was extended. Tradition depicts Gamaliel and his close advisers—Eliezer ben Hyrcanus, Joshua ben Hananiah, Akiba ben Joseph, and Elazar ben Azariah—visiting Rome from the year 95 on and engaging in debates with pagan philosophers. Gamaliel and his retinue received more than intellectual satisfaction from these visits. The visits were undoubtedly made to forfend against undesired decrees, to plead for privileges, and to discuss the implementation of those that were granted.

The Age of Jamnia marks the change from the temple-oriented Judaism comprising a variety of sects which characterized the pre-Destruction era to a Judaism structured around the decentralized synagogue, yet in other areas moving toward centralization, canonization, and uniformity. These tendencies, incidentally, are discernible in contemporary Roman government and law.

3. *The Synagogue.* The Temple was destroyed in the war. The sacrificial cult was ended, though we hear faint echoes of attempts to revive it. Prayer and legend enshrined the hope for their restoration, but this hope became a dream as it was discreetly deferred to messianic times. Messianic

[39] See H. Mantel, *op. cit.*, pp. 28 ff.

[40] See Acts 5:34 and 22:3.

[41] The relationship of Gamaliel II to John ben Zakkai has been the subject of numerous scholarly conjectures. Some of the questions posed include: 1) Was Gamaliel a pupil of John's? (Cf. b. Baba Bathra 10*b*) 2) Is the account in Gittin 56*b*, which tells of John's request to Vespasian to save the family of Gamaliel, a fact or a legend? 3) Could John have been deposed by Gamaliel? On these see W. Bacher, *op. cit.*, pp. 73 f.

ideology was now definitely a part of the rabbinic movement. For some it was a token of piety; for others, as we shall see, a practical doctrine. First-century apocalyptic, apparently discredited by the rabbis, could not enter their collection of sacred writings.

The temple was replaced by the synagogue as the focus of Jewish life, and sacrifice by prayer, now called "the cult of the heart" (*avodah she ba-lev*).[42] Prayer and ethical deeds were deemed worthy substitutes for sacrifice before the throne of the Most High.[43] The synagogue assumed the cherished prerogatives of the Temple—the right to sound the ram's horn on a New Year's day occurring on the Sabbath; the right to carry the festive wreath of Tabernacles (the *lulav*) in solemn procession on all seven days of the festival; and the right to hear the priestly benediction pronounced within its walls.[44]

4. *The Process of Centralization.* Under John and Gamaliel Jamnia became the center of scholar-judges, the inspiration for new academies burgeoning throughout the land and the fountainhead of new *halakha.*

Gamaliel and his emissaries traveled extensively in Judea and abroad to bring Jewish colonies closer to Jamnia and the authority of its Sanhedrin. Gamaliel, perhaps even more than John, insisted on supreme control of the calendar, the backbone of Jewish life and observance. With the aid of his scholars, he determined the day of the New Moon and the appropriateness of intercalating a month in his luni-solar calendar to bring it into line with the seasons. The Tosefta records a famous rescript, dictated ceremoniously by Gamaliel from the steps of the temple mount, in which he announces to the provinces of Upper and Lower Galilee, the Upper and Lower Southland (Darom), and the Diaspora of Babylonia, Medea, and elsewhere that "it is meet in our eyes and in the eyes of our associates to add thirty days to the present year." [45]

5. *The Process of Canonization.* In Gamaliel's administration the Holy Scriptures were closed with the canonization of their final section, the Sacred Writings. All over a century old, these writings already possessed *de facto* holiness, which was now made *de jure.* The controversies that had raged about the suitability of some books, like Proverbs, were now

[42] b. Ta'anit 2*a*.
[43] b. Berakhot 32*b*; *Abot d'Rabbi Nathan,* ch. 4.
[44] M. Rosh Hashana IV.1 and Sukkah III. 12; T. Rosh Hashana IV. 1f. Cf. also M. Rosh Hashana IV.4. and Sotah IX.9.
[45] T. Sanhedrin I.6. Cf. *ibid.* I.5 and b. Sanhedrin 11*a*.

over;[46] others, such as the controversies over Ecclesiastes and the Song of Songs, were now brought to an end.[47] A number of rabbis living around the middle of the second century could still question the canonicity of some books,[48] but the canon as we have it today had been determined not much later than the turn of the century.

In Jamnia the contentions between Hillelites and Shammaites were ended when, according to tradition, a heavenly voice (or *bat-kol*) declared, to no one's surprise, that Hillelite *halakha* would henceforth be the law of the land.[49] By means of hermeneutic principles, such as Hillel's or those introduced by Nahum of Gimzo, Ishmael ben Elisha, and Akiba ben Joseph, *halakha* was applied to an increasing number of life's situations and contingencies.[50]

Halakha proliferated to such an extent that academy heads, to facilitate teaching and study, compiled private collections of Oral Tradition. These collections, particularly from the schools of Akiba and Ishmael, formed the basis for the eventual official codification of Oral Law in the form of the Mishna.[51]

Under Gamaliel the liturgy, which had developed rapidly during the first century, assumed canonical status. By Gamaliel's time, it already included the call to worship, the profession of faith, a lectionary, prayers from the Bible, such as the Hallel Psalms, and prayers from the writings of the rabbis themselves. At Gamaliel's behest, Simeon the Pakulite arranged earlier prayers into the Eighteen Benedictions, the Prayer par excellence of the daily service.[52] Gamaliel is also credited with contribut-

[46] On canonization see Herbert E. Ryle, *The Canon of the Old Testament* (London, 1892). On Proverbs see b. Shabbat 30*b;* on Ezekiel b. Shabbat 13*b,* Ḥagigah 13*a* and Menaḥot 45*a*. S. Zeitlin claims that the canonicity of Ezekiel was never in question: the argument was over whether or not the book might be read in public.

[47] M. Yadaim III.2-5; T. Yadaim II.14 and b. Shabbat 13*a,* 14*a* and 116*a;* Megillah 7*a*.

[48] These included Esther (see for example b. Megillah 7*a*; Yoma 29*a-b;* Palestinian Talmud Megillah 70*a*) and Ecclesiastes (b. Megillah 7*a;* and Jerusalem Talmud Berakhot 14.15).

[49] b. Erubin 14*b;* Palestinian Talmud Berakhot 3*b* (Halakha 7). Cf. b. Berakhot 36*b*.

[50] See Moses Mielziner, *Introduction to the Talmud* (Cincinnati, 1894), pp. 124 ff.

[51] See *ibid.,* pp. 4 f., and, for a thorough review of traditional explanations Hanoch Albeck, *Mavo La-Mishnah* (Jerusalem, 1959), pp. 63 ff.

[52] b. Berakhot 28*b*. It is the commentator Rashi who first explains the words Ha-Pakoli as meaning a dealer in flax and wool. Traditionally, the composition of the Eighteen Benedictions was attributed to the men of the Great Synagogue (b. Megillah 17*b* and Palestinian Talmud Berakhot 4*d*). On this subject see Kaufmann

ing significantly to the Passover Seder ritual[53] and requiring the individual to pray thrice daily, morning, afternoon and evening.[54]

6. *The Problem of Conformity.* Like other creative periods, the Age of Jamnia produced its bitterness and conflict. In his efforts to standardize Judaism, Gamaliel clashed not only with the Shammaites, but with the budding churches of the Judeo-Christians and even with his own scholar class.

Unable to bend the various Judeo-Christian groups (the Ebionites, the Nazarenes, the Gnostics, the Elkesaites) to his control, he sought to sever them from the body of Judaism. He authorized Samuel the Small (Shemuel ha-Katan) to include in the Eighteen Benedictions a prayer against all heretics.[55] He stipulated that every Jew, to fulfill his Passover obligation, recite an explanation of the symbols of Lamb, Unleavened Bread, and Bitter Herbs that evidenced his distance from the Judeo-Christian community.[56] Rivalries between Christian and non-Christian Jews of the first century were at least as intense as those which set Pharisees against Sadducees or Hillelites against Shammaites. The execution of James, son of Zebedee, in Herod Agrippa's reign (A.D. 37-41), the execution of James, brother of Jesus, by the High Priest (62) and the Judeo-Christians' flight to Pella before the siege of Jerusalem (April, 70) created a breach between Christian and non-Christian Jew. The actions of Gamaliel widened this breach, and the impossibility of the Judeo-Christians' accepting the messianic ideals of the Bar Kokhba Rebellion in A.D. 132 severed the two groups completely.[57]

Kohler, "The Origin and Composition of the Eighteen Benedictions," *HUCA,* I (1924), 387-425; Abraham Z. Idelsohn, *Jewish Liturgy and Its Development* (New York, 1932), pp. 26 ff. On the structure and background of the ancient Jewish liturgy see Eric Werner, *The Sacred Bridge* (New York, 1959), pp. 2 ff. As Werner indicates, "Paul was aware of the categories of Jewish prayer and the similarities of early Christian prayers and contemporary or older Jewish prayers are numerous." See also L. Mowry, "Revelation 4–5 and Early Liturgical Usage," *JBL,* LXXI (1952), 75-84.

[53] M. Pesaḥim X., esp. section 5. On the basis of T. Pesaḥim X.12, which tells of the time when Rabban Gamaliel and his elders spent an entire night (the Passover Seder night?) discussing the *halakhas* of Passover at the home of Boëthus ben Zonin, it is not unreasonable to assume that Gamaliel was responsible for many more of the regulations and customs now associated with Passover and the Seder.

[54] b. Berakhot 27*b*. Cf. A. Z. Idelsohn, *op. cit.,* p. 27. The *Didache* VIII, 3 is aware of the practice of praying three times daily.

[55] b. Berakhot 28*b*-29*a*. On Samuel see T. Sota XIII.4.

[56] S. J. Fischer, "Sh'loshah D'varim," *Ha-Tsofeh,* IX-X (1925-26), 238-240.

[57] Before 70, the Jews and Judeo-Christians had been very close. See Morton Enslin, *The Literature of the Christian Movement* (New York, 1956; Part III of *Christian*

Also bitter for Gamaliel was his struggle with the scholar class, which mutinied in an attempt to check the Prince's concentration of power in his office. Joshua ben Hananiah appears to have led a *coup d'état* which deposed Gamaliel and replaced him with the young scholar-priest, Elazar ben Azariah.[58] Finally a compromise was reached, permitting Gamaliel to return as Prince and insuring a measure of autonomy for the scholars. This they exercised for the last time in many years when they stirred up messianic hopes among the people and fomented the Bar Kokhba Rebellion of 132. The rebellion was crushed in 135 and the Prince emerged with virtually plenipotentiary power.

7. *The Road to Universalism.* In Gamaliel's day one could clearly discern a change in the nature of the holidays which had been taking place since the Hillelites rose to power. The name Passover—reserved in the Bible for the first night of the festival, the remaining six nights and seven days called the Festival of Unleavened Bread—was now extended to the entire holiday. Though retaining its traditional agricultural and historical elements, Passover now stressed the Israelites' miraculous redemption and salvation through the might of God.[59] Pentecost (Shavuot) became the holiday of Revelation, associated with the Giving of the Law, perhaps to provide a counterpart to the connecting of the Holy Ghost with the Pentecost of the Judeo-Christians.[60] The New Year's Day (Rosh Ha-Shanah) and the Day of Atonement (Yom Ha-Kippurim), divested of Temple pomp, were now completely universalized. Tied to no events specifically Jewish, they were dedicated to universal man and his relationship with the Divine. The Hillelites dropped the plethora of Judean holidays commemorating national events.[61] Hanukkah, well in-

---

Beginnings), pp. 203 ff. and Millar Burrows, *More Light on the Dead Sea Scrolls* (New York, 1958), who quotes with approval Morton Smith's belief that after Jesus' death the Gospels reflect "a progressive Judaizing of Christianity." On the post-70 era, see, *inter alia* G. Alon, *op. cit.*, 184 ff. and Samuel Abramski, *Bar-Kokhba: N'si Yisrael* (Tel Aviv, 1961), pp. 73 ff. See also Leo Baeck, *Judaism and Christianity* (New York and Philadelphia, 1961) and H.-J. Schoeps, *Das Judenchristentum* (Bern-Munich, 1964).

[58] M. Rosh Ha-Shanah II.9; b. Rosh Ha-Shanah 24*b*-25*b* and Berakhot 27*b*-28*a*; Palestinian Talmud Berakhot IV.1.

[59] S. Zeitlin, "Judaism as a Religion," *Jewish Quarterly Review*, (NS) XXXIV (1943), 23.

[60] E. Werner, *op. cit.*, p. 93.

[61] For a list of these see S. Zeitlin, *Megillat Taanit as a Source for Jewish Chronology and History in the Hellenistic and Roman Periods* (Philadelphia, 1922), pp. 65 ff.

trenched, was stripped of all association with war, national pride, and even the Maccabees, and made to commemorate the miraculous survival of the flame in the sacred shrine.[62]

Gradually national and ethnic elements of the heritage yielded to the universal, and the universal name "Israel" was applied to every Jew, regardless of his provenance.[63] The rabbis even asserted that God had revealed the Torah in the wilderness to forfend against any special claims to it on the part of the Holy Land.[64]

The Prince was really an emperor. His seat was in Judea, but his dominion reached throughout the world. In the first century most Jews lived outside Judea, thriving in the Near and Middle East, North Africa, and the Mediterranean littoral of Europe. They had come as freemen or as prisoners. They had served, achieved, and earned privilege. Their numbers had grown through natural increase and proselytization.[65]

The importance of conversion in first-century Judaism cannot be minimized. Full conversion entailed baptism and circumcision, and apprehensions about the latter may have dissuaded more than a few male prospects. Yet the fact remains that conversions to Judaism were numerous in the first century, even after 70, and among the noble classes in the Roman Empire. Matthew's assertion that a Pharisee would compass sea and land to make one proselyte testifies to the Hillelites' efforts and helps to explain their success.[66] The Hillelites removed numerous

[62] The traditional account of Hanukkah is to be found in b. Shabbat 21*b*. Cf. Numbers Rabba XIII.4.

[63] See S. Zeitlin, "Judaism as a Religion," *loc. cit.* p. 221. Again, it should be remembered that our distinction between the ethnic and the religious was not current at that time. (This has been the source of much confusion including, *inter alia,* that of J. Juster, *Les juifs dans l'Empire romain* [Paris, 1914], II, p. 19). It is true that at one time after A.D. 70 Rome limited the practice of Judaism to those who, by its estimation and arbitrary decision, were members of the Jewish polity at that time. This, however, did not mean that Jews could not be Roman citizens (Juster, *ibid.*). Nor does it mean that Jewish leaders could not stress the universal elements in their tradition and hope for its acceptance by non-Jews, as in the past.

[64] Mekhilta, ed. Lauterbach, II, 198.

[65] See J. Juster, *op. cit.,* II, pp. 1 ff. On the subject of proselytization the two most comprehensive studies are those of Bernard Bamberger, *Proselytism in the Talmudic Period* (Cincinnati, 1939) and William G. Braude, *Jewish Proselyting in the First Five Centuries of the Common Era* (Providence, 1940). See particularly pp. 7-9, and 11 ff. of Braude's work.

[66] Matt. 23:15. It is interesting to note that Eliezer ben Pedat, a Palestinian teacher (Amora) of the third century, viewed Israel's dispersion as designed by God in order that proselytes might be attracted to it. See b. Pesaḥim 87*b*.

barriers to conversion; even Ammonites and Moabites could now enter the fold,[67] despite the Bible's express prohibition.[68] They fought with fair success to insure the equal status with other Jews that proselytes enjoyed in theory.[69] Some even considered it an honor to be descended from proselytes.[70] To attract those who could not wholly commit themselves to Judaism, the category "fearers of the Lord" was created for status and honor.

8. *The Impact of Hellenism.* Though removed from Judea, the Jews of the Diaspora in the first century supported Jerusalem and then Jamnia, and looked to them for guidance. Most of the Diaspora communities produced no appreciable Jewish culture of their own.[71] One did. The immense Egyptian community, boasting a million souls and fifteen per cent of the total population, created in Alexandria a culture that blended the spirit of Judea with the thought of ancient Greece. Here many creative Jews wrote their history, poetry, and drama with Jewish themes.

In the first century the Alexandrian-Jewish tradition produced three outstanding defenders of their heritage. Josephus and Philo wrote impassioned apologies;[72] the author of IV Maccabees, blending Stoic ethics and Jewish virtues, extolled martyrdom as preferable to a life lived in a pagan faith. Josephus' histories and Philo's philosophy, the greatest monuments of the Hellenistic-Jewish tradition, are the products of minds that saw in their heritage values worthy of preservation.

The Alexandrian Jews were not opposed to law: Philo's own writings make this clear.[73] They may have known of the *halakha;*[74] but halakhic

[67] M. Yadaim IV.4; T. Yadaim II.17.

[68] Deut. 23:3.

[69] See Bamberger, *op. cit.,* pp. 60 ff., and Braude, *op. cit.,* p. 34 and pp. 79 ff. That restrictions on the proselyte's participation in the cult were not any more severe than those of other Jews is made brilliantly clear by the third anecdote regarding Hillel and Shammai found in b. Shabbat 31*a* (the story of the pagan who was willing to become a proselyte on condition that he be made High Priest).

[70] Thus Shemayah and Abtalion are said to have descended from proselytes (b. Gittin 57*b*). Hillel was descended from Avital, David's wife (II Sam. 3:4; I Chr. 3:3).

[71] There is a division of scholarly opinion on the question whether the Jews of the Diaspora were ignorant of Judaism.

[72] Philo's *Apology for the Jews* is lost, except for a quotation by Eusebius, in his *Preparatio Evangelica* VIII, 11. Philo's two tracts, *Against Flaccus* and *The Delegation to Gaius,* though apparently not extant in their full and original form, are impassioned apologies of Judaism. See E. Goodenough, *An Introduction to Philo Judaeus* (New Haven, 1940), p. 35.

[73] E. Goodenough, *An Introduction . . .* , pp. 54, 200.

[74] See S. Belkin, *Philo and the Oral Law* (Cambridge, Mass., 1940), and *The Alex-*

creativity had to remain the prerogative of the center of Jewish life. The problem which absorbed Alexandrian Jews was the apparent contradiction of revelation and reason, of Torah and the wisdom of the Greeks. The effort to understand both sources of truth as identical, visible in the Septuagint, the Wisdom of Solomon, and IV Maccabees, reached its zenith with the achievement of Philo.

This is not to say that the rabbis in the Holy Land were oblivious to the challenges of Hellenistic thought. The culture of Greece had pervaded the Holy Land: in the first century its language of refinement was certainly Greek. Hellenism inspired art and architecture, including Herod's Temple. Gamaliel II had a school where five hundred youths studied Greek culture.[75] He himself also visited a bathhouse in Acre dedicated to the goddess Aphrodite; he regarded her statue not as a forbidden image, but as an object of adornment.[76] Greek proverbs entered Hebrew. Greek hermeneutics may have helped to fashion the *halakha*.[77] Greek words, perhaps in excess of two thousand, enriched the vocabulary of the early rabbis.[78]

Many rabbis, too, wrestled with the implications for Judaism of the philosophy of the Greeks, particularly the thought of the Stoa and the Academy. They emerged with a conception of God as incorporeal, omnipotent, omniscient and omnipresent, transcendent, yet indwelling in a universe that serves, so to speak, as his material home. This conception could hardly be shared by the majority of the people; they doubtless followed the rabbis who rejected the influence of Greek thought and clung tenaciously to the anthropomorphisms of the Bible.[79]

Yet in other areas of theology, the differences between the early rabbis

---

andrian Halakah in Apologetic Literature of the First Century, C.E. (Philadelphia, n.d.).

[75] b. Baba Kamma 83*a*. Cf. also b. Gittin 58*a;* Palestinian Talmud Ta'anit IV.8 and Lamentations Rabba I.51. On Hellenistic influences in the Holy Land see Saul Lieberman, *Greek in Jewish Palestine* (New York, 1942), and *Hellenism in Jewish Palestine* (New York, 1950), pp. 100 ff.

[76] M. Avodah Zarah III.4; b. Avodah Zarah 44*b*.

[77] See David Daube, "Rabbinic Methods of Interpretation and Hellenistic Rhetoric," *HUCA,* XXII (1949), 239-64.

[78] See Samuel Krauss, "Greek Language and the Jews," *The Jewish Encyclopedia* VI, p. 87: "It is estimated that more than 3,000 words borrowed from the Greek and Latin are found in the rabbinical works."

[79] On this subject see A. Marmorstein, *The Old Rabbinic Doctrine of God* (London, 1937), particularly chs. II and V.

were not great.[80] First-century rabbinic thought regarded God as perfect and holy, the source of justice, yet even more a loving Father, who placed mercy over justice in his concern for the individual man. It described man as a creature of earth bearing a spark of divinity and hence eternity; free of will, yet paradoxically not undestined; a fusion of two natures struggling for mastery of his being; prone to sin, yet capable of repentance. It expressed God's relationship to the world through the modality of the Holy Presence, or *Shekhina,* a concept not identical with the Philonic Logos, yet functionally akin to it. Reciprocally, it taught, man reaches God through wisdom gained from the study of Torah—the divine pattern for human living—and the application of its principles to every phase of his life. Rabbinic thought saw in the faithful of Israel a prophet-group, the vehicle of revelation, selected for service and impressed with the onerous task of attuning itself and others to the Will Divine, thereby to accelerate the advent of the Kingdom of Heaven.

The rabbis left no works of systematic theology. The currents of their thought must be observed through the thousands of discrete commentaries, homilies, and legends which have come down in their names, and which together are known as the *'aggadah,* or Lore.

9. *The Primacy of Ethics.*[81] Neither in the first century nor in subsequent Judaism did theology acquire the status given to *halakha.* The rabbis were less concerned with man's belief than with the kind of life he led. Their primary goal was ethical behavior; for them deed rather than creed marked the pinnacle of piety. The ethical ideals of Judaism pervaded both their *halakha* and their *'aggadah.* They saw ethical action as the summit of holiness. They interpreted the biblical precept to be holy as God is holy to mean clothing the naked, nursing the sick and comforting the sorrow-laden. Religiosity for them entailed essentially ennoblement of life and adherence to a "social gospel" with a sense of love and duty. In the minds of the early rabbis, whosoever lived by these ideals, Jew or Gentile, was assured his portion in the world to come.

Unfortunately there are occasional attempts to disparage the rabbis' achievement in the area of ethics. From time to time we read statements to the effect that the early rabbis were so burdened with the minutiae

[80] On theology, see the works mentioned in nn. 10 and 13 above.

[81] *Ibid.* See also Moritz Lazarus, *The Ethics of Judaism* (tr. Henrietta Szold), 2 vols., Philadelphia, 1900.

of ritual law as to leave the garden of ethics untended; indeed that Judeo-Christianity represented a reaction against law and a return to the ethical paradise of the prophets.[82] The ethical heritage of Judaism did indeed play a vital role in early Christianity. Equally important was the role it played in first-century rabbinic thought. To the first century and the beginning of the next belong many of the statements found in the writings known as *Ethics of the Fathers*. From this period also come the early strata of the *'aggadah,* the treasurehouse of rabbinic ideas and ideals.

An old man living in A.D. 110 could not help but marvel at the changes which had swept over the heritage of his fathers in the short span of his own lifetime. Gone was his temple and its splendid ceremonies; gone even the freedom which he and his forbears had enjoyed. But his tradition remained, speaking to him with meaning and buoying him with hope. If he only had known the impact that this tradition, through later Judaism and Christianity, would have upon the civilization of man, he would have rejoiced. For ultimately, what mattered it that his people had lost their temple, if the spirit of his tradition had gained the world to serve?

[82] Thus, for example, Rudolf Bultmann, *Theologie des Neuen Testaments* (Tübingen, 1953), pp. 10 ff., English tr., pp. 11 ff.; Hans Lietzmann, *The Beginnings of the Christian Church* (tr. B. L. Woolf, London, 1953), p. 33; Joseph Bonsirven, *Palestinian Judaism in the Time of Jesus Christ* (New York, 1964), pp. 257 f., and H. Odeberg, *Pharisaism and Christianity,* tr. J. M. Moe (St. Louis, 1964). See the review of Odeberg by Sidney B. Hoenig in *Jewish Quarterly Review,* (NS) LV (1964), 168-70.

8

G. QUISPEL

Gnosticism and the New Testament*

When we consider the problem of Gnosticism and Christianity, we must take into account certain facts about the history of the Church.

Paul's opponents in Palestine did not disappear without leaving any trace. Their views were inherited and developed by a group of Jewish Christians existing somewhere in Syria; it was this group that was largely responsible for the views expressed in the Pseudo-Clementine writings. It is, of course, exceedingly difficult to assess just to what extent the older views are present in these later writings. But there is no doubt that some continuity does exist. Attempts to deny this continuity or to explain it away by citing parallels from Gnosticism should be dismissed as apologetics. The Pseudo-Clementine writings may be somewhat fantastic, but certainly are not gnostic. They are moreover valuable to the historian of the Church, both for the concept which we find there of Jesus as the promised prophet and because they show us that animosity towards Paul continued to persist in certain Jewish Christian quarters.

Nor should we assume that the Christian community of Jerusalem—that recognized Paul, but did not accept his views on the Law—vanished into the air after A.D. 70, or even after 135. If the Acts of the Apostles say nothing about the Christian mission to Egypt or Eastern Syria and Mesopotamia, we must not conclude that nothing of the kind existed. Egypt is very near to Palestine; consequently there were many Jews living in Alexandria. So it is possible that Jewish Christians came to Alexandria at a very early date to preach the Messiah, especially to their compatriots. In any case Jewish Christians must have lived there

* Editor's Note: This paper was published, in somewhat different form, in the June, 1965, issue of *Vigiliae Christianae*. Reprinted with the permission of the North-Holland Publishing Company, Amsterdam, publishers of *Vigiliae Christianae*.

before A.D. 200, because both Clement of Alexandria and Origen quote with some respect from their Gospel, the *Gospel According to the Hebrews.*

Relations between Palestine and Edessa are better substantiated. Tradition tells us that a certain Addai, a name abbreviated from the Hebrew Adonya, was sent from Jerusalem to Edessa to preach the gospel and was very well received there by the local Jews. Burkitt and Vööbus agree that there must be some truth in this story. As a matter of fact, we must consider the Aramaic-speaking Christendom of Palestine and Syria as a special unit with its own traditions, strongly influenced by its Jewish surroundings and not very interested in the ontological interpretation of Christianity which developed on Greek soil. This isolation explains, for example, why the concept of the Holy Ghost as a Mother, a concept well attested in the Jewish Christian Gospel tradition and quite understandable in a religion of Semitic language, continued to persist everywhere in Syria and can even be found in the fourth-century Syrian mystic Makarios.

All this, of course, has nothing to do with Gnosticism. It is against this background, however, that we must see the Gospel tradition in the *Gospel of Thomas,* which for several reasons should be located in the Christian community of Edessa and dated about A.D. 140. This collection of Sayings contains evidence of a Gospel tradition transmitted in a Jewish Christian milieu. In fact, one saying is even based upon a quotation from the *Gospel According to the Hebrews* (1:2). In logion 12, James is seen as the primate of the whole church, a view also attested by the Pseudo-Clementine writings (*Rec.* 1:43); this reflects the precedence of James in the primitive community, of which Paul also gives witness when, in Galatians 2:9, he puts James before Peter. If the Western Text gives the names in the opposite order and thus shows that at a very early date somebody in Rome may have had a different opinion, this only proves that the original wording was no mere coincidence. But the *Gospel of Thomas* also shows that it was Jewish rather than Gentile Christians who brought Christianity to Eastern Syria. Its author often uses, and even inserts into his sources, the word *monachos* in the sense of "bachelor," thereby showing that this was a technical term in his milieu. As a matter of fact, this word, of central importance in the *Gospel of Thomas,* has until now not been found in any known gnostic writing unless one wants to claim that the *Gospel of Thomas* is such, and so its presence is certainly no evidence for this text being gnostic. In fact its use here tends to show that the *Gospel of Thomas* is not gnostic at all. For the word *monachos* here, as in the Bible translation of the Jewish Christian Symmachus, seems to be the translation of the Hebrew *yāḥîd,* which is invested with the same meaning of "bachelor" in some rabbinic passages. The concept continued to exist in Syrian asceticism, expressed by the technical term *iḥidaya,* which conveys exactly the same idea.

We find the same relation between Jewish Christianity and Syrian asceticism in logion 42, "become passers-by." Some gnosticizing interpreters of the *Gospel of Thomas* have translated it, "come into being as you pass away." Consideration of the Greek, Coptic, and Hebrew languages show that this translation is very impressive, incomprehensible, and faulty. Joachim Jeremias has pointed out that "passer-by" is a literal translation of the Hebrew word *'ôbēr,* which means "wanderer," "wandering teacher." The logion says, "become wanderers." Obedient to this commandment the Syrian ascetics kept wandering until the fourth century and even later.

It would seem that this ascetic mood of the Jewish Christians is responsible for the distortion of the parable of the invitations, as found in the *Gospel of Thomas,* logion 64. Following the example of certain OT prophets, Zephaniah (1:11) and Zechariah (14:21), this writing shows a certain animosity towards commerce and business. "Tradesmen and merchants shall not enter the seats (lit. places) of my Father." But exactly the same application and interpretation of the parable is to be found in Aphraates (Parisot, pp. 249-50: *qui adsumit iugum sanctorum, negotiationem a se removeat*). Vööbus was certainly right when he pointed out that Syrian asceticism and Christian asceticism in general had a Jewish Christian background. A gnosticizing, arbitrary, and unhistorical interpretation of the *Gospel of Thomas* obscures this insight into the history of the early Church.

Historians of the early Church have recently stressed the importance of Encratism and the fact that its roots lay in primitive Christianity. These two realizations have a direct bearing upon the much debated problem of Gnosticism and Christianity. Much would be gained for our study of the NT if it were established once and for all that Encratism is not the same as Gnosticism. Henry Chadwick, in an article for *Reallexikon für Antike und Christentum,* has shown that Christianity has been accompanied by Encratism since its very beginning. Perhaps it was present in Corinth, where Paul exhorts the Encratites not to give up marriage in spiritually overrating their all too human frames. Certainly it is there too in the pastoral letters, where Jewish Encratites proclaim that the resurrection has already taken place and that marriage should be abolished. Later, Encratism remained a current within the Catholic Church until finally, in some quarters of the Western Church, the Encratites were declared heretics and expelled. I must add that in Syria the Encratites in fact remained within the Church much longer. Tatian was not considered a heretic there; on the contrary his Gospel harmony, which contained Encratitic corrections, was accepted for use in the Church. The *Acts of Thomas,* written about A.D. 225 in Edessa, reflects the main stream of Syrian Christianity when it proclaims divorce as the essential Christian teaching. The Syrian *Liber Graduum,* rightly considered by its editor Kmosko to be Encratitic, shows no evidence that it was written outside the Church. The fourth-century Syrian mystic Makarios (38:1) identified the Church with its unmarried ascetics—a characteristic view of Encratitic doctrine. But although his views are certainly in tune with the specific teachings of the Syrian Messalians, we cannot prove that in his lifetime Messalianism led a heterodox existence outside the Church. Our sources show rather that their expulsion took place only towards the end of the fourth century. Messalianism then was probably a revival of a very old indigenous spirituality, which had existed in Syria for many centuries.

Encratism seems to have differed from Catholicism mainly in that it prescribed celibacy, whereas the Western Church in general only preferred it. Celibacy was for the Encratites a requirement for baptism. According to our sources they considered marriage to be fornication and corruption; from this it followed that everyone who had not left his father and his mother was to be considered the son of a prostitute. Moreover, birth was considered to be deplorable, because it inevitably led to death.

Our main source for the history of Encratism, the third book of Clement of Alexandria's *Stromateis,* reveals a more sophisticated and profound interpretation of the Christian faith and gives us reason to suppose that a certain continuity between the NT and the early Church can also be found to exist in the case of Encratism.

In the *Stromateis,* marriage is considered in its eschatological perspective. Jesus had taught that in the eschatological era marriage would not exist any more (Mark 12:25 par.). But now eschatology has been realized. Christ has risen from the dead, the faithful participate in his resurrection, and therefore marriage should be abolished. It is possible that this reasoning also lies behind the words of the Encratites in II Tim. 2:18, saying that the resurrection has already taken place.

Clement also transmits the pessimistic view of these Encratites on love and marriage; reproduction and generation only serve to nourish death. But the basis of their theology is biblical—they follow the Lord who was poor and unmarried. Redemption, moreover, is a deliverance from desire, because the Fall, according to their interpretation, was a Fall out of innocence into sexuality. The tree of knowledge, from which man ate, symbolized sexual intercourse. Jesus by his life and message delivered the Christian from this urge and drive for life.

When we have read and understood the views of the Encratites in the third book of the *Stromateis,* we clearly see that this is the real theology of the *Gospel of Thomas.* It teaches that

1) only those who are unmarried can be saved (1:75);
2) the resurrection has already taken place (1:51);
3) marriage is fornication (1:105);
4) the earthly mother produces children for death, but the heavenly Mother regenerates them for eternal life (1:101);
5) before the Fall, man lived in a state of innocence, where the differentiation between the sexes had not yet taken place (1:37, 1:11). When man returns to the sexual innocence of the child, and only then, he regains Paradise (1:22); he realizes the original unity and identity with himself which he had lost.

All this is Encratitic and in accord with the information given by Clement of Alexandria concerning the Encratites. This proves that the *Gospel of Thomas* is Encratitic. The activity of Tatian in Eastern Syria and the Acts of Thomas attest to the existence of Encratites in the Syrian Church of Edessa. The *Gospel of Thomas* proves that they were already there about A.D. 140. Unlike Gnosticism the *Gospel of Thomas* does not teach an inferior demiurge, docetism, the divine consubstantiality of the human Self, nor the mythical expression of self-experience. Where is Achamoth, where Barbelo, where are the Aeons? Those who claim that the author of the *Gospel of Thomas* was a Gnostic, must first prove that there were Gnostics in second-century Edessa and that the author of this writing was one of them. I know of no sources which contain such information. The adherents of the gnostic interpretation, moreover, must explain how the author could possibly say that the buried *corpse* could rise again (logion 5, Greek version) and that Jesus manifested himself, quite undocetically, in the *flesh* (1:28, cf. Baruch 3:38).

I think, on the contrary, that we can adduce a decisive argument to prove that the *Gospel of Thomas* is Syrian and Encratitic. Working quite independently of each other, Dom Baker and G. Quispel have recently established that the Syrian mystic Makarios knew and used the *Gospel of Thomas.* Makarios quotes one saying almost word for word: "The Kingdom of God is spread upon the earth and men do not see it" (1:113). There are, moreover, many clear allusions to the *Gospel of Thomas* and there are also very many similarities in theology. For both Makarios and the author of the *Gospel of Thomas* Christ is our Father, and the Holy Spirit our Mother; man should be one, because God is one. Man originates in the heavenly Paradise, and has fallen because he has tasted the bitterness of desire and has drunk the venom with which the serpent infected the fruit of knowledge. But now eschatology has been realized, the resurrection is already there, owing to Christ. Therefore, man should dissolve his marriage, leave his wife and children, follow Christ and identify himself with Him, in order to regain Paradise here and now.

Nobody has ever said that Makarios was a Gnostic. Then neither is the *Gospel of Thomas.* We should envision this writing in its historical milieu and thus in its proper perspective, in order to discern its message. Encratism is not Gnosticism—not even the Encratism of the NT, which should be interpreted in the light of the Encratitic sources that are available, in both Greek and Syrian, although they are of a somewhat later date.

With this in mind, we turn to the so-called *Hymn of the Pearl,* which occurs in the *Acts of Thomas* (chs. 108—113). This hymn is sometimes considered the key to the pre-Christian Iranian myth of the Saved Savior, which is supposed to lie behind the teaching of the NT, especially the

Fourth Gospel. The poem tells us about a prince, who as a child was living in the kingdom of his father. He is sent away from home with a "load" (*phortion*) of precious stones to fetch a pearl in Egypt. When he arrives there he clothes himself in the dress of the Egyptians and forgets about his mission. Then a letter is sent to him from home which reminds him of his task. He charms the serpent that guards the pearl, "the one pearl" (line 12), and he takes this pearl away and returns to his father. The robe which he had formerly worn is given back to him. In this he recognizes his real nature. He invests himself with this robe and gives the pearl to his father.

There is no doubt that this hymn is Christian in origin. It is based upon the parable of the pearl, of which it is a poetical amplification and illustration. More especially it is based upon the version of this parable contained in the *Gospel of Thomas,* 1:76. "The Kingdom of the Father is like man, a merchant, who possessed merchandise (*phortion*) and discovered a pearl. That merchant was prudent. He sold the merchandise, and bought 'the one pearl' for himself."

This parable must have existed outside the *Gospel of Thomas* in the Jewish Christian and Syrian Gospel traditions. In the Pseudo-Clementine *Recognitions* (3:62) we also read that the merchant was *sapiens* and that he bought *unam margaritam* ("the one pearl"). Likewise, *sapiens* is the reading of Ephrem Syrus and the *Life of Rabbula.* But the *Hymn of the Pearl,* too, has the variants *phortion* and "the one pearl" in common with the *Gospel of Thomas.* If the *Acts of Thomas* was written at Edessa about A.D. 225, this Christian hymn must have been composed sometime before 225 and after the introduction of Christianity into Edessa by Jewish Christians. Nor is there any doubt that its basic ideas are also to be found in the Syrian Makarios. For in Makarios as well, we find that man receives again the garment of glory that he had lost when the soul fell from its height and became the slave of the true Pharaoh (47:6). Or again he likens Christians to the sons whom a father sent to a foreign country with drugs to soothe and kill the dragons that attack them (26:24). Moreover in Makarios, ch. 39, Scripture is the letter, written by a king (39).

In this historical context the underlying idea of the *Hymn of the Pearl* is revealed. The soul, born in the heavenly Paradise, must be reminded of its task in the body, so it can return to Paradise and receive the original garment of the Spirit. The concept of the preexistence of the soul in Paradise, of Jewish origin and understandable in a Christian milieu so profoundly influenced by Judaism, persisted in Syria at least until the time of Makarios (25:7). The *Hymn of the Pearl* is not gnostic at all, but rather an orthodox Christian hymn tinged with Judaistic colors.

Perhaps these conclusions will give us some second thoughts about the apodictic and uncritical statements of George Widengren and others concerning the Iranian myth of the Saved Savior. We are reminded of the sober criticism by Gershom Scholem in his great book, *Jewish Gnosticism,* where he writes

> Theories that the origin of Gnosticism is to be found outside the scope of Judaism have been widely discussed. It is one of many marvels confronting the explorer in the field that scholars who have been looking far and wide to establish the source from which it all has come have been remarkably reluctant, or, rather, unwilling to allow the theory that Gnostic tendencies may have developed in the very midst of Judaism itself, whether in its classical forms or on its heterodox and sectarian fringes. The more far-fetched the explanation, the better. The theories of Reitzenstein in particular, on the Iranian origin of Gnosticism, have had considerable influence for some time. Even when, on closer inspection, they have been found disappointing and highly speculative, they still linger on—if only in a somewhat emasculated form. One is often left wondering about the methods used in this approach; and one is no less amazed by the stupendous ignorance of Jewish sources that warps the conclusions and even the basic approach of some of the finest scholars. Since the appearance of the excellent collection of rabbinic source material in Strack-Billerbeck's *Commentary on the New Testament,* we have, furthermore, been vouchsafed a new kind of fake scholarship, one that feeds on this work and takes it for granted that what is not in Billerbeck is not in existence.[1]

I think we must agree with Scholem. Gnosticism is not a late chapter of the history of Greek philosophy and therefore a Christian heresy, an acute Hellenization of the Christian religion. Nor is it a fossilized survival of old Iranian or even Indian religious concepts, and certainly it is not derived from a presupposed, consistent Iranian myth of the Saved Savior. It is rather a religion of its own, with its own phenomenological structure, characterized by the mythical expression of self-experience

[1] *Jewish Gnosticism, Merkabah Mysticism, and Talmudic Tradition* (New York: Jewish Theological Seminary of New York, 1960), pp. 1-2.

through the revelation of the "Word," or, in other words, by an awareness of a tragic split within the Deity itself. And as such it owes not a little to Judaism. When we try to discern the relations between Judaism and Gnosticism, the problem of Gnosticism and the NT may be seen in a new and illuminating perspective. For clarity's sake we shall distinguish between three milieus: first, circles at the outskirts of Judaism, namely in Samaria; second, the milieu of esoteric lore transmitted within the very heart of Palestinian Pharisaism; and third, certain baptist sects in Palestine which seem to have had some relation to the Jewish religion. The Hellenistic Judaism of Alexandria as represented by Philo, however, does not seem to have the same relevance to our subject.

The female counterpart of God is called "Helen" in the Gnosis of Simon the Magician, "Barbelo" in the *Apocryphon of John,* and "Silence" in the Valentinian school. Perhaps all these names are important illustrations of the syncretistic character of Gnosticism. Helen was a goddess, venerated everywhere in the Hellenistic world and in Samaria. Depth and Silence always have had, as they did then, a mystical flavor. "Barbelo" is more problematical, for its etymology is uncertain. In a magical papyrus which I acquired in Berlin in 1956, the name is found spelled Abrbelōth, together with Io, Ialtaboth (?), El, Adonai, Gabriel (?), Souriel (?), Istrael, Mikael, Ouriel, (B) ainchoooch, and Abrasax. This sounds very Jewish, but does not necessarily prove that Abrbelōth was venerated in Jewish circles. In Greek magical papyri we find such forms as these: barbarioth (Preisendanz, 1:70), Barbar Adonai (1:84), Brabēl (1:102), Abraiaoth (1:106), Abraal (1:180), Abriēl (2:43). It may be then that Abrbelōth is Hebrew and means perhaps: *ḥābēr ba'al,* "companion of the Lord." But etymologies of magical names are very uncertain. The only thing we can say is that Abrbelōth is related to Jewish-Hellenistic magic.

But the fact is that these references and affiliations do not help us very much to discern the real issue of Gnostic theology, which is to my mind the concept of the suffering God, the fallen God. Yet the Gnostic sources are quite explicit in this respect. God suffers detriment to his soul (*Ev. Ver.* 41:36); Iao redeems his soul (Iren. 1:21-3); Christ redeems his soul (*Gospel of Philip,* 9). In a way this is also the basic idea of Manicheism, that primordial Man, the Self of God, is overwhelmed by the powers of darkness and vanquished, until the call from above redeems him. God, in redeeming man, redeems himself.

We must remove the Hellenistic accretions and rigorously examine the Gnostic conception against its Jewish background, to understand what this means and what was happening in the transition from Judaism to Gnosticism. The female counterpart of the Godhead in Gnosticism is the Wisdom of Judaism, the more or less personified *ḥokmâ* of Prov. 9:1, and of the Wisdom of Solomon, who according to Jewish teaching was instrumental in creating the world; and who, according to some versions of the story, descended from heaven to dwell among man but was not accepted and so returned to her abode in heaven.

It would seem that in the Gnosis of Simon the Magician, Wisdom herself fell—that is to say, the Fall is a split within the Deity. It is true that, according to one report, Wisdom herself remained completely unknown to the Rulers of this world, and only her image was overpowered by the lower powers (Pseudo-Clementine *Recognitions* 2:12). This then would mean that already at a very early date there existed among Samaritans (heterodox Jews) the concept of a double Wisdom. In any case, that is what we find in the *Apocryphon of John.* There Barbelo, the female counterpart of God, is called the "first idea," a Stoic expression equally attributed to Simon's Helen, and understandable as a title of Wisdom; but the last of the aeons, who falls because of her lascivity, is called Sophia. And it would seem that this is a complication of the more simple concept, that Wisdom herself falls. The Valentinian system, as conceived by Ptolemaeus, is still further differentiated. There Sige, the mother of the Pleroma, is distinguished from the thirtieth aeon, Sophia, who falls because of her desire to understand God, and then brings forth a lower Wisdom who is expelled from the Pleroma. But that we have here a far echo of Jewish Wisdom speculations, is proved by the fact that this female is called Achamoth, the Jewish *ḥokmâ* (Iren. 1.4.1).

Once again we must turn to syncretism and astrology to find some explanation for the gnostic demiurge. In the *Apocryphon of John,* now available in its three Coptic versions edited by M. Krause, and in a good English translation by Sōren Giversen, we read that this demiurge, Ialdabaoth, has the aspect of a lion and a serpent. Evidently he is a monstrous figure with the head of a lion and the body of a serpent, like Chnoubis or Abrasax on magical amulets. More helpful is the information that Ialdabaoth has been borrowed from magic and represents the planet *Saturnus* (Origen, *Contra Celsum* 6:33). Ialdabaoth, says the *Apocryphon of John,* had eyes like burning lightning that flashed. He is the God, who brings about Heimarmene. All this fits in very well with astrological lore. Saturn, the highest planet with the most malignant influence, is represented in Africa as Baal Hammon with the head of a lion, and Arnobius speaks about him as the lion-headed Frugifer (*Adv. Gentes* 6:10). Saturnus as Kronos, and therefore Chronos ("time"), is described by Plutarch (*de Iside* 44.) as the creator of the world, because Time in its course brings forth everything. Saturnus is also the god of lightning. He is related to the monstrous figure in the Mithraic mysteries, with the head of a lion and covered by snakes, who symbolizes Time and Fate. And certainly it is characteristic of Gnosticism to abhor and reject time and history. "This archon who was weak had three names: the first name is Ialdabaoth; the second is Saklas; the third is Sammael. But he was ungodly in his ignorance which is in him for he said: I am God and there is no other God but me" (*ibid.,* 59:15-20). Ialdabaoth is Aramaic for "Son of Chaos," an etymology which has long been suspected, and one which does not shed much light on our problem. Sammael means "the blind one" and is a name of the devil in Jewish sources. This shows that the demiurge in the *Apocryphon of John* was identified with the devil, who in certain passages of the NT is conceived of as the Ruler of this world, or even the God of this world.

Still more illuminating is the etymology of Saklas. "Sakla" is Aramaic for "fool." This lends an Aramaic color to the story and reveals the basic idea of the writing. The *Apocryphon of John* dramatically describes the persistent struggle between Ialdabaoth and Barbelo, or some related female figure, whom he does not know. But if *sakla* means "fool," this means (in less mythological and more abstract terms) that the conflict between hidden wisdom and worldly folly is a persistent theme in history.

The original and spirited dualism of the *Apocryphon of John* is not, in the last analysis, a dualism of good and evil in the world, as in Manicheism, but of the Divine and the world. But at this point, the learned Gnostics Basilides and Valentinus follow a different course. They consider the demiurge to be an ignorant tool of a higher purpose. I think theirs is a conscious modification. It would seem to me that the original form of the myth contained in the *Apocryphon of John* is more primitive and archaic than the profound and learned elaborations of Basilides and

Valentinus. If we accept this as a working hypothesis, we may discern how much Basilides and Valentinus contributed of their own account, and how each in his own way Hellenized and Christianized an earlier Gnosis of a much more mythological character, and one which showed a relative absence of Christian elements and the strong influence of a Jewish milieu. Basilides had a speculative mind, Valentinus was enthusiastic and poetical, but they did not create out of nothing. They developed an already existing gnostic myth, which at least must have been similar to the teaching of the *Apocryphon of John.* Then we can discern that they radically changed a primitive dualism into a much more monistic setting.

Basilides was perhaps not as original or as bold as he seemed to be, when he started his system with an impressive statement about the "non-existent God." In the *Apocryphon of John* we find a similar negative theology. It might be, then, that this was the traditional way of starting a gnostic system. What is really new is that Basilides replaced emanation and fall with creation and evolution, and conceived of Christ as the exclusive, central source of revelation, whereas the *Apocryphon* seems to teach several interventions by Barbelo. The Ruler of the world is not described as a hostile monster: he serves the hidden purpose of God and is instrumental in its fulfillment. But he originates from chaos and thus reminds us of Ialdabaoth, which seems to mean "Son of Chaos." He is called Abrasax and so recalls the well-known figure of the magic gems with the head of a cock, the tail of a serpent, and a whip in his hand. Most characteristically, this highest Ruler of the world does not know that there is a God above him. So this theme seems to have been taken from an already existing gnostic system.

Valentinus appears to have followed the version in the *Apocryphon of John* more closely. It is said in a Valentinian source that Sophia suffered her passion apart from the embrace of her consort (Iren. 1.2.12); this feature also plays an important and detailed role in the newly published *Apocryphon* (Krause 135:30). Moreover, in certain Valentinian sources, she prays, and the aeons intercede for her (Hipp. 6:31). When in 1947 a reconstruction of the original doctrine of Valentinus was published, this was supposed to have been the teaching of the Gnostic teacher himself, though no document from his school had exactly preserved this sequel of events. It was moreover suggested that the scheme of the myth was borrowed from some already existing oriental gnosticizing sects.[2] It is gratifying to find, so many years later, something rather similar in the *Apocryphon of John* (61:35): "She repented with much weeping, and the whole Pleroma heard the prayer of her repentance and praised the invisible, virginal spirit for her sake." This seems to prove that Valentinus must have known this or a similar writing.

What is more, when we find in a Valentinian document that the demiurge is called "foolish," *mōros* (Hipp. *Ref.* 6.33.1; 6.34.8), like "Sakla" in the *Apocryphon of John,* we must assume that it is a traditional motif taken from an earlier Gnosis. For in the *Apocryphon* "fool" has a very special, Jewish meaning. A fool is a man who says in his heart that there is no God. But that is exactly what the Ruler of this world is thought to say. Therefore he is "foolish"; God and his Wisdom are hidden from him.

This concept that the Wisdom of God is a hidden Wisdom, seems to be of Jewish origin. It is found already in Job 28:12 ff. An adherent of Simon Magus seems to have taught that Divine Wisdom was completely unknown to the Rulers of this world (Pseudo-Clementine *Recognitiones* 2:12: *ipsam vero ut est penitus ignorarunt*). The theme of the foolish Ruler of the world seems to be traditional in Gnosticism and seems to be derived from a Jewish milieu.

This would explain its curious similarity to some views held by St. Paul. The view that Wisdom has fallen is absent from the NT. Therefore, when we find in the Synoptic Gospels (as in Matt. 11:28) that Jesus speaks as the embodiment of Wisdom, we should not explain it in terms of a gnostic influence, but rather explain it in terms of a common Jewish background. Likewise, when St. Paul in the first two chapters of I Corinthians proclaims a Divine Wisdom unknown to the Rulers of this world, he is not necessarily under the influence of Jewish gnostic sects. But he does say that the Wisdom of God is hidden and unknown to the Rulers of this world; for if the Rulers had known the hidden purpose of salvation, they would not have crucified the Lord of Glory (2:7-8). They were foolish enough to serve God without knowing it. But God in his act of salvation unmasked worldly wisdom as folly (1:20). And we might also add that the words of Paul imply that the wisdom of the

[2] "The Original Doctrine of Valentine," *VigChr,* I (1947), 43-73.

Rulers of this world is equally foolish and godless. In the light of the Cross, that wisdom which the angels of the nations supposedly transmitted to the several peoples, is shown to be worldly, autonomous, and godless wisdom—it is essentially "folly" in the Hebrew sense of the word. All this suggests that Paul did not think about earthly kings and authorities, but rather about spiritual entities located somewhere in space, the ambivalent spiritual powers behind the earthly authorities. This way of looking at things would seem to be very near to the gnostic dualism of *ḥokmâ* and *sakla*. It is not just a mythological concept of the universe that Paul and the gnostics have in common. It is rather the awareness that the profoundest motives of this world are absurd and that our rational philosophies, inspired as they are by these innerworldly motivations, are equally absurd—because our world as such is absurd.

But even if Gnosticism and Christianity shared a common Jewish background, there is yet another aspect of their relationship which bears investigation—namely, that the Gnostics may have preserved archaic Christian material not attested elsewhere. For a certain period they belonged to the Christian Church (in some congregations longer than in others) and participated in the social, liturgical, and sacramental life of the local churches. But by nature the Gnostics were not inclined to have any special appreciation for the massive objectivity of ritual acts. They tended rather to spiritualize exterior rites and thought that it was not only baptism which saved men, but also the Gnosis, "what we are, where we come from, whither we go." Therefore we have recently learned to appreciate gnostic writings, not only for the specific gnostic doctrine they contain, but also for the traces of primitive archaic theology expressing Christian views in Semitic categories which we find imbedded in the gnostic doctrine itself. Whatever interpretation one finds for these remarkable theological data, he sometimes cannot help but assume that these primitive and undoubtedly Jewish concepts and expressions sometimes lead us back a long way from Gnosticism to Palestinian Christianity, especially where sacramental views are concerned.

On the other hand, the Mandaean problem has become an open question again, since Torgny Säve Söderbergh has shown that the Manichaean *Psalms of Thomas* were based upon some extant Mandaean hymns, thus proving that the Mandaean sect in Iraq must have had a very long prehistory. Kurt Rudolph argued in his useful monograph on the Mandaeans that this sect was of Western Palestinian origin, and there is much to say in favor of his thesis. The curious expression "Lord of Greatness" in Mandaean writings has been found in the Qumran *Genesis apocryphon.* Moreover, I cannot explain the parallels between the names of Mandaean divinities and those found in the Hellenistic magical papyri unless the Mandaeans have very old Western roots. We should also note that in the Mandaean sect ritual ablutions in "living" streams of water have a central place. The Swedish scholar Segelberg has argued that there exist some curious parallels between the Mandaean and the Roman rite of baptism, and concludes that they had a common pre-Christian background in Palestine. His studies deserve very attentive consideration.

Furthermore, Niels Dahl has pointed out that justification in Paul has baptismal implications. Basing himself upon Qumran material, he has shown that in the Essene sect the same combination of ablution and justification was found as in Paul. "But you were washed, you were sanctified, you were justified in the Name of the Lord Jesus Christ and in the Spirit of our God" (I Cor. 6:11). It goes without saying that rebirth in the *Gospel of John* also has its sacramental implications. Now the *Gospel of John,* more than any other writing of the NT, has stylistic and conceptual parallels with Mandaean literature. Even if Mandaeism turns out to be neither so old nor of Palestinian origin, obligatory reading of Mandaean writings could serve students of the NT as good preparation for the right understanding of the Fourth Gospel.

All this tends to show that baptism was very important in primitive Christianity, and may have had its prefiguration in the Jewish sects of Palestine.

A primitive survival of sacramental language seems to have been preserved in the *Gospel of Philip,* Saying 12.

> One single Name they do not utter in the world, the Name which the Father gave to the Son, which is above all things, which is the Name of the Father. For the Son would not become Father except *he clothe himself with the Name of the Father.*

It has been proven long ago that the speculations about Jesus as the Name of the Father, so frequent in documents of Valentinian Gnosis, presuppose esoteric Jewish lore about the Name of the Lord and have parallels in NT passages, especially John 17:11 ("keep them in Thy name which Thou hast given me") and Phil. 2:9 ("bestowed on him the Name which is above every name"). Here the gnostics have a common background with John and Paul, a background which is Jewish or even Jewish Christian. But the curious expression "to clothe oneself with the Name" needs further clarification. There is a parallel for it in another source of Valentinian Gnosis, a sacramental formula quoted by Irenaeus 1.21.3, "The hidden Name with which Jesus the Nazarene invested himself. . . ." It is possible that these words contain an allusion to the baptism of Jesus in the Jordan, for the Valentinians thought that at that moment the Name of God had descended upon Jesus (*Excerpta ex Theodoto* 22:6). The same expression occurs in the *Odes of Solomon* which I consider to be evidence for Syrian Christianity in Edessa.

> *Put on,* therefore, *the Name* of the Most High and
> know Him:
> and you shall cross without danger,
> while the rivers shall be subject to you (39:8).

If we assume that Christianity in Edessa was of Palestinian origin, there is some possibility that the concept of the believer "putting on the Name" is of Jewish Christian origin. In any case we also find the theology of the Name elsewhere in Syria.

In the *Acts of Thomas* (ch. 27) "the holy Name of Christ which is above every name" is invoked in a sacramental content. The "true Name," that is, the *tetragrammaton* is distinguished from the conventional name "Jesus Christ." "Thou art not able to hear his true Name now at this time, but the name that is given to him is Jesus the Messiah" (ch. 163). If we find the same curious expression in the Syrian Christianity of Edessa and in circles of Valentinian Gnostics somewhere in the West, this seems to point to a common background in Jewish Christianity.

As far as I know, the expression "to put on the Name" is not found in the OT. But we find there a similar conception, that namely the Spirit of God "invests" man, so that he is "clad" with the Spirit (cf. LXX Judges 6:34 ms A; I Chron. 12:19; II Chron. 24:20). In a magical Jewish writing of later date, "describing a highly ceremonious rite in which the magician impregnates himself, as it were, with the great Name of God, i.e. performs a symbolic act by clothing himself in a garment into whose texture the Name has been woven," it is said, "Then go into the water up to your loins and *put on* the glorious and terrible Name in the midst of the water" (*Sēfer Hammalbush,* Br. Mus. 752). From this passage we may conclude that the idiomatic Hebrew phrase for "putting on the Name" was *labuš eth ha-šēm.*

The same expression was current among the Samaritans. In a Samaritan hymn it is said about Moses: "Mighty is the great prophet, who *clad* himself *in the Name* of the Godhead." [3] I think this material is relevant for the interpretation of Paul's remark, "As many of you as were baptized into Christ, you have *put on* Christ" (Gal. 3:27). The wording seems to be thoroughly Jewish. It reveals to us the Jewish perspective of Paul's sacramental convictions. It also leaves open the possibility that this drastic imagery was not personally invented by Paul, but was inherited by him from a common faith and even perhaps prefigured in some pre-Christian sect of Jewish baptists.

Gnostic materials, then, can be instrumental in our discerning the sacramental implications and Jewish presuppositions of some NT authors, if only we admit that the Mandaean problem and, more generally, the history of Jewish sects have to be taken into account.

The most important Jewish contribution, however, both to Gnosticism and to early Christianity, seems to have come from esoteric circles in the heart of Palestinian Judaism. Gershom Scholem has shown that there existed within Judaism esoteric traditions which had very old roots and went back to Pharisaic circles of the first century A.D. And he has pointed out that St. Paul as well as some Gnostics must have known these traditions. I accept his view. The Valentinian Gnostic Marcus the Magician, who gives us a phantastic description of the "body of Truth," is indebted to Jewish esoteric traditions about the measuring of the body of the Schechina. When the *Pistis Sophia* mentions a *Yahweh qātōn* and a *Yahweh gādōl,* this writing reveals a familiarity with the shocking terminology of earlier Jewish mystics. We must add that the speculations in the Valentinian *Gospel of Truth* about Christ as the "proper Name" of the hidden God must have the same origin. For in the *Apocalypse of Abraham* (ch. 10), the oldest document of Jewish mysticism, we find that

[3] A. E. Cowley, *The Samaritan Liturgy,* I, 54.

Jaoel the vicegerent of God second only to God himself has received the ineffable Name that is dwelling in him. Speculations on the Name, moreover, were characteristic of esoteric Jewish lore. I think I can mention a new argument in favor of the thesis that Jewish esoteric teaching concerning the *kābôd* as the "form like the appearance of a Man" or the "body of God" influenced Gnostic thought. It is taken from the *Treatise on the Three Natures,* the fourth book of the Jung Codex, where it is said about Christ: "He alone is truly worthy, the *Man* of the Father, who is . . . , the *form* of the formless, (the body) of the bodiless, the *face* of the invisible, the *word* of the inutterable, the *thought* of the unthinkable" (p. 66, 1:10-16).

We see then that the Gnostics have been influenced by a very specific current within Judaism, namely the esoteric traditions of Palestinian Pharisees. This should stop once and for all the idle talk of dogmatic minds about Gnosticism having nothing in common with Judaism proper. On the other hand, the comparison shows how far the Gnostics have removed themselves from these Jewish origins. The Gnostics teach the consubstantiality of God and man; the Jewish mystics underline the gulf that separates man from God, even in the ecstasy of vision. The Jewish mystics know of no split within the Deity, nor do they admit that the creator of the world is a lower demiurge.

Early Christianity, too, seems to have been influenced by these esoteric traditions. In his book, *Jewish Gnosticism,* Scholem proves that Paul is expressing himself in the terminology of the rabbinic ecstatics, when he says that he has been lifted up towards the Paradise in the third heaven (II Cor. 12:2). It is certainly reasonable to suppose that a former Pharisee knew the traditions of esoteric Pharisaism.

This perspective might also throw a new light on other passages of the NT. On this occasion I will only remark that the Western text of Luke 11:52 (paralleled by logion 39 of the *Gospel of Thomas*) shows an awareness of this secret tradition when it states that the teachers of the Law, especially the Pharisees, have *hidden* the key of knowledge, that is, the oral interpretation of the Law.

But also the Gospel of John can become more understandable in the light of these traditions. The attention of the Jewish mystics was focused upon such chapters as Isa. 6 and Ezek. 1, where the prophets described the manifestation of God upon his throne. The mystics were concerned to behold this *kābôd,* this "body" or "form like the appearance of a Man." Is it not remarkable, then, that in the Fourth Gospel Jesus reproaches the Jews that they have not seen the *eidos* of God (John 5:37), implying that God has a form?

Elsewhere (12:41) John states that Isaiah beheld the glory of Christ. This could be interpreted to mean that the prophet beheld Christ eternal upon the Throne; in that case Christ is identified with the *kābôd* which, according to the mystics, manifests itself upon the throne. This is not only a matter of parallels and historical influences. It reveals a deep affinity with the basic motives of Jewish mysticism, a common conception of God and a similar answer to the challenge of a particular historical situation. Again it is Gershom Scholem who proves to be a trustworthy guide and an eye-opener on our way. His book *Von der mystischen Gestalt der Gottheit* contains a learned discussion of the problem of the image in montheism. The latter opposes the use of images in the cultus. But this does not imply that God has no form. The Bible explicitly states that God has a "form" (Num. 12:8), and is full of anthropomorphic imagery. Under the influence of Greek philosophy, Hellenistic Judaism tried to spiritualize these conceptions and to assimilate them into the abstract generalizations of a rational world civilization.

Completely the opposite reaction to philosophy is to be found in the Palestinian circles which brought forth Jewish mysticism. In these conservative, even reactionary quarters, it is stressed that God has a "form." Anthropomorphism is reasserted in a challenging and provocative way. Such bold symbolic speech naturally leads to the break-through of authentic mythological patterns—and this did not happen at the outskirts of Judaism, but in the center of Palestinian Judaism. Such a Gnosis is completely Jewish-orthodox. Its aim is to maintain that the God of Israel is not an unmoved first mover, but a hidden God who reveals himself to man. This basic issue of the biblical religion is formulated in a radical way. The astonishing imagery serves a thoroughly conservative purpose, the preservation of the Jewish identity.

Against this background we see more clearly how Jewish early Christianity was. It was part of that movement of the "revolt of the images" on Palestinian soil, already reflected in Jewish apocalypticism and continued in esoteric Pharisaism, the eventual result of which was the birth of Gnosticism proper, at the fringe of Judaism. We may consider this movement as an endeavor in the face of the Hellenistic world civilization to maintain the faith in a living God who is moved and reveals himself. At the same time it represents a swing within the Jewish soul away from reason and moralism towards freedom and the image.

In Christianity, in contradistinction to Gnosticism, man remains man. God is moved, but not split, and the redeemer is also the creator. In spite of this, we must conclude that Gnosticism and Christianity have much in common, because they have in part a common background and a certain historic affinity for one another. Therefore careful consideration of the Gnostic materials can help us to discern how Jewish the NT is, and how lively was the Jewish mind at all times, and especially at the beginning of our era. So much so that both Judaism and Christianity would not only contrast the folly of this world with a transcendent Wisdom which lies beyond our grasp, but would stress the sacramental implications of salvation, and the possibility of beholding the glory of the hidden Lord.

ROBERT MCLACHLAN WILSON

RESPONSE TO G. QUISPEL'S "Gnosticism and the New Testament"

The subject proposed for our consideration in this session is "Gnosticism and the New Testament Writings," which is rather a large order for the time at our disposal. Even to review the researches of the past ten years would involve discussion of three books published in English alone, thirteen original Coptic documents made available within that period, and a very considerable mass of articles in various modern languages.[1] It may suffice to recall that the Nag Hammadi bibliography published

[1] R. McL. Wilson, *The Gnostic Problem* (London, 1958); H. Jonas, *The Gnostic Religion* (New York, 1958); R. M. Grant, *Gnosticism and Early Christianity* (London and New York, 1959). The Coptic documents are: the Gospel of Mary, the Apocryphon of John and the Sophia Jesu Christi, in W. C. Till, *Die gnostischen Schriften des koptischen Papyrus Berolinensis 8502,* Berlin, 1955; the Gospel of Truth, in *Evangelium Veritatis,* ed. Malinine, Puech, and Quispel (Zürich, 1956) (Supplement by the same editors with W. C. Till, 1961); the Gospel of Thomas, ed. Guillaumont, Puech, Quispel, Till, and Yassa Abdal Masih (Leiden, etc., 1959); the Gospel of Philip, in W. C. Till, *Das Evangelium nach Philippos* (Berlin, 1963); the Epistle to Rheginus, in *De Resurrectione,* ed. Malinine, Puech, Quispel, and Till (Zürich and Stuttgart, 1963); an anonymous treatise, in A. Böhlig and P. Labib, *Die koptisch-gnostische Schrift ohne Titel aus Codex II von Nag Hammadi* (Berlin, 1962); five apocalypses, in Böhlig-Labib, *Koptisch-gnostische Apokalypsen aus Codex V von Nag Hammadi* (Halle-Wittenberg, 1963). In addition a German translation of the Hypostasis of the Archons, based on the photographic edition published by Labib in 1956, has been published by H. M. Schenke in *TLZ,* LXXXIII (1958), 661 ff. Three further versions of the Apocryphon Johannis have been published by M. Krause and P. Labib, *Die drei Versionen des Apokryphon des Johannes im Koptischen Museum zu Alt-Kairo* (Wiesbaden, 1962). Of the texts above mentioned the following are available in English: the Gospel of Mary and the Apocryphon Johannis (Berlin text) in R. M. Grant, *Gnosticism: An Anthology* (London and New York, 1961); the Apocryphon Johannis (from Nag Hammadi Codex II), ed. S. Giversen (Copenhagen, 1963); the Gospel of Thomas (separate English ed.), the Gospel of Truth and the Epistle to Rheginus (tr. in ed. listed); and the Gospel of Philip, ed. R. McL. Wilson (London, 1962), (New York, 1963) (also tr. by C. J. de Catanzaro, *JTS,* XIII [1962], 35 ff.). The Gospel of Truth has also been edited by Kendrick Grobel (Nashville and New York, 1960), and translated in Grant's *Anthology.* The Gospel of Thomas has been edited by R. M. Grant and D. N. Freedman (London and New York, 1960), and translated in Hennecke-Schneemelcher, *NT Apocrypha* i (English tr., 1963), to which reference may be made for further information on the Gnostic Gospels and related documents.

by Søren Giversen,[2] covering the fifteen years from 1948 to 1963, includes some 640 items. Admittedly this list incorporates reviews as well as independent books and articles, but even so the sheer quantity of the material is somewhat daunting. Some narrowing of the field is therefore inevitable.

I propose accordingly to approach the subject from the point of view of a NT scholar with an interest in the historical problems relating to Christian origins, in the whole process of development out of which there emerged in the early centuries the Catholic Christianity of the Great Church on the one hand, and Gnosticism as traditionally defined on the other. And right at the outset it must be noted that we have an ambiguity in our very title, for if the NT writings are clearly defined and delimited by the NT canon, Gnosticism remains something of an unknown quantity. It is as well that we should be clear as to what we are discussing.

On the traditional definition, which saw in Gnosticism simply a Christian heresy of the second century, the movement of course is in one direction only. There can be no thought of "Gnostic" influence on the NT, and the only question concerns the use that was made of the NT documents by the second-century Gnostics, how and why they came to interpret them, or misinterpret them, as they did. Broadly speaking, this has been the position adopted by British scholars, and it has been maintained within the last decade by R. P. Casey.[3]

In the course of the present century, however, German scholars in particular have widened the range of the term "Gnosis" to include a great deal more than the second-century Christian heresy. At the one end they have brought in Manichaeism and Mandaeism; at the other they have pointed to the affinities with Gnosticism in the traditional sense which exist, for example, in the writings of Philo, in the Corpus Hermeticum, and in the NT itself. The convergence of evidence from many different sources has led them to postulate a pre-Christian "gnosis" which lies

[2] *Studia Theologica,* XVII (1963), 139 ff.

[3] *The Background of the New Testament and Its Eschatology,* ed. W. D. Davies and D. Daube (Cambridge, 1956), pp. 52 ff. Cf. earlier his article in *JTS,* XXXVI (1935), 45 ff. So also the late A. D. Nock wrote that the relation of the Gospel of Truth and other texts to the NT seemed "to vindicate completely the traditional view of Gnosticism as Christian heresy with roots in speculative thought." See *HTR,* LVII (1964), 255 ff. (quotation from p. 276).

behind them all, and which has influenced the NT writers, in particular Paul and John. Gnosticism, says Bultmann, "first appeared and attracted the attention of scholars as a movement within the Christian religion, and for a long time it was regarded as a purely Christian movement, a perversion of the Christian faith into a speculative theology, the 'acute Hellenization of Christianity.' Further research has, however, made it abundantly clear that it was really a religious movement of pre-Christian origin, invading the West from the Orient as a competitor of Christianity." [4]

This procedure however raises problems. For one thing, Bultmann's translators use the term "Gnosticism," as I have just done, where he himself speaks of "die Gnosis"; this can only be confusing to the English-speaking reader who is thinking in terms of the traditional definition. Again, what is the historical relationship between this postulated pre-Christian "gnosis" and the traditional Gnosticism? Is it, for example, legitimate to construct a synthetic picture from second- and third-century sources, and use it for the interpretation of NT ideas in the first century? In the entire chapter devoted to Gnosticism in Bultmann's *Primitive Christianity* there is not a single reference to any document which can be dated prior to the NT. This is not in itself sufficient to invalidate his reconstruction, since many particular ideas can in fact be traced back to an earlier period; but it must raise the question whether it was not the associations which these ideas came to have *within the Gnostic systems* which gave to them their "Gnostic" character. At an earlier point, in his discussion of astrology, Bultmann lists a number of redemptive religions which either competed with or assimilated star worship: the mystery religions, Gnosticism, "finally" the Christian gospel, and Christian Gnosticism. The unwary reader might assume, particularly in view of the "finally," that these religions are listed in chronological order, but the quotation for the mysteries is drawn from Apuleius, and those for Gnosticism from Lactantius and the Corpus Hermeticum—all somewhat later than Paul's letter to the Galatians, which is quoted after them. It is not of course suggested that Bultmann is guilty of a deliberate attempt to mislead. What is in question is the validity of the approach, the as-

[4] *Primitive Christianity in Its Contemporary Setting* (New York, 1957), p. 162. Cf. also his *Theology of the New Testament,* I (London, 1952), pp. 164 ff.

sumptions and the methodology which come into play in discussions of "Gnostic" influence on the NT.

The problem is complicated by the fact that we have but one adjective, "gnostic," to do duty both for the traditional Gnosticism and for the phenomena ascribed to pre-Christian Gnosis, which makes it all too easy to read back conceptions of a later period and assume that what was Gnostic in the second century is already Gnostic in Paul.[5] We must distinguish a merely descriptive sense of the term from its use to indicate derivation. Johannes Munck has recently proposed an alternative,[6] that we should describe the pre-Christian phenomena as syncretistic rather than Gnostic, but this too presents problems. The term "syncretism" may be legitimately used both of Christianity and of Judaism, but in these two cases it does not have quite the same meaning as in the case of the Hellenistic mystery religions. A third shade of meaning might only make confusion worse confounded.

These problems call for the probing of a lancet, not for the slash of a cavalry sabre. Their investigation for the moment requires not sweeping generalizations but detailed and meticulous study and clarity of definition. How far can we in fact speak of a pre-Christian Gnosis, and in what sense? What are the criteria by which it is to be defined? It is not uncommon, for example, for the student of Gnosticism to detect a very Gnostic ring in some of our hymns, particularly the hymns of certain periods; but are they really Gnostic, or merely the outcome of a Platonizing interpretation of Christianity? Platonism is not Gnosticism, although it may have made a considerable contribution. Or again, take the characteristic Gnostic contrast of light and darkness. Are we to assume a Gnostic influence wherever these terms occur? In the Qumran War Scroll, for example, or in Amos when he speaks of the day of the Lord as darkness and not light, or Isaiah when he says, "The people that walked in darkness have seen a great light"? Or take the key word "knowledge" itself: what of the statements, "The Lord is a God of

[5] The late Professor Kendrick Grobel suggested that in writing, at least in English, the adjective should be capitalized when it refers to Gnosticism, and the lower case used when it refers to *gnosis*. This, if generally adopted, would have its advantages, but it would be impossible in other languages, notably German; which would only add to the problems of translators!

[6] In *Current Issues in NT Interpretation,* ed. Klassen and Snyder (New York, 1962), pp. 224 ff. (also in *Studia Theologica,* XV [1961], 181 ff.).

knowledge," or "One who is perfect in knowledge is with you"? Taken apart from their contexts these might readily be thought typically Gnostic—the second indeed contains two characteristic Gnostic terms—but one is from I Sam. 2:3, the other from the book of Job (36:4). Study of a concordance will produce many other examples. Knowledge and ignorance, light and darkness, truth and error—these are commonplace Gnostic contrasts. But at what point do they *become* Gnostic? If such concepts are employed by Paul or John, are they already Gnostic, or necessarily due to Gnostic influence?

I would suggest that there may be a certain area of common ground, a stock of ideas which is neither specifically Gnostic nor specifically Christian but shared by both, and by other religions also. Such ideas obviously cannot be of any help in determining whether there has been an influence one way or the other. There may, however, be other ideas which are specifically Gnostic, which are not to be found in the earliest strata of the NT, but only in the later stages; and there may be ideas which cannot be traced back beyond the NT, but can only be described as the result of Christian influence upon the developing Gnostic movement.

Here I think it is important to underline a point made by Bultmann—that Gnosticism *grew*.[7] It is, I think, a fundamental mistake to assume that the movement emerged in all the glory of its later development, as Athene in ancient Greek mythology sprang full-armed from the head of Zeus. We have to reckon with a process of growth and development, of which such documents as we possess may reflect different stages. Ernst Haenchen, for example, distinguishes two stages in the relationship between NT Christianity and Gnosis.[8] In the first, "Gnostic" ideas and concepts are employed, but any further penetration of Gnosis is resisted, whereas in the second Gnosis is treated simply as false doctrine, and any *Auseinandersetzung* with it is forbidden. This would seem to point in the right direction, although I must reserve the right to question whether some of the "Gnostic" conceptions which he adduces were not in fact

[7] Thus in a review (*JTS*, NS, III [1952], 22) he speaks of "themes already germinant" in late-Hellenistic philosophy and in Philo which later "reach their full expression in Gnosis." It should be added that in discussing "Gnostic" influences on the NT writers Bultmann is careful to note the differences—a point often overlooked both by his followers and by his critics.

[8] *RGG* 3rd ed., II, 1652 ff.

conceptions which only became Gnostic through their use in the Gnosticism of the second century. It is in any case probable that the lines of division were not in the first instance very clearly defined, that there was a period during which ideas later stigmatized as Gnostic could be tolerated and employed by the most orthodox of writers,[9] and that it was only with the passage of time that the issues became distinct. Such a course of events would not be by any means unusual.

The resultant picture may for the moment be neither neat nor tidy, but it may be more accurate, more true to the facts of our knowledge, than some other presentations have been. And its very untidiness may be a stimulus to further investigation, to the clearing up of those areas which as yet must be designated "largely unexplored": the relation of Gnosis and Gnosticism, for example, to Jewish apocalyptic, or to Jewish heterodoxy, or to Jewish mysticism; or the tracing of the precise lines of connection between one movement and another, and the recognition of the stages of development at which particular influences came into play. There is among English-speaking scholars an increasing recognition that there was in some sense a pre-Christian Gnosis,[10] but we must still seek for a clear definition of its character. Only then can we really go on to formulate the further questions: a) how far has it actually affected the NT writers, and b) how far can we trace a direct continuity and development from this pre-Christian Gnosis to the schools of the second century and later? And here there are further questions which demand investigation. How far is second-century Gnosticism influenced by the NT itself—in other words, to what extent is it in fact a Christian heresy? How far do we find in the second-century schools ideas from the pre-Christian Gnosis which have passed into traditional Gnosticism *through Christian-*

[9] The closest parallels to certain passages in the Gnostic Gospel of Philip, for example, occur in the writings of Irenaeus; this neither makes "Philip" orthodox nor Irenaeus a Gnostic.

[10] Thus Nock can speak of a "Gnostic way of thinking" but no Gnostic *system* apart from the Christian movement, and suggest that it was the emergence of Jesus and of belief in him that "precipitated elements previously suspended in solution" (*op. cit.*, p. 278). At the very least it must be admitted that there was a good deal of "gnosticising" speculation in the period, difficult as it may be to identify clearly Gnostic elements or trace the process of development.

K. Rudolph's comprehensive survey "Stand und Aufgaben in der Erforschung des Gnostizismus" (*Tagung für allgemeine Religionsgeschichte 1963. Sonderheft der wiss. Zeitschrift der Friedrich-Schiller-Universität Jena,* pp. 89 ff.) reached me only after the present paper was complete.

ity, and have taken on a Christian coloring in the process? And how far can we determine the social, political, and other factors which may have contributed to the development?

Such questions could be multiplied, but those which have been raised may serve to indicate the complexity of the problems, and to warn against superficial and facile solutions.

HANS JONAS

RESPONSE TO G. QUISPEL'S "Gnosticism and the New Testament"

This response to Professor Quispel's paper consists of two parts. Part I is devoted to a refutation of his views on the Hymn of the Pearl and is also meant to serve as a methodological preface to the much larger theme of Part II: this is to deal with the alleged Jewish origins of Gnosticism.

I

Quispel holds that the Hymn of the Pearl in the apocryphal Acts of Thomas is (a) not gnostic at all, (b) orthodox Christian tinged with Judaistic colors, and (c) based upon the parable of the pearl in Matt. 13:45-46, which reads: "Again, the kingdom of heaven is like a merchant in search of fine pearls, who, on finding one pearl of great value, went and sold all that he had and bought it." Of this, Quispel says, the Hymn is "a poetical amplification and illustration." Maybe it is, but then we must ask: what kind of amplification? What does it do with the given? Merely expand, or also add to it? Merely add, or also modify it? Merely modify, or perhaps entirely remake it? Each of these contingencies is a possibility. For it needs hardly saying that we have to distinguish between the constancy of a symbolical term (image) and the variability of meanings which it may be used to express. The meaning must in each case be determined from the context in which it figures; and if we should find the same symbolical term, such as the "pearl," serving two significantly different meaning contexts, then we must turn our attention to those contexts and ask how *they* stand to each other, e.g., whether one is an outgrowth of the other, or both are variations of one generic theme, or whether they are substantially heterogeneous. And when found to be heterogeneous, then we may sometimes, from an immanent comparison of two such contexts, form a judgment as to which is the more natural habitat of the simile in question: where it seems more genuine, more at home, in more adequate and congenial surroundings, allowing it as it were to spread its wings and unfold its full implications; or, seen from the standpoint of the whole: where the imagery in question is crucial and where perhaps a mere casual choice; where integral to the total meaning and where easily interchangeable with other similes. And this we must try to determine by pure morphological comparison of the two contexts, irrespective (within reason) of the chronological accidents of surviving testimony: so that it *can* happen that the earlier witness, e.g., that of the Gospel, turns out to represent a more derivative and attenuated use of the simile in question than a later representation we happen to possess. At least this is what the less compelling version *might* indicate: an atrophied version; though it may as well indicate the subsequent intervention of a new force which from such scanty cues freely and arbitrarily created the different, compelling version. In either case, this latter would represent a genuine conception of its own; and, in the matter under review, this may turn out to be what is commonly called a gnostic version.

With these considerations in mind, let me confront the Hymn of the Pearl first, not with the older source, the Gospel, but with one slightly later than itself, viz., the allegory of the pearl in the Manichaean *Kephalaia.* There[1] the simile is spelled out to the last dot on the i's, for Mani was anything if not explicit; and in the bright light of his didactic explicitness one realizes that in the Hymn the symbolism of the pearl itself, though vital to the story, is rather presupposed than really developed: but presupposed it is with its full connotations. This the later source makes clear, not the earlier, however much the historian would prefer it the other way around.

I summarize the extensive Manichaean allegory ("On the Holy Church") thus: the raindrop falls from on high into the sea; down there, in an oyster shell, it forms into a pearl; divers descend into the deep and bring up this pearl; the divers hand it on to the merchants; the merchants give it to the kings. Thus far the metaphor. Then comes the explanation, a kind of allegorical dictionary, symbol by symbol, as follows: the *raindrop* is "the spoil that was carried off [in the beginning, namely], the living Soul" (i.e., that part of the god Man which was lost to the powers of darkness in the primordial battle and swallowed up by them—the one "soul" now dispersed in the world); the *oyster shell* is "the flesh of man-

[1] A. Böhlig and H. J. Polotsky (ed. and tr.), *Kephalaia,* Kap. LXXXIII, Stuttgart, 1940, p. 204.

kind in which the soul is gathered and laid up" as pearl (the pearl, therefore, is the specifically human, redeemable form in which the incarnated soul exists in the world); the *divers* are "the apostles of God" (such as Mani himself), sent down for the pearl; the *merchants* are "the luminaries of the heavens" (i.e., mainly sun and moon, which in the Manichaean myth are conveyors of souls from this to the other world and thus a link in the chain of salvation); lastly, the *kings and nobles* to whom the pearl is finally transmitted, are "the Aeons of the Greatness" (i.e., the world of light from which the pearl came and to which it is now restored).

Thus far the Manichaean exposition, to which I may just add the key for one more term of the symbolic code: the *"sea"*—quite fittingly the element in which pearls are found, but having, besides, its own fixed code-meaning as the *world of matter and darkness* into which the divine has sunk. So well-attested is this symbol of the Sea or the Waters throughout gnostic literature that I can spare myself examples.[2] But I mention it here to throw light on the otherwise gratuitous addition, in the Hymn, of the "sea" as abode of the pearl to "Egypt," itself a widespread gnostic symbol for the world of matter: landlocked as the Prince's itinerary seems to be, the "sea" was called for by gnostic usage, by the authentic associations of the pearl image, and also as the only dwelling place for the fearful serpent who guards the pearl, the great dragon of primordial chaos which from times immemorial had been associated with the waters of the deep and the world-girdling ocean (no relation of the small, intellectual serpent of the paradise story). But why this grim guard over the pearl, the fierce resistance to letting it go? The whole Manichaean myth is an answer to this question, but so again are many gnostic myths long before Mani, once the equation of the pearl with the fallen and engulfed portion of divinity, i.e. with the totality of our spiritual selves, is recognized: the presence of this alien element is vital to the cause of the archons—if not to their own survival, at least to that of their work. As a Mandaean text puts it: "The treasurers of this world assembled and said 'Who has carried away the pearl which illumined the perishable house? In the house which it left the walls cracked and collapsed.'" [3]

[2] Cf. H. Jonas, *The Gnostic Religion,* Boston, 1958, p. 117 f., and the references *s.v.* "Wasser" in the Index to *Gnosis und spätantiker Geist* I, 3rd ed., Göttingen, 1964, p. 444.

[3] Left Ginza III 8: Mark Lidzbarski, *Ginza. Der Schatz oder das Grosse Buch der Mandäer,* Göttingen, 1925, p. 517. For the more extreme view, held also by Mani,

Finally, lest it be objected that all this came after the Hymn, I add one piece of earlier evidence. The Naassenes as quoted by Hippolytus speak of the "live" elements in the universe—"words and minds and men"—as "the pearls that are the progeny of the Formless one cast [4] into the formation" (*Refut.* V 8, 32).[5]

"Formation" (*πλάσμα*, as in the Gospel of Truth) denotes the material creation; the Unformed (*ἀχαρακτήριστος*) is the highest deity, First Man, whose lowered image, second Adam, subjected to shape (*κεχαρακτηρισμένος*) and enclosed in the earthly formation (*πλάσμα χωϊκόν*), is "the God that inhabits the flood" (Ps. 29:10), immersed in the "many waters" of "much-divided mortal becoming," from which his voice cries up to the Unformed one, his unfallen original, Primal Man (Hippol. V 8, 14 f.).

---

that the very life of the archons, not only the continuance of their creation, depends on the retention of this element, see the gnostic teaching recorded by Epiphanius, *Panar.* 40, 2: "They say that the *Soul* is the food of the archons and powers without which they cannot live, because she is the *dew from above* and gives them strength." We see how consistent the imagery is: the "dew from above" is the "dew of light" which according to the Ophites fell from the overflow of the (female) "Holy Spirit" into the waters below, whence it assumed a body, and which to extract again from the nether powers is the saving work of the Christ (Irenaeus, *adv. haer.* I 30): here we have the "raindrop" of the (later) Manichaean pearl-allegorism still really "falling" in a movement of its own, as behooves the image, while the adaptation to the Manichaean myth of the primordial war had to make it, somewhat incongruously, a victim of violence—"the spoil carried off in the beginning": Mani, or his disciple, here as elsewhere slightly recasts an *earlier gnostic* imagery. But as the "hurling" of the pearls in the Naassene example shows (cf. next footnote), the violent picture alternated, already before Mani, with that of "sinking."

[4] *ἐρριμένους* from *ῥίπτω*: flung, hurled—a rather violent term, recalling the *που ἐνεβλήθημεν* of the Valentinian formula in *Exc. Theod.* 78, 2 "whereinto we have been thrown." Cf. also Hibil's lament "How long shall I pour living water . . . into the muddy water? . . . how long shall I abandon *pearls* to the perishable . . . ? When will at last this world come to an end?" (M. Lidzbarski [ed. & tr.], *Das Johannesbuch der Mandäer,* Giessen, 1915, p. 197).

[5] This is offered as the exegesis of an apocryphal logion, viz., "If you ate dead things and yet made (of them) live things, what might you not make once you eat live things?" which is also found in the *Gospel of Thomas,* but there in a stunted and unintelligible form, to wit "In the days when you ate dead things you made them alive. When you are in the Light, what will you do?" (82, 19-22). Clearly in this rendering the logion, so perfectly clear in the Naassene rendering, is ruined: the parallelism is destroyed, the contrapuntal argument has vanished. The saying has literally become pointless, since its point consisted in the double use of the idea of "eating," and that idea has now been dropped from the second half of the statement. I mention this merely in passing as an instance of the very doubtful value which the *Gospel of Thomas,* as presently extant, has as a source for apocryphal logia: it strengthens the suspicion one has in many other instances where we have no second tradition to compare with, viz., that their mysterious obscurity is due not to profundity of meaning but to plain, dumb textual corruption.

This, in the final analysis, is the "pearl cast into the formation"—*one* pearl in essence, as the god sunken in the waters is one according to the theological myth.

Here, then, is one coherent "meaning context" for the pearl symbol and thus one candidate for the office of key to the Hymn. Let's call it "context A." Our next step must be to determine the meaning context of the NT parable, which Quispel claims to be the key, and our next then to determine which of the two (if they are two) better fits and unlocks the story of the Hymn.

Now the parable of the pearl in Matt. 13:45 is one in a long string of parables about the kingdom of heaven: the sown field, the mustard grain, the leaven, the treasure, the pearl. Directly preceding it is that which likens the kingdom to "a treasure hidden in a field which a man found and covered up; then in his joy he goes and sells all that he has and buys that field." The pearl parable, apart from omitting "field" and "hidden," makes the following variations in the metaphor: "merchant" for man, "searching" for (perhaps) accidental finding, "pearl" for treasure unspecified. Is the last switch significant? Hardly, for the merchant is said to search for "fine pearls" (in the plural), obviously signifying precious objects as such, and then to find one object more precious than all the rest: no associations peculiar to "pearl," as distinct from "treasure" in general, are called into play. Nor is there a suggestion that the pearl is where it should not be, that it got there by some inimical fate and must be rescued hence and restored to its right place and owners; nor that the merchant was *sent* for that or any purpose affecting the pearl's condition: his own salvation is the issue. And so "the one pearl" just stands (as does the "treasure") for the surpassing *value* of that which the finder will own when he is wise enough to acquire it: a place in kingdom come—a good bargain for the price of all the treasures of the world.

This, then, is the meaning context for the pearl simile in the parable—let's call it "context B." And now we can ask and answer a number of plain questions.

(1) Are contexts A and B significantly different? They surely are. One is the context of the messianic kingdom to come, the other that of the lost and retrieved portion of God.

(2) To which of the two is the Hymn closer? Surely to context A,

that represented by the Manichaean, Mandaean, and Naassene examples where the symbolism of the pearl is so richly unfolded and so fully utilized: all that the Hymn story has in excess of the Gospel parable (the prince being sent, the pearl's location far from the heavenly land, down in the sea, in alien custody, jealously guarded by hostile powers, difficult to rescue and finally to bring home, etc.) are without exception covered by the other context.

(3) This context A, which step by step fits the narrative of the Hymn—is it, or is it not, gnostic? It surely is, by a convention of speech I see no reason to subvert; but by whatever name we choose to call it, orthodox-Christian it is certainly not. Incidentally, it is with respect to this kind of context that competent Iranologists claim an Iranian background, or at least a contributory Iranian influence,[6] and I do not see good reasons for non-Iranologists (be it Scholem or Quispel or myself) to dismiss that claim lightly and summarily—as little, I hasten to add, as I would advocate at other points a like dismissal of expert Judaistic claims. Both, of course, and others perhaps as well, are mutually compatible when properly understood, especially in the case of Judaism which was itself so wide open to Iranian influences and may often have been the channel for their transmission. What we must beware of in these championships of causes is the fallacy of exclusiveness, the lure of fashion, and the hasty identification of any one with "the origin" of Gnosticism. This applies also to the present Judaistic mood of which I have to say something in the second part of this paper. But let me first finish our exercise in the model example, the pearl symbol, because it so well illustrates points of method vital in the study of Gnosticism.

(4) The next question would concern the genetic relationship between the two contexts: can one be considered a derivate from the other by way of immanent development? Here I can only, once more, record my conviction that they are really heterogeneous, of different pedigrees, each an original conception of its own and neither reducible to the other in point of genesis as well as meaning.

(5) But this still leaves room for the question of whether the *pearl simile* (given the well-known mobility of coined symbols) might not have passed from one context to the other, granted the prior existence

[6] A small point: the opponent of Iranian background must explain the partiality for Parthia shown in the Hymn.

of the contexts themselves; and if so, which side would more probably be the borrower in such a transfer. Now if we compare the full-fledged and vital role of the pearl simile in the gnostic context [7] with its limited and casual role in the Gospel context,[8] then, much rather than see in the former an outgrowth from that slender and differently pointed cue, we might see in the latter a faint and vestigial echo of the former, i.e., of a fuller symbolism already abroad at the time: in which case we must also allow the meaning context which alone gives it full scope—the gnostic context—a contemporary existence with the logion. I say, not that I do assume this, but that I find it easier to assume than a certain alternative. Easier still (too easy perhaps to the taste of some) it is to accept a mere coincidence of metaphor, seeing that the pearl *is* after all a thing of prized value and beauty and might just on that account (the only one utilized in the parable) have been picked by Jesus, without prompting from a symbolic tradition. Most difficult I find it to imagine the process suggested by Quispel whereby in effect the parable in Matthew would become the source not only for the Hymn in the Acta Thomae but for the whole spread of symbolical language centered around the pearl through Naassene, Mandaean, Manichaean literature—surely an overload of consequences for a modest impromptu not even especially emphasized in its original company. Not that such a process is *per se* impossible *as a feat of exegesis:* the Gnostics amply demonstrate what they can do in this respect. But Quispel was not thinking of such fanciful exegesis, but of orthodox amplification and illustration—which simply will not do.[9] And that other kind, the exegetical alchemy which *might* have transmuted the pearl of the parable into the extensive symbol-

[7] Let us recall what, in addition to the mere preciousness of a gem, qualified the pearl in particular to become the symbol of the lost divine soul in the gnostic scheme: the purity of its white lustre in contrast to the darkness of its natural surroundings; the coarseness of its animal shell; its immersion in the waters of the deep; the dangers of bringing it up. And, indeed, whenever "pearl" is used as simile for the "soul," it is with the connotation of the lost pearl.

[8] Which makes use of just one, and for that matter the most interchangeable aspect of the pearl: its preciousness (and perhaps smallness?), which other gems supply just as well.

[9] Unfortunately for his thesis, not even the fanciful exegesis, when we do find it practiced in support of the gnostic pearl symbol, happens to turn to *this* logion: the Naassenes (Hippol. V 8, 33) quote Matt. 7:6 "do not throw the pearls before the swine" in connection with "the pearls of the Unformed one flung into the formation." Generally, the "lost sheep" serves the Gnostics as scriptural reference for the lost portion of divinity.

ism of our texts? (We have no evidence that it did, but it admittedly might.) Well, this once again would *presuppose* the meaning context which could inspire and guide such a transmutation, supplying the intention in whose service its ingenuity would be employed—the gnostic context, in short. And once we grant this as a living force, we might even credit it, *horribile dictu,* with the invention of some of its own symbols.

The point of this discussion is still the same I tried to make long ago in my first study of Gnosticism: that it is the meaning context, taken in its wholeness and integrity, which matters, and not the traffic in single symbols, figures, and names. With this I leave the pearl and for the remainder of this paper briefly comment on the Judaic theme, on whose much larger terrain some findings of the limited case study may prove pertinent.

II

Let me first mark the area of agreement. On one point there can surely be no quarrel: the Gnostics, as a matter of plain fact, made liberal use of Jewish material; they must therefore have been acquainted with it; and in some cases this knowledge and use extends to Jewish mystical thought currents that ran alongside the more official and better known mainstream of biblical and rabbinic and even apocalyptic Judaism. This last point has been effectively established by G. Scholem. But even without this valuable addition to what had been known or mainly considered before, the abundance of OT exegesis alone is evidence of a proximity, even a fascination with Jewish themes, that could not be, and in fact never was, overlooked. Thus I am not sure whose "idle talk" about Gnosticism having "nothing in common with Judaism" Quispel deems to have been stopped "once for all" by the results of Scholem's investigations. I personally can only voice agreement when Quispel speaks of certain things in Gnosticism being *"derived* from a Jewish 'milieu,'" of its "owing not a little to Judaism," even of "a strong *influence* of Jewish conceptions," etc. And, of course, I wholeheartedly agree with his "on the other hand"—*my* original thesis, after all: that Gnosticism is a religion of its own,[10] dominated by the idea of a tragic split within

[10] Precisely this, and what follows, was the view I expounded in *Gnosis und spätantiker Geist,* vol. 1 (1934!) as a novel conception against the prevailing *syncretistic* views of Gnosticism. It is gratifying to find this once heretical view now

the Deity and the concept of the fallen God (which he rightly terms "the real issue of Gnostic theology"), and his underscoring of how far the Gnostics have removed themselves, with this dualism of theirs, with the consubstantiality of God and man, etc., from what he terms the Jewish origins and what I would less committingly term the Jewish antecedents. So far, so good. My difficulty begins with relating, in Quispel's presentation, these two sets of statements, the "on the one hand" and the "on the other hand"; or, what amounts to the same, my difficulty is with the essential vagueness and ambiguity of the terms "derived from," "influenced by," "transition from A to B," which figure in the first set of statements. And here would apply much of what I have said in the first part of this paper apropos of "amplification," "meaning contexts," and the transfer of symbols from one to the other. Let me illustrate this on one point in the present larger issue.

Quispel has said that the Apocryphon of John, an archaic document compared with the more sophisticated Valentinian Gnosis, shows "a strong influence of Jewish conceptions." And so it does, as in the following example: Ialdabaoth the creator, after expelling Adam and Eve from paradise into black darkness because they had acquired knowledge of their higher origin in defiance of his command, became inflamed with lust for the virgin Eve, raped her, and begot with her two sons: Jahve the bear-faced, and Elohim the cat-faced, among men called Cain and Abel to this day. Elohim the "just" he set over fire and wind, Jahve the "unjust" over water and earth: together they rule over the tomb, i.e., the body. This, as a piece of OT exegesis, is strong meat, but no more than a fair sample of the kind of use the Gnostics—and the more so the more familiar they show themselves with Jewish sources—habitually make of the Jewish material they incorporate into their speculation; or, to use Quispel's words: of what happened in the transition from Judaism to Gnosticism. And what is the spirit of this use? Why, it is the spirit of vilification, of parody and caricature, of conscious perversion of meaning, wholesale reversal of value-signs, savage degrading of the sacred—of gleefully shocking blasphemy. It is as if the Gnostics had been speaking thus to the Jews: You say your God is the creator of heaven and earth? He is—and so yours is an inferior and obtuse god. He proclaimed himself

---

become so general that it can be voiced from a platform shared with me without there seeming a need any longer to connect it explicitly with its early champion.

the highest and only god? Proof of his presumption and ignorance. He made man in a likeness? A sly and blundering imitation of the envied, dimly perceived superior Godhead. He forbade the fruit of the tree? Sure, to keep man in darkness about his true being. He later issued the law? The better to secure his stranglehold over him. He rules the universe? Look at cosmic Fate, the *heimarmene* of the planets, and you know what to think of this sinister tyranny. He chose you for his people? By becoming it, you have cast your lot with unenlightenment. And so it goes on and on.

Is this merely exuberant license, pleasure in the novel and bizarre? No, it is the exercise of a determined and in itself thoroughly consistent tendency. Does its exercise merely add a flourish, an interesting gloss, to the original? No, it is a total turning upside down. And its result—is it marginal or central to Gnosticism itself? It is its heart and soul, without which it would be a limp and flabby body, a motley of mythologumena and theologumena not worth the study we spend on it. I add: it is also its pepper and salt without which it would be a stale and insipid dish; but this is a matter of personal taste.

In short, and with the oversimplification excused by extreme shortness, the nature of the relation of Gnosticism to Judaism—in itself an undeniable fact—is defined by the *anti-Jewish animus* with which it is saturated. "The greatest case of metaphysical anti-Semitism!" exclaimed Scholem once when we talked about these matters soon after the appearance of my first volume on Gnosis: that was in the thirties (and in Jerusalem) when one was very much alive to this aspect of things. Professor Wilson too, in his beautifully judicious chapter on Judaism and Gnosticism,[11] repeatedly uses the term "anti-Semitism" in that context (minus the "metaphysical"—a reflection perhaps of the national difference in philosophical backgrounds between the two gentlemen). Not once did this term, or any reference to the phenomenon it names, appear in Quispel's story today.

So far I have not said or implied that the anti-Jewish animus *constitutes* the essence of Gnosticism, nor even that it was its originating cause: I have merely said that it is of the essence of Gnosticism, in a confrontation with Judaism, to react with that violent and insulting hostility; and

[11] R. McL. Wilson, *The Gnostic Problem*. London, 1958, ch. VII.

it seems that such confrontations took place very early, perhaps even right from the beginnings of the movement. But perhaps the matter does go farther than that, and we have to consider the following scale of hypotheses, each more specific than the preceding one:

1. (As stated before:) Gnosticism as an evolving state of mind *reacted* against Judaism when and where it encountered it.
2. Gnosticism *originated* out of a reaction (that is, *as* a reaction) to Judaism.
3. It was so originated *by Jews.*

Hypothesis 1 is uncontroversial: the massive evidence of anti-Jewish use of Jewish material leaves no doubt of the reaction as such. And needless to say, an anti-relation *is* a relation, and hate involves, and in turn can induce, its own familiarity, even intimacy with the object of it.

Hypothesis 2: that this reaction is itself the generative cause, at least the midwife, of Gnosticism—who knows? The record does not preclude it, and the ubiquity and force of Judaism at the time give it a certain plausibility. One may feel, as I do, that it takes too narrow a view of Gnosticism and of its basis in the contemporary world; also, by making it merely reactive, it is an inadequate view of its autonomy as a spiritual cause. And, like all negative genealogy, it leaves us with the question of the positive ground from which the reaction was determined: at least the "gnostic disposition" so to react, so to feel provoked by Judaism, must be presupposed. In that sense, the hypothesis begs the question. We are caught here in the fine question of whether a No produces a Yes, or presupposes one. Possibly both. Anyway, in some such polemical sense, Judaism may have been a focal fact in the genesis of Gnosticism. One observation which might be construed in this sense, but which should give pause to the proponents of Jewish origins, is that the more archaic the source, the more vehement the anti-Judaism. The comparatively conciliatory, mitigating views of a Valentinus are clearly second thoughts, and not the first thoughts. Whatever this observation, which I cannot enlarge upon here, may signify otherwise, it throws an interesting light on the next question.

So, then, the third hypothesis, somehow at the back of the mind of those who advocate the Jewish origins of Gnosticism: Was that reaction perhaps begotten, incubated, and brought forth in the midst of Judaism itself—by Jews? Who would say that this is impossible? We have learned that almost nothing is impossible in human psychology, not even anti-Semitism among Jews. And what an exciting, nay soul-shaking spectacle that would be: the greatest iconoclasm before modernity erupting in Judaism—Jews themselves turning against their holiest, tearing it down, trampling it into the dust, revelling in its utter humiliation, proclaiming the complete devaluation of all traditional values—Nietzsche, Sartre, Saint Genet rolled into one: how fascinating, how modern. Of all the many genealogies of Gnosticism tried out so far, this would surely be the most interesting. But before we surrender to the lure of mere possibility, we ask for evidence. Of what could it consist in the given state of our historical testimony? I can think of two tests, not indeed supplying proof (which would be asking too much), but either of them at least *indicative* one way or the other.

The first test is applied by asking: Are there *Hebrew* writings of that period which are Gnostic in the sense here specified? Now if Scholem's book,[12] which I read very differently from the way Quispel seems to read it, has demonstrated one thing to me, it is that there are not. And here I trust my friend Scholem: if he, with his avid appetite for the unorthodox and aberrant, his exquisite nose for the scent of it, and his unique knowledge of the field, has failed to bring up from this hunting trip even one example of that kind of "unorthodoxy," I am satisfied that it wasn't there. Scholem himself is at pains to differentiate between "Jewish Gnosticism . . . which was striving . . . hard to maintain a strictly monotheistic character" (p. 42), and "Gnostics" pure and simple or "antinomian Gnostics" who "frequently borrowed such material and deliberately changed it" (p. 72), "used and turned [it] upside down" (p. 73); he, too, speaks of "parody" [13] and, rather disarmingly, of a "deterioration" which Jewish esoteric teaching suffered at the hands of its Gnostic appropriators who "put it into false context" (p. 34). I find "false context" charming. Never is there a suggestion that those who did this were Jews, and it is only unfortunate that he insists on calling those to whom it was done, the Jewish mystics, also "Gnostics." But he leaves no doubt about *their* essential "orthodoxy," even if not in the rabbinic sense. And Quispel follows him when he says, "This Gnosis (sc. of

[12] Gershom G. Scholem, *Jewish Gnosticism, Merkabah Mysticism, and Talmudic Tradition* (New York: The Jewish Theological Seminary of America, 1960).

[13] In this case "calculated to put the prophet Elija to shame" (p. 73).

esoteric Pharisaism) is completely Jewish-orthodox"; and yet he goes on to say that it "eventually *led to* the origin of Gnosticism, *properly speaking,* at the *fringe* of Judaism." Led to . . .: here we see the semantic disservice which Scholem did to clarity when he called his Palestinian Hekhaloth mysticism a "Gnosis." An innocent enough label in its literal meaning, it encourages the view of a smooth "transition" instead of a decisive break, a mere mutation in the same genus. And what real process is designated by "eventually leading to"? How impersonal and abstract! Almost like a gnostic emergence of aeons from aeons. But Jewish-orthodox "Gnosis" of itself just cannot lead to something basically different from itself. *Somebody* must have taken it and *made* it into something new, *turned* it upside down. *Who* did so? Gnostics ("properly speaking") to be sure. Who were they? Perhaps Jews? This is a concrete and straightforward question of "Whodunit." In the spirit of generosity after the holocaust, our (the Jews') credit for creativity has been vastly extended; and Jewish vanity, which of course is not lacking, might be pleased to welcome into the record even the disreputable, which in the present climate (with all the alienation going around) enjoys its own paradoxical prestige.

However, since we have drawn a blank on the first and more ambitious test, viz., the existence of "properly" gnostic Jewish (i.e., Hebrew) writings, let us try the second, more modest test of asking: Are there at least any Jewish *names* among the many recorded names of gnostic authors and teachers? It is a rather simple-minded question, I admit, but the older I get, the more I favor simple-minded questions. I need not tell this audience that in all the patristic lists there are none, with one interesting half-exception: Simon the Magician from Samaria, a Hebrew name indeed and, as it happens, the earliest of them all. Small wonder that he looms large in the argument for the Jewish origins of Gnosticism. But quite apart from his obtrusive paganism (evident in the Helena-Selene worship) which almost obliterates his residual Judaism, we must not forget that he was the member of a very specially placed community, a group discriminated against, rejected, despised. Here we have a palpable motive for a response of *ressentiment,* aggression and spite; and here for once we can connect a definite meaning with the much-invoked, hazy term "fringes (or, outskirts) of Judaism," "at" which, we are told, Gnosticism originated, a term that usually prompts me to ask: inside or outside the line? The Samaritans were partly in and partly out, and some of them apparently very far out. This is a rich field for non-sequiturs. Quispel takes the fact of Simon's teaching the fall of Wisdom and thus a split in the Deity to mean "that already at a very early date there existed among Samaritans (heterodox Jews) the concept of a double Wisdom." Unless this is a tautology, merely saying that if Simon, a Samaritan, taught so and so, there was at least one Samaritan who taught so and so, if it is to mean that Simon's teaching what he taught testifies to a Samaritan development, then it is a non-sequitur. For Simon might have been the first, he might have been unique, he might—*sit venia verbo*—have been original. But the non-sequitur is compounded (in reversed chronology) by Scholem when, after classing the Samaritans (mainly on Simon's account) as "heretical Judaism," he argues: "Once we admit that such a development could take place within the Samaritan variant of Judaism, the possibility of analogous developments within the main branch of Pharisaic or Hasidic Judaism must equally be admitted." [14] Not at all! Samaritans had reasons for kicking against official Judaism, for an antagonistic posture, which those in the main branch had not. No bonds of loyalty bound them; at least they were much weakened in their case. It is these particular circumstances of an alienated group driven into opposition which for me have always lent great credibility to the tradition on Simon Magus, at a time when it was much more the fashion to mythify the whole outrageous figure including his lovely whore. He indeed is the first individual Gnostic our records permit us to discern. But we should surely hesitate on that account to place—in a throwback to Irenaeus—the burden of having started the mighty gnostic tide on the frail shoulders of the very localized Samaritan group. They do not measure up to such an influential role in the world of their time. Much rather should we say that they, or some of them, generally ready for heterodoxy, were especially receptive for the anti-Jewish animus, or the anti-Jewish possibilities, of the incipient Gnostic flood.

All this is not to deny that Judaism was a powerful factor in the formation, perhaps even in the nativity of Gnosticism. In a sufficiently loose and non-committal sense of "fringe" one may safely say (but it says

[14] *Op. cit.*, p. 4.

little) that it did originate "at the fringes" of Judaism. I prefer to say: in a zone of proximity and exposure to Judaism, where the Jewish share—besides the contribution of much transmissible material—was in essence *catalytic* and *provoking*. To the breathtaking possibility of its even being positive begetter of the essence, I keep an open mind but will not lower my price. A Gnosticism without a fallen god, without benighted creator and sinister creation, without alien soul, cosmic captivity and acosmic salvation, without the self-redeeming of the Deity—in short: a Gnosis without divine tragedy will not meet specifications. For those are the things we have to account for when truly asking for the origins of Gnosticism. A Gnosis merely of the heavenly palaces, of the mystical ascent, the ecstatic vision of the Throne, of the awesome secrets of the divine majesty—in short: a *monotheistic* Gnosis of the *mysterium numinosum et tremendum,* important as it is in its own right, is a different matter altogether. I would be thrilled to the bone if the first could be shown to have been engendered within Judaism. It would add the last touch to the kind of violent and defiant impulse I see at work behind Gnosticism; and its revolutionary aspect, which I have emphasized from the first, would be enhanced beyond my wildest imagination. So far there is not a shred of evidence that this is what happened. Yet this, and only this, is to me the really relevant and challenging sense of the phrase: Jewish origin of Gnosticism. All the other senses, conducive as they may be to particular lines of scholarly research, are apt to obscure the decisive issue at stake.

9
Archaeology and the Future of Biblical Studies

DAVID NOEL
FREEDMAN

The Biblical Languages

Introduction

When the Society of Biblical Literature and Exegesis was founded in 1880, archaeology was already firmly entrenched in the Near East. Napoleon's conquest of Egypt and neighboring lands opened the way for the recovery of man's most ancient civilizations, while the effusions of romantic poets such as Byron and Shelley stirred adventure in the souls of cultivated and daring Europeans. Before long intrepid gentlemen-explorers and travelers were penetrating the inmost recesses of the Turkish domain. Paul Emile Botta and Austin H. Layard pioneered the heroic age of Near Eastern archaeology, uncovering the abandoned cities of the Assyro-Babylonian monarchs. Faithful to their homelands, they stuffed room after room at the Louvre and the British Museum with cargoes of priceless loot: the monumental art and innumerable inscriptions from ancient Khorsabad and Kouyounjik. Decipherment went hand and hand with discovery and by 1850 the essential solution to Assyro-Babylonian cuneiform had been achieved through the efforts of Grotefend, Rawlinson, Hincks, Oppert, and others. The publication of the Babylonian creation and flood stories by George Smith (in 1876) created a sensation among biblical scholars and the general reading public. Equally startling was the discovery and decipherment of the Moabite Stone (since 1868), by far the most important royal inscription ever found in Palestine. Not only was the king, Mesha, known from the biblical record, but the language of the inscription was so close to Biblical

Hebrew, that it could be read with comparative ease. The contents served to supplement the biblical narrative (II Kings 3) and also present a point of view entirely at variance with that of the Israelite author. Doubtless the conversations at the early meetings of the Society of Biblical Literature and Exegesis touched on the recent discoveries and their implications for the future of biblical studies.

Looking back now, we can confidently affirm that in spite of the extraordinary and unrepeatable finds of the early years, the greatest days of archaeological research were in the future. Eighty-four years later there is no discernible diminution of interest in or recognition of the contribution of archaeology to the study of the Bible. Since the end of World War II the tempo of archaeological activity—surveys, surface explorations, small and large excavations, reports ranging from provisional to permanent, from brief summaries of work in progress to monumental multi-volume compendia—has steadily increased, in spite of disturbed conditions all over the Near East; and the point of diminishing returns is nowhere in sight. Chance discoveries continue at an unexampled rate, and even previously excavated sites never fail to yield a rich harvest to diligent seekers. Rarely does an expedition exhaust the possibilities of a small tel, while the larger mounds would require decades of intensive digging to complete the work of excavation. In spite of very extensive operations at Megiddo, much work remains to be done there; and the same can be said of Lachish, Hazor, Gezer, and the other sites in Palestine. C. Schaeffer has been digging at Ugarit since 1929 without drying up the immense resources of that ancient mound. The picture is the same at many other sites in Syria and Mesopotamia, where the only barriers to perpetual excavations are local and human ones—lack of money and skilled manpower, unsettled political, social, and economic conditions. In addition there are thousands of classified sites of ancient occupation which are waiting to be excavated; and new ones are being listed all the time. The supply seems inexhaustible, and I am sure that at the 200th meeting of the Society a similar estimate of the situation will be made.

Along with the general increase in the amount and rate of excavation, there has been constant refinement in the techniques and procedures of archaeology. A notable transformation has taken place from the early days of destructive treasure hunting to the present controlled research, with highly skilled technicians keeping meticulous records, and analyzing everything turned up including the dirt. The discovery and development of the basic principles of stratigraphy and typology (pottery sequence-dating) changed archaeology from a hit-and-miss search for valuable antiquities and museum pieces into a relatively exact science. The innovations and contributions of leading archaeologists such as W. Flinders Petrie, C. R. Fisher, W. F. Albright, and more recently K. Kenyon have greatly enhanced the reliability of work in the field and the value of excavation reports. Methods are constantly being improved with significantly better results. The adaptation of equipment and use of techniques derived from various physical sciences have provided archaeology with tools of research, like radio-carbon dating, which were undreamed of two generations ago. Much material that was formerly discarded or ignored is now studied for clues to the former inhabitants and their way of life. The scientific revolution in archaeology is only well started and the future will bring more advanced procedures, and more effective control of materials. We should not minimize the difficulties in the development of scientific instruments and their efficient use, nor the disappointments that have attended many brave experiments, but physical scientists working in this area have some remarkable achievements to their credit, and it is only a matter of continued application until universal success is attained. I can visualize the excavation of the future in which electronic devices will thoroughly explore a site and its contours, plot its strata and classify its contents without removing a spadeful of dirt. But before we get lost in a future we can mold to our wishes, let us return to the more refractory past.

Archaeological research has served to illuminate the Bible; it has helped to supply a frame of reference for modern students which the biblical writers presupposed and with which their audiences were presumed to be familiar. Here and there discoveries have tended to confirm or illustrate specific passages in the Bible—such as the inscription of Sargon II found at Ashdod in 1963 which corroborated Isa. 20:1, or the inscription in the Siloam water-tunnel which amplifies II Kings 20:20.

Occasionally archaeological data contradict the biblical account, or seem to. One of the most spectacular examples is Jericho, where the most painstaking archaeological investigation has failed to yield evidence of a substantial wall or city (as described in the Bible) in the 13th century B.C., i.e. the time of Joshua. Responses to the negative archaeological evidence have been varied: from acceptance at face value which involves denial of the biblical record, through different attempts at harmonization, to straightforward rejection of the archaeological information and affirmation of the Bible. It may help the cause of progress in the truth to note that neither the archaeologists nor the biblical writers are necessarily infallible, and that neither or either or both may be correct with regard to the presentation or interpretation of ancient events.

In general, however, archaeology has tended to support the historical validity of the biblical narrative. The broad chronological outline from the patriarchs to NT times correlates with archaeological data. Allowing for occasional anachronisms and other lapses, the biblical writers correctly describe the cultural patterns and mores of the period to which they refer. Thus archaeology confirms the setting of the patriarchal stories in the Middle Bronze II period (first half of the second millennium B.C.) while the exodus and conquest are correctly placed in the transition from Late Bronze to Early Iron (13th century B.C.). Future discoveries are likely to sustain the present moderate position that the biblical tradition is historically rooted, and faithfully transmitted, though it is not history in a critical or scientific sense. Attempted reconstructions of biblical history by modern scholars—e.g., Wellhausen's view that the patriarchal age was a reflex of the divided monarchy; or the rejection of the historicity of Moses and the exodus and consequent restructuring of Israelite history by Noth and his followers—have not survived the archaeological data as well as the biblical narrative. Radical rearrangements or reassessments of the material are not likely to be substantiated by future excavations.

Archaeological correlation with the historical patterns and chronological outline of the Bible does not extend to details as a rule, since evidence for or against the actuality of the latter is rarely obtained. And in the area in which the Bible is most concerned, i.e., religious truth, the reality of God, faith and commitment, archaeology can deal only with the impress or effect of such factors on human life as these are reflected in the material remains of a civilization.

Archaeology can also provide a tangible frame of reference for the Bible, a setting in time and place, social and economic, historical and political, and culturally articulated through the synthesis of countless artifacts uncovered in hundreds of excavations. On the basis of the evidence already in hand it has been possible to outline the cultural history of Palestine from earliest times to the present, and to report the factual conditions of life throughout the biblical period. Such syntheses will always be provisional in view of the continuing flow of new data from every corner of the country, as well as from sites in neighboring nations, but they already offer a substantial picture in place of the largely ephemeral and evanescent structures which have been mortised by biblical scholars in the past to serve as a setting for the biblical narrative.

The weakness of every such pattern—from Wellhausen's artificial Hegelian structure, through the liberal British and American evolutionary theories, to the form critical school's hypothetical life or rather cult situations—is that the frame of reference is constructed out of the biblical materials, which are then interpreted in the light of the structure, or the presuppositions which underlie it. Surely no one will quarrel with the manifest usefulness of classifying literary materials according to their several forms, or with the development of working hypotheses to explain their function and meaning. But a working hypothesis requires some external evidence to sustain it.

Methodological decency would seem to require an external hook on which to hang circular reasoning. The standard of judgment for all such reconstructions must be the actuality of life preserved in the soil and recovered by archaeology. The Bible is the story of people who occupied a certain geographic territory, who lived and died on it, who worked and worshiped there, who struggled with their neighbors and with each other; and who left tangible evidence of their presence. Any theory of the Bible or reconstruction of the history of Israel must deal with that reality, i.e., the material culture whose remains have survived in hundreds of sites and millions of artifacts all bearing witness to what they were and did, thought and felt. Before archaeology there was no adequate alternative to the creation of hypothetical frameworks for the biblical narrative; but as the factual evidence has become available, there is less and less excuse for such exercises in ingenuity, and in due course there will be none.

Archaeology and the Biblical Languages

Archaeological discovery has had an immediate and direct impact on the interpretation of the biblical languages. While these languages—

Hebrew and Aramaic in the OT, and Aramaic and Greek in the NT—were never forgotten in the sense that Egyptian hieroglyphics or Babylonian cuneiform or many other ancient languages were, nevertheless there are many difficult passages in the Bible, some of which were corrupted through errors in the transmission of the text, and others the true meaning of which was forgotten in the course of time and which were no longer understood by the early translators and commentators. In various ways archaeology has contributed to a clearer understanding of the biblical materials.

The discovery of ancient manuscripts of the OT and NT has been of direct material aid in elucidating the text. Occasionally an early manuscript will have a different, older, and superior reading to any preserved in the extant manuscripts. In such cases the difficulty in the received text is seen to be the result of a scribal error, and the problem is resolved by substituting the preferred reading of the newly found text. Or the manuscript may have a variant reading, which though not to be preferred to the standard text nevertheless provides a clue to the interpretation of the passage, and opens the way to a solution of the crux. Non-biblical manuscripts of a similar genre which are dependent upon or related to biblical materials may offer help in the interpretation of difficult passages, or may help to clear up grammatical, syntactic, or lexicographical problems through the use of the same or related terms in different contexts. The possibilities are practically unlimited, so that the discovery of inscribed texts almost always results in some positive gain in the interpretation of biblical passages. That is why the search for inscriptions remains the principal objective of biblical archaeologists. And the relative paucity of written materials turned up in Palestine has only increased the avidity of excavators. Practically every Hebrew inscription found, however brief, has contributed in some measure to the elucidation of the Bible. Needless to say, the reverse is also true, and in greater measure.

It should be added that archaeology contributes indirectly to the clarification of the Bible in many ways. Artifacts may concretely illustrate a biblical passage, especially one dealing with *realia*. Archaeological data about the common activities of life may help to clarify incidental allusions and references in the biblical text which are not otherwise explained. Knowledge of the cultural setting in which the biblical books find their place can be provided in part by archaeology. An adequate interpretation and rendering of biblical passages requires control of a wide range of related data. Sometimes considerably more than the determination of the text is involved in the clarification of a passage. Thus, for example, the text of the first verses of Genesis is not in question—presumably it has been transmitted unchanged from the autograph of the Priestly writer—but the interpretation of the material is the subject of perennial scholarly controversy.

Our concern now is with archaeological data which directly illuminate the biblical languages. We will attempt to deal with the relevant materials in roughly chronological order:

1. The Patriarchal Age: Middle Bronze II—second millennium, first half. As yet no texts of any length in Amorite, the presumed language of the patriarchs, have turned up. But certain expressions, personal and place-names, do occur in Akkadian texts of this period. The principal source is the thousands of Mari tablets from the eighteenth century B.C. Through careful examination of the many Amorite names, some of which are identical with or very similar to biblical names of the patriarchal period, it has been possible to work out a basic vocabulary and grammar of this ancestral Northwest Semitic dialect which is closely related to Canaanite on the one hand and Aramaic on the other.

In addition there are the so-called pseudo-hieroglyphic inscriptions from Byblos, which may be somewhat older. Though a definite decipherment has not yet been published, G. E. Mendenhall has made sufficient progress toward a solution to describe the script as syllabic and the language as Canaanite, bearing marked resemblances to Ugaritic and Phoenician, and to Biblical Hebrew, though with some notable deviations.

We mention in passing the execration texts of the Twelfth Dynasty in Egypt (nineteenth and eighteenth centuries B.C.), in which are found the names of contemporary Canaanite cities.

2. The Amarna Age: Late Bronze II A—fourteenth century B.C. There is now a great abundance of material in Northwest Semitic dialects from this period, though neither of the principal deposits was known at the time of the founding of the Society of Biblical Literature and Exegesis. The first group of Amarna letters was discovered in 1887, and it was not until 1929 that the first Ugaritic tablets were found.

a. The Amarna letters, found in the ruins of the capital city of the pharaoh Akhenaten, constitute part of the royal diplomatic archives. They were written in Akkadian, the official language of international correspondence in the fourteenth century B.C. Many of the extant letters were sent by kinglets of the city-states of Canaan, the pharaoh's puppet rulers of Byblos, Jerusalem, Megiddo, Shechem, and other cities. While these letters are principally important as first-hand cultural documents describing and reflecting political, military and socio-economic conditions in Palestine a century or so before Moses and Joshua, they are also very valuable sources for the contemporary Canaanite language. The local dialect of the scribes often shines through the Akkadian formalities; and they regularly inserted Canaanite words and phrases to facilitate the expression of their meaning, and possibly to help the translators in the Egyptian foreign office, who presumably knew Canaanite better than Akkadian. It need not be added that the transcription of Canaanite words in Akkadian provides a dividend for the attentive scholar. In Akkadian words are vocalized, thus offering a clue to the vowel structure, whereas in alphabetic inscriptions in Canaanite of this and even later periods no such help is given; only consonants are indicated. The cuneiform alphabet used in Ugaritic is a partial exception (*'aleph* alone of the consonants is regularly vocalized). Thus in the Amarna letters we have a rare glimpse, in relatively full dress, of the immediate ancestor of Biblical Hebrew.

b. By far the most extensive early source for Northwest Semitic is the Ugaritic texts—a vast quantity of tablets written in alphabetic cuneiform dating from the fourteenth and thirteenth centuries B.C. Since excavations began, thousands of tablets have been recovered, and there seems to be no diminution in the rate of return. The most important of these are mythological epics in poetic form, which provide direct documentation of Canaanite religious belief, long known only from the hostile descriptions of the Bible and late classical sources. There are other literary texts, but the great bulk of the remaining tablets are official documents of various kinds, including numerous lists and others dealing with a wide variety of matters. The mythological poems have so far made the principal contributions to biblical studies, but the great accumulation of prose texts, many as yet unpublished, gives promise of substantial additional help in interpreting the Bible.

While occasional voices are raised in protest at the classification of Ugaritic as a Canaanite dialect, there is a growing consensus that it belongs to the Northwest Semitic family of languages (as its location, and the contents of its literature would suggest), with very close affinities to Amarna Canaanite and Biblical Hebrew. This contention is borne out fully by a careful comparison of biblical poetry with that of Ugarit (a similar comparison of biblical prose with the Ugaritic prose texts is also in order), and the recognition, only now gaining headway, that many features of Ugaritic syntax, morphology, and lexicography hitherto regarded as setting it apart from Biblical Hebrew, actually occur in biblical poetry. But these features, practically all archaic and long since abandoned in classical Hebrew prose, passed unrecognized by editors and scribes, and were thus accidentally concealed, partially erased or altered through misrepresentation and misinterpretation. Fortunately the scribes were generally faithful in their work, even when they did not comprehend the text; and a sufficient number of examples of archaic usage have survived to make the identification with characteristic Ugaritic features certain. Thus the occurrence of enclitic *mem* in Hebrew poetry (and in passages based on poetic originals) is now universally acknowledged, and hundreds of convincing cases have been discovered. But the phenomenon in Biblical Hebrew was not even suspected until after it was observed in Ugaritic, and later noted in the Hebrew Bible. The same is true of other features: e.g., the asseverative use of initial *l;* the prepositions *b* and *l* with the meaning "from"; the use of double-duty particles which occur only once in a poetic couplet or bicolon, but exert force in both cola: these include prepositions, pronominal suffixes, negative particles and of course verbs and nouns; the alternation of perfect and imperfect forms of the verb without the use of *waw* consecutive, and in which the tense or action of the verb must be determined from context and not according to familiar prose rules. There are close similarities in lexicography as well. Traditional pairs of words are common to both Hebrew and Ugaritic poetry; in these not only are the pairs made up of the same words, but the order of words (which appears first and which second) is also constant. It is now becoming clear that Hebrew poetry made use of a special vocabulary quite different from ordinary prose, which it shared with Ugaritic; and it has been possible to identify certain of these roots on the basis of Ugaritic cognates.

None of this should come as a surprise. Hebrew poetry is noticeably different from Hebrew prose. Students who breeze through a course in

Hebrew reading confined to the narrative portions of the OT find Hebrew poetry much more difficult. Biblical poetry employs a more complex vocabulary, often uses rare words and archaic forms, and indulges in difficult syntactical constructions: features which are common to poetry of many languages, but are avoided in prose. It is therefore no accident that archaic or archaizing Hebrew poetry should have close affinities with somewhat older Canaanite poetry.

I may add that M. Dahood of the Pontifical Biblical Institute in Rome is just finishing work on the Anchor edition of the Psalms, interpreting them in the light of Ugaritic lexicography, morphology, and syntax. While the first volume, which will appear in about a year, covers only Pss. 1–50, it is already clear that the results of his highly original work are rather startling. In any case his enterprise should mark the end of the period of wholesale emendation of the text, which mars the work of practically all modern critical commentators, and the abandonment of many speculations based upon such drastic treatments. Dahood has made an effective case for dealing with the text essentially as it has been handed down, and has been able to clarify decisively many passages which have hitherto proved impenetrably obscure. His work, however, is only a logical extension of the pioneering effort of other Ugaritic specialists who had previously pointed out the close affinities between Hebrew poetry and the poems of Ugarit. Once this principle is established then it is only a matter of making the right combinations, and using the available materials with skill and caution. On the basis of Dahood's proposals, even if only a fraction stand the test of scholarly criticism, it should be impossible in the future to ignore or minimize the importance of Ugaritic for the study of Hebrew poetic materials.

c. Canaanite alphabetic inscriptions. Apart from the Ugaritic tablets in their special script, there are a number of inscriptions written in the Canaanite alphabet, which is the direct ancestor of the well-known Phoenician, Aramaic, and Greek scripts of later centuries. They date from about the seventeenth century B.C. on, and constitute an invaluable corpus for tracing the evolution of the alphabetic scripts. This subject is of importance in its own right for the study of the transmission of the biblical text, since all extant manuscripts are written in alphabetic scripts, and often scribal errors and other variations can be explained on the basis of epigraphic considerations. Most of these early inscriptions are very brief or fragmentary and offer little in the way of linguistic material. The proto-Sinaitic inscriptions of the fifteenth century B.C., however, are an exception. Many scholars have had a hand in their decipherment, most recently W. F. Albright and Frank M. Cross, Jr., whose contributions have appeared in various journals. A comprehensive treatment of the inscriptions by Albright, including much new material, is now in the press and will appear in the near future. For the bearing of these rather remote texts on biblical studies we may refer to Cross's study, "Yahweh and the God of the Patriarchs,"[1] in which a pattern of divine titles or address is established partly on the basis of a reading in the proto-Sinaitic texts.

3. The First Commonwealth: ca. 1200-600 B.C. A large number of inscriptions in a variety of dialects including and related to Hebrew and Aramaic comes from this period. Taken as a group they constitute an important witness to the linguistic situation in Palestine-Syria during the time when the bulk of the OT was composed. We can only mention the most important items:

a. Phoenician inscriptions: 1) The royal inscriptions from Byblos of the tenth century B.C. These are our best witness to the state of Canaanite at the time when Hebrew letters flourished at the court of David and Solomon. The affinities between the so-called Byblian dialect and Israelite are particularly marked. 2) From the ninth century on, Phoenician inscriptions are found all over the Mediterranean world, reflecting the rapid expansion of Phoenician maritime interests, and extensive colonization.

b. Aramaic inscriptions from the ninth century on. These were written in a variety of dialects, since it was not until much later that the dialect of Damascus became the official Aramaic language, first of the Aramean empire and then of the western provinces of the Babylonian and Persian empires. The earliest inscription in Damascene Aramaic is the Ben-Hadad stele dating about 850 B.C. Other dialects are represented by inscriptions from Hamath, Sujin, and Zinjirli. Mention should also be made of the recently published Saqqara papyrus, which dates from about 600 B.C. and indicates that Aramaic was by that time the language of foreign affairs in Palestine.

[1] *HTR,* LV (1962), 225-59.

c. The Moabite Stone has already been mentioned. It remains the most important of all the Palestinian inscriptions, not only for its historical data, but because of its formal characteristics as a royal inscription, and its linguistic features as the only extensive document in official Moabite, a close cousin of Hebrew. A second Moabite inscription from the same period has recently been published;[2] in our judgment it should be attributed to the same king.

d. We can only mention the very numerous seals and stamps in Hebrew and neighboring dialects; the quantity is constantly increasing as the result of recent excavations, and a separate work would be required to catalogue and evaluate them. But more must be said about the Hebrew inscriptions from Israel and Judah, which are a prime external source for the language of the Bible in pre-exilic times. The number of these of any length or importance is not large, but it is growing as new discoveries are constantly being made. Their importance is too obvious to require comment. Among other data, they have provided information concerning dialectal differences between Israel and Judah respectively. Thus the Gezer Calendar and the Samaria Ostraca are witnesses to the Israelite form of Hebrew, which had close affinities with Phoenician, while the Siloam inscription (discovered in the year that this Society was founded) and the Lachish letters are the principal witnesses to the Judahite form of Hebrew, in which the biblical materials were finally set down and transmitted.

Recently there has been a spate of new finds including ostraca from Hazor, Beth-shan, Tel Qasile, Ashdod, and Arad. The most important single item is the letter of a protesting peasant from Yavneh-yam, which dates to the last quarter of the seventh century B.C. It is written in relatively good Hebrew (with numerous echoes of biblical usage), and has an interesting point of contact with certain legal passages in the Pentateuch, especially the law on the return of a pledged garment in Exod. 22:26-27. A number of ostraca have been found in successive seasons at Arad. They are in Hebrew and Aramaic and date from the ninth to the fourth centuries B.C. One bears the name Arad written several times, and in different directions. Like the inscribed sherds from Gibeon bearing the

[2] W. L. Reed and F. V. Winnett, "A Fragment of an Early Moabite Inscription from Kerak," *BASOR,* CLXXII (Dec. 1963), 1-9; cf. D. N. Freedman, "A Second Mesha Inscription," *ibid.,* CLXXV (Oct. 1964), 50 f.

name of that city (and another from Beth-shan with the name of that city), it may presage a new and welcome trend in the hitherto complicated business of identifying archaeological sites. Another Arad ostracon has a tantalizing reference to the "king of Judah," while still another has the reading *bêt yhwh*—extraordinary because it may refer to a temple at Arad.

Lastly, mention should be made of the inscribed clay tablets found at Deir ʿAlla this past spring and just published by H. Franken. They are provisionally dated to the twelfth century B.C., and are written in an unknown script which may be related to Linear A. They may turn out to be written in the long-lost and long-sought Philistine language; if true, we would have preferred to have them turn up at Ashdod, where we have been looking hard for just such inscriptions. However, Ashdod has produced inscriptions in four other languages, so there is no cause for complaint.

4. The period of the Second Commonwealth: fifth century B.C. on. In the post-exilic period the stream of materials turns into a flood, and it would be a hopeless task even to try to list them. It may be noted that for the earlier part of this period, the fifth and fourth centuries, practically all the texts are in Aramaic. There seems to be a definite break in Hebrew inscriptions from the sixth century to the third century B.C. It was not until the time of the Maccabees that Hebrew was revived on a large scale, as the official language of the country, and for literary and religious purposes. At least one colloquial dialect of spoken Hebrew is attested in this period as well. From the second century B.C. until the end of the Second Commonwealth, to which must be added the period of Bar Kochba's revolt, Hebrew continued in regular and widespread use, though it never displaced Aramaic as the common language of the population of the whole area, and the medium of commerce and diplomacy through this long period. From the fourth century B.C. on, Greek became increasingly important in the same area, and it is now clear that all three languages played significant roles in the life of Palestine with intersecting and overlapping jurisdictions.

a. For the earlier period the principal sources are the fifth-century Aramaic papyri from Elephantine initially discovered in 1893 seqq. but not fully published until 1953 (when E. G. Kraeling published the Brooklyn Papyri). These documents brought to light the existence, previously unsuspected, of a heterodox Jewish colony at Elephantine in Egypt, who worshiped the God Yahu (abbreviated from Yahweh) in their own temple. It is clear that they diverged far from the normative Judaism of Ezra and Nehemiah, and even from the less orthodox Samaritans in the north of Palestine. Some of the letters are of special importance for clarifying the puzzling situation in Judah during the fifth century B.C., though as is generally the case new problems have been raised in the process of resolving old ones. The value of the papyri as a source for the official Aramaic of the fifth century B.C. is rivaled only by the diplomatic correspondence of the Satrap Arsames (published by G. R. Driver in 1954). They offer a solid basis of comparison with the Aramaic portions of Ezra. So far as language is concerned, there is no reason to doubt the authenticity of the reports in the biblical book. We may also mention an Aramaic ostracon from Ashdod belonging to the fifth century, in which the name Zebadiah appears. It is interesting to note that the only occurrences of this name in the Bible are in post-exilic sources: Ezra and Chronicles.

From the fourth century B.C. we have the so-called Samaria papyri, which were found a little more than a year ago in a remote cave in the Wady Adaliyeh region. A preliminary report by Frank M. Cross, Jr., indicates their considerable importance for biblical studies, especially as this period is largely passed over in the Bible. The occurrence of the name Sanballat is especially intriguing.

b. From the period from the third century B.C. until the second century A.D. the principal archaeological data are the Dead Sea Scrolls, including both the Qumran Scrolls and the other extensive manuscript finds from the Wady Murabba'at and other caves in the Judean desert. The almost incredibly vast quantity of material involved, which nevertheless does not begin to match the literature about them, makes any comment here seem faintly ridiculous. They constitute not only the most important, but also the most unexpected of all the discoveries made in Palestine. Since hundreds of documents, and thousands of the fragments are of biblical books, and since many of the other documents either quote from or allude to biblical materials, there is no need to argue the case for their relevance to OT studies. Since as a group they are also the principal contemporary source for the language and literature of Judaism in this period, and provide the essential background for the NT literature, their importance for Intertestamental and NT research is equally clear.

Perhaps we can escape with three observations: 1) The Scrolls are of basic significance for the history of the text of the Hebrew Bible. They are especially valuable for Septuagint studies, settling certain questions decisively and throwing important light upon others. There are at least three fragmentary manuscripts of biblical books which can be dated as early as the third century B.C. on paleographic grounds. Through the determination and comparison of text-types, an even earlier state of the Hebrew text can be projected. In the case of Ecclesiastes and Daniel we have manuscripts which are reasonably close to the presumed autographs. The fragments of Ecclesiastes come from the second half of the second century B.C., probably within two centuries of the original. The fragments of Daniel belong to the first quarter of the first century B.C., or less than a century after the autograph which must have been written in 165 B.C. 2) Another principal value of the Scrolls lies in the fact that they are primary documents of Judaism in the period from 150 B.C. to A.D. 70. They constitute the religious literature of the Essenes, and are thus firsthand evidence for the way of life, the faith and practice of a major Jewish sect. 3) It is in connection with the NT that the Scrolls should make their largest contribution to biblical studies. Early Christianity had very close affinities with and arose out of apocalyptic Judaism, a form of which is faithfully reflected in the Scrolls. Not only is the thought-world and biblical exegesis of the NT represented in the Scrolls, but much of the theological vocabulary of the NT is a rendering in Greek of the Hebrew terminology of the Scrolls. There are points of contact with the Scrolls throughout the NT; it is perhaps surprising that the Johannine and Pauline writings, as well as the Epistle to the Hebrews, have especially close parallels in the Qumran treatises.

The Scrolls, and here we include the later documents of the latter part of the first century and the early part of the second century A.D., confirm the view that Palestine in this period was multilingual. Not only are there documents in Hebrew (both the archaizing "biblical" dialect of many of the Qumran Scrolls and the contemporary colloquial Mishnaic, as in the Copper Scroll), Aramaic, and Greek, but also in Latin and Nabatean.

c. We cannot close this abbreviated presentation without some reference to the vast amount of manuscript material which bears directly or indirectly on the text and language of the NT. Since the founding of this Society, which marked the triumph of the so-called Neutral text favored by Westcott and Hort, a large number of papyri containing portions of the NT have been found. Many of these are older than the great uncial manuscripts of the fourth century which form the basis for the present critical editions of the NT; one is so old that in terms of mathematical probability it bears on the question of the date of original composition, i.e. it helps to fix a *terminus ad quem* for the autograph. I refer to the John Rylands fragment of the Gospel of John which is conservatively dated on epigraphic grounds to the second quarter of the second century. Thus it lends support to the view held by certain scholars that John is one of the earlier NT writings. Other NT papyri from the third century (the principal collections are the Chester Beatty and Bodmer papyri), reveal a mixed textual situation antecedent to the emergence of the standard text-types.

In addition to the manuscripts of the NT text and versions there are many other ancient documents less directly related to the NT, but showing dependence on its contents through quotations or allusions. Thus the great hoard of Gnostic Christian codices found at Chenoboskion in Egypt are of particular value for NT studies. These manuscripts were written in Coptic, and date from the fourth century A.D. It is clear however, that they are translations or adaptations from Greek documents of the third and second centuries. Many of them show direct dependence upon the canonical gospels (especially John) and other NT writings. They differ so markedly in character from the NT that it is difficult to escape the conclusion that by the time of their composition the NT was already complete and had achieved authoritative if not canonical status. Briefly we may say that just as these works derive from the second century and following, the NT is clearly a product of an earlier period, the first century.

With respect to the language of the NT, a principal contribution has come from the thousands of non-biblical papyri of the same period. It is at once clear that the Greek of the NT is essentially the same as the Koine of the papyri. Many expressions in the NT have been clarified by the papyri, and interesting nuances and overtones detected in the same fashion. On the other hand, there is a specifically biblical cast to the language of the NT, as comparison with the Septuagint shows. Further, the Septuagint, through its rendering of key OT terms, provided the basic theological vocabulary for the NT writers. A third factor is present also; the specifically sectarian vocabulary of the Scrolls is matched in the Greek of the NT. There is no question of priority since the Scrolls all antedate the NT books, but both may derive from a common source in Hassidic Judaism. In any case, the language of the NT, which is Greek, is nevertheless thoroughly grounded in biblical, Jewish, Palestinian soil —where we may add that Greek had also been deeply rooted since the fourth and third centuries B.C.

Conclusion

It will be seen from this survey that a vast amount of material has been unearthed which bears on our understanding of the biblical languages. Much work has been done, but much more remains to be done before the importance of these materials can be fully appreciated. In view of the constantly increasing supply of data, and the fantastic rate of accretion, it is, however, a losing battle. At the moment we need more workers on the material found, than finders of new material. Nevertheless, remarkable progress in decipherment, interpretation, and application has been made, and the future looks even brighter.

In the discussion of the biblical languages, it should be remembered that they were never lost. A continuous tradition of interpretation accompanied the transmission of the text. And this is reflected in the versions and commentaries from earliest times. Nevertheless, in the process certain lexicographical and grammatical points were forgotten or misconstrued. There was inevitable modernizing in orthography, diction, and other features of the language, whereby obsolete and archaic elements tended to be sloughed off. Fortunately in the case of the Bible there was an equally powerful resistance to change, and scribes faithfully reproduced the text before them whether they understood it in detail or not, and even when it posed serious problems to the interpreter. Because of this tenacity in transmission scholars have been able to recover, with the help of the inscriptional evidence, words and forms, meanings and constructions, which had long been forgotten. Thus archaeology makes its principal contribution to the study of the biblical languages in two areas:

1) The non-biblical materials help to give a clearer picture of the

dimensions and character of the languages which are only partially represented in the Bible. Since the inscriptions also come from a variety of places and periods, they provide a basis for analyzing the biblical languages according to a historical perspective, and thereby yield clues as to date and authorship. It is also possible to recover lost words and lost meanings, grammatical devices and uses: in short, to do justice to the biblical material. This is especially true of Hebrew poetry where we have much to learn about the canons which governed its composition.

2) Sensational discoveries in the past decades have provided us with very old manuscripts of the books of the OT and NT. For the OT, we are now in a position to practice serious text criticism, i.e., the classification of manuscripts and comparison of standard text-types in the preparation of an eclectic critical edition of the Hebrew Bible. When finally established (at least for the historical books), it will reflect the best manuscript tradition of the second, third, and even fourth centuries B.C. rather than being the resultant text of the first and second centuries A.D.

For NT studies, the papyri have made it possible to penetrate beyond the standard text-types to the earlier stages of text transmission, when variations from the autographs and early copies first appeared and began to congeal into groups. Just what will emerge from these studies is not yet clear, but the chances are excellent for ultimately recovering or reconstructing an archetypal text not more than a generation or two from the autographs.

There can be little question of the value or usefulness of archaeological data in the determination of the biblical text and the clarification of its meaning. Presuppositions and methods must constantly be checked and revised and refined, and there is always danger of misuse and misinterpretation. Movement and progress unfortunately are not the same. Still there has been both movement and progress, and there will be more of both.

It is my understanding that among the founders of the Society of Biblical Literature and Exegesis were members of the American Committee for the revision of the King James Version of the Bible, the English edition of which appeared in 1885, to be followed in 1901 by the American Standard Version. These revisions signaled a change in the scholarly climate, a basic shift in mood and approach. The translators stood at the end of a long line of dedicated scholars and were heirs of a great tradition. Their work reflected that fact. But they also stood at the threshold of a new era, marked by accelerating change, and stimulated by archaeological discovery. In the 84 years since the founding of the Society vastly more information about the Bible and its world has come into our hands than in the preceding 840 years or more. The rate of Bible revision and translation has increased rapidly. Even current translations are outmoded soon after they appear because of the new materials literally spilling out of the earth all the time. For we are just in the preliminary stages of scholarship so far as the biblical world is concerned. I am confident that the future will see such strides made and gains secured as will make past efforts seem tepid and timid.

JAMES BENNETT PRITCHARD

Culture and History

When this Society was founded, biblical archaeology was limited to exploration on the surface of the Holy Land and to study of antiquities picked up at random or from holes dug into a few ancient sites. During the first three decades of the life of our Society, however, this discipline took on a new dimension: by digging below the surface of a number of tells such pioneers as Petrie, Bliss, Macalister, and Reisner found a new kind of data that could be controlled and utilized in the study of the Bible. These beginnings in scientific excavations made before the outbreak of World War I, just fifty years ago, may seem small in retrospect, yet they set a pattern for what has become a major discipline within biblical studies.

The achievements made after World War I are well known: major assaults upon Megiddo and Beth-shan and probes at Jericho, Samaria, Jerusalem, Shechem, Beth-Shemesh, Bethel, Ai, and Lachish. The names themselves conjured up in the popular mind dramatic episodes from the biblical past, with the result that financial support for these projects was readily available. Highly significant during the period between the two Wars was the excavation of a site relatively obscure in biblical narrative, Tell Beit Mirsim, thought to be the ancient Debir. At this place, for which no miracles or dramatic events are recorded, W. F. Albright found and brilliantly utilized a key of stratigraphy and typology that miraculously opened up possibilities for applying archaeological results to the problems of biblical history. One could hardly have expected that Tell Beit Mirsim would have been more informative in the long run than the major sites of biblical history; yet Tell Beit Mirsim became a key site which supplied the chronological framework to a host of others far better known to readers of the Bible.

Since World War II there has been a further application of archaeological technique to sites that played a less dramatic role in biblical narratives but which often contained better stratification than the familiar cities: Tell el-Far'ah, Dhiban, Deir 'Alla, Hazor, Arad, Ashdod,

Ramat Rahel, Tell Qasile, Qumran, and Tell es-Sa'idiyeh. Besides these new excavations there has been a careful reexamination and further exploration of such important sites as Shechem, Jericho, Taanach, Jerusalem, Bethel, and others. Measured by any standard—money and manpower expended, sites dug, and publications—the achievements of the past seventy-five years are impressive.

One might say that the past century of biblical study has been characterized by attempts to find firm points of independent reference outside the text of the Bible itself, positions from which biblical tradition could be tested and better understood. Cuneiform and Ugaritic studies are examples of new approaches that have been enormously productive; other schools of study have stimulated fruitful discussions: the study of pre-Islamic Arabia, comparative folklore, myth and ritual, the traditio-historical approach, and the Dead Sea Scrolls, the discovery of which in 1947 infused the colorless but important field of textual criticism with drama and adventure. Thus, it is fair to say that over the last century the main stream of biblical studies has been joined by many tributaries. Although some have diminished in volume after the first flash floods of initial enthusiasm, they have nevertheless left their marks on the prevailing picture of what the Bible is and says.

The question that concerns us now, however, is whether archaeology is an independent vantage point for seeing and testing the historical framework of the Bible. To be sure, archaeology has been successful in charting the long history of Palestine; but what has it contributed to an understanding of the history and culture of the Bible? Have the results of excavations confirmed or controverted the written record? Has archaeology provided some new perspective for old problems? These are our immediate concerns.

Before attempting to answer these questions it may be useful to consider briefly three observations about the nature of the archaeological evidence which is at our disposal.

1. Support for the costly work of excavation and its publication has generally come from those who have a deep concern for the tradition preserved in the Bible. Sites which are at the center of biblical narratives have generally had more appeal than those lying on the periphery. What relates directly to the relatively short segment of biblical history is of more concern generally than that which illuminates the history of the

Amorites, the Canaanites, or the Nabataeans, for example. One might say that popular interest in the Bible is both the principal base of support for archaeology and at the same time a potential source of distortion.

2. Rarely, if ever, do historical judgments emerge from the ground. They are usually deduced by archaeologists from observed evidence. Such tangible objects as pots, walls, floor, etc., take on meaning for history only as the context in which they are found can be controlled, identified, and related to other contexts by the excavator and his colleagues. This process of interpretation involves opinion, common sense, and logic. To remember these human variables, the components of any archaeological equation, is to guard against an unwarranted authoritarianism.

3. The reliability of archaeological evidence varies. Techniques have developed in the past seventy-five years, so that it is possible to extract more solid historical information today from a single trench than from an entire hill of debris a generation ago. Unless the elements of the highly diversified material found in a tell are distinguished for what they are and recorded in sections by strata, the resulting picture of human occupation may be seriously distorted.

In the appraisal of results pertinent to biblical study we can pass over quickly, with a mere mention, two obvious accomplishments. First, there is the placing of biblical geography on a firmer basis. The pioneer work of Edward Robinson in 1838 and 1853 has been built upon by excavations as well as by the surface explorations of Albright and Glueck, and more recently by those of members of the annual seminars of the Deutsche Evangelische Institut.

Secondly, excavations have illuminated and illustrated the written record of the Bible. It is to the credit of archaeology that we now have actual examples of city defenses, water systems, houses; industrial installations for the manufacture of such products as wine, cloth, copper, pottery; examples of writing and engraving in hard stone and ivory; tools, weapons, weights, bronze vessels from the biblical period. No one can deny the value of this obvious gain in knowledge, which has brought to light the economic and social life of a people who a century ago were known only from written descriptions.

We shall pass over these undisputed increments of archaeology to consider in more detail another area of importance. What has biblical archaeology contributed to our understanding of the traditions about history and religion as described in the OT? The answer to this question cannot be as specific as the answers to the questions about the cultural background. Yet the answer is of considerable importance for appraising the tradition about events and the origins of Israel's religion.

Let us suppose that one were to come to a study of the mass of data recovered from the excavations of the past seventy-five years in Palestine without any knowledge of the literary sources preserved in the OT. What impression would he have of Israelite history, religion, and culture? He would know of the existence of the kingdoms of Israel and Judah from the accounts of Assyrian invasions, and he would be aware of the name of the national god Ya or Yahu from the theophorous components of dozens of personal names that appear on ostraca, graffiti, and seals. From many stratified remains he could easily discern the differences between the assemblages of artifacts from the various periods of occupation; he could note the evidence for continuity in cultural patterns as well as the intrusions of influences from outside through trade and conquest. In fact, the early segment of the known history of Palestine is entirely dependent upon archaeological sources such as these.

It would be apparent that on several occasions Palestine was invaded and settled by new peoples bearing with them distinctive customs and techniques. Two illustrations of such a break in the continuity of the culture of the land will suffice. The first is at the beginning of the Middle Bronze Age and the other shortly after the advent of the Iron Age.

Sometime about the end of the third millennium B.C. in a period variously labeled as Middle Bronze I, the Intermediate Early Bronze-Middle Bronze, or the Caliciform period, there was an invasion and settlement of a new people in central and southern Palestine. They are known best from several hundred rock-cut shaft tombs located at Tell el-ʿAjjul, Lachish, Jericho, and Gibeon, as well as from remains at several less prominent sites. Suddenly there appears throughout the land an entirely new repertoire of pottery vessels, of which the graceful caliciform jar is the most distinctive, a new type of bronze javelin with a curled tang, four-nozzle lamps, and an elaborate provision for the burial of the dead. Since these elements are radically different from those which make up the culture of the preceding Early Bronze Age, the unanimous verdict is that these remains evidence unmistakably an intrusion into the land of a new people. Even without a written tradition it is obvious that there was a decided discontinuity in culture. Although we must be content to know the intruders only as the "Caliciform" people, there can be no doubt that, at about the twenty-first century B.C., the Early Bronze culture came to a definite end with the arrival of a new wave of settlers.

The second example of discontinuity is more widely known. The remains of the twelfth century B.C. evidence the appearance at a number of archaeological sites along the coast of Palestine and in the adjacent regions of assemblages of distinctive pottery locally made; iron tools and weapons make their first appearance and there is evidence for burials in anthropoid coffins. This new cultural pattern appears suddenly, breaking the continuity of the preceding centuries at a period for which we have two literary traditions, each independent of the other. One is the testimony of inscriptions of Ramses III at Medinet Habu of the invasion of the Sea Peoples, one constituent of which is the Philistines; the other tradition is the well-known biblical accounts of the Philistines. Here then in the twelfth century, as also in the twenty-first, there exists tangible evidence for a break in the continuity of the cultural history of Palestine, and the observations of this change made by the archaeologist can be matched by biblical and Egyptian traditions about a break in the ethnic continuity of the settlement.

Since we have seen that there have been examples of discontinuity in the history of human culture in Palestine, and that invasions and settlements of new peoples can be detected by means of archaeological method, we may pose an important question: what evidence is available from archaeological remains for the strong biblical tradition preserved in the book of Joshua for the conquest and settlement of the land by a new and different people?

It is apparent, I am sure, to this audience that the long debate over the archaeological evidence for the conquest has moved from a discussion of its date to the more basic question of the very evidence itself, since Miss Kenyon's convincing demonstration of the early date for Garstang's walls at Jericho.[1] To the scant evidence for Late Bronze Age remains at Jericho and the now recently reconfirmed gap in occupation at Ai extending over the entire Late Bronze period, there must be added an account of the present state of our knowledge of the occupational history at Gibeon.[2]

[1] K. M. Kenyon, *Archaeology in the Holy Land,* 2nd ed. (London, 1965), pp. 210-11.
[2] J. B. Pritchard, *Winery, Defenses, and Soundings at Gibeon,* 1965.

In the course of the fourth of the five seasons of excavations at el-Jib there appeared what seemed to be evidence for the existence of the Late Bronze Age Gibeon, which figures so prominently in Josh. 9 and 10. Within seven tombs on the west side of the tell there appeared funerary deposits which belonged unmistakably to the Late Bronze period. Surely, we thought at the close of the 1960 season, when we saw our first Late Bronze Age pottery at el-Jib, there was a city standing on the tell in the period before the beginning of the Iron Age.[3] In the fifth season, 1962, we had as a major objective the clearance of the Bronze Age cemetery at the west and the cutting of test trenches in areas of the mound not previously explored in an attempt to find the Late Bronze Age city. Alas, there were in the large cemetery of fifty-five rock-cut tombs, no more burial deposits of the Late Bronze Age. When the contents of the tombs were studied more carefully for publication, it was clear that the seven deposits of Late Bronze material had been made in tombs hewn from the rock in the Middle Bronze period, and not one of the tombs containing this later material had been prepared especially for the Late Bronze burials. A more careful study of the pottery forms forced us to date them in the fourteenth century, with a possible overlap into the thirteenth century.[4]

When we examined the evidence from excavations made through the debris to the bedrock of the tell in all the major areas[5] there were nowhere the remains of a wall, room, floor level, or house which could possibly be identified as belonging to the Late Bronze period. Among the hundreds of thousands of sherds which were washed and examined there were not more than a half dozen which could be assigned definitely to the Late Bronze Age. Time and time again we found Iron Age occupation overlying that of the Middle Bronze period, without any intervening settlement.

Thus, two results emerge as relatively certain. First, el-Jib is to be identified with the biblical Gibeon of Josh. 9 and 10 through general topographical features as well as by the discovery of twenty-six jar handles

[3] The situation at the close of the 1960 campaign was described then as follows: "The Late Bronze tombs have provided the first evidence for the Canaanite city which is described in chapters nine and ten of the book of Joshua" (*The Illustrated London News*, Sept. 24, 1960, pp. 518-19).

[4] J. B. Pritchard, *The Bronze Age Cemetery at Gibeon* (Philadelphia, 1963), p. 72.

[5] Areas 22, 10, 8, 17, 16, and 28.

inscribed with Gibeon, a find which has fixed beyond cavil the identification of el-Jib with Gibeon. Secondly, there was no extensive city on the tell from the end of Middle Bronze until the beginning of the twelfth century. The Late Bronze tombs of the fourteenth century belonged either to a very small settlement, limited to some small section of the mound as yet untouched, or to the temporary camps in the vicinity. There can be no doubt, on the basis of the best evidence available, that there was no city of any importance at the time of Joshua.

The apparent anomalies found in the archaeological results from three sites which figure prominently in the narratives in the first part of Joshua suggest that we have reached an impasse on the question of supporting the traditional view of the conquest with archaeological undergirding.

There is, however, another approach to the question of the history of the conquest of Canaan by Israel. It involves the break in the continuity of the basic culture of Canaan—that totality of observable components of cultural remains such as burial customs, cultic furniture, and charms, as well as artifacts of everyday life.[6] In short, when and in what areas did the characteristic features of the Iron II period begin to be differentiated from the configurations known from the Late Bronze period? Since it is demonstrably possible to isolate as intrusive the Middle Bronze I and the Philistine cultures, can we identify the people of Israel described in the Bible by artifacts and mark their emergence into Palestine?

The evidence for answering this question is unfortunately as yet extremely limited, because of the lack of evidence from sites where there is a continuous occupation, or the delay in publication of what has been reported.

At Tell Beit Mirsim the abundantly documented Stratum C is followed by a meager selection of B 1 sherds from silos 14 and 24;[7] at Beth-

[6] The definition of a "phase" by Willey and Phillips would seem to correspond to what is intended here by the basic culture: "An archaeological unit possessing traits sufficiently characteristic to distinguish it from all other units similarly conceived, whether of the same or other cultures or civilizations, spatially limited to the order of magnitude of a locality or region and chronologically limited to a relatively brief interval of time" (G. R. Willey and Philip Phillips, *Method and Theory in American Archaeology*, p. 22).

[7] *Annual of the American Schools of Oriental Research*, XII (1930-31), 58-60. Six more cisterns of the period are reported but the contents are not published (*ibid.*, p. 60).

Shemesh the destruction of the Late Bronze Stratum IV is followed by unmistakable Philistine occupation; the sequence of LB to Iron I is not well documented at Lachish; and the evidence at Tell el-Hesi is not sufficiently trustworthy to be used with any confidence.

During the 1958 season at Hazor the gap between layers of the tell proper and the extensive lower city was closed by the excavations in Areas A and B.[8] The material from these two areas is now known from summaries in preliminary reports as well as from the plates and catalogue of *Hazor III-IV*,[9] of which I have had the use through the courtesy of Y. Yadin.

The Canaanite city at Hazor which was destroyed sometime in the second half of the thirteenth century was succeeded by Stratum XII in both Area A and B and by Stratum XI in Area B. Both of these strata are taken by the excavator to be remains of Israelite occupation at Hazor. Thus at Hazor, for almost the first time, we have a representative sequence of settlements from Late Bronze through the Iron Age; and it comes from a site which is said in the book of Joshua to have been taken by Israel. This fortunate occurrence of a continuous sequence makes it possible to see if there is a contrast between Canaanite and Israelite culture, provided, of course, that Hazor fell to the Israelites at the end of the Late Bronze Age. What evidence is there, then, for a discontinuity in the culture of these two periods?

A comparison on the basis of everyday wares found in the Late Bronze and Iron I levels at Hazor reveals a slight development in the latter of forms and techniques well established in the Late Bronze Age. No real discontinuity can be detected in the forms of cooking pots, bowls, lamps, craters, pilgrim flasks, or pyxides. There are recognizable differences to be sure, but there remain in the Iron Age the essential hallmarks of the potters who had made these vessels during the preceding two or three centuries. When we compare the more specialized articles of cultic use—a sensitive area where one would normally expect to find a definite break in continuity—the picture is essentially the same. Incense stands, tubular in form with apertures and decoration so common in the Late Bronze periods,[10] are characteristic of the assemblages of the Iron I Age Strata

[8] *IEJ*, VIII (1958), 280 ff.; IX (1959), 74.
[9] Y. Yadin, *Hazor III-IV*, Plates, 1961.
[10] Eighteen examples appear in *ibid.*, Pls. 268:1-4, 276:9-16, and 282:3-8.

XII and XI.[11] Furthermore the bronze figure of a seated god found in the Iron Age "high place" of Stratum XI of Area B [12] is within the Late Bronze tradition of Megiddo and other sites. The only discernible intrusion of an entirely new ceramic feature in the Iron Age strata is that of the collared store-jar.[13] While this is a new tradition in the repertoire of pottery it is not identical with that long familiar from the Iron I Age at Gibeah and Bethel.[14]

Thus at the one site where there is good evidence for a fairly continuous occupation throughout Late Bronze and Iron I, there seems to be a continuity in the assemblages of artifacts. Those who built after the destruction of Stratum XIII may have been poorer than their predecessors, but exhibited basically the same ceramic technology and the same traditions in the making of cultic articles.

This is the place, perhaps, to suggest a possible strategy for the future. We have seen how in the last half century excavators have become concerned with the sites of importance for the stratified record which they contain as well as with those of colorful memory. The development of human culture in Palestine has become of interest for its own sake as well as for the association with the Bible. It is now high time for us to differentiate carefully between the changes which take place within certain well-defined districts of Palestine—Esdraelon, the hill country, Negev, and the Jordan Valley—and to seek to identify the cultural components of the periods associated historically with Canaanites, Israelites, Philistines. From the resulting picture of change and continuity we may be able to gain an independent vantage point from which the biblical record can be better understood and interpreted.

Archaeology is beginning to contribute new evidence which is relevant for a study of the development in Israelite religion. Here again we are dealing with the problem of continuity or discontinuity in the material evidence for the cult in Palestine during the Late Bronze and Iron Ages. What change can be detected in the places of worship, in iconography, in

[11] *Ibid.*, Pls. 169:17, 204:1-5.

[12] *Ibid.*, Pl. 205:2.

[13] *Ibid.*, Pls. 167—168.

[14] See *Annual of the American Schools of Oriental Research,* Vols. 34-35 (1954-56), Pl. 20 for Periods I and II at Tell el-Ful. For contrary opinion see R. Amiran, *IEJ*, VIII (1958), 280.

symbolism, in cultic furniture over this period of a thousand years? Are there radical breaks in the sequence of datable material, or evidence for conflicts between one religious system and another? If so, when did such changes take place? Where? These are some of the questions that have been asked repeatedly of the textual tradition. Let us now ask them of the archaeological data thus far available.

By far the most important discovery made during the recent excavations at Hazor is the series of Canaanite temples found in Area H, to which we have referred above. Although the final plans have not been published it is already clear from the preliminary reports [15] and the excellent aerial photographs [16] that the general arrangement of the three rooms—porch with bases for two columns, hall, and holy of holies—is similar to that of the Jerusalem temple of Solomon as described in the book of Kings. The Canaanite cult was housed in three of these temples, 2, 1*b,* 1*a,* throughout the Late Bronze period. Although Syrian parallels for Solomon's temple have long been known from later periods, the Late Bronze temples at Hazor are the first striking illustrations of the plan followed by the Jerusalem temple to emerge from Palestine itself. It is now certain that the famed shrine of Israel was firmly fixed within a tradition indigenous to Canaan.

In addition to this newly found plan at Hazor it is now apparent that at Beth-shan, Level V, the ground plan of the north temple of Ramses III was within the same general tradition.[17] At Arad, according to preliminary reports of Aharoni, a sanctuary with a holy of holies containing a raised platform, three stelas, and a stepped entranceway flanked by two stone altars,[18] has been uncovered belonging to the period between the ninth and second half of the eighth centuries.[19] The surprising fact is that here in the period of the divided monarchy, within the kingdom of Judah, there was a temple of large dimensions—obviously not a high place or a small shrine—of three adjoining rooms, apparently with an orientation similar to that of the Jerusalem temple.

It is obvious that the hundreds of small clay figurines of the nude

[15] *IEJ,* IX (1959), 81-84.
[16] *Hazor III-IV,* Pls. 101-103.
[17] S. Yeivin, *VT,* XIV (1964), 339.
[18] *Archaeology,* XVII (1964), 53.
[19] Strata X—VIII; *IEJ,* XIII (1963), 336.

female found in strata extending through the Canaanite Late Bronze and the Israelite Iron Age strata had no utilitarian functions. They were hardly produced and circulated as works of art. They must therefore have performed some magical or cultic function.[20] From their first appearance in Middle Bronze to the end of Iron II at about 600 B.C. there were changes in decoration, hairdress, methods of manufacture, and symbolism, but there is a basic continuity in the persistent emphasis upon distinctive female features of reproduction. The emphasis is always, in every known type, upon fertility. Thus the appearance of these distinctive objects in late Israelite strata is a measure either of the syncretism within Israelite religion or of apostasy from the Israelite cult which sought to differentiate itself from the older Canaanite ways of worship.

What then are we to conclude about the place of archaeology in biblical studies? It has had its enthusiasts. Yet the rapidly growing science of Palestinian archaeology is, I predict, something more than a temporary enthusiasm. For while the points of specific contacts between the results obtainable from the soil of the Holy Land and the chapter and verse of Scripture are few indeed, there are other more valuable contributions that archaeology can make and is making to biblical studies. In short it provides a vantage point that is completely independent of the written text for viewing the events and the cultic practices described in the many-stranded and often-revised tradition preserved finally in the biblical text. As we have seen this evidence provides a clue to the state of affairs which is termed "Conquest"; it is able to measure the rate of acculturation of newer peoples who came into the land of Palestine; and it can provide a new source for learning of the development in the cult of ancient Israel.

Some of the enthusiasms of the past century of OT research seem to have reached the point of diminishing returns. Either the materials available have been rather exhaustively culled or theories have been pushed as far as they can without dissolving into pure speculation. Archaeological research, on the contrary, has not yet reached the limits of its possibilities.

Biblical archaeology involves the reevaluation of former results in the light of new evidence. One has but to recall such seemingly sure conclusions as Garstang's Late Bronze walls at Jericho, Solomon's stables at

[20] J. B. Pritchard, *Palestinian Figurines* (New Haven, 1943).

Megiddo, the Jebusite wall at Jerusalem, and the Semitic high places to be reminded that the interpretation is not static.

Besides, the resources for further work are almost limitless. Of the hundreds of tells in Palestine, only one has been rather fully excavated, and those on which extensive work has been done remain as possibilities for rechecking the history within them by means of the greatly improved scientific methods now available. New techniques of digging and controls over the dating of strata through pottery, carbon 14, and possibly by thermoluminescence, promise to make for even greater precision. Although there has been the often repeated lament that so little epigraphic material has come from Palestine, it must be remembered that almost every major excavation has produced some evidence for writing. Canaanite, Egyptian, Ugaritic, Akkadian, Hebrew, and the Deir ʻAlla script are all attested as having been used in the land during the biblical period of its history. The means for a systematic search for the history of the land of the Bible are now increasingly available. Given a period of peace in the land there is every reason to expect an enlarged vista of the past, a new measure of certainty in results, and a continued flow of the kind of unexpected surprises which has characterized archaeological work for the past decades.

10

New Testament Textual Researches Since Westcott and Hort

(PAPERS OF THE AMERICAN TEXTUAL CRITICISM SEMINAR)

KURT ALAND*

The Significance of the Papyri for Progress in New Testament Research

The common heading of the papers presented at this conference is "New Testament Textual Researches Since Westcott and Hort," thus taking as their starting and reference point the work accomplished by those two scholars. I shall begin with a remark which will probably startle you. I come from a country where every NT scholar speaks of Westcott and Hort with great respect. He is conscious of their importance for the history of the NT text and he does not miss an opportunity of enforcing this fact upon his students. Indeed, we all have grounds to be indebted to the work of Westcott and Hort, not least through our work with Nestle's edition of the Greek NT. But the number of NT scholars who possess a copy of the Westcott-Hort NT edition of 1881—to say nothing of their use of it—could be regarded as insignificant, and few of us will presumably have read their Introduction to that edition, in spite of its primary importance. I do not believe that the situation will be much different elsewhere on the European continent.

As I was preparing this paper, I read again, carefully, the three hun-

* I wish to express my appreciation to Paolo Ferreira, B.D. for his work in translating this paper, and to Miss Margaret Lee for assisting him.

dred pages of Westcott-Hort's Introduction. I found that the word papyrus is not even once mentioned in them. The papyri were still outside Westcott and Hort's range of vision. This is valid not only for Westcott and Hort, but also for most of their contemporaries. When C. R. Gregory published the First Part of the third volume of his Prolegomena to Tischendorf's *editio octava maior* in 1884, he knew of only one papyrus, Q^p, which contains fragments of I Corinthians. In 1862 Tischendorf had identified in Leningrad only part of the fragments which Porfiri Uspenskij had brought from the Near East. The five fragments he identified contained I Cor. 1:17-20; 6:13-15, 16-18; 7:3-4, 7, 10-11, 12-14, and were dated in the fifth century (Gregory, *Prolegomena,* pp. 434 f.). It took nearly a hundred years to have this papyrus almost completely edited. I had the chance of examining it in Leningrad, and, as far as the time and primitive aids at my disposal allowed, of separating and reconstructing some of its fragments, which I had the opportunity of publishing later in *NTS,* III (1956-57), 269-78. There were now seventeen fragments, containing portions of all the first seven chapters of I Corinthians. Had I had enough time and the proper aids, I could have separated some of the fragments which were still sticking together, thus increasing their number. Incidentally, the papyrus is now dated from the seventh century and presents interesting reconstruction problems. As late as 1884 Gregory writes: "Praeter haec folia nullum habemus textum Graecum Novi Testamenti uncialibus litteris in papyro scriptum" (p. 435); and even ten years later one could still read in Scrivener-Miller: "This is the only papyrus manuscript of the NT written with uncials" (*A Plain Introduction to the Criticism of the NT,* I, 186). Miller mentions P^{14} and P^{4} only briefly in the appendix of his book (pp. 396 f.). He counted P^{3} as a lectionary, without a reference to its contents (p. 358, as Nr. 502). If this was still the case in 1894—Gregory had also reached this position with the Third Part of his Prolegomena (according to him P^{3}=evl 348, cf. p. 734; P^{4}=evl 943, cf. p. 1312; P^{14}=714, cf. p. 1308)—it is not surprising that Westcott and Hort did not refer to the papyri in their Introduction, published in 1882. But the number of NT papyri increased rather slowly. In the third Part of his *Textkritik,* published in 1909, Gregory mentions 14 papyri. In 1912, their number had increased to 19. In 1933, there were 48, whereas now we know of 80. Thus, the NT papyri constitute, almost without exception, a phenomenon of the twentieth century: in this century they have been found and/or published. Only five papyri were published before 1900, of three of which, however, there were known only isolated fragments.[1] But none of them played an important role in the criticism of the NT text. In the second edition of his introduction to the Greek NT, published in 1899, Eberhard Nestle refers to the papyrus as writing-material, in two places (pp. 35 and 40-42), but only mentions the NT papyri in one and a half lines, in which he alludes briefly to P^{11} and P^{14}. P^4 and P^3, which he must have known by that time, are not even mentioned by him. The papyri were, in fact, scarcely taken into consideration in the nineteenth century.

But not only regarding the papyri is our situation today fundamentally different from that of Westcott and Hort. As far as other important problems of the tradition of the NT text are concerned, we are also working under conditions which are entirely different from theirs. Westcott and Hort do not provide any exact details about the material at their disposal. But it is possible to reconstruct this material with a considerable degree of certainty, partly on the basis of the information they supply, partly in view of the fact that they did not collate any manuscripts, but availed themselves of the works of others.[2] We may assume with some confidence that the list, given in tabular form on page 15 of the Introduction, must have included practically all the uncial manuscripts Westcott and Hort actually used, i.e. 19 uncials in all. Elsewhere, they mention 19 manuscripts for the Gospels, 9 for Acts, 7 for the Catholic Epistles, 9 for the Pauline Epistles and 5 for the Apocalypse, which, as they say, had been preserved "in fair completeness" (p. 75). To these manuscripts must be added of course several fragments [3]; but, on the other hand, the four great uncials ℵABC are included each time, in every one of the five groups mentioned, exception being made of B in the Apocalypse, so that the total of 44 manuscripts, which is reached by adding together the above-mentioned numbers, would, in fact, have

[1] This is valid for P^{11} and P^4, which gained recognition only after it was published (Marcell, 1938). The other four papyri to be considered are P^3 (Wessely, 1882), P^{14} (Harris, 1890), P^5 (Grenfell-Hunt, 1899 and 1922), and P^{10} (Grenfell-Hunt, 1899).

[2] "We have no considerable private stores to add to the common stock" (p. 89).

[3] "The number given for the Gospels, Acts, and Pauline Epistles do not include some more or less considerable fragments" (p. 75).

to be reduced by 15, making 29. But Westcott and Hort could not have known of more than about 45, because the number of manuscripts cited by Tischendorf in his eighth edition of the Greek NT lies within this range.[4] The number of cursives to which Westcott and Hort had access is easier to determine. They know of the existence of about 900 to 1,000.[5] This number is purely theoretical and has to be drastically reduced, because they declare "the full contents of about 150 cursives, besides Lectionaries, may be set down as practically known from these sources." [6] The number of manuscripts actually examined and taken into account by Westcott and Hort almost certainly lies below it, but we will take it as a basis.[7] To these should be added the lectionaries, "of which above 400 have been catalogued," according to Westcott and Hort.[8] But, considering that they add, "Comparatively few Lectionaries have as yet been collated" [9]—an assertion which remains valid one hundred years later—we may, without doing them an injustice, estimate the number of lectionaries they actually used as being rather low.

This is the basis on which Westcott and Hort operated. What is ours? The numbers can be stated quickly: 78 papyri, 224 uncials[10] (these

[4] Tischendorf used more manuscripts, about 60 in all, than Westcott and Hort, but a large number cannot be reconstructed from his edition.

[5] "If each manuscript is counted as one, irrespective of the books contained, the total number is between 900 and 1,000" (p. 76).

[6] p. 77.

[7] This, I believe, does justice to Westcott and Hort's position, even assuming that they could have used a few more cursives, known to them. "A much larger number are known in various degrees of imperfection, some perhaps almost as well as those included in this first class, from the labours of a series of collators, of whom Mill, Wetstein, Greisbach, Birch, Scholz, and Muralt deserve special mention. Many others have been examined only in selected passages, by which rough presumptions, but hardly more, can be formed as to the general character of the text" (p. 77).

[8] p. 76.

[9] p. 76.

[10] This number will probably surprise the reader, but the reason for its being lower than the number of the last uncial in the List is that the uncials have been counted anew. In the List there are 253 uncials named, but through identification and investigation of the relationships of some manuscripts, 6 were eliminated (0149, 0152, 0153, 0192, 0194, 0195). In earlier generations, it often happened that, when a manuscript was found, it was added to the list without being checked for the possibility of belonging to an already-known manuscript.

The investigation of relationships of uncial manuscripts has already led to the elimination of 24 other manuscripts from the list of uncials. The following have already been grouped:

029 + 0113 + 0125 + 0139
059 + 0215

numbers are lower than those mentioned in the "List of Manuscripts," because in some instances fragments of the same manuscript are listed there under different numbers; the number of uncials in the "List" is, for example, 30 more than the above-mentioned figure), about 2,650 cursives, about 2,000 lectionaries—that is, approximately 5,000 Greek manuscripts as against the nominal figure of about 1,500, supposedly known to Westcott and Hort. Of course, not all of these manuscripts can be regarded as complete; about 450 contain fragments of the manuscript group [11] or of the NT manuscript to which they belong. But no one can possibly overlook the fact that the number of Greek manuscripts known to us at present is at least more than three times the number of manuscripts known to Westcott and Hort—among these were also some fragments! Perhaps I ought to have said: this fact *should* not be overlooked, for it often happens that scholars refer to Westcott and Hort as if our situation today, although in many ways different from theirs, were fundamentally the same. A gulf separates us from them, which can no longer be bridged. The only thing we can do is to attempt to ignore it.

---

063 + 0117
064 + 074 + 090
070 + 0110 + 0124 + 0178 + 0179 + 0180 + 0190
0191 + 0202
073 + 084
083 + 0112 + 0235
089 + 092a
095 + 0123
0102 + 0138
0106 + 0119
0136 + 0137
0186 + 0224

The following 24 numbers will have to be crossed out of the list: 074, 084, 090, 092*a*. 0110, 0112, 0113, 0117, 0119, 0123, 0124, 0125, 0137, 0138, 0139, 0178, 0179, 0180, 0190, 0191, 0202, 0215, 0224, 0235.

The above-mentioned numbers 6 and 24 make 30 uncials. It should, however, be noted that although 092*a* is to be taken out of the List, 092*b* will continue to be included. Therefore, the number 253 given in the List, will be reduced by 29 instead of 30. The number of existing known uncials is therefore 224, a number which will probably soon be altered (by further investigation of the relationships of the manuscripts and revision of the List).

[11] Meant are e a p r, but normally a manuscript contains only one of these groups. As far as the earlier period is concerned, it may be expected that a manuscript may have only one NT book or parts of the four groups. It is not by accident that only 57 of the manuscripts known to us contain the whole NT, i.e. all groups e a p r; 224 contain only three groups (the order of the groups varies); 326 two groups (the order of the groups also varies); but 2,402 contain only one group. This arrangement is a result not only of the technical conditions, but also of church requirements.

It is the purpose of this paper to expound this problem in detail and to try to evaluate its results. If the papyri have been mentioned at the beginning, this has not happened inadvertently, but for quite definite reasons. The first is the shifting of the time limit caused by their discovery. Those who have a relationship with NT textual research, more theoretical perhaps than practical, may argue that it is not the number of manuscripts that matters, but the value of their text. This argument is just as valid as it is ingenious, for the main problem of NT textual criticism lies in the fact that little more than their actual existence is known of most of the manuscripts so far identified, and that therefore we constantly have problems with many unknowns to solve. We proceed as if the few manuscripts, which have been fully, or almost fully, studied, contained all the problems in question and all the text-types to be considered, like a child, who, having picked up stones or shells on the shore and brought them home, then seeks to determine from the collected specimens the kinds of stones or shells which can be found on that particular shore. This child might have had the good fortune to collect specimens of all the important kinds of stones or shells to be found on that shore, so that a thorough examination of this shore would merely add few and unimportant new kinds to those already known. It may be that, in NT textual research, we are in a position similar to that of this child. But who knows it with certainty and who can really take it for granted? The naiveté of Westcott and Hort's judgment is not allowed to us, for we cannot ignore the enormous increase of manuscripts (about 900 alone in the last 30 years!) and the results of the investigation of many of them. Westcott and Hort could speak of the "wealth of documentary evidence now accessible," [12] and, in spite of their recognition of the "large amount of present ignorance respecting the contents of cursives," they go on to say, "But enough is already known to enable us to judge with reasonable certainty as to the proportional amount of valuable evidence likely to be buried in the copies as yet uncollated," and further, "Nothing can well be less probable than the discovery of cursive evidence sufficiently important to affect present conclusions in more than a handful of passages, much less to alter present interpretations of the relations between the existing documents." [13] Both statements

[12] p. 14.
[13] All quotations from p. 77.

have been repeatedly shown to be false. The shortness of time does not permit me to expound this point further, and it is indeed unnecessary for me to do so, since this fact is well and widely known.

Westcott and Hort speak here of the cursives, but, in fact, they also mean the other manuscripts. They do not mention expressly the uncials and the lectionaries, because they are confident of their knowledge of the former and they do not regard the latter as very important. Their closing statement makes plain the extent of their error: "it would be an illusion to anticipate important changes of text from any acquisition of new evidence." [14] The discovery of the papyri has been decisive in shifting the time limit of the field of NT research to an earlier date. The same applies to the discovery of new uncials. Westcott and Hort declare about the latter: "Few of this number belong to the first five or six centuries, none being earlier than the age of Constantine." [15] In fact, however, they had had access to only two manuscripts of the fourth century, the Vaticanus and the Sinaiticus, and for the fifth century to only four: viz., the Alexandrinus and the Codex Ephraemi Syri rescriptus, as well as Q (=026) and T (=029), both of which contained fragments from the Gospels of Luke and John.[16] Today, we know three uncial fragments from the third century: 0212 (the famous Diatessaron fragment from Dura/Europos), 0220 (containing verses from Rom. 4 and 5), and 0232 (containing 9 of the 13 verses from the second Epistle of John). We have now 21 uncials from the fourth century, 2 from the fourth/fifth century, 30 from the fifth century[17] and 7 from the fifth/sixth century. That means, instead of six manuscripts from the time prior to the sixth century known to Westcott and Hort, today we know 63. There is, of course, none which surpasses ℵ, A, B, or C; nevertheless, among them we find the two Freer manuscripts, I (=016, with the letters of Paul) and W (=032, with the Gospels), Θ and others. From the sixth century, we know today more than 47 uncials. Westcott and Hort mention 9 and remark: "Some lesser fragments are not reckoned." [18]

[14] p. 285.
[15] p. 10 f.
[16] 029 has increased in the meantime.
[17] Westcott and Hort probably knew still other fragments, besides the 4 abovementioned manuscripts.
[18] p. 75.

Considering now the NT papyri, we note that we have about 50 different manuscripts and fragments dated from the time prior to the sixth century. They must all be added to Westcott and Hort's material and to the above-mentioned figures. The number of papyri dated from the fifth century, which is rather high in the case of the uncials, is relatively low. There are only four: P^{14} (from the fifth century), P^{54}, P^{56} and P^{63} (from the fifth/sixth century). The number of papyri increases as we go back to the fourth and third centuries. We have 14 papyri from the fourth century, or fourth/fifth century (P^{6}, P^{8}, P^{10}, P^{17}, P^{24}, P^{25}, P^{35}, P^{62}, P^{71}, from the fourth century; P^{19}, P^{21}, P^{50}, P^{51}, P^{57}, from the fourth/fifth century). From the third century, or third/fourth century, we have 31 papyri (6 from the third/fourth century: P^{13}, P^{16}, P^{18}, P^{37}, P^{38}, P^{72}; from the third century, 25 papyri: P^{1}, P^{4}, P^{5}, P^{9}, P^{12}, P^{15}, P^{20}, P^{22}, P^{23}, P^{27}, P^{28}, P^{29}, P^{30}, P^{39}, P^{40}, P^{45}, P^{47}, P^{48}, P^{49}, P^{53}, P^{65}, P^{69}, P^{70}, P^{75}, P^{78}). The time limit once seen in Constantine's epoch has thus been pushed backwards. With the last four papyri, P^{32}, P^{46}, P^{64+67} and P^{66}, which date from about A.D. 200, or from early in the third century, we come now into the second century. Besides the fact that the dating, "about A.D. 200," represents a mean value, covering the time immediately after as well as immediately before 200, one must assume that the text of a manuscript which is copied from others represents normally a text which is at least one generation older. P^{77} (second century) and P^{52} (about 125) lead us far back into the second century, thus fulfilling expectations which our predecessors could not even dream of. Certainly, many of the papyri known so far contain only a few verses, but the percentage of the NT text covered by them is astonishingly high. This can easily be shown by the following numbers: 12 papyri, dated from before the fourth century, contain fragments of the Gospel of Matthew, in particular, of its second half[19]; 1 contains about seven chapters of the Gospel of Mark; 4, the Gospel of Luke; 11, the Gospel of John; 8, the Acts of the Apostles; 4, the Epistle to the Romans; 2, the First Epistle to the Corinthians; 1, large portions of the Second Epistle to the Corinthians and of the Epistle to the Galatians, the text of which is almost complete. For each of the Epistles to the Ephesians and to the Philippians, we have 2 papyri; for the Epistle to the Colossians, 1; for

[19] The fourth century (but not the fourth/fifth century) is included here because of the connection with the Vaticanus (cf. the following paragraphs).

the First Epistle to the Thessalonians, 3; for the Second Epistle to the Thessalonians, 1; for Titus, 1; for Hebrews, 4; for James, 2; for the First and Second Epistles of Peter and the First Epistle of John, 1 each; for Jude, 2; for Revelation, 3. None of these papyri dates from later than the fourth century. Only Philemon and the Second and Third Epistles of John do not appear in old papyri and there is not a single papyrus containing the First and Second Epistles to Timothy. When the separate parts of the edition of the "New Testament on Papyri," in preparation at the Institut für neutestamentliche Textforschung in Münster, have been published, the extent of parallel text traditions on papyri will become apparent. It will be seen that sometimes three, or even four papyri, may have the same text. And it is worth noting that among these are the Chester Beatty papyri, P^{45}, P^{46}, P^{47}, containing important portions of the Gospels, of Paul's Epistles and of the book of Revelation, and the Bodmer papyri, P^{66}, P^{75} and P^{72}, containing the Gospel of John twice, the Gospel of Luke once, the First and Second Epistles of Peter, and Jude.

Again, objections could be raised here on the basis of the theory of textual criticism. But we need not mention the fact that the oldest manuscript does not necessarily have the best text. P^{47} is, for example, by far the oldest of the manuscripts containing the full or almost full text of the Apocalypse, but it is certainly not the best. But what was the situation in Westcott and Hort's time and before the discovery of the larger papyri? Indeed, what is still the situation of many a NT scholar today? We need only think of von Soden's edition of the Greek NT and of other text editions and critical essays which followed it. The special importance given in them to the Old Latin and Old Syriac versions can only be explained and justified as an attempt to get over Constantine's time, back to the third and even to the second century. "Cum mihi constet ex consensu veteris syriacae et veteris latinae plerumque lectionem primitivam restitui posse, has versiones constanter allegavi," writes Merk,[20] whom I mention as an illustration of the point of view, held by many others. Considering Merk's statement, we can also understand why so much weight is attributed to the connection of D with the Itala, and to the Syriac versions of Sinai and of Cureton. (I hope that, since I have spent much time and effort in editing further Jülicher's Itala, nobody

[20] In the Praefatio to the last (5th) edition of his NT (1943), cited according to p. 6 of the 9th edition of 1964.

will suspect me of being against the Old Latin and Old Syriac traditions.) It remains valid for both of these traditions, that the documentary evidence available to us does not go back beyond Constantine's time. As far as the Old Latin manuscripts are concerned, we may say that most of them date from an even later period, reaching far into the late Middle Ages. And we should not forget completely that both the Codex Bezae Cantabrigiensis and the Codex Claromontanus are dated from the sixth century. Regarding the Latin and Syriac versions, the same complaint seems to have been made within both traditions. In Hieronymus' letter to Damasus, as in the Vita of Rabbula, we read that the reason for the new translation was the large number of different variant readings in the manuscripts which had been in circulation up to that time. In the case of the Syriac versions, it ought to be noted that, possessing only two manuscripts of the Old Syriac, we are left with an inexact and oversimplified picture and, although the documentary evidence is very much wider in the case of the Vetus Latina, we are here just as much in danger of building upon too narrow a basis. In view of the papyri now at our disposal, which contain large portions of the NT Greek text of the third and even of the second centuries, the Vetus Latina, the Vetus Syra and D have been deprived of their earlier exclusive significance. We do not doubt that the text of these three, where they agree, reflects a very old text, but this is but *one* of a wide number of texts which circulated in different forms in the second and third centuries.

The early papyri illustrate well how the NT Greek text had been circulating in many and divergent forms, proceeding in different directions, at about the same time, in the same ecclesiastical province. In my opinion, an entirely new phase began in NT textual criticism when this began to be recognized. This new phase can be seen as beginning in the thirties, when the Chester Beatty papyri had become known and were being discussed. Or, to put it more cautiously, scholars should then have begun to be more aware of the change which these papyri had introduced in the field of textual criticism. One of the important results of this change has been, for instance, that Westcott-Hort's so-called "Western non-interpolations" have been, so to speak, stripped of their original nimbus and that, although interesting, they are no longer regarded, or should no longer be regarded, as authoritative.

Let me proceed by repeating what I have often, since the publication of the Bodmer papyri, maintained among my colleagues, in particular, in connection with the work on a new edition of the NT. P^{66} confirmed the observations already made in connection with the Chester Beatty papyri. With P^{75} new ground has been opened to us. Earlier, we all shared the opinion, in agreement with our professors and in accord with NT scholarship, before and since Wescott and Hort, that, in various places, during the fourth century, recensions of the NT text had been made, from which the main text-types then developed. That seemed plausible, since, in the Constantine era, with its numerous church buildings, there had been a great demand for biblical manuscripts. A large number of manuscripts, especially those kept in the great churches of the episcopal sees, had been destroyed during the persecutions, probably a rather high percentage. Now that the church had ceased to be illegal or, if you wish, half-legal, it could not only obtain, or arrange for the production of, the needed manuscripts, but also could seek to enforce a definite form of text. A Scriptorium, which was charged with the production of copies of a manuscript, selecting a particular manuscript for this purpose, propagated thereby this particular manuscript. This may have been the case of the Scriptorium at Caesarea, which Constantine had entrusted with the production of fifty manuscripts. But, at the beginning of the fourth century, the number of Scriptoria existing for the purpose of producing copies of Christian documents could not have been very high. Nothing was more natural, then, than that the bishop of an ecclesiastical province, and/or the theologians who advised him on such matters, should have taken this opportunity for ordering the production of a new text free from old corruptions. So we thought, and, in this sense, we spoke of recensions and text-types, and if this was not enough, we referred to pre-Caesarean and other text-types, to mixed texts, and so on.

I, too, have spoken of mixed texts, in connection with the form of the NT text in the second and third centuries, but I have always done so with a guilty conscience. For, according to the rules of linguistic philology, it is impossible to speak of mixed texts before recensions have been made (they only can follow them), whereas, the NT manuscripts of the second and third centuries which have a "mixed text" clearly existed before recensions were made. But, up to now, no better or more accurate term has been found, which would more adequately describe the situation of the text in the second and third centuries. "Text in flux," and "unfixed text," or similar terms, do not hit the mark either. In any case, P75 shows such a close affinity with the Codex Vaticanus that the supposition of a recension of the text at Alexandria, in the fourth century, can no longer be held. It is not possible to continue with the idea that at that time, a meeting of philologically trained theologians, or the reverse, took place, in order to produce a new text. This can be assumed with a reasonably high degree of certainty: they did not create a new text-form out of the existing manuscripts, taking recourse to philology. What they apparently did was to take those manuscripts which they regarded as reliable—for Luke and John a manuscript such as P75—and to correct text errors and corruptions or what they thought to be such. That is, they carried out a revision of the texts of the selected manuscripts. At least the Egyptian text appears to have originated from a local text. Or, rather it seems that from the existing local texts one was selected, revised, and, through the production of copies of the revised manuscript, enforced as the dominating text in this particular ecclesiastical province. If this was so in Egypt, which had in Alexandria a recognized center of philological science, why should it have been different elsewhere? The text thus favored and put into circulation did not, of course, immediately become the dominating text, if in fact it ever did. For other manuscripts, which did not disappear or were not destroyed during the Diocletian persecutions, still continued to be used and copied. In certain areas, for example, in the occidental districts governed by Constantius Chlorus, the persecution caused relatively few losses and the old text forms could therefore continue to circulate practically without restriction (bilinguals!).

Of course, one can speak of an Egyptian or an Alexandrian text-form, as well as of an Antiochian or Byzantine text-form, however you may name them. These are, it seems to me, the only text-types which may be regarded as certain, and that only since the fourth century. Everything else is extremely doubtful. It is impossible to fit the papyri, from the time prior to the fourth century, into these two text-types, to say nothing of trying to fit them into other types, as frequently happens. The simple fact that all these papyri, with their various distinctive characteristics, did exist side by side, in the same ecclesiastical province, that is, in Egypt, where they were found, is the best argument against the existence of any text-types, including the Alexandrian and the Antiochian. We still live in the world of Westcott and Hort with our conception of different recensions and text-types, although this conception has lost its *raison d'être,* or, it needs at least to be newly and convincingly demonstrated. For, the increase of the documentary evidence and the entirely new areas of research which were opened to us on the discovery of the papyri, mean the end of Westcott and Hort's conception. We can no longer take their conception as valid, as long as its *raison d'être,* even under the new conditions, has not been proved. And it certainly cannot be proved by opening new agencies of the old Firm, as von Soden did with his Jerusalem text or as was done with the claim for a Caesarean text-type—anyhow a remarkable proposal. A gulf of several centuries separates the manuscripts belonging to this so-called Caesarean text, from the time when it is supposed to have originated. And, although it seems likely that Caesarea (with Origen, Pamphilus, and Eusebius) became the center of a particular text-type, it would be a help if this text-type could be fully traced in Eusebius, or, if a plausible explanation could be offered for the remarkable fact that, very often, opposing readings of a particular text can be found in Origen. The assertion that Origen cites from memory, and therefore inexactly, is not convincing. Different readings of any one text, cited in his writings, are not likely to have been due to a weak memory, for they do not all originate from his Caesarean days, when he was older, but also from Alexandria, when he was much younger.

NT textual research has no doubt achieved wonderful results in the last one hundred years, for example, in the identification of groups of manuscripts and in determining the relationships of different texts. But I am afraid that this happened more or less accidentally, in that those aspects upon which the light of the scholar's lamp falls are objects of the most careful and painstaking study, whereas others are neglected or ignored, simply because they lie outside the lighted area. The last attempt made towards a comprehensive examination of the whole material, questions and problems, which are the object of NT textual research, was made by Hermann von Soden, fifty years ago, and it failed. It failed because it was carried out with inadequate means and because he wanted too much too quickly. I do not need to comment upon these inadequate resources and means; enough has been said in the scholarly discussions of von Soden's edition of the Greek NT (cf., for example, the dispute between Lietzmann and von Soden). It should be noted, however, that the inaccuracy and unreliability of his information is understandable, in many cases, if you consider the rather precarious conditions prevailing at that time. When a large number of assistants has to be entrusted with the collation of manuscripts, the quality of work will naturally vary from individual to individual. Furthermore, the unfavorable conditions in many libraries have a negative influence upon their efficiency. Think, for instance, of the monastery libraries on the Athos. The collation of a particular manuscript by one assistant, without another collation of the same manuscript with which to check it, is not always without error, regardless of how good that assistant may be. As a result of the development of techniques, we find ourselves today in a much more favorable position. We need no longer travel to the places where the manuscripts are kept; the manuscripts come to us in the form of microfilms, provided, of course, that men can be found who are capable of photographing them, including those manuscripts which are kept in libraries to which access is difficult. In the five years of its existence the Institut für neutestamentliche Textforschung in Münster, has not only discovered several hundreds of manuscripts, and thereby increased our difficulties, but also has made our task easier by bringing together complete microfilms or photos of over 3,500 manuscripts, most of which we photographed ourselves. We now have in Münster, photocopies or microfilms of

71 papyri,
208 uncials,
1,910 cursives and
1,320 lectionaries.

Of course, we also have to cope with many deficiencies and problems in our work. In some cases, it is very difficult, if not impossible, to obtain photos or film of a manuscript. Fortunately, we have sufficient data about all old manuscripts, with exception of one papyrus and 14 uncials, most of which have been lost or destroyed. However, the Institut für neutestamentliche Textforschung will proceed with its work, endeavoring to obtain photographs of existing manuscripts and to rediscover lost ones. In 1965, we hope to get at least 500 manuscripts on microfilm. These will probably come in approximately equal parts, not only from libraries situated in remote places, not easily accessible and away from civilization, but also from a library in one of the great centers of Western culture, from which it is extremely difficult to get films of manuscripts.

I would like to think that the aim of 4,000 NT manuscripts, which we have set ourselves, will soon be achieved. After that, our collection will perhaps increase slowly, but it *will* increase, and I hope for the assistance of scholars from all parts of the world. For as soon as we can open a collection of manuscripts in microfilm which is as complete as possible, the situation in NT textual research will be entirely different, since we will have at hand a mass of documentary evidence which we never had before. It will be possible to collate manuscripts at leisure and to check these collations. It will be possible to examine, side by side, all manuscripts belonging to a particular group. The different families of manuscripts will meet, so to speak, at the same table, and the family members will talk to each other, making it possible for an attentive and careful observer to reach certain conclusions concerning their relationships.

But, what about that frighteningly large number of manuscripts, to which I referred at the beginning? 5,000 is an appalling number. 4,000 is almost as large; and even in the case of the 3,500 which we already have on microfilm, the hope of ever bringing our immense task to an end almost deserts us. We all know that most of these manuscripts belong to the Byzantine text-type, but, it has been shown over and over again that among the pebbles precious stones often lie hidden, the value of which we can compare with that of our great uncials. Only after we have got to know all the existing evidence, can we feel fairly confident that the conclusions we now are able to reach in NT textual research, are not going to be greatly modified by any sudden discovery of new manuscripts. It is urgently necessary that collations of all existing manuscripts be made, before an edition of the Greek NT is published, which may justly claim to have universal validity. Unless this is done, the textual evidence supplied in our editions of the Greek NT will continue to be unreliable. What are we going to do about this situation? We cannot allow ourselves to regard the still-known manuscripts with the same naiveté and self-confidence that characterized the Westcott and Hort approach. He who is not yet convinced of this would do well to consider the fate of the editions of von Soden and Legg.

In the situation in which we find ourselves today, it is not surprising that the voice of the eclectics carries greater weight and appears to be more attractive. Their argument is both right and ingenious, as were the two with which we dealt at the beginning. According to them, any manuscript can hold the correct variant reading. Who questions that? It is quite right, theoretically here we find ourselves, once more, concerned with the *theory* of textual criticism. Theoretically, the original reading can lie hidden in a single manuscript, thus standing alone against the rest of tradition. To this we must add that we are bound to be eclectic, because the guiding light of the Neutral text, which Westcott and Hort confidently followed, no longer shines, and also because we have no possibility of working out a genealogy of manuscripts which might throw some light on the history and tradition of the text.

Every decision concerning the text has to be taken on its own. With regard to every group of variant readings, we are compelled to reexamine the whole internal and external evidence. If, then, we cannot avoid eclecticism, why do we not make it a principle? Of course, we could do that, but it will depend on what we understand by eclecticism. Seeing those eclectics at work who seem to regard the language of the NT writings as fixed and who merely seek in the tradition of the text the group of manuscripts, or the particular manuscript, or the version, which they need for their text, I must doubt, not only the scientific value of their method, but also the principle upon which that method is based. It is a well-known fact that, in our age, scholars have devoted themselves to studying the use of language in the NT as never before. But, if our text is to be corrected on the basis of their findings, it would mean that we would be regarding as conclusive results which must still be proved. As yet, we do not have the tools necessary for investigating the use of language in the NT. Both of the great Greek concordances, upon which word statistics rely, are based on editions which are about one hundred years old and which do not, therefore, take into account either the manuscripts found in this century, or the research of many scholars since Westcott and Hort. When the complete concordance to the Greek NT, on which we are working at the Institut für neutestamentliche Textforschung is ready, which I hope will be in 1966, word statistics will be given a new basis, more in accordance with our knowledge and requirements. But, although our knowledge of word-usage in the NT will be greatly increased by a concordance such as this, it will be important to remember that the language and the style of the NT writers cannot be made to fit in with the theories worked out in the scholar's study. Just the reverse: these must be related to, and made to fit in with the former.

It is true and generally known, that the principles of stemmatology (*rezensierende Philologie*) cannot be applied to the NT. At least, the scholars who have attempted to do so have been unable to state their case convincingly. But, if the establishment of genealogies of NT manuscripts does not seem possible, there is no reason why we should ignore the method used, and the conclusions reached, by stemmatology in the classification of other manuscripts, and thus, so to speak, throw away the basin with the water. Rather, we believe, that stemmatology can render us an important service, provided that its limitations are well defined beforehand. Von Soden wanted too much too quickly and, for that reason, could not achieve his aim. He wanted to throw light upon the whole history of the text, even upon each ramification of the Koine-Text. Apart from the fact that his starting-basis did *not* prove to be right —the recensions J, H, K, and the assumption that their agreement is a guarantee for the original text—the collations of manuscripts made under his supervision were neither comprehensive nor accurate enough, so that he could conclude from these collations which manuscript belonged to a particular group or groups. Yet, that is what he actually did. No one doubts, however, that on certain points he was able to make important contributions, doing the work of a pioneer. Many essays on NT textual criticism of today are based on von Soden's work and very often they constitute no more than a development of it. If we wish to avoid the danger which caused von Soden's failure, we must observe two things: we must have a single aim in view, and not several at a time, and we must make sure that our work has a solid basis.

Let us consider for a moment the aim which we want to achieve. This can be so defined: to establish the original text of the NT, that is, the text-form in which the NT writings were officially put into circulation. Already Westcott and Hort have striven to reach this goal. They rejected the text of the fourth century as insufficient: "It is no longer possible to speak of the text of the fourth century."[21] They claimed "to present exactly the original words of the NT, so far as they can now be determined from surviving documents"[22] . . . "the closest possible approximation to the apostolic text itself."[23] Their aim was to determine "the original words of the Apostles and writers of the NT."[24] We would not define ours in such terms. For, by means of textual criticism we can only get back as far as an early redactional stage, if so far. In the case of the Gospel of John, for example, we can only determine the form in which it had been circulating after a redactor, or however you may choose to call him, had added chapter 21, i.e. the form preserved in the copies of the redactor's exemplar and in subsequent copies of these. Similarly, in the case of Paul's letters, we can only get back to the time when a collection of these letters was made by some unknown person in the first century, after the death of the Apostle. The text-form of the collector's original exemplar, which was then propagated and gained universal acceptance, sets the limit beyond which we cannot penetrate, by using the method of textual criticism. But we aim to reach this limit. In comparison with this aim, other questions and problems of NT textual criticism are secondary, including the special problems of the later tradition of the text. So much for the first aspect of our task.

The second aspect is connected with the first one. Although our whole heritage concerning the tradition of the text has become questionable, or needs at least to be proved anew, no one doubts the existence of a Koine text, or of the Byzantine text, whichever name you give to it. This Koine text, which, by way of precaution, we call the Majority-text (siglum: M), is by no means monolithic, but went through different stages of development and was influenced by various factors. But it constitutes a closed and distinct unit, sufficiently differentiated from the manuscripts which do not contain it, even where, as often happens, its evidence disagrees or is divided into two opposite branches of tradition. It can therefore be said to have a tradition of its own.

With a view to reducing the large number of uncollated cursives, the Institut für neutestamentliche Textforschung in Münster is trying, by

[21] p. 288.
[22] p. 1.
[23] p. 288.
[24] p. 16.

means of test-collations, to prove which of these cursives actually belong to the Koine-Text. For a manuscript which has been found to have this Majority-text need not, according to the principles of stemmatology, be considered further. I have decided to lay down a net of passages from NT writings as a basis for our investigation. The Apocalypse will not be taken into account for two reasons: first, because of the particular character of the history of its text in the Greek-speaking church. (Only later, in A.D. 367, when Athanasius first included it in his canon, did it begin to gain official acceptance, although it still continued to meet with strong opposition.) Second, because a complete examination of the manuscripts containing it has already been made by Hoskier and, recently, by Josef Schmid.

1,000 passages have been selected from the Gospel of Mark, the Gospel of John, the Acts of the Apostles, the Catholic Epistles, and the Epistles of Paul, as follows:

Gospel of Mark	199
Gospel of John	338
Acts of the Apostles	105
Catholic Epistles	103
Epistles of Paul	255
	1,000

The chosen passages are widely scattered throughout each of these writings, except those in the Gospel of John, which have been selected only from chapters 1-10 (without the pericope of the adulteress). 1,000 passages will therefore be collated in a manuscript containing the four Gospels, the Acts of the Apostles, the Catholic Epistles, and the Pauline Epistles (e, a, p); 537 in a manuscript containing only the four Gospels; 208 in a manuscript containing the Acts of the Apostles and the Catholic Epistles; and 255 in a manuscript containing the Pauline Epistles. Such variant readings have been selected, in which the two previously mentioned text-types clearly disagree, as well as variant readings, apparently not originating independently or under the influence of a parallel-passage, which suggest a relationship of the manuscripts containing them. If a manuscript has the Majority-text in all passages as indicated above, or if the number and the character of the variant readings in which it disagrees with the Majority-text is relatively insignificant, it may be henceforth neglected. Only the manuscripts which disagree with the Majority-text on a larger number of more important variant readings, will be examined further. Often the selected manuscripts have more than one text-group, and, accordingly, the figures relating to different text-groups have to be added together. Hence, a manuscript containing all text-groups may have the Majority-text up to 1,000 times, i.e., as many times as the number of passages selected for our purpose.

1,000 cursives have already been collated in this way at the Institut für neutestamentliche Textforschung. The results of these test collations, the number of which far surpasses the number normally made by classical philologians, are now being prepared for publication. They will again be examined and checked in various ways, but we hope that they will be ready for print in 1965. If so, the second series of collations will soon be started in the Institut. It is our purpose to collate all cursives of which we can obtain microfilms. Of course, the collation of *one* manuscript in the way described above, costs very much time and effort, but this is only a *small* fraction of the time and effort required for a complete collation of this manuscript. However, with the publication of the work I have just described, "1,000 cursives examined in 1,000 passages with a view to evaluating their text," I hope some valuable information which may serve as a starting-point for further investigation will be put at the disposal of scholars. I, myself, will probably be content, at first, with the elimination of the representatives of the Majority-text. These make up about 90 per cent of known cursives. Think of what that means, in relation to the large number of existing manuscripts; from 2,700 cursives, 2,400 can henceforth perhaps be practically disregarded, to wait for someone with the required capacity, energy, and time to study the history of their text and their relationships. We can, then, concentrate our efforts upon the remaining 300. Among these, we may expect to find representatives of all forms of the "mixed-text," showing the more or less far-reaching influence of the Majority-text.

The history of the Majority-text may also be studied in the numerous representatives of this text among the 224 uncials and the 78 papyri. Thus, not only the Majority-text, but each Greek manuscript relevant to the early tradition of the text, will be fully and carefully examined, and the conclusions will not be based just on theory or hypothesis, but on the complete collation of manuscripts. The material is still large enough: about 300 cursives, 224 uncials, and 78 papyri. To these must be added the old versions, the quotations of NT passages made by the Fathers, and a number of lectionaries which must still be assessed by experts. Regarding the lectionaries, we must choose those which, as in the case of the cursives, will not only show the movement within one and the same text-group, which is irrelevant to the problem of the original text of the NT writings, but also throw light upon the later stages of the tradition of the text. I need not say anything in reference to the old versions of the NT. Bruce Metzger deals with this subject in his paper. I only wish to point out the increasing significance of the Coptic texts, which the Institut für neutestamentliche Textforschung has also been collecting for some time. A theme in itself would be the deplorable neglect generally occurring in NT textual research of patristic quotations, and the use of outdated editions of the Fathers (following Tischendorf's and others' citations). But I hope that this field of research will soon be better provided for, with the help of experts in patristics. A large quantity of new material has, incidentally, been collected by the Institut für neutestamentliche Textforschung and made available for the work about which I have spoken. This is no doubt a great task, not only concerning the aim to be achieved, but also regarding the work itself. We should not allow ourselves to be frightened by the numbers mentioned. Many of the 300 cursives do not contain the whole NT; 4/5 of the uncials and a still higher percentage of papyri are only fragments. Leaving out the old versions and patristic quotations, between 150 and 175 complete collations of the whole NT will have to be made. That is a rough estimate of the work to be done.

This task will not be completed from one day to the next, but, with hard work and concentration of effort, it may be completed in the foreseeable future, since the new edition will consist of a number of volumes, to be prepared separately. The critical apparatus, if we follow the proposed method, will be kept within limits, and at the same time, be so comprehensive as to include all the material relevant to the original text of the NT, to the tradition of the text up to about the fifth century, and, to a lesser degree, to the later tradition of the text. The material in the critical apparatus could not, then, be suspected of being based on theory, but on reliable and complete collations of documentary evidence. Both the text and the critical apparatus can only be prepared with the cooperative effort of all experts in the field of NT textual criticism who are willing to take part in this work. Even the Institut für neutestamentliche Textforschung would not be able alone to cope with the immense amount of work involved. That such cooperative effort can be valuable and successful will be apparent to all, when the edition of the Greek NT, begun on the initiative of the American Bible Society and prepared under the patronage and supervision of the International Bible Societies, by Matthew Black (St. Andrews), Bruce Metzger (Princeton), Allen Wikgren (Chicago), and myself, is published. It is, of course, obvious that this edition, with its very short critical apparatus, provides us only with a pattern for the larger edition, to which I have referred, but it *does* provide us with a pattern. And I would not have the courage to stand here and speak to you of the great task I have in mind or, let me say, I am dreaming of, if enough preparatory work had not already been done and sufficient material were not in our hands, to make the achievement of our aim seem possible in the foreseeable future. Of the urgency of the task, I need say nothing.

Let me finish with an illustration of our present position in NT textual research. In 1881, when Westcott and Hort published their edition of the Greek NT in a final form, after it had appeared in separate volumes during the years from 1871-1876, people still crossed the Atlantic in wooden sailing-ships. In 1875—if my nautical knowledge is sufficient—the first full-rigged ship with four masts and iron hulk was built. With time sailing-ships began to give way to steamers, but a voyage across the Atlantic still took several weeks. *Today* a person can cross the Atlantic in a very short time, either by liner or by jet. *None* of us would entrust himself to a ship of the year 1881 in order to cross the Atlantic, even if the ship were renovated or he were promised danger money. Why then do we still do so in NT textual criticism?

BRUCE M. METZGER

Recent Contributions to the Study of the Ancient Versions of the New Testament

A comparison between what was known concerning the ancient versions of the NT almost a century ago, when Tischendorf's eighth edition (1869-72) and Westcott and Hort's critical text (1881) were in the making, and what is known today is both encouraging and embarrassing. It is, on the one hand, encouraging because progress has been made in the acquisition of further information concerning several of the versions (such as the Syriac, the Coptic, and the Georgian) as well as because of the discovery of manuscript remains of certain hitherto unknown versions (such as the Nubian and the Sogdian versions). But it is also, on the other hand, embarrassing because in several cases very little attention has been given to what has been available to scholars for a long time (such as the materials for the Armenian, Ethiopic, and Arabic versions).

In what follows an attempt will be made to describe and assess the significance of contributions to the study of the ancient versions of the NT which were published during the past ten years (1955-64).[1]

[1] For a comprehensive general treatment of the subject, see Arthur Vööbus, *Early Versions of the New Testament, Manuscript Studies* (=*Papers of the Estonian Theological Society in Exile,* no. 6; Stockholm, 1954). For a bibliographical survey of the chief literature published during the first half of the twentieth century, reference may be made to the present writer's contribution to a symposium held at the University of Chicago in honor of E. J. Goodspeed, and published in *New Testament Manuscript Studies,* ed. M. M. Parvis and A. P. Wikgren (Chicago, 1950), pp. 25-68 and 177-208; this was subsequently supplemented by an article surveying the research of the next five years (1950-54), entitled "A Survey of Recent Research on the Ancient Versions of the New Testament," published in *NTS,* II (1955), 1-16.

The ancient versions of the Bible have been treated in a number of dictionaries published during 1955-64; e.g. *RGG,* 3te Aufl., vol. 1 (1957), cols. 1193-1224; *Lexikon für Theologie und Kirche,* 2te Aufl., II (1958), 375-411; *IDB,* IV (1962), 749-60; and *Dictionnaire de la Bible, Supplément,* vol. 6, fasc. 33 (1962), cols. 807-881. The last mentioned article, "Orientales de la Bible (Versions)" is of permanent significance and the several contributions on individual versions are mentioned at appropriate places below.

I
The Latin Versions

During the past decade a considerable number of publications have appeared which deal with the Old Latin and Vulgate versions of the NT. Those which pertain chiefly to aspects of textual criticism include:

(a) *The Old Latin*

In 1963, vol. 4 of Adolf Jülicher's *Itala* was finally published, after many delays arising from circumstances beyond the control of the continuing editor, Kurt Aland.[2] It contains the evidence of eighteen Old Latin manuscripts of the Gospel of John, along with Wordsworth and White's text of the Vulgate.

Much more extensive is the Vetus Latina project sponsored by the Monastery of Beuron in Hohenzollern. Begun in 1908 when Pfarrer Josef Denk outlined plans for a new Sabatier, *Bibliorum Sacrorum Latinae Versiones Antiquae,* the project has been carried on by many dedicated workers who have produced and filed in scriptural sequence more than one million slips containing patristic citations of Old Latin Bible texts.[3] Under the capable guidance of Bonifatius Fischer, the present director of the Vetus Latina project, the information is being digested and edited, and transferred to the printed page. Thus far fascicles have appeared containing Genesis, the Petrine Epistles, and portions of Ephesians and Revelation. The layout of the large page (9 x 12 inches) supplies several lines of Latin text, with the Greek Vorlage, at the top of the page. Underneath is a section devoted chiefly to orthographic variant readings. The rest of the page contains extensive quotations from patristic authors.

A companion volume, which serves as an index to the Latin authors whose works are cited in the edition, has now appeared in a second edition.[4] Likewise, several monographs have been published as subsidiary studies by scholars who have utilized the materials at Beuron. These include an analysis of the vocabulary of the Latin text of the Johannine

[2] *Itala. Das Neue Testament in altlateinischer Überlieferung. IV, Johannes-Evangelium* . . . ed. Ad. Jülicher . . . Walter Matzkow und Kurt Aland (Berlin, 1963).

[3] *Vetus Latina, Die Reste der altlateinischen Bibel,* nach Petrus Sabatier neu gesammelt und herausgegeben von der Erzabtei Beuron.

[4] Bonifatius Fischer, *Verzeichnis der Sigel für Kirchenschriftsteller,* 2te Aufl. (Freiburg, 1963).

Epistles,[5] a study of the Latin text of Paul used in Ireland,[6] and an investigation of the origin and subsequent text-critical history of the extant Old Latin manuscripts of Paul.[7]

One of the treasures in the Spanish Cathedral of León is a palimpsest manuscript that contains in a tenth-century Visigothic minuscule hand Rufinus's translation of Eusebius's church history. The underwriting is a seventh-century uncial text of portions of the Scriptures, mostly in Jerome's Vulgate but with an Old Latin text of the books of the Maccabees, the Catholic Epistles, and the book of Acts. Only two folios of the last have been preserved, containing the text of Acts 8:27—11:13 and 14:21—17:25. Bonafatius Fischer provides a transcript of this material as well as an analysis of its textual relationship, which is closest to the Spanish Liber Comicus.[8]

Several monographs have appeared during the past decade devoted to the isolation and analysis of the NT text used by various Latin church fathers. That veteran textual critic, Heinrich Josef Vogels, whose researches over the years have included many investigations of Old Latin texts of the NT, has edited the Corpus Paulinum of Ambrosiaster, based on the collation of thirty manuscripts.[9]

Following the methodology of his teacher, Karl Th. Schäfer, Heinrich Zimmermann has published an extensive investigation of the history of the Old Latin versions of II Corinthians.[10] He finds two main types of text, (1) that preserved in the Latin version of the bilingual manuscripts D E F G, along with the commentaries of Ambrosiaster and Pelagius as well as the citations of many Latin Fathers, and (2) that of the Freisinger Fragments and the text of St. Augustine.

Another study, likewise begun under Schäfer, is confined to a similar

[5] Walter Thiele, *Wortschatzuntersuchungen zu den lateinischen Texten der Johannesbriefe* (Freiburg, 1958).

[6] H. J. Frede, *Pelagius, der irische Paulustext, Sedulius Scottus* (Freiburg, 1961).

[7] H. J. Frede, *Altlateinische Paulus-Handschriften* (Freiburg, 1964).

[8] "Ein neuer Zeuge zum westlichen Text der Apostelgeschichte," *Biblical and Patristic Studies in Memory of Robert Pierce Casey,* ed. J. Neville Birdsall and Robert W. Thomson (Freiburg, 1963), pp. 33-63.

[9] *Das Corpus Paulinum des Ambrosiaster* (=*Bonner biblische Beiträge,* 13; Bonn, 1957). A preliminary study of several of the manuscripts was published earlier under the title, *Untersuchungen zum Text paulinischer Briefe bei Rufin und Ambrosiaster* (=*Bonner biblische Beiträge,* 9; Bonn, 1955).

[10] Heinrich Zimmermann, *Untersuchungen zur Geschichte der altlateinischen Überlieferung des zweiten Korintherbriefs* (=*Bonner biblische Beiträge,* 16; Bonn, 1960).

investigation of the text of I Timothy in the bilingual manuscripts D E F G and in the commentaries of Ambrosiaster and Pelagius.[11]

Unlike the previously mentioned monographs the work of Muncey on the NT text of St. Ambrose must be used with great caution. Handsomely printed by the Cambridge University Press in the second series of *Texts and Studies,* under the general editorship of C. H. Dodd, the volume embodies the results of what were undoubtedly long years of devoted research.[12] It is to be regretted, however, that the author displays a shocking laxity of accuracy of detail in his citations of quotations from the works of Ambrose; he also gives only the most meager attention to the previously published investigations of Rolando and Caraglione on the text of Ambrose (published in *Biblica* in 1945 and 1946).

One of Augustine's exegetical works was an *Expositio epistulae Iacobi.* Though it is no longer extant, from a variety of quotations from Augustine's other treatises Walter Thiele seeks to ascertain how far Augustine was a reviser of the current Latin text (s) of this epistle.[13]

In the course of preparing a critical edition of *The Turin Fragments of Tyconius' Commentary on Revelation,*[14] the late Francesco Lo Bue, a young Waldensian scholar of great promise, published a brief study on "Old Latin Readings of the Apocalypse in the 'Wordsworth-White' Edition of the Vulgate." [15] Among other things Lo Bue points out that a few quotations from the Apocalypse, which are embedded in Tyconius' exposition preserved in several Turin fragments, have been apparently neglected both by Vogels and by the Editor of the Oxford Vulgate.

(b) *The Latin Vulgate*

Taking the publication of the final fascicle of the Wordsworth-White *editio maior* of the Latin Vulgate as his starting point, Fischer makes a

[11] Franz Hermann Tinnefeld, *Untersuchungen zur altlateinischen Überlieferung des I. Timotheusbriefes. Der lateinische Paulustext in der Handschriften D E F G und in der Kommentaren des Ambrosiaster und des Pelagius* (=*Klassisch-philologische Studien,* 26; Wiesbaden, 1963.

[12] R. W. Muncey, *The New Testament Text of St. Ambrose* (=*Texts and Studies,* Second Series, vol. 4; Cambridge, 1959). For devastating critiques of the book, see Jean Duplacy, "Citations patristiques et critique textuelle du Nouveau Testament," *Recherches de science religieuse,* XLVII (1959), 391-400; S. Lundström in *Gnomon,* XXXII (1960), 640 ff.; and P. G. van der Nat in *VigChr,* XVI (1962), 55-56.

[13] "Augustinus zum lateinischen Text das Jakobusbriefes," *ZNW,* XLVI (1955), 255-58.

[14] *Texts and Studies.* Second Series (Cambridge, 1963).

[15] *VigChr,* IX (1955), 21-24.

broad survey of the critical method and selection of witnesses used in that edition.[16] The first volume, which contains the Gospels, suffered particularly from the editors' inexperience.

In a study devoted to Codex Amiatinus and to Cassiodorus, Fischer points out the diverse types of text which underlie the several parts of that famous codex: for the Psalms, a poor Irish text; for the Gospels, a good Neopolitan lectionary; for the Catholic Epistles, a local British text; and for most of the biblical books, good Italian manuscripts.[17]

Several years of painstaking research have gone into the making of a detailed descriptive catalogue of 138 early Latin Gospel Books; the compiler sets forth information concerning the order of the prefatory and Gospel texts, the layout of these texts on the page and their distribution in quires, as well as the way in which they are introduced by pictures, initials, and varying scripts.[18]

Éduard Massaux has edited two fragments of a sixth- or seventh-century manuscript containing the Vulgate text of Luke 6:48—7:5, 11-13 and John 12:39-49, 13:6-15.[19]

Among the medieval Castilian translations of the Latin Vulgate is a thirteenth-century manuscript in the Escorial Library.[20] What makes it noteworthy for the textual critic is the presence in it of unusual readings which doubtless go back to Old Latin texts. Thus, in the Lord's Prayer (Matt. 6:11) the fourth petition "Nuestro pan cotidiano nos da oy" follows the Old Latin *cotidianum* rather than Jerome's *supersubstantialem*.[21] It also contains a number of readings which are unique in Latin manuscripts, a few of which agree with Old Syriac witnesses.

[16] Bonifatius Fischer, "Der Vulgata-Text des Neuen Testamentes," *ZNW*, XLVI (1955), 178-96.

[17] Bonifatius Fischer, "Codex Amiatinus und Cassiodor," *Biblische Zeitschrift*, N.F., VI (1962), 57-79.

[18] Patrick McGurk, *Latin Gospel Books from* A.D. *400 to* A.D. *800* (Paris, Brussels, Amiens, and Amsterdam, 1961). Cf. Ludwig Bieler, "The New Testament in the Celtic Church," *Studia Evangelica*, III, ed. F. L. Cross (=*Texte und Untersuchungen*, 88; Berlin, 1964), pp. 318-30.

[19] "Deux Fragments d'un manuscrit oncial de la Vulgate," *Ephemerides Theologicae Lovanienses*, XXXVII (1961), 112-17 (with two plates).

[20] Thomas Montgomery, *El Evangelio de San Mateo, según el manuscrito escurialense I.I.6. Texto, gramática, vocabulario* (=*Anejos del Boletín de la Real Academia Española*, VII; Madrid, 1962). The present writer draws attention to several of the more noteworthy readings in his review of the volume in *Erasmus*, vol. 16 (1964), cols. 334 ff.

[21] According to a study of "The Lord's Prayer in Irish Gospel Manuscripts" by

II
The Syriac Versions

(a) *The Diatessaron*

In September, 1957 the information was made public that A. Chester Beatty had acquired a Syriac manuscript which contains about three-fifths of Ephraem's Commentary on the Diatessaron;[22] since the commentary had hitherto been known only through an Armenian translation of Ephraem and in brief quotations preserved in other Eastern Fathers, the new acquisition aroused much interest. The Syriac text has now been published by Dom Louis Leloir in a handsome edition with a Latin translation.[23] The editor dates the manuscript in the late fifth or early sixth century. A comparison of the Syriac and Armenian texts discloses that the latter is, on the whole, a reliable rendering of the original. It apparently was not made from a form of text identical with that preserved in the Beatty manuscript, for occasionally the latter presents supplementary paragraphs, involving both lemmata and commentary, and occasionally it lacks material that is present in the Armenian translation. In view of the large lacunae in the Syriac manuscript, the Armenian version as well as patristic quotations are still indispensable for our knowledge of those portions lacking in the Beatty manuscript.[24]

G. G. Willis, about one-third of the Irish Latin texts read *cotidianum* in the Matthean form of the Lord's Prayer (*Studia Evangelica,* III, ed. F. L. Cross [=*Texte und Untersuchungen,* 88; Berlin, 1964], pp. 282-88).

[22] See L. Leloir, "L'original syriaque du Commentaire de S. Éphrem sur le Diatessaron," *Analecta Biblica,* XI (=*Studia Biblica et Orientalia,* vol. II; Rome, 1959), 391-402 (=*Biblica,* 40 [1959], 959-70).

[23] *Saint Éphrem, Commentaire de l'Évangile concordant, text syriaque (manuscrit Chester Beatty 709)*, édité et traduit par Dom Louis Leloir (=*Chester Beatty Monographs,* No. 8; Dublin, 1963).

[24] See *Saint Éphrem, Commentaire de l'évangile concordant, version arménienne* (=*Corpus Scriptorum Christianorum Orientalium,* vol. 145; Louvain, 1954); *idem, L'Évangile d'Éphrem d'après les oeuvres éditées. Recueil des textes* (=*CSCO,* vol. 180, *Subsidia,* 12; Louvain, 1958); and *idem, Le Témoignage d'Éphrem sur le Diatessaron* (=*CSCO,* vol. 227, *Subsidia,* 19; Louvain, 1962).

The article by Louis Mariès, "Pour l'étude du Diatessaron," *Recherches de science religieuse,* XLIV (1956), 228-33, describes Leloir's edition of the Armenian text of Ephraem's commentary on the Diatessaron.

One of the tertiary witnesses to Tatianic readings is the Medieval Persian Harmony of the Gospels, edited by G. Messina (Rome, 1951); for discussions of its character and significance, see A. J. B. Higgins, "The Persian and Arabic Harmonies," *Studia Evangelica,* ed. K. Aland *et al.* (=*Texte und Untersuchungen,* vol. 73; Berlin, 1959), pp. 793-810, and B. M. Metzger, "Tatian's Diatessaron and a Persian Harmony of the

The question why Bp. Victor of Capua referred to Tatian's Diatessaron as *diapente* has puzzled many scholars. Some have thought that the expression was chosen in order to indicate obliquely that, in addition to the canonical gospels, Tatian utilized a fifth source. Frequently this fifth source has been supposed to have been the Gospel according to the Hebrews (so, e.g., Grotius, Mill, and, more recently, Baumstark, Peters, and Quispel); occasionally it has been identified with the Protevangelium of James (e.g. Messina, in part). Others have suggested that *diapente* is nothing more than a *lapsus calami* and therefore not to be taken seriously (so, e.g., Zahn).

Another suggestion, first proposed by Isaac Casaubon, that *diapente* be understood as a musical term, is explored at length in a monograph by Franco Bolgiani.[25] On the basis of information derived from Martianus Capella, Fulgentius, Macrobius, and others, Bolgiani shows that διὰ τεσσάρων and διὰ πέντε are technical terms used in ancient musicology, one referring to an interval of three notes, and the other to an interval of four notes. He therefore interprets Victor's comment to mean that Tatian's "harmony" of the four evangelists involves not merely individual notes but one of the fundamental elements of symphonic harmony, the *diapente*. Thus both terms, Diatessaron and Victor's metaphorical use of *diapente*, are appropriate descriptions of Tatian's Harmony of the Gospels.

Several scholars have given renewed attention to problems concerning the order and arrangement of Tatian's Diatessaron. Taking Ephraem's commentary on the Diatessaron as a basis, Leloir compared the sequence of material in the Arabic, Latin, Dutch, Italian (Venetian), and Persian harmonies.[26] He also collected a considerable number of Tatianisms preserved in the work of Ephraem and supported in either the Old Armenian version or the Old Georgian version.

In a study of the sequence and character of the Diatessaron, Ortiz de Urbina pointed out that, when one tabulates according to each Gospel

Gospels," in *Chapters in the History of New Testament Textual Criticism* (Leiden and Grand Rapids, 1963), pp. 97-120.

[25] Franco Bolgiani, *Vittore di Capua e il "Diatessaron"* (=*Memoire dell'Accademia delle Scienze di Torino*, Cl. di Scienze Morale, Storiche e Filologiche, Serie 4ª, no. 2; Torino, 1962).

[26] Louis Leloir, "Le Diatessaron de Tatien," *L'Orient syrien*, I (1956), 208-31 and 313-34.

the material quoted by Ephraem, the verses cited appear in disorder so far as the sequence of each Gospel is concerned.[27] When, however, one considers the sequence of material within the Diatessaron, it is obvious that Tatian grouped passages from the four Gospels that pertain to the same context, whether of episode, parable, dialogue, or preaching of Jesus.

The influence of Tatian's Diatessaron in the early church was felt far and wide, either directly or indirectly. It is natural that, soon after the publication in 1956 of the Coptic Gospel of Thomas, an investigation should be made of the question whether the newly discovered text has any appreciable connection with Tatian's work. According to Quispel the Gospel of Thomas discloses influence from the Jewish-Christian Gospel according to the Hebrews, which was a fifth source used by Tatian, portions of which are embedded in the Medieval *Heliand*.[28] The latter part of Quispel's investigation was severely attacked by the Germanist Krogmann, who tested passages adduced by Quispel from the *Heliand* and concluded that they are totally insufficient to support Quispel's thesis.[29] In turn Quispel published a lengthy rebuttal of Krogmann's strictures, maintaining that a careful comparison shows that the *Heliand* is based on a very distinctive and ancient text of the Diatessaron, some of whose variants are shared by the Gospel of Thomas. Although a Germanist, Quispel acknowledges, may judge differently about this or that parallel, yet the resemblances, he urges, are so numerous that they cannot be accidental.[30]

The relationship of the text of the Gospel of Thomas to Tatian was investigated independently by another Dutch scholar, Tjitze Baarda.[31] Setting forth in tabular form data of about 130 variant readings, Baarda shows that it is the Arabic Diatessaron that supplies the greatest number of agreements with Thomas (about 60 agreements) and that the Liège

[27] I. Ortiz de Urbina, "Trama e carattere del Diatessaron di Taziano," *Orientalia Cristiana Periodica,* XXV (1959), 326-57.

[28] Gillis Quispel, "Some Remarks on the Gospel of Thomas," *NTS,* V (1959), 276-90; and *idem,* "L'Évangile selon Thomas et le Diatessaron," *VigChr,* XIII (1959), 87-117.

[29] Willy Krogmann, "Heliand, Tatian und Thomasevangelium," *ZNW,* LI (1960), 255-68.

[30] "Der Heliand und das Thomasevangelium," *VigChr,* XVI (1962), 121-53.

[31] See Baarda's chapter on "Thomas en Tatianus," in R. Schippers, *Het Evangelie van Thomas* (Kampen, 1960), pp. 135-55.

Diatessaron[32] and the Persian Harmony have each about 50 agreements. The Venetian and Toscan Harmonies agree about 30 times. Ephraem's commentary on the Diatessaron accounts for about 20 agreements.

(b) *The Old Syriac Version*

The earlier work of Molitor[33] in assembling Ephraem's quotations from the Old Syriac text of the Pauline Epistles has been carried further in a recently accepted dissertation at the Gregorian University.[34] In a summary of his dissertation the author concludes that the influence from Marcion on the Old Syriac text of Paul has often been overestimated. An analysis of the Old Syriac text of Paul confirms the generally held opinion that it presents a typically Western type of text, "in a line with Tyconius, Tertullian, many treatises of Augustine, etc. Especially noteworthy are agreements with Irenaeus. But direct relationship cannot be established with certainty." [35]

Carrying his researches further, Kerschensteiner investigated the Old Syriac text of Acts, and found that for this book also there was a widely disseminated, unified text in the fourth century which differed from what came to be known as the Peshitta version.[36]

Announcement has been made by Arthur Vööbus[37] that his researches of the past thirty years are now approaching completion, namely his *Vetus Syra: New Materials for the History of the Old Syriac Version of the Gospels.* The first two volumes will contain Prolegomena on the manuscript evidence and will present the Syriac texts with a Latin translation. A third volume, which will be devoted to the patristic evidence, is to follow later.

[32] After a lapse of a quarter of a century the publication of *The Liège Diatessaron,* edited with a Critical Apparatus by D. Plooij, C. A. Phillips, and A. H. A. Bakker, has been resumed under Miss Bakker's supervision; Part VI has appeared in *Verhandelingen der koninklijke nederlandsche Akademie van Wetenschappen,* Afdeeling Letterkunde, Nieuwe Reeks, Deel 31 (Amsterdam, 1963), pp. 481-576.

[33] Josef Molitor, *Der Paulustext des hl. Ephräm* (Rome, 1938).

[34] Josef Kerschensteiner, *Der altsyrische Paulustext.* Diss. Pont. Univ. Gregorianae, 1961-62.

[35] "Neues zum altsyrischen Paulustext," *Studiorum Paulinorum Congressus Internationalis Catholicus,* 1961, I (=*Analecta Biblica,* vols. 17-18; Rome, 1963), 531-38.

[36] "Beobachtungen zum altsyrischen Actatext," *Biblica,* XLV (1964), 63-74.

[37] See A. Vööbus, "Completion of the Vetus Syra Project," *Biblical Research,* VII (1962), 1-8.

(c) *The Syriac Peshitta*

On the much debated question of the relation of Bp. Rabbula to the Peshitta version, Kerschensteiner observes that there appears to be no trace of the Peshitta text of Paul prior to the time of Rabbula. In a thorough analysis of the form of Gospel quotations in Rabbula's biography, Tjitze Baarda concludes that both Burkitt and Vööbus were wrong in holding that the biographer used the Peshitta.[38] Rabbula's text of Matthew and Luke was less revised than either the Old Syriac or the Peshitta, while his text of John had indeed been revised but was not identical with the Peshitta. Baarda interprets these data as supporting Vööbus's opinion that the Peshitta did not become official until the end of the fifth century. But the existence of the somewhat revised text of John (and the Lord's Prayer) suggests to Baarda that Rabbula may after all have been responsible for a partial revision of passages, particularly in John, that figured in the Christological controversies.

Finally, attention should be drawn to an excellent descriptive summary of what is known today of the Syriac versions of the Scriptures written by Cl. Van Puyvelde for *Dictionnaire de la Bible*.[39]

III
The Coptic Versions

During the past decade portions of the NT have been published in several of the Coptic dialects, including Sahidic, Middle Egyptian, Fayyumic, and Bohairic. Two of these are in the possession of the Swiss bibliophile, Martin Bodmer, and were edited by the French pastor, Rodolphe Kasser.

In 1958 Kasser published a papyrus codex containing the Gospel of John and the opening chapters of Genesis in Bohairic.[40] Though the first few folios are badly damaged, beginning at about the middle of the fourth chapter of John the text is much better preserved. It is of interest that passages which textual scholars previously recognized as critically suspect (such as the statement concerning the angel moving the water

[38] "The Gospel Text in the Biography of Rabbula," *VigChr*, XIV (1960), 102-27.
[39] *Supplément*, vol. 6, fasc. 33 (Paris, 1960), cols. 834-81.
[40] Rodolphe Kasser, ed., *Papyrus Bodmer III. Évangile de Jean et Genèse* I-IV, 2 *en bohairique* (=*Corpus Scriptorum Christianorum Orientalium*, vol. 177 [the text], and vol. 178 [French translation]; Louvain, 1958).

in John 5:3*b*-4, and the pericope of the adulterous woman, 7:53—8:11) are not present in this manuscript.

The editor is inclined to date the codex in the fourth century. When it is recalled that fifty years ago several scholars were of the opinion that the Bohairic version was made in the seventh or even eighth century (such was the opinion, e.g., of Forbes Robinson, Burkitt, Leipoldt, and Baumstark), the importance of the Bodmer codex is hard to overestimate. Even if it should turn out that subsequent investigation should modify Kasser's early dating, the manuscript will retain its interest for the Coptist because of the paucity of early Bohairic manuscripts. In fact, besides this codex only two other literary documents written in Bohairic, or semi-Bohairic, are known to come from a date prior to the ninth century; one is a school text (Pap. Mich. 926) and the other a parchment fragment of some verses from Philippians found at Bala'izah.

The other Bodmer manuscript is a parchment codex which contains the second half of Matthew (14:28 onward) and the opening part of Romans (1:1—2:3) in the Sahidic dialect.[41] It is written in a very careful hand of the so-called Biblical uncial, similar to the hand of codex Sinaiticus. On palaeographical grounds the editor dates the manuscript in the fourth or fifth century. It is thus among the most ancient copies of Matthew and Romans in Coptic.

A leaf of parchment, dating from the eighth or ninth century and containing some verses from the ninth chapter of Luke in Sahidic, has been edited by Roca-Puig.[42] Though the fragment presents no particularly noteworthy reading, it is valuable as supplying still another witness for the Sahidic version of Luke. Several short portions of Matthew (14:21-22, 25-27, 30-31, 36; 16:8, 12, 15-16, 20) in Sahidic are described[43] and transcribed[44] in the journal published by the Coptic Institute at Cairo.

[41] Rodolphe Kasser, ed., *Papyrus Bodmer XIX. Évangile de Matthieu* xiv, *28*-xxviii, *20. Epître aux Romains* i, *1*—ii, *3 en sahidique* (Cologny-Geneva, 1962).

[42] R. Roca-Puig, "Un pergamento copto en Barcelona. P. Barc. inv. núm. (Lc. 9, 29-32. 36-39. 42-45. 48-50)," *Estudios eclesiásticos,* xxxiv (1960), 837-50, with 4 plates.

[43] Sylvestre Chanleur, "Sur un papyrus portant un fragment de l'Évangile selon saint Matthieu decouvert en Egypt," *Les Cahiers Coptes,* XV (1957), 3-4.

[44] Jules Garrido, "Un nouveau papyrus de l'Évangile de saint Matthieu en copte sahidique," *Les Cahiers Coptes,* XV (Cairo, 1957), 5-16. The same author also draws attention to a small papyrus fragment containing Matt. 14:20-22 in Sahidic; "Hallazago de un papiro del Nuevo Testamento en copto sahídico," *Estudios Bíblicos,* seg. ép., XVII (1958), 107-8.

Since the Fayyumic version of the NT is represented by only a relatively few documents,[45] scholars must be grateful to Elinor M. Husselman for her edition of a portion of the Gospel of John (6:11—15:10) now in Kelsey Museum of Archaeology at the University of Michigan.[46] In the format of a single-quire codex, the manuscript, which is dated by the editor in the early part of the fourth century, has some 25 readings peculiar to it alone; it agrees with the Sahidic against the Bohairic 68 times, and agrees with the Bohairic against the Sahidic 30 times.

What is perhaps the most exciting discovery among Coptic NT manuscripts is a parchment codex from the fourth or early fifth century which contains on 107 leaves the text of Acts 1:1—15:2. The language belongs to the comparatively little-known archaic Coptic dialect which Kahle designated "Middle Egyptian Proper." [47] The manuscript, which is no. G67 in the Glazier Collection in the Pierpont Morgan Library, New York, is valuable as an early witness to the Western form of text in Egypt.[48] Many typically Western readings, hitherto known from codex Bezae, the Fleury Old Latin manuscript (*h*), and the margin of the Harclean Syriac version, are now found to have been current also in Egypt. Examples include the following:[49]

Acts 1:1 chosen] + to preach the gospel
2:37 what shall we do?] + Show us!
5:36 claiming to be *a great* somebody
6:15 an angel] + standing in their midst
12:21 began to address them] + and he came to an agreement with the Tyrians
13:43 + The Word however spread through the whole city
14:25 Attalia] + and they preached to them.

[45] For a list of the Fayyumic manuscripts of the NT, see Paul E. Kahle, *Bala'izah, Coptic Texts from Deir el-Bala'izah in Upper Egypt,* I (London, 1954), 279-90.

[46] Elinor M. Husselman, ed., *The Gospel of John in Fayumic Coptic* (*Mich. inv. 3521*) (Ann Arbor, 1962).

[47] Kahle, *Bala'izah,* I (London, 1954), 220-24.

[48] A preliminary description of the manuscript is given by Theodore C. Petersen, "An Early Coptic Manuscript of Acts: An Unrevised Version of the Ancient So-Called Western Text," *CBQ,* XXVI (1964), 225-41.

[49] These examples are cited from Petersen's article. It is understood that Petersen intends to prepare a complete edition of the manuscript.

Another parchment manuscript containing on 238 leaves the Gospel of Matthew in the same dialect (Middle Egyptian proper), now in the possession of Otto Schäfer, a business executive of Schweinfurt, is being edited by Dr. Julius Assfalg of Munich.

There are also many other readings which remind one of typically Western accretions but which are not found in any other known witness. Examples include the following:

2:25 David says] + in the Psalms

6:1 The Hebrew deacons were neglecting the Greek widows

7:31-34 (The text is amplified by several extensive accretions from the Pentateuch.)

7:42 the book of the prophets] Amos the prophet

7:48 prophet] + Isaiah

8:35 Then Philip *took his* beginning from the Scripture, *and now he was in the spirit,* [and] *he began to explain to him from the Scripture,* [and] preached *the Lord* Jesus *Christ* to him.

8:39 When they came up out of the water *the Holy Spirit came upon the eunuch. But* the *Angel* of the Lord took Philip away *from him. . . .*

11:30 to the presbyters *who are in Jerusalem*

12:8-9 . . . and follow me. *But he seized him and drew him along before him and came out with him,* and *Peter* followed . . .

Several years ago the University of Mississippi acquired a single-quire papyrus codex of 52 leaves or 104 consecutive pages. The manuscript contains a miscellaneous assortment of documents written in Sahidic, among which is the complete text of I Peter. According to William H. Willis, who described the manuscript in a report read before the International Congress of Papyrologists meeting at Oslo in 1959, the date of the manuscript is no later than the turn of the third and fourth centuries.[50] It is therefore among the very oldest copies of I Peter in Greek or Coptic. At present Willis is engaged in preparing a variorum edition of the Sahidic text of I Peter.[51]

In conclusion, attention should be directed to (a) an invaluable index entitled "Coptic Biblical Texts Published after Vaschalde's Lists," drawn

[50] Wm. H. Willis, "The New Collections of Papyri at the University of Mississippi," *Proceedings of the IX International Congress of Papyrology* (Oslo, 1961), pp. 382-89. See also George D. Kilpatrick, "The Bodmer and Mississippi Collection of Biblical and Christian Texts," *Greek, Roman, and Byzantine Studies,* IV (1963), 33-47.

[51] See Willis' report in the 1963 *Yearbook* of the American Philosophical Society (Philadelphia, 1964), pp. 627 f., and his article, "An Unrecognized Fragment of First Peter in Coptic," in *Classical, Mediaeval and Renaissance Studies in Honor of B. L. Ullman,* ed. Charles Henderson, Jr. (=*Storia e Letteratura,* XCIII; Rome, 1964), pp. 265-71.

up by the late Walter C. Till,[52] and (b) a useful summary by B. Botte of what is known of the Coptic versions of the Scriptures.[53]

IV

The Gothic Version

Streitberg's standard text of the Gothic Bible has been issued in a fourth, unaltered printing.[54] Basing his researches on 512 variant readings in Streitberg's apparatus, Friedrichsen investigated the difficult question of what Greek text should be printed as the *Vorlage* of the Gothic "when either of the alternative readings would have resulted in the same Gothic rendering, and when the readings differ only by the presence or absence of a particle, or by the different renderings of introductory particles or conjunctions such as *καί, δέ, οὖν, γάρ,* the representation of which in the Gothic text especially of St. John seems to be subject to irresponsible variation." [55] The result of Friedrichsen's analysis is to show the limitations of the use of the Gothic in reconstructing the underlying Greek text.

In another analysis of 157 readings of the Greek text underlying the Gothic version of Luke, Friedrichsen tabulates 16 agreements with the Syrian (Byzantine) type of text, 68 agreements with pre-Syrian types of text, and 32 agreements with isolated uncial manuscripts against the Syrian type of text.[56]

After discussing a characteristic feature of Gothic syntax, Dr. Henss, the librarian of the University of Heidelberg, points out certain consequences in making judgments respecting the relation of the Gothic and Old Latin versions of the NT.[57]

[52] Published in *BJRL,* XLII (1959), 220-40.

[53] *Dictionnaire de la Bible, Supplément,* vol. 6 fasc. 33 (Paris, 1960), cols. 818-25. A. Joussen's dissertation, *Die koptischen Versionen der Apostelgeschichte. Kritik und Wertung* (Bonn, 1963), was not available to me.

[54] *Die gotische Bibel,* ed. Wilhelm Streitberg (Heidelberg, 1960).

[55] G. W. S. Friedrichsen, *Gothic Studies* (Medium Ævum Monographs, VI; Oxford, 1961), p. 2.

[56] G. W. S. Friedrichsen, "The Greek Text Underlying the Gothic Version of the New Testament. The Gospel of St. Luke," *Mélanges de linguistique et de philologie; Fernand Mossé in Memoriam* (Paris, 1959), pp. 161-84.

[57] Walter Henss, "Gotisches jah und -uh zwischen Partizipium und Verbum finitum," *ZNW,* XLVIII (1957), 133-41.

In 1960 Bennett edited and translated the *Skeireins,* fragments of a Gothic com-

V
The Armenian Version

It is not generally realized how abundant are the manuscripts of the Armenian version of the NT. Contrary to a rather widespread impression of their rarity,[58] more manuscripts of this version are extant than of any other ancient version, with the exception only of the Latin Vulgate.

A tool which will be of great assistance to scholars in the study of the Armenian version is Rhodes's annotated list of Armenian NT manuscripts.[59] After consulting scores of printed and handwritten catalogues of Armenian manuscripts and culling out those which contain all or part of the NT (except lectionaries and commentaries on the NT text), Rhodes lists 1,244 manuscripts and supplies information concerning their location, contents, physical description, scribes, place and date of writing, as well as references to previous lists and monographs in which the manuscripts have been cited.[60]

Continuing his earlier lists of Armenian manuscripts in the collection of Harry Kurdian of Wichita, Kansas, Allen Wikgren[61] describes ten additional items, supplementing Rhodes's catalogue. The Kurdian collection now contains sixty-nine NT manuscripts.

Catalogues of other collections of Armenian manuscripts have been

---

mentary on the Gospel of John, comprising 800 lines averaging about 13 letters each. Though the chief value of the commentary is the additional light it sheds on the Gothic language, occasionally it offers the possibility of making text-critical judgments regarding the Gothic version itself; see William Holmes Bennett, *The Gothic Commentary on the Gospel of John* (New York, 1960).

[58] Cf., for example, F. G. Kenyon's *Our Bible and the Ancient Manuscripts,* 5th ed. (London 1958), p. 237.

[59] Erroll F. Rhodes, *An Annotated List of Armenian New Testament Manuscripts* (Ikebukuro, Tokyo, 1959).

[60] It is to be hoped that Rhodes, who teaches in St. Paul's University, Tokyo, will find time and energy to continue his search for Armenian manuscripts. A few years ago it was reported that the Scientific Academy of the Armenian Soviet Socialist Republic had been moving manuscripts from outlying districts to its central repository at Erevan, and that there are now 1,500 Gospels manuscripts and 100 complete Bible manuscripts, not to mention incomplete and fragmentary manuscripts, in this institution alone. Inasmuch as Rhodes lists 267 manuscripts in the Erevan collection, it will be seen that there is room for a revised and enlarged edition of his useful catalogue.

[61] "New Armenian Manuscripts of the New Testament in the Kurdian Collection," *JBL,* LXXIX (1960), 52-56.

published by Sirarpie Der Nersessian,[62] K. Roszko,[63] J. Assfalg and J. Molitor,[64] and by a number of contributors to the Armenian journal, *Handes Amsorya*.[65]

In an analysis of the textual complexion of the Armenian version of the Epistle to the Ephesians,[66] Molitor finds that the text rests upon an Old Syriac version, traces of which have been transmitted in the Peshitta version. These Syriacisms are often represented in the variant readings which Zohrab cites under the siglum "many [manuscripts]" in the apparatus of his edition.

Finally, attention should be drawn to Louis Leloir's useful survey of what is known of the Armenian version of the Scriptures, published in *Dictionnaire de la Bible*.[67]

VI
The Georgian Version

In 1955 Canon Brière[68] published the Old Georgian version of the Gospel of Luke, thus bringing to a conclusion the work begun by Robert

[62] Miss Der Nersessian has published a catalogue of the Armenian manuscripts in the Case Memorial Library at Hartford in *The Hartford Foundation Library Bulletin*, No. 19 (1955); she has also published the volumes entitled *The Chester Beatty Library. A Catalogue of the Armenian Manuscripts* (London, 1959), and *Armenian Manuscripts in the Freer Gallery of Art* (Washington, 1963).

[63] Roszko's catalogue of Armenian (and Georgian) manuscripts in Polish libraries is vol. III of *Katalog rekopesów orientalnych ze zbiorów polskich*, ed. S. Strelcyn (1959). Roszko gives a brief account of the work of assembling the catalogue in *Przeglad orientalistyczny*, 4 (24) (1957), 307-12.

[64] *Armenische Handschriften: Verzeichnis der orientalischen Handschriften in Deutschland*, IV (Wiesbaden, 1962).

[65] P. N. Akinian lists and describes the Armenian manuscripts in Cyprus (at present in Antilias, Lebanon), *Handes Amsorya*, LXIX (1955), 170 ff.; the Armenian manuscripts in the Armenian Hospital of St. Blasius in Rome, *ibid.*, LXXI (1957), 282-91, 420-39, 537-58; and in the Pont. Leoniano Collegio in Rome, *ibid.*, LXXII (1958), 49-82; T. Balian, the Armenian manuscripts at the Monastery of St. Karapet in Caesarea, *ibid.*, LXXIII (1959), 253-74, 421-43, 540-51; LXXIV (1960), 81-99, 241-87, 416-35; and at the Monastery of St. Daniel in Caesarea, *ibid.*, LXXIV (1960), 537-50; P. J. Kossian, the Armenian manuscripts at the Arznian School in Erzerum, *ibid.*, LXXV (1961), 102-36, 312-29; LXXVI (1962), 30-57, 174-82, 339-52; and in the villages of Erzerum, *ibid.*, LXXVII (1963), 23-37, 207-21, 371-91, 505-15; LXXVIII (1964), 29-37, 153-60; and P. H. Oskian, the Armenian manuscripts of the Capuchin monastery in Beirut, *ibid.*, LXXIV (1960), 550-67; and in the University Library at Graz, *ibid.*, LXXVIII (1964), 479-85.

[66] "Der armenische Epheserbrief und die syrische Textüberlieferung," *Handes Amsorya*, LXXVIII (1964), 301-10.

[67] *Supplément*, vol. 6, fasc. 33 (Paris, 1960), cols. 810-18.

[68] Maurice Brière, *La Version géorgienne ancienne de l'évangile de Luc, d'après les évangiles d'Adich avec les variantes des évangiles d'Opiza et de Tbet'* (=*Patrologia orientalis*, XXVII, fasc. 3; Paris, 1955).

P. Blake (*Mark,* 1928; *Matthew,* 1933; *John,* 1950). As in the case of the previous fascicles, variant readings from two other Old Georgian manuscripts are supplied, as well as a literal Latin translation of the text and the variants. According to Brière, the text preserved in the Adysh manuscript (A.D. 897) represents the form of the Old Georgian version shortly after it was first translated from the Armenian in perhaps the fifth century. A somewhat later form of Georgian text is represented in the other two manuscripts (Opiza, A.D. 913, and Tbet', A.D. 995), from which Brière cites variant readings.

In the same year Garitte[69] made available the text of the book of Acts in the Old Georgian version, drawn from two tenth-century manuscripts; he also supplied a Latin translation. This edition was soon made the object of a study by Tarchnišvili,[70] who concluded that the text edited by Garitte was translated in the fifth century very shortly after the Old Georgian version of the Gospels represented by the Adysh manuscript.

In 1961 the Georgian scholar Imnaišvili published the Old Georgian version of the book of Revelation.[71]

Besides these three major editions, several other texts have been either made available or described. These include fragments which are identified by certain characteristic linguistic features; viz., the terms Khanmeti and Haemeti refer to the archaic use of the velar fricative letter *Khan* and of the aspirate *Hae* in certain verbal forms and in the comparative form of adjectives.[72]

Theodor Klug describes certain external features and the sequence of material in two manuscripts of the Apostolos, both of which he dates in the seventh or eighth century.[73]

[69] Gérard Gariette, *L'Ancienne version géorgienne des Actes des Apôtres, d'après deux manuscrits du Sinai* (Louvain, 1955).

[70] Michel Tarchnishvili, "A propos de la plus ancienne version géorgienne des Actes des Apôtres," *Muséon,* LXIX (1956), 347-68.

[71] I. V. Imnaishvili, *L'Apocalypse de Jean et son commentaire: Ancienne version géorgienne* (=*Travaux de la chaîne d'ancien géorgien,* 7; Tiflis, 1961) [in Georgian].

[72] See Joseph Molitor, "Die altgeorgischen Chanmeti- und Haemeti-Bibelfragmente," *Lexis,* IV (1954), 79-84.

[73] "Über zwei altgeorgische neutestamentliche Handschriften," *Novum Testamentum,* I (1956) 304-21. J. Molitor's article "Eigenart und Bedeutung des altgeorgischen Hadischi-Tetraevangeliums," *Revue de Karthvélilogie,* XXX-XXXI (Paris, 1958), 55-63, was not available to me.

After many years of labor, Joseph Molitor published[74] a collection of texts entitled *Monumenta Iberica Antiquiora. Textus Chanmeti et Haemeti ex Inscriptionibus, S. Bibliis et Patribus.* The volume contains eighteen Khanmeti fragments of the four Gospels, Romans, and Galatians, and twenty-three Haemeti fragments of the four Gospels. Subsequently Molitor began publishing in *OrChr* a series of studies comparing textual and linguistic features of the several Khanmeti fragments.[75]

In 1960 the editors of *Muséon* wisely reprinted an important article by Tarchnišvili which had appeared during World War II in what is today an almost inaccessible journal.[76] The article describes two fragments of Old Georgian Lectionaries, dating from the fifth and eighth centuries. The older fragment preserves quotations of Matthew, Luke, John, Romans, and Galatians; the later fragment supplies rubrics for most of the month of November and for the first day of December.[77]

Since 1953 Molitor, with indefatigable industry, has been publishing currently in *OrChr* a Latin translation of the Adysh manuscript of the Gospels, which is more consistently literal than the rendering of Blake and Brière.[78]

In addition to making Old Georgian texts available, Molitor has also devoted considerable attention to studying the nature of the Old Georgian version. In an analysis of the text of Mark 1, he concluded that the translation was not made from the Greek text but from the Old Armenian version, perhaps in the form of a harmony.[79] On the other

[74] In the series *Corpus Scriptorum Christianorum Orientalium*, vol. 166; *Subsidia*, 10 (Louvain, 1956).

[75] "Chanmetifragmente. Ein Beitrag zum Textgeschichte der altgeorgischen Bibelübersetzung," *OrChr*, XLI (1957), 22-34; XLIII (1959), 17-23; XLIV (1960), 17-24; XLV (1961), 115-26; XLVI (1962), 19-24.

[76] *Kyrios; Vierteljahresschrift für Kirchen- und Geistesgeschichte Osteuropas*, VI (1942), 1-28.

[77] Michel Tarchnishvili, "Zwei georgische Lektionarfragmente aus dem 5. und 8. Jahrhundert," *Muséon*, LXXIII (1960), 261-96.

[78] "Das Adysh-Tetraevangelium. Neu übersetzt und mit altgeorgischen Paralleltexten verglichen," *OrChr*, XXXVII (1953), 33-55; XXXVIII (1954), 11-40; XXXIX (1955), 1-32; XL (1956), 1-15; XLI (1957), 1-21; XLII (1958), 1-18; XLIII (1959), 1-16; XLIV (1960), 1-16; XLV (1961), 1-19; XLVI (1962), 1-18; XLVII (1963), 1-15.

[79] "Zur Harmonistik des altgeorgischen Evangelientextes," *Biblische Zeitschrift*, N.F., I (1957), 289-96.

The expression "othch-thavi" (i.e. "four-chapter") used in reference to the Old Georgian tetraevangelium seems to imply, as Strobel points out, that the earliest form of the Gospels in Georgia was that of a Harmony; see A. Strobel, "Der Begriff des

hand, Molitor's examination of the NT quotations in an Old Georgian patristic text of homilies discloses traces of influence from both Greek and Armenian texts; he also discovered one Tatianism.[80] In a summary of the characteristics of the Old Georgian text, Molitor points to evidence of the influence from Greek, Armenian, and Syriac on the language, style, and text of the version.[81]

Finally, reference should be directed (a) to D. M. Lang's informative survey and evaluation of textual and linguistic research on the Georgian NT, including bibliographical references to related works on Georgian palaeography, manuscript illumination, and hagiography,[82] and (b) to Louis Leloir's useful article on the Georgian version of the Scriptures.[83]

VII
The Ethiopic Version

Of work on the Ethiopic version of the NT there is, unfortunately, not much to report. The chief work, undertaken by Josef Hofmann, is an investigation into the influence of the Arabic version (s) on the Ethiopic translation of the book of Revelation.[84] On the basis of an examination of the text of Revelation in twenty-six Ethiopic manuscripts, dating from the fifteenth to the nineteenth centuries, the author finds that they fall

'vierkapiteligen Evangeliums' in Pseudo-Ephraem C," *Zeitschrift für Kirchengeschichte,* LXX (1959), 112-20.

[80] "Evangelienzitate in einen altgeorgischen Väterfragment," *OrChr,* XL (1956), 16-21. Cf. *idem,* "Synoptische Evangelienzitate in Sinai-Mravelthavi von 864," *ibid.,* XLVIII (1964), 180-96.

[81] "Die Bedeutung der altgeorgischen Bibel für die neutestamentliche Textkritik," *Biblische Zeitschrift,* N.F., IV (1960), 39-53, and "Zur armenischer Vorlage der altgeorgischen Version des 1. Johannesbriefes," *Handes Amsorya,* LXXV (1961), 415-29. Molitor's earlier article, "Zur Frage der Vorlage des altgeorgischen Bibeltextes," *Bedi Karthlisa,* XXVI-XXVII (1957), 23-27, was not available to me.

[82] "Recent Work on the Georgian New Testament," *Bulletin of the School of Oriental and African Studies,* XIX (1957), 82-93. For an interesting account of the history of "Georgian Studies in Oxford," reference may be made to Lang's contribution with that title in *Oxford Slavonic Papers,* ed. S. Konovalov, VI (Oxford, 1955), 115-43. For an evaluation of the contributions by Brière and Molitor to the study of the Old Georgian version, see S. Lyonnet, "L'ancienne version géorgienne des Évangiles," *Biblica,* XXXIX (1958), 492-96.

[83] *Dictionnaire de la Bible, Supplément,* vol. 6, fasc. 33 (Paris, 1960), cols. 829-34. Leloir's earlier survey, "La version géorgienne de la Bible," in *Pazmaveb,* CXVI (1958), 197-203, was not available to me.

[84] "Der arabische Einfluss in der äthiopischen Übersetzung der Johannesapokalypse. Textkritische Untersuchung auf Grund von Handschriften," *OrChr,* XLIII (1959), 24-53; XLIV (1960), 25-39.

into three families. One group of manuscripts preserves the Ethiopic vulgate text, and the other two groups present texts which are the result of two revisions made on the basis of Arabic text (s). Even in the oldest manuscripts of the Ethiopic vulgate there are sporadic traces of Arabic variants, which have been influenced by the Bohairic.

Several Biblical manuscripts are included (pp. 1-9) in Ullendorf and Wright's catalogue of Ethiopic manuscripts at Cambridge.[85]

Mention may be made also of B. Botte's survey in *Dictionnaire de la Bible* of what is known of the Ethiopic version of the Scriptures.[86]

VIII
The Arabic Versions

One hundred years ago Paul de Lagarde wrote in the Preface of his edition of the four Gospels in Arabic, "There are more Arabic versions of the Gospels than can be welcome to theology, with its press of work." [87] Recently Joseph Henninger provided a historical survey of the Arabic translations made from the seventh to the fifteenth centuries for Melchites, Maronites, Nestorians, Jacobites, and Copts. He also describes the chief Arabic printed Bibles down to the nineteenth century.[88]

Covering the major printed Arabic Bibles, John A. Thompson deals at length with the basic texts and methods used in producing (1) the Arabic version in the Paris Polyglott of 1645 and in the London Polyglott of 1657; (2) the Propaganda Version published at Rome in 1671; (3) the Smith-Van Dyck Version published at Beirut in 1865; and (4) the Jesuit Version completed in 1880 also in Beirut. The survey was written in connection with Thompson's work, in collaboration with Butrus Abd-al-Malik, in revising the 1865 version.[89]

[85] Edward Ullendorf and S. G. Wright, *Catalogue of Ethiopic Manuscripts in the Cambridge University Library,* with a contribution by D. A. Hubbard (London, 1961).

[86] *Supplément,* vol. 6, fasc. 33 (Paris, 1960), cols. 825-29.

[87] Paul de Lagarde, *Die vier Evangelien arabisch* (Leipzig, 1864). For a classification of five or six main groups of Arabic versions, see B. M. Metzger in *New Testament Manuscript Studies,* ed. M. M. Parvis and A. P. Wikgren (Chicago, 1950), pp. 47-49.

[88] Joseph Henninger, "Arabische Bibelübersetzungen vom Frühmittelalter bis zum 19 Jahrhundert," *Neue Zeitschrift für Missionswissenschaft,* XVII (1961), 201-23.

[89] John A. Thompson, *The Major Arabic Bibles, Their Origin and Nature* (New York, 1956); the several chapters were first published as articles in *The Bible Translator,* VI (1955), 1-12, 51-55, 98-106, and 146-50.

For a survey of what is known of the Arabic versions of the Scriptures, reference may be made to B. Botte's article in *Dictionnaire de la Bible.*[90]

IX
The Old Slavonic Version

One of the principal manuscripts of the Old Slavonic version, the codex Marianus, which is usually assigned to the eleventh century, has been made more readily available through the photographic reprinting of Vatroslav Jagić's edition, *Quatuor evangeliorum versionis palaeoslovenicae codex Marianus glagolithicus.*[91]

Recently the Czech scholar Horálek reexamined the opinion expressed a century ago by K. I. Nevostrujev that St. Cyril's translation of the Old Slavonic Gospels shows influence from the Syriac version. Though rejecting as indecisive some of the examples adduced by Nevostrujev, Horálek concludes that enough evidence remains to prove that Cyril was acquainted with the Syriac (Peshitta) version; in fact, Horálek thinks that perhaps Cyril also made use of an Aramaic translation of the Gospels (!).[92]

The study of the Old Slavonic version is complicated by the circumstance that the extant manuscripts preserve texts that have undergone a certain amount of linguistic modification that reflects local dialectal developments in Slavic. Josip Vrana of Zagreb has investigated "The Relation of the Gospel of Miroslav [which dates from about the twelfth century] with the Old Slavonic Lectionaries and Tetraevangelia."[93] Continuing his analyses, Vrana published a study of "The Types, Redactions, and Mutual Relationships of the Old Slavonic Gospels,"

[90] *Supplément,* vol. 6 fasc. 33 (Paris, 1960), cols. 807-10.

[91] Graz, 1960. Jagic transcribed the glagolitic text in Cyrillic characters. According to F. Repp, this important manuscript was written in the western area of the Balkan peninsula ("Zur Kritik des Codex Marianus," *Zeitschrift für slavische Philologie,* XXIV [1956], 271-76). For a discussion of criteria for determining the date of early Slavonic manuscripts, reference may be made to Horace G. Lunt, "On Slavonic Palimpsests," *American Contributions to the Fourth International Congress of Slavicists,* Moscow, September, 1958 ('s-Gravenhage, 1958), pp. 191-209.

[92] Karel Horálek, "Sv. Kirill i semitskie yazyki," [*Festschrift*] *For Roman Jakobson, Essays on the Occasion of His Sixtieth Birthday . . . ,* compiled by Morris Halle *et al.* (The Hague, 1956), pp. 230-34. For a brief summary (in French) of the article see A. Dostál in *Byzantinoslavica,* IX (1958), 391.

[93] "O odnosu Miroslavljeva evandelja prema staroslovjenskim evandelistarima i ceveroevandeljima," *Slavia, casopis pro slovanskou filologii,* XXV (1956), 306-12.

in which he sets forth in convenient tabular form statistics concerning the variations in seven of the most important manuscripts of the Old Slavonic Gospels.[94]

Surveying the results of earlier textual analyses of the Old Slavonic Gospels, Horálek contributes a balanced and informative account of the present status of scholarly opinion on this subject.[95] For another survey, which includes also an examination of the historical and legendary traditions concerning the work of the translator (s) of the Old Slavonic version, reference may be made to the present writer's volume, *Chapters in the History of New Testament Textual Criticism.*[96]

X
Epilogue

In what respects and to what degree are the ancient versions of the Scriptures useful to the modern scholar? Running counter to the generally accepted opinion concerning the great importance of the versions for the textual critic of the NT, A. F. J. Klijn[97] calls attention to certain features of some of the versions that seriously limit their usefulness. Though the origin of the oldest Latin, Syriac, and Coptic versions goes back to the middle or end of the second century, the manuscripts in which they are preserved are usually later than the oldest Greek texts. Furthermore, from internal as well as external evidence, it appears that several of the early versions had their origin as targumim. One should therefore not be surprised that in such texts some very remarkable readings occur. Hence, Klijn concludes, only when a versional reading is supported by an early Christian Greek author of about A.D. 200 (Clement, Origen), can we assume with confidence that we are dealing with a variant which was found in the Greek text of that period.

Though the textual critic should recognize that he must use versional evidence with circumspection in his effort to ascertain the original text,

[94] "O tipovima, redakcijama i medusobnom odnosu staroslovjenskih evandelja," *Slavia, casopis pro slovanskou filologii,* XXVI (1957), 321-36.

[95] "Zum heutigen Stand der textkritischen Erforschung des altkirchenslavischen Evangeliums," *Zeitschrift für slavische Philologie,* XXVII (1959), 255-74.

[96] Being vol. 4 of *New Testament Tools and Studies* (Leiden and Grand Rapids, 1963), pp. 73-96.

[97] "The Value of the Versions for the Textual Criticism of the New Testament," *The Bible Translator,* VIII (1957), 127-30; translated by Harold H. Oliver from Klijn's article in *Nederlandsch theologisch tijdschrift,* VIII (1953-54), 165-68.

versions frequently supply scholars with invaluable information in other areas. They obviously assist one in tracing the history of the transmission of the scriptural text, with its subsequent modifications and corruptions.[98] They also occasionally throw light upon such matters as divergent traditions concerning the punctuation of the text. For example, the Sahidic manuscript 604 in the Morgan collection is apparently the only Coptic evidence which supports the placing of a full stop after ὁ πιστεύων εἰς ἐμέ of John 7:37-38.[99] Related to this kind of information is the evidence preserved in Gothic manuscripts pertaining to section-divisions, cola, and other features of format associated with Euthalius. In fact, it now appears that the Gothic evidence antedates all other information bearing on Euthaliana.[100]

In a still wider area, the ancient versions of the Bible often throw welcome light on questions concerning syntactical and lexical influence of one language on another.[101] The scientific study of the ancient versions, therefore, remains both a necessary and a fruitful discipline to which biblical scholarship would do well to devote renewed attention.

[98] For a list of eight kinds of alterations revealed by an examination of manuscripts of the Vulgate (additions, omissions, modifications, transpositions of verses, sentences, or words, erroneous renderings, and divergences in interpretation, in punctuation, and in verse numeration), see Lincoln Ramos, "A Vulgata e o Texto Primitivo dos Evangelhos," *Revista eclésiastica brasileira,* XVI (1956), 356-79.

[99] K. H. Kuhn, "St. John vii.37-8," *NTS,* IV (1957), 63-65.

[100] James W. Marchand, "The Gothic Evidence for 'Euthalian Matter,'" *HTR,* XLIX (1956), 159-67.

[101] Besides occasional examples which have been cited above in other connections, attention may be drawn to H. Birnbaum's "Zum periphrastischen Futurum im gotischen und altkirchenslavischen," *Byzantinoslavica,* XVIII (1957), 77-81, in which the author admits lexical influence but denies syntactical influence in respect of the periphrastic future. For a linguistic evaluation of the Armenian version of the Gospels, see P. G. Scardigli, "Per una valutazione linguistica della versione armena dei Vangeli," *Rendiconti di scienze morali della Accademia Nazionale dei Lincei,* Ser. VIII, XIV (1957), 307-12.

ERNEST
CADMAN
COLWELL

Scribal Habits in Early Papyri: A Study in the Corruption of the Text

The dead hand of Fenton John Anthony Hort lies heavy upon us. In the early years of this century Kirsopp Lake described Hort's work as a failure, though a glorious one. But Hort did *not* fail to reach his major goal. He dethroned the Textus Receptus. After Hort, the late medieval Greek Vulgate was not used by serious students, and the text supported by earlier witnesses became the standard text. This was a sensational achievement, an impressive success. Hort's success in this task and the cogency of his tightly reasoned theory shaped—and still shapes—the thinking of those who approach the textual criticism of the NT through the English language.

I do not mean to suggest that this influence is undeserved. Hort's second volume is still the best statement of theory and method in this field of study. His knowledge was comprehensive, and his judgments were marked by a wisdom so unusual as to merit the word "unique." Any one who would think constructively here must first rethink Hort's thoughts.

But I would be the last to suggest that his system was a perfect one. Many years ago I joined others in pointing out the limitations in Hort's use of genealogy, and the inapplicability of genealogical method—strictly defined—to the textual criticism of the NT. Since then many others have assented to this criticism, and the building of family trees is only rarely attempted. Therefore we might assume that the influence of Hort's emphasis upon genealogical method is no longer a threat. But this assumption is false.

Hort's brilliant work still captivates our minds. So when confronted by a reading whose support is minimal and widely divorced in time and place, we think first and only of genealogical relationships. Hort has put genealogical blinders on our eyes that keep us from recognizing the major role played by scribal corruption.

True, Hort's basic dictum was "identity of reading implies identity of origin," but he at times slips into the argument that identity in *a* reading implies identity of origin. This is not true, nor is it Hort's real position. He recognized the importance of extensive agreement in numerous readings, as also of agreement in distinctive readings.[1] But the followers of Hort commonly fall into the fallacy of assuming that any agreement in readings demands the assumption of a common ancestry. We forget to ask "How much agreement is significant?"

From his study of the manuscript tradition of Cyprian, Bévenot emphasizes the importance of quantity in agreements: "But whether correct or not," he says, "and whether recognizably correct or not, a great number of such common readings reveals a *connexion* between these two MSS, either by direct transcription or by borrowing, whereas a small number of such common readings indicates little or no connexion." [2]

The influence of Hort limits our vision in another way. For him the external evidence of documents was as important as it was for the champions of the Textus Receptus. His prudent rejection of almost all readings which have no manuscript support has given the words "conjectural emendation" a meaning too narrow to be realistic. In the last generation we have depreciated external evidence of documents and have appreciated the internal evidence of readings; but we have blithely assumed that we were rejecting "conjectural emendation" if our conjectures were supported by some manuscripts. We need to recognize that the editing of an eclectic text rests upon conjectures. If these conjectures are to be soundly based, they must rest upon transcriptional probability as well as intrinsic probability. If the conjectures as to transcriptional probability are to be soundly based, they must rest upon a knowledge of scribal habits.

A careful study of what scribes actually did, with a resultant catalogue

[1] For a discussion of these criteria for the grouping of MSS, see my article, "Method in Locating a Newly Discovered Manuscript within the Manuscript Tradition of the Greek New Testament," *Studia Evangelica,* I, (Texte und Untersuchungen, Band 73, Berlin: Akademie Verlag, 1959), 757-77.

[2] Maurice Bévenot, *The Tradition of Manuscripts* (Oxford: Clarendon Press, 1961), p. 128.

of readings produced by scribes, is essential for textual criticism. Two outstanding scholars have emphasized this need. Maas claims that "To reach firm ground in this field it would be necessary to prepare a catalogue of all peculiar errors arranged in classes according to the different periods of history, types of literature, and the scripts used in the different localities. . . ." [3] And Dain, after praising Havet's work on the Latin texts, admits that in an effort to apply this to the Greek texts he found nothing new except minor matters of historical character.[4] But the degree of our specialization is such that until we have the equivalent of Havet with Greek data, critics of the Greek NT will be handicapped and inadequate in struggling to remove corruptions from the text.

The Present Study

This study is an initial step toward meeting the needs which have been mentioned. Its primary purpose is to gain knowledge of an individual scribe's habits, and thus to increase skill in the evaluation of that manuscript. Also its purpose is to gain knowledge of the habits of scribes in general—of the processes of corruption—and thus to increase skill in the evaluation of readings. Ultimately it will sharpen tools for establishing the kinship of MSS; it will disencumber the *apparatus criticus,* and will support both conjectural emendation broadly defined and an increased use of external evidence.

The singular readings of P [45], P [66], and P [75] constitute the material for this study.[5] Since in most readings, the student cannot determine whether or not the scribe copied or originated the reading, this study is restricted to singular readings (readings without other MS support) on the assumption that these readings are the creation of the scribe. The restriction of this study to singular readings can be made with confidence in view of the wealth of manuscript attestation for the Greek NT. A singular reading has been defined as a reading which has no Greek sup-

[3] P. Maas, *Textual Criticism,* tr. B. Flower (Oxford: Clarendon Press, 1958), p. 14.

[4] A. Dain, *Les Manuscrits* (Paris: Belles lettres, 1949), pp. 38 ff. with reference to L. Havet, *Manuel de critique verbale appliquée aux textes latins* (Paris: Hachette, 1911). Dain presents from the teaching of Desrousseaux a superb analysis of copying as four acts: reading, remembering, saying it to oneself, and writing.

[5] *The Chester Beatty Biblical Papyri: Gospels and Acts,* Frederic G. Kenyon, ed., vol. 2 (London: Emery Walker, 1933); *Papyrus Bodmer II,* Nouvelle édition augmentée et corrigée (Genève: Bibliothèque Bodmer, 1962); and *Papyrus Bodmer XIV-XV,* 2 vols. (Genève: Bibliothèque Bodmer, 1961).

port in the critical apparatus of Tischendorf's 8th edition. It is true that some witnesses unknown to Tischendorf may support some of these readings, but it is also highly probable that many readings with minor support in Tischendorf are scribal creations. Where the support of recent finds was known, the reading was eliminated from our list; but no rigorous effort was made to go beyond the evidence of Tischendorf's apparatus.

Before turning to statistical summaries, one word of caution. In many passages a clear decision as to the presence of a singular reading was not possible. In some cases this was due to the gaps in the papyrus and the hypothetical reconstruction of the text. The density of singular readings is the greatest where the text is complete. Thus our figures probably understate the case. In other cases the complex nature of the attestation and the difficulty of identifying the unit of variation made decisions difficult, and statistics only approximately accurate. But no major conclusion of this study depends upon an exact tabulation.

The total number of readings in these three papyri but unsupported by Greek witnesses in Tischendorf is 1,649: 482 in P 66, 275 in P 45, and 257 in P 75 (plus 635 itacisms to which we shall come presently).

The primary classification of these readings must be based upon their genesis—not upon formal descriptive categories, nor upon the presence or absence of intention, nor upon the bodily organ responsible for error (whether eye, ear, or mind). "Sound textual criticism [is] founded on knowledge of the various classes of facts which have determined variation," said Hort.

But since the process of study of a manuscript of the NT usually began by collating the manuscript with the Textus Receptus (or some other edition) taken as a base, readings were classified in formal descriptive categories as (a) omission, (b) addition, (c) transposition, or (d) substitution. When the classification of readings is based upon these descriptive categories, the student has tacitly assumed knowledge of the original text (or of the text used by this scribe), a knowledge which he has not yet attained. Thus the common use of these categories is to be abandoned. Moreover, the use of these categories does not aid in removal of the wrong reading which is the primary goal of textual criticism. To speak of omissions, transpositions, etc., does not help us to understand the habits of scribes. Scribes were not addicted to omission or addition or transposition or substitution as such.

To base a primary classification of readings upon the presence or absence of intention is to anticipate the establishment of probabilities which must be established in other ways. There is always the risk of reading deliberate intention into unintended error. A secondary classification of readings based upon the presence or absence of intention plays a valuable role in textual criticism but only if it itself rests upon a classification based upon the genesis of readings.

Why Singular Readings?

We begin, then, with the difficult question of "Why?" Why did the scribes of these papyri create this mass of singular readings? The first reason is their lack of ability to spell. Their spelling in certain restricted areas is regularly irregular.

Scholars have long known that one cause of corruption is the spelling habits of the individual scribe. These show up clearly in his singular readings where the interchange of similar sounds in diverse spellings is frequent. The three early papyri studied here underline the insignificance of variant readings of this type.

These "itacistic spellings" are numerous. More than 635 have been tabulated in the three papyri: P 45 has approximately 90, P 75 about 145, and P 66 has 400. Exact comparisons as to frequency are difficult, due primarily to the consistently fragmentary nature of the pages of P 45, and to the wide variation in the amount of text per page. If number of pages be taken as a base, P 45 has 60 (all more or less imperfect), P 66 has 148, and P 75 has 199. If the number of verses be taken as a base, P 45 has 795 ("at least in part"), P 66 has 808, and P 75 has 1,406. In general, P 75 has the fewest itacisms per square inch, and P 66 has the most.

These papyri differ also in their favorite spellings. Tischendorf's 8th edition was taken as the base for identifying divergence, an admittedly arbitrary procedure. But lest it be too easily assumed that the recorded divergences are only the "regular" spelling for the scribe in question, note that every word in a particular papyrus which is spelled in divergence from Tischendorf is also spelled in agreement with Tischendorf in the same papyrus. Accurate generalization as to spelling customs in the second century will require very extensive and careful study.

Some general comments on these itacisms may be of value. P 45 and P 75 agree (against P 66) in changing iota to epsilon-iota in approximately three-fourths of all their itacisms. In these two papyri, no other single spelling change is frequent.

In P 66, on the other hand, the most frequent variation is from epsilon to alpha-iota; with the change from epsilon-iota to iota running it a close second. These two variations total about two-thirds of the itacisms of P 66. But there is another frequent change in P 66—from iota to epsilon-iota about 70 times. It may be worth noting that the interchange of omicron and omega is very infrequent: 10 times in P 75, 5 times in P 66, one time in P 45.

The differences are striking. P 75 has alpha-iota for epsilon once, P 45 none, P 66 at least 150 times. Where P 45 and P 75 move from iota to epsilon-iota, P 66 moves in the reverse direction from epsilon-iota to iota. Since the documents come from the same period and from the same general area, these differences may be identified as scribal in origin and of little significance for the history of the text. The removal of all such spelling variations from the critical apparatus to the realm of special studies would give us more valuable editions of the Greek NT. If the itacisms are to be cited at all in our *apparatus criticus,* they should all be cited; for the availability of a comprehensive survey of evidence is essential in such a highly variable area. But stop and think what that means. If these three papyri, fragmentary as they are, give us more than 600 itacisms to record, the total for all witnesses would crowd hundreds of pages with relatively insignificant lore that would be a stumbling block to the reconstruction of the original text and the establishment of manuscript relationships.

Let us then remove these itacisms from our list of Singular Readings in P 45, P 66, and P 75. The total of 1,649 is reduced to 1,014: P 66 has 482, P 45 has 275, P 75 has 257 singular readings exclusive of itacisms.

For the sake of increasing our acquaintance with the individual manuscript, let us digress to note the distribution of their Singular Readings between Sensible Readings and Nonsense Readings. The Nonsense Readings include words unknown to grammar or lexicon, words that cannot be construed syntactically, or words that do not make sense in the context.

In P 66, two out of five Singular Readings are
Nonsense Readings—40 per cent;
in P 75, one out of four—25 per cent;
in P 45, less than one out of ten—10 per cent.

If these Nonsense Readings were to be removed from consideration, the number of Sensible Singular Readings remaining would be:
in P 66, 289; in P 45, 250; in P 75, 190.
Thus P 75 (the most extensive MS) has the fewest, and P 45 in spite of its fragmentary nature almost equals the longer P 66. Another way of saying this is that when the scribe of P 45 creates a singular reading, it almost always makes sense; when the scribes of P 66 and P 75 create singular readings, they frequently do not make sense and are obvious errors. Thus P 45 must be given credit for a much greater density of intentional changes than the other two.

How shall we begin a classification of the Singular Readings of the MSS based upon the nature of the origin of the readings? Dain in his invaluable manual states that the most frequent scribal errors are (1) the leap from the same to the same (homoioteleuton and homoioarcton) and (2) the omission of short words.[6] New faults tend to accumulate from copy to copy—but books destined for libraries alter little. Our scribes have a worse than average record.

The leap from the same to the same is a familiar phenomenon to all students of MSS. It is really the case of the misplaced scribe. The scribe loses his place, looks around and finds the same word, or at least the same syllable or letter, and starts from there. If he looks ahead to find his place, the result is a gap in the text. If he looks back, the result is a text twice written (dittography). A special case of a gap caused by the leap is that where a word or at least a syllable, or a letter is repeated immediately in the text. The writing of only one of these (haplography) causes the loss of the other.

P 66 has 54 leaps forward, and 22 backward; 18 of the
forward leaps are haplography.
P 75 has 27 leaps forward, and 10 backward.
P 45 has 16 leaps forward, and 2 backward.
From this it is clear that the scribe looking for his lost place looked ahead

[6] *Op. cit.*, pp. 43 f.

three times as often as he looked back. In other words, the loss of position usually resulted in a loss of text, an omission.

Harmonization

Our manuals all mention the scribal habit of harmonizing the text with parallel passages. The importance of the Synoptic Problem, and the concentration of textual studies upon the Gospel of Mark under the influence of the Lakes and Streeter and the Caesarean text have led to a focus upon remote parallels, parallel passages in other Gospels, or in the OT.

Harmonization to Remote Parallels

Although they are not frequent, harmonizations to remote parallels do occur. Ten occur in our MSS. Peter's confession in John (6:69, P 66) is enriched by adding "The Christ" from Matthew 16:16. In Luke (11:12, P 45) the hungry son asks for Matthew's bread, while Matthew's "birds of the air" (6:26) are added to Luke's ravens (12:24, P 45). In both P 66 and P 75 the Baptist's statement of his unworthiness in John uses the language of the Synoptic Gospels.

Harmonization to the Immediate Context

Our three papyri show clearly that scribes were much more addicted to *harmonization to the immediate context.* The influence of a neighboring word, of a balancing clause in the same sentence, of the familiar phraseology of the Gospel in question, was evidently inescapable. Harmonization to immediate context is usually mentioned incidentally in our manuals. It needs to be given headlines on the front page. There are 104 cases of harmonization creating singular readings in our three papyri, and 83 of them are harmonizations to immediate context.

These run the gamut from a change of tense in the answer to a question to harmonize with the tense in the question (John 11:27, P 66), to adding a verb to the second clause of a sentence to balance the verb in the first clause (Matt. 25:43, P 45), to picking "Herod" out of the context to replace the title "King" (Mark 6:22, P 45). They include changing the genitive (*υμων*) to the dative (*υμιν*) after the *εν* of *εσωθεν* (Luke 11:39, P 75), repeating the prepositional prefix of a verb after the verb

(Luke 13:13, P 75), changing the "door" to the "shepherd" (John 10:7, P 75), changing the case of a noun to agree with the case of the following possessive pronoun (John 11:5, P 75). Harmonizations range to writing πανθρωπον for ανθρωπον (John 1:9, P 66) under the influence of the preceding word, παντα, or μεψαντα for πεμψαντα (John 7:18; 7:33; 13:20, P 66) under the influence of the word which follows (με), which P 66 liked so well he did it three times.

Harmonization to General Usage

A third type of harmonization is equally well attested, occurring eleven times. This leads to "correctional formulas." Και εγενετο is added before an infinitive phrase in Luke (9:36, P 45). In John (6:57, P 75) the bare words "The Father" have the usual possessive "my" added. In Jesus' interview with Nicodemus the "Amen, Amen, I say to Thee" is harmonized to the prevailing plural "I say to you" (John 3:3, P 66).

Harmonization of all kinds occurs; but the dominant type to which the textual critic needs to be especially alert is harmonization to immediate context.

The Individual Scribe: Attitudes and Habits

The characterization of these singular readings can go no further until the individual scribes have been characterized. Their peculiar readings are due to their peculiarities. This has been well said by Dain.[7] He reminds us that although all scribes make mistakes and mistakes of the same kind, yet each scribe has a personal coefficient of the frequency of his mistakes. Each has his own pattern of errors. One scribe is liable to dittography, another to the omission of lines of text; one reads well, another remembers poorly; one is a good speller; etc., etc. In these differences must be included the seriousness of intention of the scribe and the peculiarities of his own basic method of copying.

On these last and most important matters, our three scribes are widely divided. P 75 and P 45 seriously intend to produce a good copy, but it is hard to believe that this was the intention of P 66. The nearly 200 nonsense readings and the 400 itacistic spellings in P 66 are evidence of some-

[7] *Ibid.*, p. 46.

thing less than disciplined attention to the basic task. To this evidence of carelessness must be added those singular readings whose origin baffles speculation, readings that can be given no more exact label than carelessness leading to assorted variant readings. A hurried count shows P 45 with 20, P 75 with 57, and P 66 with 216 purely careless readings. As we have seen, P 66 has, in addition, more than twice as many "leaps" from the same to the same as either of the others.

Influence of Similar Forms

These are surprisingly few in number. Here the progression goes from the fewest in P 45 through P 75 to P 66 which has the largest number. There are a bare half dozen in P 45. Two seem to be the textbook type of visual confusion, the misreading of very similar forms. In Acts 13:46 αυτους is read for εαυτους. And in Acts 15:4 the finite verb followed by τε becomes the participle ending in τες. In two cases words with similar beginnings are confused—the more interesting occurring in Luke 10:30, where Jericho becomes a priest. In another case the augment of the finite verb is added to the participle. But the total of these cases is so small in this MS as to be insignificant.

In P 75 there are no examples of the visual confusion type, of misreading very similar forms. In this papyrus, only one letter is involved, more often a vowel than a consonant. Basically these are errors due to carelessness or perhaps fatigue; and the role of the similar word or form is simply that of giving some superficially responsible form to the misread or misremembered word. Eighteen times in P 75 a similar word has influenced the shape of the error. In Luke 11:11 fish (ιχθυν) has become strength (ισχυν); and in John 3:8 the verb "blows" has been turned into the *nomina sacra* type of abbreviation for "spirit" ($\overline{\pi\nu\epsilon\iota}$ for πνει). In thirty-six other passages in P 75 the *form* of a word has been changed to a similar form.

In P 66 it is necessary to distinguish carefully between readings involving confusion with similar words or forms and a large number of changes which are very similar but lack any possible reference to confusion with similar words. Here (as in P 45) there are two cases of possible visual misreading as the basic cause of a variant. In John 12:1, P 66 reads "five days before the Passover" instead of "six days before. . . ."

Père Boismard felt that this possibly represents an ancient tradition.[8] But it is more easily explained as a misreading of "six." Scribes in this period used a bold rough breathing with a long horizontal stroke over confusable forms such as "six" (εξ). If "six" were thus written in the exemplar of P 66, the horizontal stroke above the letter epsilon would easily suggest the numeral "five" to the scribe of P 66, and he would write "five" (πεντε). Half a dozen times, P 66 confuses similar words; e.g., in John 20:14 he changes "Jesus" to "Lord." A dozen times, he writes a similar form of the word. Thus, in John 18:34, he writes "he said" (ειπεν) for "they said" (ειπον), even though the subject is clearly plural.

On the avoidance of careless error, P 45 would be given top rating. But if we look at the basic method of copying, the rating of the three papyri changes. In general, P 75 copies letters one by one; P 66 copies syllables, usually two letters in length. P 45 copies phrases and clauses.

The accuracy of these assertions can be demonstrated. That P 75 copied letters one by one is shown in the pattern of his errors. He has more than sixty readings that involve a single letter, *and* not more than ten careless readings that involve a syllable. But P 66 drops sixty-one syllables (twenty-three of them in "leaps") and omits as well a dozen articles and thirty short words. In P 45 there is not one omission of a syllable in a "leap" nor is there any list of "careless" omissions of syllables. P 45 omits words and phrases.

Another clue to the nature of a scribe's work can be obtained from a study of his transpositions. Since word order in Greek is very free, it may be assumed that most changes in word order are due to scribal error. I suggest three causes of transposition: A. By a leap the scribe jumps over a word, copies the following word, looks back at his exemplar, catches his error, and writes in the omitted word out of order. I have noted five of these in P 45, [9] four in P 66, [10] and four in P 75.[11] B. Even more rarely, a scribe omits a word, the corrector interlines it slightly out of order, and the next copyist produces the transposition. One of these in-the-making occurs in these papyri. C. The third and commonest cause of transpositions is a carelessness as to word order.

[8] M.-É. Boismard, review of *Papyrus Bodmer II, RB,* LXX (January, 1963), 120-33.
[9] Luke 10:38; 12:11; 12:36; Acts 10:32; 16:37.
[10] John 5:6; 10:4; 10:31; 13:34.
[11] Luke 14:10; John 4:9; 7:18; 14:19.

In carelessness as to word order P 45 come first with 37, P 66 second with 21, and P 75 least with 11 (these are over and above transpositions due to "leaps").

The transpositions in P 66 and P 75 are explicable as abortive omissions, caught in the act and immediately corrected. These are errors, lapses on the part of the scribe—as usual more frequent in P 66, less frequent in P 75.

But the transpositions in P 45 are capable of a very different explanation. This scribe does not actually copy words. He sees through the language to its idea content, and copies that—often in words of his own choosing, or in words rearranged as to order. The length of text transposed differs from P 45 on the one hand to P 66 and P 75 on the other. In P 66 and P 75, transpositions usually involve two words, occasionally three. But out of the 37 transpositions of P 45, 20 involve more than three words. This is true of only three cases in each of the other papyri. The inference is plain: P 45 bites off three to five words at a time; he copies phrases where P 66 usually copies syllables, and P 75 letters. A second inference is equally clear: P 45 copies with great freedom and his freedom springs from his basic attitude as a scribe. From one point of view, P 66 is as free as P 45. He certainly creates more readings than P 45 does. But his freedom is failure to live up to his accepted task; whereas for P 45 it *is* his task. P 66 gives the impression of working in a controlled situation. If he catches a transposition while he is writing, he erases the out-of-order-word and writes the correct-order-word over it. If the transposition is caught later, strokes between lines correct it. This never happens in P 45. He feels free to make the order of words what he wants to make it, and he is a careful workman. He does not fall into the slips and nonsense that P 66 does. Thus, though P 45 and P 66 are alike in treating their sources with freedom, their freedoms are very unalike. P 45 gladly is free of any obligation to reproduce *words* faithfully, but P 66 has accepted that obligation and regrets his failures to live up to it.

In P 75 the text that is produced can be explained in all its variants as the result of a single force, namely the disciplined scribe who writes with the intention of being careful and accurate. There is no evidence of revision of his work by anyone else, or in fact of any real revision, or check. Only one of five of his singular readings (including nonsense readings) is corrected. The control has been drilled into the scribe before he started writing.

P [45] gives the impression of a scribe who writes without any intention of exactly reproducing his source. He writes with great freedom—harmonizing, smoothing out, substituting almost whimsically. Here again, there is no evidence whatever of a second party control—less than three singular readings per hundred are corrected—nor in fact of external controls of any kind.

P [66] seems to reflect a scribe working with the intention of making a good copy, falling into careless errors, particularly the error of dropping a letter, syllable, a word, or even a phrase where it is doubled, but also under the control of some other person, or a second standard, so that the corrections which are made are usually corrections to a reading read by a number of other witnesses. Nine out of ten of the nonsense readings are corrected, and two out of three of all his singular readings. In short, P [66] gives the impression of being the product of a scriptorium, i.e. a publishing house. It shows the supervision of a foreman, or of a scribe turned proofreader.

In short, P [75] and P [66] represent a controlled tradition; P [45] represents an uncontrolled tradition. P [75] and P [45] are, according to their own goals, careful workmen. P [66] is careless and ineffective—although he is the only calligrapher of the three. He uses up his care, his concern, in the production of beautiful letters.

If P [45] represents an uncontrolled tradition and the others do not, there must be evidence of this in the pattern of sensible singular readings. That evidence will lie in the amount and range of editorial readings. I use this term advisedly. These three papyri are enough to show that scribes made changes in style, in clarity, in fitness of ideas, in smoothness, in vocabulary. They created readings which can properly be called "editorial." The role of the editor (the maker of a text-type) was to select rather than create readings and to gain consistency in the application of the ideals of good style, clarity, etc.

Editorial Changes: Logical Harmonization

If "Harmonizations to General Usage" be slightly extended to include logical harmonization to the general context, we have crossed into the realm of editorial changes. One type of these is usually identified as "doctrinal." But the so-called doctrinal changes seem to be only part of a more general class—a class in which the fitness of idea-content is appraised and improved. It is this fitness as much as a specific parallel that changes Jesus as the door of the sheep to the shepherd of the sheep, that changes "a" prophet to "the" prophet when it refers to Jesus.

Editorial Changes: Conciseness in P 45

As an editor the scribe of P 45 wielded a sharp axe. The most striking aspect of his style is its conciseness. The dispensable word is dispensed with. He omits adverbs, adjectives, nouns, participles, verbs, personal pronouns—without any compensating habit of addition. He frequently omits phrases and clauses. He prefers the simple to the compound word. In short, he favors brevity. He shortens the text in at least fifty places in *singular readings alone.* But he does *not* drop syllables or letters. His shortened text is readable.

Many of his omissions are striking—not to say startling. In P 45 the 5,000 do not sit down "by hundreds and by fifties," nor are we told how many loaves and fishes there were. In Mark 6:48 he does not bother to tell us that it was the fourth watch "of the night" since vs. 47 has already made it evening. In Acts 15:20, "unchastity" is absent from the list of prohibitions, and unfortunately the parallel in 15:29 is in a gap. The Ethiopian Eunuch (Acts 8:36) does not say "See, here is water!" since the water has already been mentioned. In Luke 10:21 there is no repetitive address to God, "Yea, Father." P 45 does not make Caiaphas High Priest "that year." In this papyrus, Jesus does not say "I am the Resurrection and the Life"; he says more briefly, "I am the Resurrection." If the subject of the verb can be understood, it is not expressed—whether it be the dumb demoniac, or Jesus. One word is made to serve for several. "His son" replaces "The Son of God" (John 11:4); and "to men" serves for "into the hands of men" (Mark 9:31).

As an editor P 45 is interested in clarity. In Mark 7:5, for example, he points out that the hands were "defiled" because they were "unwashed." At the tomb of Lazarus he adds the common form of the imperative "Come" to the command (John 11:42). In Acts 14:15 the over-concise Greek is clarified by the addition of a verb, "turn away from." By the judicious addition of a pronoun or a conjunction or a change in order or form, other passages are clarified (see John 11:2; Acts 9:39; Mark 7:7; 7:28; 7:33; Luke 13:32; Acts 16:33).

Should the removal of the difficulty from a difficult saying not be classified as clarification? In Luke 9:50, P 45 straightens out the hard saying that the man who is not against us is for us by making it read that he is neither for us nor against us.

That P 45 attempted stylistic improvements is unquestionable. The appropriate label for his improvements is not easily found. Occasionally he makes the text "smoother" or "simpler." In Mark 9:28 he anticipates the Textus Receptus by relating a genitive absolute to a verb (which incidentally he supplies). His sentence is much smoother than the original (see Luke 10:37; 12:48). In Acts 10:11 the vision of the vessel let down from heaven is either simplified or made smoother by omitting the comparison to a sheet. In two passages he transposes a word or phrase an incredible distance, perhaps for better style: in Luke 10:40 the pronoun *μου* is advanced, and in John 10 the words "in the scripture" are moved ahead from vs. 35 to 34.

Style may be responsible for the dozen changes in verb forms. At least three times the tense is changed to the aorist. In another dozen passages words are replaced with synonyms—although *ηλθεν* for *εγενετο* in Acts 10:10 is not quite equivalent! Most of his changes are to the familiar and the common.

While certainty awaits further study, the use by P 45 of conjunctions, the article, prepositions, and negatives does not seem to be caused by a concern for style, although his frequent substitution of one conjunction for another *may* be a matter of style. In twenty-four passages, ten conjunctions are omitted, six are added, and eight are changed. The same ones are added, omitted, and interchanged. The article is added six times, but omitted nine others. As a whole P 45 seems to be a typical scribe with some freedom to add or omit articles and other words. Both P 66 and P 75 exhibit similar changes in many ways. All three scribes omit articles more often than they add them. P 45 and P 75 omit more conjunctions than they add; P 66 does not. But P 66 and P 75 add *οτι* several times at the beginning of a quotation; and P 45 does not. Variations in the use of these words seem to be due to scribal license rather than to stylistic considerations.

The resemblance between these three in these matters may be due to their participation in the larger common error: the omission of short words. Dain notes this as one of the two errors common to all scribes. He found it especially in the linking words, the conjunctions, particles, prepositions, the verb "to be," and even negatives. But the evidence of these papyri in their singular readings points to license rather than to the habit of omission alone.

The editorial readings of P 45 include those aimed at concise expression, at clarity, and at a good style. The most distinctive of these is the intended omission of dispensable words. That this striving for concise expression is intended and conscious is shown by the absence of any large number of unintended omissions. In the "leaps" from the same to the same P 45 with only 18 cases is well below the others, P 75 with 36 and P 66 with 76.

Editorial Changes in P 75

P 75 shares the concern of P 45 for clarity and for style, but lacks the passion of P 45 for conciseness. In 14 passages there are clarifying changes in P 75. In Luke 11:34 a second hand adds the word "eye" before "evil." P 75 gives the name of the rich man in Luke 16:19. In Luke 8:21, Jesus replies, logically enough, to the questioner rather than the crowd. And once at least (Luke 8:32) the legion of demons is referred to in the singular. In P 75 (Luke 11:32) Jesus is a greater *person* than Jonah. Some of these are slight, superficially logical harmonizations to context; e.g., the perfect tense in John 9:39 and the substitution of "he will be raised up" for "he will recover," John 11:12. (Cf. Luke 16:18; John 7:52; 8:55; 14:9).

P 75 is probably striving for better style in changing verb forms, which he does about as often as P 45 (though in a much greater amount of text). Only three times does he substitute synonyms, and one of these looks like harmonization to immediate context. Twice he prefers the simple to the compound word. A half dozen times he chooses brevity, possibly for style. The best example is John 12:38 where in "the word which he said" the redundant "which he said" is omitted. There are a couple of changes of case and number. One of his habits is to omit personal pronouns; he drops more than a dozen and adds one. This could be stylistic, but is probably related to the occasional carelessness of P 75 in regard to short words. In P 75 the scribe's impulse to improve style is for the most part defeated by the obligation to make an exact copy.

"Editorial" Changes in P 66

Wildness in copying is the outstanding characteristic of P 66. This makes it very difficult to decide whether particular readings are due to editorializing on the part of the scribe or rather are due to his general laxity and inefficiency. As I catalogued his singular readings, I marked 43 as due to clarification, to smoothing out the text, to simplification or to logical agreement with context. Some of these exhibit a preference for the more familiar word or idiom: *επ αυτω* for *εν αυτω* (John 12:16), *και* for *τε* (John 2:15), "Jesus answered" becomes "Jesus answered and said" (John 18:37). In John 3:3 *αρχην* became *πρωτην* because "first" is clearer here.[12] P 66 corrects the broken syntax of John 8:40, "a man who I have spoken the truth," to agree with RSV "a man who has spoken the truth." In John 8:48 the tense of a verb is put back into the past to fit the fact (cf. John 7:20). There are other "logical" changes of this sort (cf. 9:4; 13:1).

There are rearrangements of the Greek text that are almost certainly stylistic. Note the smoother feeling of *πολλοι ουν των ακουσαντων μαθητων* of P 66* contrasted with *πολλοι ουν ακουσαντες εκ των μαθητων αυτου* (John 6:60) of P 66 corr and the others. There are half a dozen similar if less successful rewritings.

In P 66 some additions look stylistic. In John 5:29, "And those who have done evil," which Boismard ascribed to carelessness, RSV again follows the first hand of P 66. In 7:40 *εκ του οχλου ουν* becomes *πολλοι εκ του οχλου οι*. The very difficult passage John 8:25 is cleared up by prefixing "I said to you."

In John 13:33 trouble lies in the unconnected *και υμιν λεγω αρτι* at the end of the verse. P 66 would end 13:33 with *και υμιν λεγω*; he has a high point after *λεγω*. And he begins 13:34 with *πλην αρτι εντολην καινην*. MSS 1 and 565 on the other hand end vs. 33 with *αρτι* and begin 34 with *πλην*. These corruptions are alternative ways of clearing up the difficulty.

[12] RSV agrees with the first hand of P66.

Again it may be style, a feeling for simplicity, that leads P 66 * to change "what the things were which he was saying to them" to "what he was saying to them." The significance of the agreement of the Old Latin (exc q) is diminished by the agreement of RSV.

Simplification probably explains the omission of *τις* in John 11:49 *εις δε τις εξ αυτων* where RSV again agrees. But more rigorous editing (or erroneous harmonization) is needed to explain 15:4, where "neither can you unless you abide in me" is reduced to "so also (is) he who abides in me." I join Boismard in labeling as "fantasy" the substitution in 5:28 of "desert" for "tombs."

I have already pointed out general agreement of P 66 with the others in readings involving omission or alteration of conjunctions and the article. He favors *ην* instead of *η* for the third person singular of the present subjunctive. One further detail, in his general omission of short words: he omits personal pronouns eighteen times, and adds them six times.

Enough of these have been cited to make the point that P 66 editorializes as he does everything else—in a sloppy fashion. He is not guided in his changes by some clearly defined goal which is always kept in view. If he has an inclination toward omission, it is not "according to knowledge," but is whimsical and careless, often leading to nothing but nonsense.

And finally (if I may use that most hopeful of all adverbs), I present a list of suggestions drawn from this study of corruption. Some of these are no more than hypotheses for further study; some are firm conclusions.

I. Singular Readings should not be included in any *apparatus criticus*. They belong to special studies.

II. The singular readings of a particular MS should be studied not against Tischendorf or Nestle or the Textus Receptus, but rather against the consensus of the Text-type to which the MS belongs. The singulars of P 75 should be studied with reference to the Beta Text-type (Vaticanus and friends).

III. Since corruption was universal, identical singular readings with only minor scattered support elsewhere should be assumed to be coincidental in these agreements—unless other external evidence establishes relationship.

IV. The corruption of the text in P 45 sheds light on the process of corruption in an uncontrolled tradition. In that tradition a particular kind of freedom exists. It occurs where Greek sophistication is in short supply—in the backwoods where few knew Greek—and results in the making of an independent translation. In these areas appeal to a "standard" text was impossible, for the very idea did not exist.

V. A translation to be good must be free. The translator is always tempted to extend that freedom unjustifiably. The result is inevitably agreement between any translation and a MS whose text was corrupted either intentionally or through carelessness. Boismard in a study of the readings of the first hand in P 66 suggests kinship between P 66 * and various versions, including half a dozen. Since the makers of the RSV did not use P 66, I compared the *Singular Readings* of P 66 with RSV. In fifteen passages RSV follows P 66 singulars, and in four others a relationship is possible (cf. John 2:20; 5:29; 5:36; 8:40; 9:30; 9:33; 9:34; 9:37; 10:6; 11:27; 11:49; 12:2; 12:47; 13:1; 15:12; and as possibilities 1:27; 2:11; 5:22; 8:51). No one will suggest a genetic kinship here, but if the agreement of P 66 were with an Old Latin MS . . . ?

VI. The relationship of P 66 to established text-types should be reconsidered with the nature and extent of P 66 corruptions kept vividly in mind. P 66 might then look like a corruption of the Beta Text-type rather than like a mixed text.

VII. A study of P 45 and Codex Bezae concentrating on the nature of their corruptions might clarify the nature of the so-called Western text-type. Kenyon's elimination of D's major variants from that comparison invalidates his conclusions, for it is these very major variants that he depends upon elsewhere to establish the existence of a Western text-type.

VIII. P 66 should not be cited as evidence for the omission of a short word, except where its kinship with a group that omits the word has been established.

IX. P 45 should not be cited as evidence for a transposition, except where its kinship with a group that supports the transposition has been established.

X. A study of the presence or absence of the article should determine whether scribal usage had enough consistency to justify the citation of the individual codices (even when supported by others, unless those others are members of the same established group).

XI. A study of general scribal practice in the omission of personal pronouns might provide a guideline for the use of evidence in this matter.

XII. Readings that are identifiable as harmonizations to immediate context should not be cited unless they characterize a group.

XIII. The publication of a commentary on the singular readings of these papyri and of other important MSS would be most valuable.

XIV. Of the writing of many books there is no end, and much study is a weariness of the flesh.

INDEX